# Visual Basic
# SAP R/3
## Programming

**Oleg Ovanesyan**

**Wrox Press Ltd.** ®

# Visual Basic SAP R/3 Programming

Published by Wrox Press Ltd. Arden House, 1102 Warwick Rd, Birmingham, B27 6BH
Printed in USA
ISBN 1-861002-7-85

## Trademark Acknowledgements

Wrox has endeavored to provide trademark information about all the companies and products mentioned in this book by the appropriate use of capitals. However, Wrox cannot guarantee the accuracy of this information.

## Credits

**Author**
Oleg Ovaneysan

**Managing Editor**
Chris Hindley

**Editors**
Craig A. Berry
Lisa Stephenson

**Development Editor**
Dominic Lowe

**Project Manager**
Tony Berry

**Copy Edit**
Diane Parker

**Index**
Diane Brenner
Andrew Criddle

**Technical Reviewers**
Ron Frank
Ulrich Homann
Peter Keiner
Glenn Quisler
Ben Trinh
Craig Welch
Christian Zalto

**Design/Layout**
Tom Bartlett
Dave Boyce
Mark Burdett
William Fallon
John McNulty

**Cover**
Chris Morris
Concept by Third Wave
Photo by Alan Klein Photography

In memory of my father...

# Acknowledgements

I would like to thank some people whose efforts and cooperation made this book possible.

Everyone at Wrox, this was the best experience I ever had. I want to thank Dominic – this book started from his email – for his support and enthusiasm. John Franklin for his guidance and support. Tony Berry for putting up with his daunting task to manage me as an author. Craig and Lisa for dealing with what I though I wrote in English. All reviewers for their valuable remarks.

I would like to also thank Guangwei Li and Rajeev Madnawat at SAP for their valuable feedback.

Special thanks go to Ulrich Homann at Microsoft for his patience and guidance, and JJ Shefcik at Microsoft – I would not have the SAP connection without his efforts.

Special thanks go to Ron Frank for introducing SAP R/3 to me, and initially directing my curiosity to the SAP web site and being the most critical reviewer of this opus.

I would also like to thank my family, friends and colleagues for their support and patience – I was not a pleasure to be around.

# Table of Contents

# Chapter 2: SAP R/3 Business Objects and BAPI 33

# Chapter 8: Calling RFCs and BAPIs 215

# Chapter 12: DCOM Component Connector Object Builder Functionality 359

# Introduction

The topic of SAP R/3 has traditionally been outside the mainstream of books involving Visual Basic programming. Moreover, SAP R/3 has remained by-and-large, a black box for Windows programmers in general, and Visual Basic programmers in particular.

SAP R/3 programming always has been, and still is, the domain of ABAP/4 programmers, simply because no other language works in SAP R/3. That's why all books on SAP R/3 programming are about ABAP/4. This may well be the first book on developing external Visual Basic applications using SAP R/3, and integrating SAP R/3 into existing systems using Visual Basic and the extensibility tools provided by SAP.

The first task for me, as author of this book, is to correctly communicate its purpose, scope and structure.

## The Challenge

The biggest challenge for me, throughout the whole writing and editing process, was to keep this book from falling into either the "yet another general Visual Basic book" category or a failure-bound attempt to trivialize SAP R/3. I tried very hard not to make this an "SAP book" or a "Visual Basic book". This was not an easy task, given that the book is essentially about how to develop applications using Visual Basic that integrate with the SAP R/3. Then why is it necessary?

First of all, I did not plan to write a book explaining SAP R/3 functionality. That would be an enormous task, and I'm sure that no single individual possesses adequate knowledge to write about every aspect of SAP R/3.

On the other hand, I did not want to turn this book into another tips-and-tricks Visual Basic book. There are plenty of such books available, and there is only so much you can write about Visual Basic.

# The Objective

I have said what this book is not. Now it's time to say what this book is.

> **This book has one single objective – the introduction of the new SAP extensibility technologies.**

These are namely:

> ➤ SAP R/3 Business Object Framework, BAPI development and SAP Desktop Integration tools – SAP Automation

> ➤ SAP R/3 COM integration tools – SAP DCOM Component Connector

SAP R/3 has always been notorious for non-trivial data access, data exchange and integration techniques. Any attempt to integrate SAP R/3 into existing corporate Information Systems used to require extensive effort, involving ABAP/4 programmers, SAP consultants and business analysts.

I tried to keep the objective of this book as close as possible to the objective of SAP on this matter:

> **To enable general programmers who are not intimately familiar with the SAP R/3 architecture or functionality, to develop meaningful applications using SAP R/3.**

As you progress into this book, you will appreciate the effort that SAP has put into the integration technologies.

# Who will Benefit from this Book

The main area of growth for the SAP R/3 market is now in mid-sized companies – all the "big guys" already have SAP R/3 and it's not something you buy every year. The Windows operating system has a very strong presence in mid-sized companies, plus they're less able to find multi-million SAP R/3 implementation budgets. SAP, recognizing this trend, developed the technologies we'll discuss in this book.

As I have already stated, this book is not intended to teach you either SAP R/3 or Visual Basic. I assume that the reader is sufficiently versed in Visual Basic. Familiarity with SAP R/3 is preferred but not required. I also assume that there will be an ABAP programmer available for you to consult as the need arises.

There are three categories of readers who will benefit the most from this book. The first category is Visual Basic programmers employed by companies that have implemented SAP R/3. For this group, the book will serve as a reference source and introduction to the technology. If you're a Visual Basic developer working with traditional data processing applications, you will easily gain reasonable expertise on the subject and be able to leverage your existing skills. In addition, this book offers you an introduction into the SAP R/3 and Enterprise Resource Planner (ERP) market in general – something not every Visual Basic programmer can boast knowledge of.

The next category is institutional ABAP/4 programmers and ABAP/4 consultants. If you belong to this group, you'll have already accumulated expertise on internal SAP R/3 functionality and enjoy relative stability in the job market. Nevertheless, for ABAP/4 programmers to be gainfully employed, it is imperative that the SAP R/3 customer base grows, boosting demand for their very specific skills. This book offers you an excellent opportunity to diversify your skills with Visual Basic and leverage your SAP R/3 expertise at the same time. No matter how hard SAP tries to make the specifics of SAP R/3 transparent to external programmers, it can't make it 100% transparent. This is where ABAP programmers who learn integration with Visual Basic can really shine.

The third group is Project Leaders, Technical Directors and all other managerial level professionals concerned with the development of corporate software involving SAP R/3. This book will help you to understand the technologies available and their implementations, giving you more perspective to make intelligent choices.

# How this Book is Structured

This book basically has three parts:

> An introduction to SAP R/3 from a technological perspective, and an overview of the technologies discussed

> The SAP Automation Toolkit

> The SAP DCOM Component Connector

You may find some overlapping and repeated explanations in the book. This is intentional, and they involve SAP R/3 specific aspects only. The idea is to introduce the material in a spiral fashion, gradually expanding the scope and depth. Most books are structured linearly – from simple to more difficult material. The linear approach usually works fine, and in many instances it the only feasible one – for example, to teach programming languages. However, for an SAP R/3 integration technology overview that assumes knowledge of Visual Basic, the linear approach would be inadequate. That's why strictly SAP R/3 material (e.g. screen shots, terminology etc) is interwoven with purely Visual Basic or SAP Automation / DCOM Component Connector topics.

I have also tried to make this book task-centered rather than tool-centered. We will programmatically replicate the functionality of SAP developed tools such as the SAP Assistant and the DCOM Component Connector. This keeps us within the SAP suggested and supported paradigm, plus it teaches you the functionality of all the necessary components provided by SAP. It's very easy to get carried away with features rather than application domain problems when dealing with new areas such as SAP R/3 integration. I tried to avoid this trap, since it would contribute very little to your actual knowledge.

Another distinction of this book is that it does not elaborate on integrating with the Microsoft family of products. You will not find chapters like "SAP R/3 and SQL Server" or "SAP R/3 and Microsoft Access". This is logical if you recall our main objective – an introduction of the *technology*, not a case study description. Moreover, there is no component or methodology specific to any particular application, such as Access or SQL Server, in either SAP Automation or DCOM Component Connector.

You may elect any tool or application to be integrated with SAP R/3 – the way you use SAP integration components and technology will not change. The DCOM Component Connector takes advantage of Microsoft Transaction Server, but you don't program against MTS, you simply use MTS as part of the infrastructure. I do provide general implementation samples using Visual Basic, but I purposely refrain from suggesting implementation scenarios.

There is no information on Microsoft Knowledge Base on Visual Basic and SAP R/3, and the information provided by SAP is sketchy and fragmented from the Visual Basic programmer's standpoint. That's why it was imperative for me to present you with accurate code and information about the technology and components.

# What You Need to Use this Book

I expect you to implement various SAP R/3 integration scenarios, and you will need some applications available to do so. To work through this book, you will need to have access to, or have installed the following:

- ➢ Access to an SAP R/3 system, preferably release 4.5 or higher
- ➢ SAP R/3 front-end application
- ➢ Visual Basic 6.0
- ➢ The SAP Automation Toolkit
- ➢ The DCOM Component Connector (RFC SDK)

*The Automation tools and the DCOM Component Connector can be downloaded from* `www.sap.com` *or* `www.saplabs.com`

It is also suggested that you have:

- ➢ Microsoft Data Access Components 2.1
- ➢ Microsoft Repository SDK
- ➢ Microsoft Transaction Server
- ➢ Microsoft Access

My objective is to deliver you knowledge on the enabling technology and demonstrate it using Visual Basic.

# Conventions Used

I have used a number of different styles of text and layout in this book to help differentiate between different kinds of information. Here are some of the styles you will see, and an explanation of what they mean:

> **These boxes hold important, not-to-be forgotten, mission-critical details, which are directly relevant to the surrounding text.**

*Background information, asides and references appear in text like this.*

➢  **Important words** are in a bold font.

➢  Words that appear on the screen, such as menu options, are in a similar font to the one used on screen, for example, the File menu. Some options in the SAP R/3 front-end GUI may be in this format, Customer.

➢  Keys that you press on the keyboard, like *Ctrl* and *Enter*, are in italics.

➢  All filenames, function names and other code snippets are in this style: DblTxtBx

Code that is new or important is presented like this:

```
Private Sub Command1_Click

    MsgBox "The Command1 button has been clicked!"

End Sub
```

Whereas code that we've seen before or has less to do with the matter being discussed looks like this:

```
Private Sub Command1_Click

    MsgBox "The Command1 button has been clicked!"

End Sub
```

# Source Code

All the projects that are given in this book can be downloaded from Wrox's web site at:

http://www.wrox.com

# Tell Us What You Think

I hope that you find this book useful, and that it will make your journey into the ERP world a little easier. You are the one that counts and I would really appreciate your views and comments on this book. You can contact me either by email (feedback@wrox.com) or via the Wrox web site.

# SAP R/3 in Enterprise Computing

Modern enterprise computing has reached the stage where traditional tools and techniques are not sufficient to find solutions for business problems. For around 40 years, the enterprise computing concept and approach has remained almost unchanged. In a perpetually changing world, business applications were implemented like a daguerreotype image – a very long exposure that led to outdated results.

Another important thing has been missing from enterprise computing all along – the time dimension. All processes have been implemented in a static manner, and the most important characteristic of continuous processes – the event chain – has been virtually ignored. Computers have been used as powerful, yet dumb, calculating devices. But this approach has begun to change.

## Developments in Enterprise Computing

It has become commonplace for people to attribute the most positive changes in modern computing to Personal Computers and Microsoft Windows – and that's not entirely wrong. However, one other software package has had a major role in changing the way we approach enterprise computing. This software package was developed by SAP AG, and it eventually evolved into **SAP R/3**.

> **The name SAP stands for Systems, Applications, Products in Data Processing. There are two system identification codes: the R/2 system, developed as a mainframe system, and R/3, a multi-user client-server system.**

# Enterprise Programming – The Basic Problem

Before we begin any exploration of SAP R/3, it would be beneficial to review some of the basic problems that are being solved by programmers in general, and Visual Basic programmers in particular.

It's very easy to get carried away by technology and the dazzling variety of modern development tools, but the fact of the matter is that programming is still an automation of relatively mundane tasks that can be handed over to an electronic device. Every program is developed to solve a particular business and scientific problem, and is not a self-serving entity.

Most business computer programs are data-processing applications. Old mainframe programs and the latest Java wonders are performing essentially the same task – entering data into some data store and retrieving it on demand. This statement doesn't imply that existing applications lack sophistication, it simply emphasizes their nature.

# Enterprise Information Systems – The Challenge

It's time to get down to a more detailed analysis. Our assignment is to develop and implement an enterprise wide, distributed, multi-user **online transaction processing** system – **OLTP**. This hypothetical system will process business transactions and have reporting capabilities. We might like to assume a few things as given:

> ➢ Microsoft Windows is the operating system of choice
> ➢ The entire system has to be developed in Visual Basic
> ➢ The back-end database is Microsoft SQL Server 7.0

However, we would probably only have this carte blanche scenario in an ideal situation. The reality is that there is always some great legacy system that was developed 15 years ago, works almost perfectly, and is the backbone of the entire company. As you go further, it turns out that there are several heterogeneous data stores and applications generating the data. These are spread all over the company, with some of them sitting on individual desktops.

Depending on your point of view, this is either a disaster scenario or a case study for Microsoft's Universal Data Access strategy. In any case, to overcome all the differences and incompatibilities of the various components that comprise an enterprise information system will require a substantial effort from the architects and software developers.

This scenario becomes more complex if we want an online or real-time solution, as opposed to a batch processing one. Most Visual Basic programmers have entered the industry oblivious to the differences between real-time and batch processing, simply because the Windows core is event-driven and real-time by design. Moreover, until very recently, Visual Basic programmers usually developed stand-alone applications that were not integrated into existing information systems. Let's clarify these arguments using the following scenario.

## Company X

Company X is a value-added reseller of networking equipment and software. It maintains a warehouse and employs many salesmen, who get a basic salary plus commissions from sales volume. The company has a legacy order processing system, which is mainframe based; an accounting application that uses Oracle on Unix; and a new SQL Server 7.0 based human resources (HR) application (developed entirely in Visual Basic) for the HR department's NT workgroup.

When a salesperson makes a sale this has to trigger different processes in different parts of the enterprise information system. It has to update the inventory, order merchandise if needed, generate the appropriate invoices, update the accounting database, calculate commissions and update the HR database.

What happens, in most cases, is that orders are entered but not processed until the next business day – a mainframe **batch process**. Then some COBOL program dumps records into a flat file. This file gets taken over to some Unix server, where it either gets processed by a C/C++ application and eventually entered into the Oracle database, or it stays as a flat file. After all that, VB either reads Oracle and imports a flat file, or some other semi-manual mechanism allows everything to get updated.

It's very difficult and resource consuming to support such a system – anybody who has ever been involved in the technical support of one can attest to this. It has too many points of failure and has no built-in capability to adapt to changes. Any modification requires an extensive effort from business analysts and software developers and may involve substantial code modification. This in turn can lead to unpredictable results.

This scenario is complex enough for a relatively small company. Imagine scaling it up to the size and complexity of Citibank or IBM. Now imagine being given an assignment to make it all a real-time environment. You can start to appreciate the problem.

## Universal Data Access Strategy

The Company X example illustrates how the requirements of modern business are far more demanding than ever before. In order to stay competitive, companies are forced to constantly revise and modify their information systems. There are two main approaches to this type of problem. One is to move all corporate data into one gargantuan database and implement all business rules on the database level or externally. Another approach is to access data where it resides.

The latter is the main premise of Microsoft's **Universal Data Access (UDA)** strategy. This has many strong points, but it doesn't resolve the main problem – real-time transaction processing. It allows you to access data, but you still have to write all the components yourself and it doesn't bridge binary and other differences among heterogeneous data stores.

# Enterprise Resource Planner Systems

The biggest challenge in implementing an enterprise information system is to enable all components to communicate with, and respond to changes in, each other. Even the latest tools and utilities require developers to create software to implement all the business rules and to enforce data integrity. Companies are forced to maintain and support various platforms and software components, and to maintain a large and diverse population of programmers. This all costs businesses a large amount of money and still doesn't guarantee success.

One very interesting observation is that the wide variety of business applications that exist in different companies are all doing essentially the same thing. If we focus on any industry, it's possible to list all the required software applications and lay out their interoperability. It turns out that every enterprise is pretty much the same when it comes to functionality.

A business is merely a combination of the following activities:

> Production
> Sales
> Employment

Therefore, every company needs some human resources system, which cannot and should not do much beyond managing personnel records. It also needs some accounting system that's all about account receivables and payables. Businesses are just like people – every one is unique personally and identical physiologically.

The hypothesis that every enterprise requires similar applications to implement its functionality leads to an important conclusion:

> **Every enterprise may be implemented, to a certain extent and with a certain approximation, by a common set of modular, functionally interconnected software components that use some common data storage.**

This hypothesis brought to life **Enterprise Resource Planner** systems – **ERP**. The lion's share of this market belongs to the German based enterprise software manufacturer SAP AG. The other major players are PeopleSoft, Baan and Oracle. The focus of this book is on SAP R/3 – the flagship product of SAP AG.

*Note that there are other popular versions of this software: the mainframe based SAP R/2, and many releases of SAP R/3 itself. However, this book will concentrate on the SAP R/3 releases 4.0 and 4.5. Bear in mind that the first releases of the SAP software were for mainframe computers.*

We won't discuss other ERP systems in detail in this book. However, we will outline some general concepts relevant to cross-ERP development and other emerging technologies. There are many compelling reasons to begin an analysis of ERP systems from SAP R/3. For one, SAP R/3 is the most mature and established product in its category. I also believe that it is the best when it comes to implementation of the enterprise.

# Microsoft in Enterprise Programming

Meanwhile, Microsoft Windows has become a *de facto* standard desktop operating system for the modern enterprise. Microsoft Windows did what no other operating system could do – it offered robust computing capabilities to the ordinary user. The rapidly evolving line of Windows NT, and the advent of Windows 2000, will thrust Windows into the enterprise orbit as fast as Windows 95 did for the desktop segment.

Windows applications have always used an event-driven mechanism and object-oriented programming concepts. Microsoft has developed many very successful user-oriented applications (such as Microsoft Office) and development tools (such as Visual Studio).

Microsoft Visual Studio includes tools for virtually every possible need of enterprise application development. Visual Basic came into play in the early nineties, and has quickly established itself as one of the most effective front-end generators for the Microsoft Windows platform. I consider Visual Basic to be the best tool for Windows client-specific application development. Visual Basic has evolved with Microsoft Windows, and as Windows transforms into an enterprise operating system, Visual Basic becomes an enterprise development tool too. At this moment, there are very few problems that you can't solve using Visual Basic. The catch – your system will work only on Microsoft Windows.

Visual Basic applications have evolved from single user, Access database front-ends to enterprise strong, data processing systems in practically four years – 1993 to 1997. This leap has taken the large community of Visual Basic programmers to a new level – that of enterprise software developers. Visual Basic programmers have started to venture into traditionally C++ programmers' areas: operating system specifics, cross-platform implementations (your application will still be limited to Windows but it now has to interact with non-Windows based systems and server-side development). As Windows continues to expand and evolve, Visual Basic becomes more popular. And with Microsoft's release of the Windows 2000 platform, Visual Basic will become even more widespread.

Microsoft Office includes tools for every aspect of the modern business, and has one of the most robust scripting languages incorporated into its core – Visual Basic for Applications. It has the best synthetic desktop RDBMS (Relational Database Management System) – Microsoft Access – based on Jet technology. These tools give business users the power to perform all the tasks necessary in the due course of their business.

Microsoft also created the SQL Server RDBMS which, with release 7.0, will surely win many programmers and database administrators from competing products. It's not only a pleasure to look at and work with, but it also performs very well. SQL Server 7.0 offers multi-dimensional data cubes and Data Transformation Services.

And that's not all. The Microsoft Back Office family of products includes tools such as Microsoft Transaction Server, Microsoft Message Queue Server and Microsoft Internet Information Server. All these tools are geared towards serious enterprise computing and are made to use the power of Windows 2000.

Finally, what may, but should not, escape us is the fact that Microsoft also developed the **Component Object Model (COM)**. COM is the only reliably functioning, well-documented standard for reusable component development natively integrated into the Windows operating system.

We have seen some of the general problems faced in modern business programming, and introduced some of the solutions available. Now let's take a closer look at SAP R/3 and its role in enterprise computing.

# SAP R/3 – A General Overview

In order to perform development using SAP R/3 in any shape or fashion, it's imperative to first gain some understanding of the purpose and functionality of SAP R/3 – a task that has always been a major hurdle for any Visual Basic programmer.

*As there is a lot of confusion about terminology and concepts when it comes to SAP R/3, one of the primary objectives of this chapter is to clarify the most important concepts and help a Visual Basic programmer to not get lost in this conceptual nebula. I have attempted to separate the things that we will use in programming, and things that you can find in the literature and in documents available from the SAP web site.*

## The SAP R/3 System

Let's define the SAP R/3 system itself:

> **SAP R/3 is a self-sufficient, real-time, multi-user, client-server and multi-platform modular ERP information system that emulates virtually every aspect of a modern enterprise. SAP R/3 allows a certain degree of customization while enforcing a variety of strict data integrity driven rules. It has its own internal programming language (ABAP/4) and uses a variety of database back-ends (SQL Server, Oracle, Informix, etc.). SAP R/3 implemented event-chains and data objects well before event driven programming became a reality.**

Another way of looking at what SAP R/3 has to offer is to remind ourselves of an important functionality that every business depends on – decision making based on data processing. This is exactly what SAP R/3 does – it offers multi-dimensional views of data for various reporting purposes. SAP R/3's implementation of the enterprise workflow and the stimulus-response paradigm allows it to implement virtually every conceivable business scenario.

We'll begin to explore the SAP R/3 system by dissecting our definition.

### SAP is Self-Sufficient

SAP R/3 doesn't need any companion software to function (although it obviously needs a correctly set-up operating environment and communications). It comes complete with a bulletproof GUI front-end and other peripheral components.

Another strong benefit of using SAP R/3 is that it's highly version compatible. In other words, different releases and revisions of SAP R/3 will cooperate just fine – if you want to upgrade just one module, that's not a trivial task, but it is possible.

## SAP is Real-Time

This is one of the most important characteristics of SAP R/3. It has been historically developed as a **real-time** application that doesn't require any batch processing to perform transactions. Every data modification in SAP R/3 triggers an immediate chain of events, and these in turn run transactions to perform other necessary data modifications. For example, if you enter a sales order, it will affect inventory and accounting data immediately.

Don't get the impression that just because SAP R/3 is a real-time system, it doesn't have scheduling functionality for processes. It does have such functionality.

## SAP is Multi-User

SAP R/3 allows multiple concurrent logins governed by the licensing. It has a very solid security system and allows you to manage users. The important point is that SAP R/3 encapsulates the back-end RDBMS so completely that it doesn't delegate any user rights or other issues to the RDBMS – it does it all internally and transparently to the user.

## SAP is a Client-Server System

SAP R/3 is a case study on how to implement true client-server systems. It is a very powerful and resource consuming system and, to minimize network traffic and load on client workstations, it implements a really tiny client that doesn't process much itself. The Internet Explorer on my workstation demands more resources than the SAP R/3 front-end.

SAP was first developed for mainframe systems that don't have "client workstations". This is an alien concept for the majority of Visual Basic programmers, who learnt Visual Basic as their first programming language, using Microsoft Windows as OS and personal computers as hardware specification. We got used to the fact that any monitor with a GUI is connected to a full capacity PC, not all that different from the server computer.

At the beginning of the Visual Basic era, the emphasis was on client-side processing. In the server-side processing based mainframe world, the terminal was nothing more than the monitor and the keyboard, and all processing was carried out by the system on the mainframe. Mainframe 'clients' were so tiny and dumb that they only acted as entry points for the system.

SAP R/3 adopted this paradigm: it is a thin-client, fat-server system. This is implemented as a three-tier client-server system:

> A front-end
> An Application Server layer that implements all functional logic
> A database server that implements data storage

The SAP R/3 front-end takes advantage of the Windows OS, but it still only marshals requests to the server and displays results to the user. SAP R/3 offers robust component management capabilities and behaves very well under Windows. It doesn't halt I/O devices, doesn't freeze an interface and doesn't drain all resources from your PC.

**13**

Another advantage of the SAP R/3 thin-client architecture is that the same front-end component works with different versions and releases of the SAP R/3 server – it has backward compatibility. This is a result of the SAP R/3 strategy to not change a function's interface for the server component. That strategy will be explored in more detail once we get into BAPI programming.

## SAP is Multi-Platform

This is the area where SAP R/3 really shines. This book is for Visual Basic programmers and the OS is obviously Windows. However, SAP R/3 Unix installations outnumber Windows installations. (Note that when I refer to the Operating System that SAP R/3 is installed on, I mean the SAP R/3's system, not its GUI front-end.)

> *As more and more new installations are using Windows NT as the platform of choice, I suspect we'll soon seen Windows NT take over as the main OS for SAP R/3.*

Many Unix based software components are still inaccessible to Visual Basic programmers, because Unix is not a COM environment. However, the SAP R/3 architecture and design make it possible to communicate with SAP R/3 from virtually any platform, using any language that is capable of making a function call.

This SAP R/3 feature bridges a cross-platform development gap that always haunts Visual Basic programmers. One of the few "last resort" types of arguments that Visual Basic's opponents have is that Visual Basic programs can only run on Windows, and are therefore limited. SAP R/3 is capable of accepting remote function calls from a Windows environment while being on a Unix or other non-COM compliant operating system.

## SAP is Modular

SAP R/3 can be looked at as a collection of logical **business modules**. Each module implements a certain segment of an enterprise – for example, Financial Accounting, Logistics, or Material Management. I purposely use the word logical to introduce modules, because the physical implementation of SAP R/3 is beyond the scope of this book. To an external programmer, the physical implementation of any particular SAP R/3 functionality is transparent. All modules are closely interconnected and they share information and data integrity concepts.

> **Every business module can be looked at as a program that emulates a certain part of an enterprise.**

# SAP R/3 and Data Storage

We've seen that the core of SAP R/3 comprises programs that implement a very specific segment of an enterprise. Each module is a big system in itself, and it requires a good knowledge of a business component to successfully use and program a module. The areas covered are accounting and controlling, production and materials management, quality management and plant maintenance, sales and distribution; human resources management, and project management. For example, Materials Management handles the creation of new materials and other inventory related functionality. Sales Orders are created from Sales and Distribution. The important point is that those two modules work in close cooperation. The Sales and Distribution module will not let you create a Sales Order for a material that doesn't exist in the Materials Management module.

All these modules access data in the back-end RDBMS used by the SAP R/3 installation via a well-defined business and data integrity rules layer. The most interesting characteristic of SAP R/3 is that all the data is subjected to validation rules, and these rules are applicable across SAP R/3 as a system. In other words, if the data being entered make sense for the module they're being entered from, but are invalid for some other module, the data will be rejected.

This takes an enormous burden off an external programmer who is creating programs to load data into SAP R/3. It happens because SAP R/3 has various entry points for the inbound data, but all data are channeled through the same validation, regardless of the source.

If SAP R/3 had validation only for data entered directly, all external programs would have been forced to mirror SAP R/3 rules. Those not familiar with SAP R/3 can take my word on this, or ask an SAP R/3 expert: mirroring SAP R/3 business and integrity rules externally is tantamount to rewriting SAP R/3 itself.

Another very interesting thing about SAP R/3 has always been the way it relates to its own back-end database. SAP R/3 uses various database management systems, depending on the user's choice or OS limitations. Regular information systems use some kind of RDBMS and can have a very creative application layer around their back-end databases. However, these databases remain standard in terms of access and management.

For SAP R/3 (and all other releases of this product), the back-end database is completely shielded from external access. If, for example, you install SAP R/3 with Microsoft SQL Server, its database will not become your regular database for you to execute stored procedures or directly access data objects. SAP R/3 completely encapsulates its data storage and won't allow external applications to directly access its data. This is an absolute must for something of the complexity of SAP R/3, otherwise it wouldn't be able to guarantee data integrity.

SAP R/3 implements many check tables that contain lists of all possible values for predefined fields. For example, you can't enter a value for the Country – e.g. USA – if it doesn't exist in one of the check tables. The SAP R/3 GUI will present you with a drop-down selector for the fields that have predefined values or values that can be selected from some other list. After all the selections are made, SAP R/3 will perform all necessary validations that involve different modules to ensure integrity of the data. You can't, for example, sell merchandise that doesn't exist in the inventory, or to an unknown customer.

# The SAP R/3 Internal Environment

All these rules and routines are implemented as **ABAP Function Modules**.

> **ABAP (or Advanced Business Application Programming Language) is a proprietary SAP programming language – it is not used anywhere else.**

You can think of it as a scripting language or an SAP R/3 VBA. SAP R/3 acts like a host engine for this language, and you can feed an ABAP module into SAP R/3 and trigger its execution. To have one more parallel, we can compare this setup to ASP technology – the script is not compiled into executable components and requires Microsoft Internet Information Server or Personal Web Server to run.

ABAP is, to some extent, related to COBOL. It's easy for COBOL programmers to learn as a language, but the whole concept of SAP R/3 has always made it hard for anybody to actually utilize it. Even if you master the syntax of ABAP, you're still not likely to be able to use it effectively, because the language is very specific to the internal SAP R/3 functionality. This is the reason that ABAP programmers are in demand and compensated beyond industry standards. Because of SAP R/3's narrow scope of availability, you can't learn it unless you work with it. The real value of an ABAP programmer is in their understanding of particular SAP R/3 business modules and their interoperability.

The majority of these function modules can't be freely modified, because they comprise the core of SAP R/3's functionality. SAP has very cumbersome licensing policies and procedures that govern development for SAP R/3 and usage of it. Additionally, SAP R/3 implements special mechanisms and procedures to modify code or to apply service pack-like fixes, and you can't bypass these mechanisms. I won't elaborate on this here, as it is way beyond the scope of this book.

SAP R/3 implements an ABAP editor that allows you to create user programs. This editor lacks many of the modern code editor's features, but it lets you create the code – and that's all you need from a code editor anyway. The ABAP programming facilities also let you see the code for the SAP R/3 function modules that already exist in the system.

*It's important to understand that, while most of SAP R/3 is developed in C++ and C, ABAP is SAP R/3's internal scripting language. This is just like MS Access, which hosts VBA but is not developed in it. This paradigm allows SAP R/3 to enforce a strict developmental architecture for its internal needs. Because no other programming language works in SAP R/3, it can maintain universal ABAP based data types, logic and all other programming language constructs.*

All SAP R/3 data objects are accessible via the **ABAP Workbench Data Dictionary** facility. Data objects may be as simple as a field or as complex as a table. From the standpoint of learning SAP R/3 and developing applications in Visual Basic, the most important feature of the Data Dictionary is the ability to drill down the hierarchy of a data object. This exercise reveals the complexity of the internal SAP R/3 data architecture. It demonstrates that the data object may include other data objects as parts of it, and so on. All eventually comes down to a physical field in the back-end database, but the path may be long and complex.

All data objects are closely integrated with function modules. Data objects are available for function modules; function modules do not comprise data objects. Function modules carry out data manipulations. Instead of having data validation and business rules hot-wired to triggers on the database level, SAP R/3 implements a much more flexible and technically correct method of the client component – interacting with the application layer, not directly with the database. This is an obvious design choice, made necessary because SAP R/3 supports many different DBMS's.

A pictorial representation of this architecture is shown below:

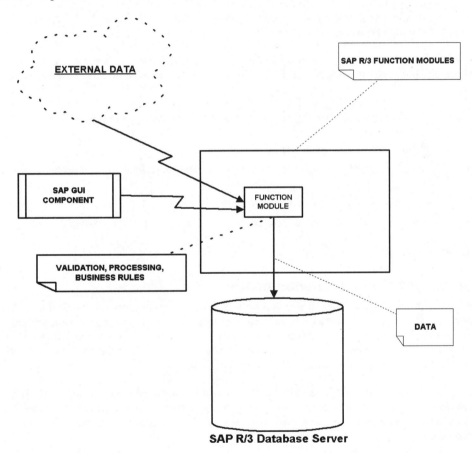

**SAP R/3 Database Server**

This architecture provides an opportunity to encapsulate all the code needed for any given business module and treat the business module as an object itself. This concept requires a more detailed exploration.

# The SAP R/3 Open Business Framework

Any software vendor that develops enterprise software of the SAP R/3 scope, price range and complexity has to plan very carefully the architecture of that software.

Companies don't buy SAP R/3 every quarter or every year – it's a huge investment of time and expensive labor. To get SAP R/3 up and running as a system, not just as a binary executable, requires substantial effort from people with a very detailed knowledge of the subject, who were involved in at least two previous large scale SAP R/3 implementations. The SAP AG consulting arm does a robust business with every customer that buys SAP R/3.

Even after a company has successfully implemented SAP R/3, it has to undertake a substantial training effort for all personnel involved with the system, and hire or train ABAP programmers to implement company specific applications.

It's very hard to justify the cost and effort involved if you're not running a company the size of IBM or Microsoft. That's why the list of SAP R/3 customers reads like a "Who's Who in the Global Economy".

To go some way towards justifying this expenditure, SAP maintains several principles:

> ➢ Integration with existing environments
> ➢ Easy modification of existing systems as business changes, without compromising those existing systems
> ➢ A common internal communication mechanism
> ➢ The ability to deal with future development and technological evolution of platforms

Let's take a closer look at these issues.

## Integration with Existing Environments

One aspect that can't be overlooked is that SAP R/3, like any other software, doesn't exist in a vacuum. Every large enterprise has a wide variety of applications, including mission critical applications that run on a variety of platforms and operating systems. All this software has to be integrated or even converted. Otherwise, instead of the benefits of the ERP package, the company will be left with very expensive and pretty useless software.

SAP R/3's ability to resolve the Year 2000 problem and to move data from legacy mainframes into a modern SAP R/3 environment attracts many companies. However, any software package that is not extensible and capable of being integrated into mainstream environments is much less attractive than one that can.

## Ease of Modification

One goal of SAP R/3 was to achieve a high level of maintainability. The major issue with enterprise software is that its very functionality has to be changed, or at least modified, with time. As new business practices and whole new industries and markets arrive on the scene, enterprise software has to evolve accordingly. These changes may go beyond simply altering coefficients in calculations – they may require modifications to algorithms or data structures. This type of change can have a ripple effect on the entire system.

To ensure maintainability, SAP implemented a modular design in its R/x line of products. Although I refer to SAP R/3 4.x in this book, the same principles are true for earlier releases as well. All internal functions in SAP R/3 are well defined and have clearly defined input and output. Functions are grouped by the business aspects of an enterprise – Sales and Distribution or Material Management – and are in fact well-defined interfaces for SAP R/3 internal modules.

This approach allows any functionality to be changed without ruining the whole module or the connection to other modules. The concept is familiar to Visual Basic programmers. We might design an ActiveX/COM component, and later decide to change its internal functionality without modifying the way it's being used externally. We do so by modifying the internal functionality, not the definitions for functions that are called externally (the component's interface).

This is the SAP R/3 customer's view of things. SAP also has to address many of the same issues during its development and planning cycle. Like any other popular software, the SAP R/x line evolves over time. There's much more to modifying something like SAP R/3 compared to upgrading conventional software.

> *Upgrades normally address bug fixes or add features to the application – they don't modify the core of the application.*

Microsoft Window NT is itself comparable to SAP R/3 in complexity and component interdependence. In the Windows OS, all components exist as separate units and implement a well-defined functionality. However, changing any Windows components may have a dramatic impact on the whole system. Moreover, these circumstances may be unforeseeable at the moment of design and implementation.

In the case of SAP R/3, this scenario could lead to data corruption and violation of business rules integrity, and that has to be avoided at any cost. Customers will not hesitate to pay the premium for software that's not going to corrupt mission critical data, and SAP R/3 promises exactly that.

## Internal Communication

Another important principle is a common interface standard. This is conceptually analogous to the COM standard. Every SAP R/3 function communicates with other functions using a standard mechanism and standard data types. If we scale it up to a business module level, it starts to resemble the way ActiveX/COM components communicate under the Windows operating system.

## Ability to Cope with Evolving Technologies

SAP has successfully addressed another very important issue – keeping up with technological change. Recall one thing that everyone takes for granted – SAP R/3 works on almost any platform and is now capable of communicating with components written in practically any major programming language. The fact that different technologies develop at a different pace under different platforms is therefore a significant issue.

SAP R/3 has a built-in abstraction layer that shields internal processes from external technology change. Think of it as of the Hardware Abstraction Layer in the Windows OS. It shields applications from the details of implementing access to hardware. This can also be said about OLEDB Data Providers and ODBC Data Drivers that abstract application developers from the specifics of a particular RDBMS implementation.

# The SAP R/3 Business Framework Environment

After outlining some key principles, we can proceed to the objective of this topic – the **Open Business Framework** of SAP R/3. Behind this name stands a simple yet powerful concept: extending SAP R/3 and making it possible to integrate it into diverse business information systems.

The main assumption behind this concept is that business components develop at a much slower rate than technologies. For example, we expect the functionality and logic of financial accounting to remain unchanged for years, whereas data representation on the platform that SAP R/3 runs on may change rapidly. If this is true, then it's possible to encapsulate a business component (for example an employee) and provide a well-defined interface for it. This guarantees cross-release compatibility, and the ability to utilize well-defined and robust SAP R/3 business objects in non-SAP R/3 applications.

At the core of the SAP R/3 Business Framework is the concept of the SAP R/3 **business object**. The business object will be discussed in much greater detail in Chapter 2. In this chapter, we'll introduce business objects from the more conceptual standpoint, to lay the foundation for a more technical discussion.

The very nature of an **object** – an encapsulation of logic and data – fits very well into the internal implementation of SAP R/3 functionality. Every operation in SAP R/3 is performed via a well-defined channel of execution using code modules. SAP R/3 identifies particular function modules and data structures responsible for implementing particular functionality.

We're all familiar with the object as a programming construct and implementation of a defined functionality. However, we're used to dealing either with components that implement some operating system functionality, like a File List box, or we implement some business rules ourselves, defining them in class modules. SAP R/3 introduces something new.

> **The business object implements a predefined business process or entity and exposes an interface for external communications. These objects are not defined in a familiar environment, and we can't handle them the way we do familiar COM compliant objects.**

SAP effectively grouped logically related functionality to make it accessible externally. In other words, all the functionality relevant to a customer or material can be implemented via corresponding business objects.

*A direct analogy: instead of forcing you to program against ODBC API directly, Microsoft introduced ODBC and DAO – a layer of well defined objects that abstract external programmers from internal implementation, yet allows them to perform all the same functionality.*

The concept of the SAP R/3 business framework permits us to build entire information systems based on well-defined, robust and refined SAP R/3 business objects. Instead of attempting to reinvent an employee or a customer every time, we can borrow the definition from SAP R/3's stock of business objects and use it across the system.

To expose the functionality implemented in business objects, SAP created **BAPI – Business Application Programming Interface** functions. These are nothing more than methods of business objects. Every business object has BAPIs defined in it, just like methods in regular objects. For example, the Database object has an `OpenRecordset` method, the Customer business object has the `CreateFromData` BAPI (used to create a Customer in SAP R/3).

Business objects have been defined in SAP R/x all along, and the emergence of these new technologies is due to an effort from SAP to extend its R/3 product to mainstream applications. The technologies that we're discussing are in the process of development and are subject to change from release to release, but SAP has strongly committed itself to the business object technology. With every release, more and more business objects are exposed, and this gradually opens up SAP R/3 for external use.

The best thing about SAP R/3 is that, because of the abstraction layer, it's possible to use any technology alongside SAP. This includes messaging and transaction tools. Later in this book, I'll introduce and discuss the SAP R/3 **DCOM Component Connector** that works with Microsoft Transaction Server – the openness of SAP R/3 will then become more apparent.

Because all the SAP R/3 business objects are defined inside SAP R/3 and we have well-established communication channels, we can use any object oriented or enabled programming environment to implement SAP R/3 business objects. They perfectly translate into the COM paradigm, and this book is built around this possibility.

# Microsoft Windows and SAP

We've seen that SAP and Microsoft both have flagship products with a commanding presence in modern enterprise computing. After reading this far, it should not come as a surprise to hear that they have started to work together.

SAP has implemented a robust communication mechanism, and developed a set of external libraries and tools to enable external access to its SAP R/3 system. The best developed and easiest to use are the ActiveX or COM based controls and COM compliant libraries that work seamlessly with Visual Basic. This mechanism is enabled in the **SAP Automation toolkit** – we'll be looking at this in great detail in later chapters.

The focus of the new SAP technological initiatives discussed in this book is to enable native integration of SAP R/3 into existing business applications and environments. All ERP vendors – namely SAP, PeopleSoft and Baan – are notorious for not supplying any comprehensive data exchange mechanism for external applications. Moreover, all mechanisms available from SAP R/3 totally disregard the external implementation of data access. For example, in Windows the native data access technology is ODBC, and emerging is OLEDB – ADO. Prior to the new tools outlined in this book, all data exchange mechanisms available from SAP were totally oblivious to Windows and its data access technologies. What's more, they required intimate knowledge of SAP R/3 internal functionality to implement any data exchange.

The problem of integration is very important, and after corporations solve Y2K related problems, it will become the next enterprise developmental priority. Every company that has purchased and implemented SAP R/3 has already invested very heavily, and has probably had to reinvent some of its business strategies to fit into the SAP R/3 implementation of enterprise.

On the software development side, it's worse. Any large or mid-size enterprise typically has complex heterogeneous data storage and business logic applications. They are most likely running on mainframes, different flavors of Unix, midrange – IBM AS/400 and increasingly on MS Windows NT. This list also applies to possible platforms for SAP R/3 installation. What happens most of the time is that the information exchange among different parts of the IS infrastructure is at best delayed, hampering the decision-making process. Many of these applications are well developed and are the core for the successful performance of the enterprise.

# Why Microsoft?

However, the desktop and workgroup segment belongs to Microsoft Windows. With the increasing power and robustness of Windows and the introduction of COM+, Windows will definitely gain popularity in the enterprise segment of development. As I said earlier it is already the *de facto* corporate standard for desktop operating systems.

The increasing popularity of Microsoft productivity tools (such as Microsoft Office 2000) and enterprise servers family (BackOffice 4.5, including the very powerful SQL Server 7.0) ensures that the first target of integration will be, and in fact is, Microsoft Windows.

Another extremely important factor is that SAP R/3 bridges the platform gap exposing COM-compliant interfaces on non-COM platforms. Windows implements transaction support with MTS, and MTS will become integrated into COM+ with Windows 2000. It also has messaging support (MSMQ) and supports Internet development (IIS and ASP). Windows has the SNA Server for mainframe/midrange support, SQL Server 7.0 for enterprise strong RDBMS with OLAP services, and implements OLEDB for Universal Data Access. It also has Visual Studio, that allows the development of virtually any kind of software for Windows.

New technologies such as OLEDB will drive further the cooperation of SAP R/3 and Visual Basic. This applies to areas of data representation rather than data access. In other words, it's not likely that SAP will develop an OLEDB provider for SAP R/3. This is because all OLEDB providers assume relational data storage and implement SQL compliance, which is simply impossible with SAP R/3 because it does not assume direct access to its data storage.

Microsoft Repository and its heavy presence in SQL Server 7.0 also creates new opportunities for SQL Server 7.0 based data warehousing solutions centered on the Microsoft product family.

These factors surely contribute to the fact that the SAP implementation of its Automation SDK is the best for Windows. It also suggests that the integration of the Windows platform based applications with SAP R/3 will be the most popular and necessary. It makes perfect sense from the business perspective. If a company has already developed a Windows-based decision support system, it can easily integrate SAP R/3 into it. Another factor that contributes to the integration of SAP R/3 is the conceptual, and to a certain extent architectural, compatibility between COM and the SAP implementation of business objects.

# Benefits of SAP and Microsoft Integration

The convergence of SAP R/3 and the Microsoft family of products creates enormous opportunities to implement real-time, event driven enterprise information systems. Some of the most obvious benefits are:

> - A unique knowledge base of SAP in enterprise computing
> - An enormous pool of business users comfortable with Microsoft Windows
> - A large pool of skilled Visual Basic and other Microsoft oriented programmers
> - The popularity of Microsoft SQL Server
> - The availability of Microsoft Office and VBA skills of its power users
> - Comfortable Visual Basic learning curve for COBOL and ABAP/4 programmers
> - Microsoft Windows' dominance in the midsize and small enterprise market segment
> - The availability of Microsoft Enterprise development tools
> - The robust SAP R/3 architecture and its stability
> - Emerging trends in cross-platform implementation of Microsoft products and SAP R/3 already being implemented on all major platforms
> - Unique SAP R/3 fit into the Microsoft Universal Data Access paradigm
> - The heavy presence of Microsoft in e-commerce, and SAP R/3's e-commerce capabilities
> - Enormous cost-effectiveness (in reducing labor/training costs by utilizing existing skills )

BAPI technology and SAP's commitment to its business object implementation makes possible the close integration of SAP R/3 into existing information systems, and the building of principally different ones. SAP has committed enormous effort to BAPI and business object architecture development, and the number of BAPIs increases with every release of its SAP R/3 product – from around 400 with version 4.0 to more than 700 with version 4.5. Moreover, there is a huge advantage in using SAP R/3 Workflow functionality and custom BAPI design. They extend SAP R/3 functionality and open possibilities to create self-adapting information systems.

# SAP R/3 and Visual Basic

In this book, I will attempt to introduce readers to SAP R/3 application development using Microsoft Visual Basic 6.0. I will also try to outline and illustrate as much as possible the integration of the new SAP R/3 technologies into Microsoft products such as Microsoft Office and SQL Server.

This book will focus on one thing:

> **What is available to a regular corporate Visual Basic programmer to develop robust enterprise applications based on SAP R/3, or integrate it into existing systems?**

One of the strongest points of Visual Basic is that there are very few aspects of Visual Basic development that you can't learn and master at home or in school. With SAP R/3, it's a totally different situation. It reminds me of the time when we didn't have personal computers, and the only way to learn programming or any software was to get a job with a company that had them. SAP R/3 is not your friendly and affordable business application – it's anything but.

As we discussed earlier in the chapter, SAP R/3 is very resource consuming, and I don't mean only computing resources. It needs a substantial investment of time, money and training. That's also why SAP are keen to seize any opportunity to utilize existing skills.

Another problem arises from of the lack of availability of SAP R/3 to mainstream programmers – there's too much hearsay and not enough facts about SAP products. This is made worse because periodic publications targeted at mainstream Visual Basic programmers don't discuss ERP issues or SAP R/3 in particular.

One of the objectives of this book is to dispel some myths about SAP R/3 and outline the basic principles of SAP R/3 functionality. It is not an objective of this book to teach you SAP R/3 as a system or an application in detail. This is a very important distinction.

*Another important clarification: as we progress into this book, I will introduce some definitions of a variety of subjects, including those related to SAP R/3. All these definitions are for clarification or illustration purposes. This book is not an academic exercise, and I have no intention of inventing any theoretical concepts. What I have to do is to comprehensively bridge the gap between the general Visual Basic development paradigm and SAP R/3 without any aberrations or excessive simplification.*

# Introduction to the SAP Front-End

So far, we've not seen any screen shots of the SAP R/3 front-end GUI. This was so as not to distract you from the conceptual paradigm of SAP R/3 as a system. However, now that we've almost finished Chapter 1, it's appropriate to start to familiarize ourselves with the SAP R/3 front-end GUI component.

This section should not be looked on as an SAP R/3 tutorial – it's not. The aim is simply to break the initial barrier for a Visual Basic programmer – I've got the SAP R/3 front-end, now what? The initial reflex of any Windows user or Visual Basic developer is to find some kind of GUI component "attached" to implemented functionality. Because we're used to Windows' intuitive GUI implementation, it's natural to start learning from the GUI.

To reproduce illustrations from this chapter you need:

> Access to SAP R/3 release 4.5A (4.0 will not be different from this perspective)

> Correctly installed SAP R/3 front-end software on your workstation. (The version used here is 4.0B.)

> A valid account for SAP R/3

*Note that data displayed on these screen shots might be different from what you see.*

If you have installed the SAP front-end component on your workstation you are most likely to have the **SAP Frontend 4.x** element under the **Start | Programs** group on your desktop. You should have an **SAPlogon** in that group:

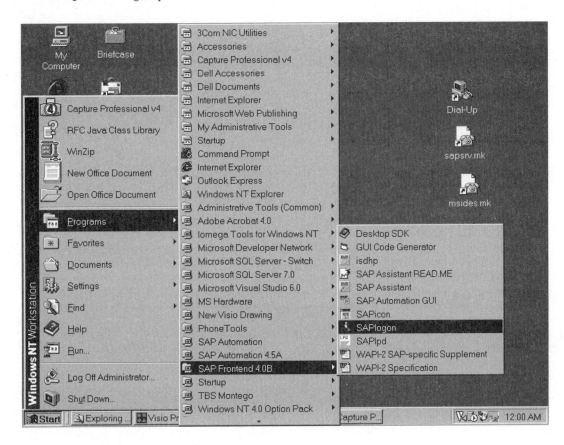

Select the **SAPlogon** element, and you
should see something like this:

Then select the SAP R/3 installation you want, and logon.

> *If you don't have the **SAPlogon** choice, or it's blank, ask your SAP programmer or
> administrator to help you with it.*

The first screen you will see
is the login screen, which is
presented to you upon
successful connection of the
front-end client to the SAP
R/3 server:

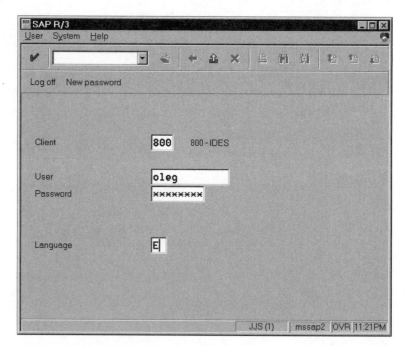

After successful
login, you should be
presented with the
SAP R/3 main
screen:

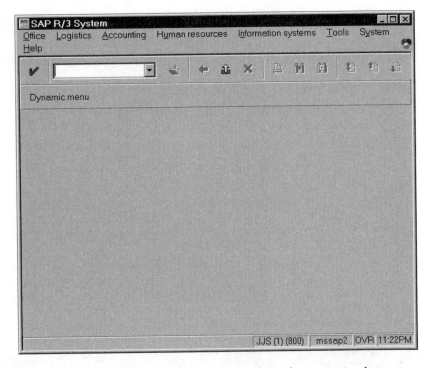

Note the top-level menu items – these are related to the business modules that comprise the system.

The SAP R/3 front-end software, like any GUI, reflects the internal functionality. What we are going to see is a visual representation of our discussion on SAP R/3 modules earlier in the chapter. Until now, they were very abstract and might have made little sense. Now we can see the implementation of these modules, and other SAP R/3 functionality.

I have already referred to the Financial Accounting module: now we'll look at the first couple of screens that SAP R/3 will offer you in this module.

Start by selecting **Accounting**. Then follow the **Financial accounting | Accounts receivable** menu choices as illustrated:

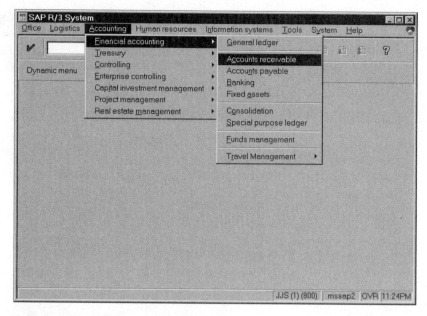

You should see the following screen:

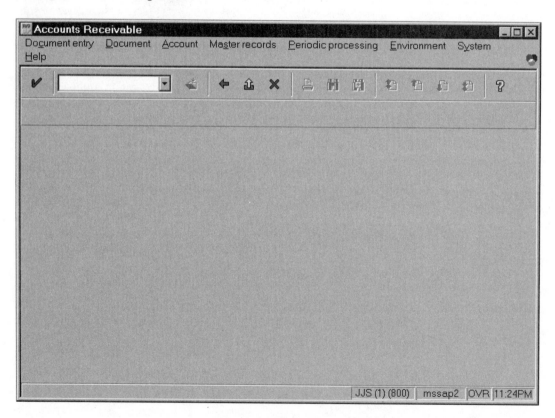

Intuitively, you can guess that **Accounting** deals with account receivables, and those who pay you are your customers. This feeds directly into our discussion about how SAP R/3 implements enterprise and business functionality. You are obviously going to have customers, and therefore SAP R/3 provides you with the functionality to perform all operations involving customers. And as we have discussed, SAP R/3 logically groups functionality into modules, and modules are exposed to the user via the GUI component:

To get into the **Customers** screen, select the **Master records | Display** menu items:

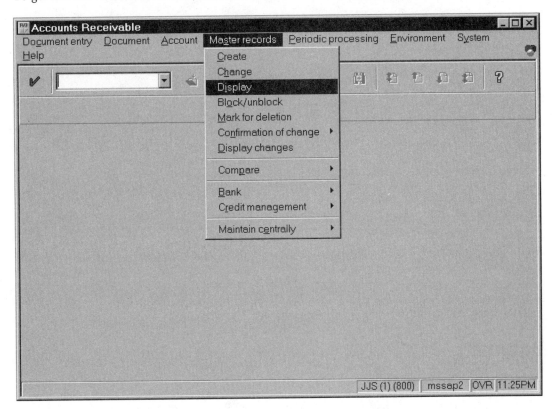

After you select the Display function, you will be presented with the following screen:

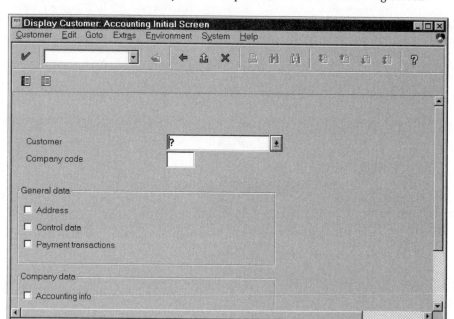

This is a customer information display screen that allows you to search for a particular customer using different criteria.

This exercise was supposed to give Visual Basic programmers an initial glimpse of the SAP R/3 system, and to illustrate the SAP R/3 front-end tool.

## Summary

In this chapter, we introduced SAP R/3 as a system. We looked at some of the problems encountered in enterprise programming, and how SAP R/3 is used by modern enterprises. We outlined the conceptual, and to some extent technical, details of SAP R/3. One of the most important concepts introduced is that of SAP R/3 business objects and how they are used to emulate an enterprise.

We also started to learn how and why SAP R/3 is being integrated with Microsoft Windows products, in particular Visual Basic.

Finally, we introduced the SAP R/3 front-end GUI component.

In the next chapter, we will expand our view of SAP R/3 as an implementation of an enterprise. We'll continue to explore business objects and BAPIs, and their relation to technologies familiar to Visual Basic programmers. We will address the similarities between SAP R/3 business objects and COM objects.

We will also continue our gradual introduction to the SAP R/3 front-end component, and display some of the internal implementation of SAP R/3.

# 2

# SAP R/3 Business Objects and BAPI

To fully understand the concept of the **SAP business object**, it's necessary to first comprehend the concept of SAP R/3's implementation of an enterprise. Like many other things described in this book, SAP R/3 is *counter-intuitive* to the traditional application programmer. It's not a traditional object model; it's not specific to any programming language; and it's not a purely hypothetical concept either. The best place to start is with a conceptual model of SAP R/3 itself.

## The Nature of SAP R/3

> **SAP R/3 is an *application* – it is *not* an operating system, platform or language.**

From a programmer's standpoint SAP R/3 is a *huge* application. SAP R/3 ABAP programmers may argue that SAP R/3 is a set of applications, and indeed internally SAP R/3 is implemented as a set of applications, but to a Windows application programmer SAP R/3 is more conceptually similar to, say, a SQL Server-based client-server system. This may sound heretical, but let's analyze my point here.

SAP R/3 has a back-end database – although it may use several different RDBMS for this purpose, including Microsoft SQL Server. SAP R/3 also has an **Application Layer** built around its physical data store. This layer shields the physical data store from direct external access. In its Application Layer, SAP R/3 implements a very complex set of business rules and internal function modules.

This doesn't mean there is no access to the data store but rather SAP R/3 implements methods of communication between the data store and external programs, written in common languages such as C++, and implemented on common platforms such as Unix and Windows. This sounds very much like our typical three-tier client-server system, albeit a huge one.

> **Ultimately, SAP R/3 is, in fact, a very well designed, scalable, multi-user distributed client-server system.**

A highly schematic view of an SAP R/3 implementation and its layers is provided below:

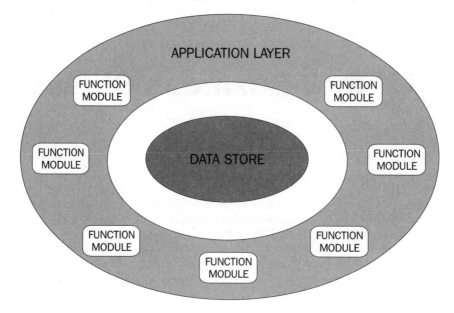

But if SAP R/3 is basically just an application why is there so much confusion about it? The answer is very simple: SAP R/3 is a *non-trivial* application.

> **SAP R/3 emulates an entire enterprise, not a single process like most regular business applications. SAP R/3 manages to implement virtually *every* conceivable business scenario and integrates them using complex rules to ensure data integrity.**

Moreover, SAP R/3 provides a somewhat arcane but bulletproof GUI to perform everything from data-entry to system management. More importantly, SAP R/3 implements an enterprise **continuously,** while most regular applications only implement variations on a snapshot of a given business segment. This may sound like some book on management rather than Visual Basic, but welcome to the world of ERPs.

For example, if you have your typical Information System and you are a big and/or old enough enterprise, you probably have a mainframe system, as well as Unix or Windows NT based applications. It requires considerable effort to integrate these systems to provide real-time functions and to implement logical dependencies of those applications – Sales influences Inventory and so forth. Using SAP R/3 alleviates you from having to implement such a system yourself.

SAP R/3 has always been and still is a set of well-integrated business related modules such as Financial, Logistics, Material Management and so on. These modules allow a company to define its own framework. Any given company may use SAP R/3 implemented modules to emulate its business workflow and processes. These modules provide all the data integrity functionality and allow for business related flexibility.

> *Moreover, if a company had already implemented one module it can add other modules without interrupting an already implemented module, while enjoying full integration.*

The only problem is that all ERPs are notorious for being inflexible when it comes to integration with any other software. With ERPs in general, and SAP R/3 in particular, they are most effective when the company does conduct, or changes the way it conducts, its business to conform to the ERP – SAP R/3 – standards.

# SAP R/3 Implementation

SAP R/3 implements all of its functionality using very complex data structures and **function modules**. This book is not intended to delve deeply into the specifics of SAP R/3 implementation, but some background detail is necessary.

In SAP R/3 you cannot directly see the data objects as you would in Microsoft SQL Server's Enterprise Manager window.

> *In fact, SAP R/3 does such a superb job in encapsulating its data objects that you won't even know which table is supplying the data to your application.*

This scenario is incompatible with traditional systems where Windows programmers may develop queries dynamically or invoke stored-procedures on the back-end RDBMS. In order to do this you need to know the underlying data structure, including relations, triggers and so on. With SAP R/3 you don't even know which internal table or function module is supplying the information to the SAP R/3 front-end GUI element you are in. Until very recently, all relevant Windows programmers were rendered obsolete the day SAP R/3 went live at any company.

As you may gather from the above paragraphs, the situation with SAP R/3 was rather unpleasant for IS departments. Consider this: you have an extremely complex ERP that does everything that you can possibly think of, but it is self-enclosed and you cannot integrate your existing applications into it without considerable modification. SAP R/3 has always provided ways to integrate external applications with it but the problem lies in having to know ABAP to do it. Plus, you have to tailor the external application to accommodate SAP R/3 specific communication procedures and data exchange formats. True integration, however, shouldn't require you to alter your existing applications.

Another issue is that to truly integrate two applications we have to be able to preserve key technologies used by either side. For example, if our Windows application uses ADO to access data we don't want to implement any other data access or processing technology in order to integrate it with SAP R/3.

Another way would be to load all your corporate data into SAP R/3 – a very labor intensive and expensive task – and use SAP R/3 exclusively for all your needs. This is contrary to the concept of integration meaning heterogeneous data dispersed in applications across the enterprise.

> **To enable integration of anything into anything else, components need to have some *common* interface and mechanism to communicate.**

SAP has created just such an interface, as we are about to learn in this chapter.

SAP R/3 by its very nature is **business process specific**. In other words, every module implements a *specific* business process of the enterprise. Every business process can be viewed as continua of related sub-processes. For example, in order to have a Sales Order you have to first have a defined *Customer* and available *Inventory*. An *Inventory* comprises *Material* items and so on. SAP R/3 implements *Customers* and *Material Management* in different modules but these modules need to be closely integrated. SAP R/3 performs this **cross-module integration** using very complex algorithms and internal processing. Moreover, this integration is not exposed to any external applications, so there is no way an external application can be aware of the background processing performed by SAP R/3.

Now let's analyze what we just said in the above paragraph. When we say that some software implements anything related to real-life, the only way we can think about it is as **abstraction**. In order to define anything we have to *abstract* it from everything irrelevant to its core nature. This leads us into the area of **objects**.

As you know, an object is something that abstracts a real-life concept or subject and can contain data and functionality to perform manipulations on that data. This definition serves the purpose of business implementation well.

Let's analyze a customer. We can define an abstract *Customer* object that will have all the necessary functionality to provide us with the data for any particular customer. If we achieve this, we would not care about how exactly the object gets the data and where it gets it from. We can also abstract ourselves from the way it is implemented. Moreover, all objects can expose a common interface to enable cross-object and external communication.

*This last statement essentially summarizes the basic principles of COM.*

# SAP R/3 and Business Objects

The major conceptual point about an object is that it abstracts real-life situations and scenarios. Since we operate in the world of ERPs in general, and SAP R/3 in particular, the "real-life situations and scenarios" we need to abstract can be rephrased as **business scenarios**.

Since SAP R/3 implements an enterprise it would be logical to look at it as an assembly of objects that abstract the different business functionalities of SAP R/3. Another characteristic of an object, that fits perfectly into the SAP R/3 internal implementation, is the fact that objects normally encapsulate functionality that accesses data. This is exactly what the function modules in SAP R/3 do – they encapsulate access to the data store.

Every Visual Basic programmer routinely uses objects to implement various tasks. As we all remember, objects merely encapsulate some functionality. You may have objects implementing GUI presentation – an object that implements chart plotting; user access functionality – an object that validates users; database access – an object that encapsulates all database access functionality; and business logic objects – objects that implement the business logic of your enterprise.

SAP took a different route with its **business objects**. The business objects implemented in SAP R/3 encapsulate business functionality only. SAP did this primarily because the main functionality of SAP R/3 is to implement various aspects of a business. It would make no sense for SAP to implement anything else. Encapsulating business functionality into business objects fits well into one of the major characteristics of SAP R/3 – abstracting the user or external programmer from internal functional implementation.

> **We can say that the SAP R/3 has various internally defined business objects encapsulating particular business functionality.**

SAP R/3 has always had everything needed to implement business objects. It has always provided an object-oriented approach to business data and it was a natural progression for SAP R/3 to clearly define business objects. These business objects benefited from SAP R/3's mature implementation of business processes and data structures. With the business object, SAP once again reinvented enterprise implementation.

With R/3, SAP started to implement all **atomic business entities** as business objects. Let me clarify what I mean by an "atomic business entity". The very word *atomic* suggests something that cannot be further divided meaningfully. If you start taking apart a car it will cease to exist as a car. You may get a wheel or a door but you need to put them all together to get a car. In the same way you cannot further break down a Customer, Purchase Order or Employee without losing something integral to their very nature. These are the sorts of Lego blocks that SAP defined. As with actual Lego blocks you can theoretically build an infinite number of combinations provided that you comply with the rules.

It is important to understand that atomic does not mean primitive or elementary. A business object may be very complex and implement a great deal of functionality but it will still be an atomic entity.

> **Every business object represents an atomic entity for a particular business process. Every business object uses existing function modules and data structures to get data or to update the underlying data structures.**

The following diagram shows how an SAP R/3 business object relates to function modules:

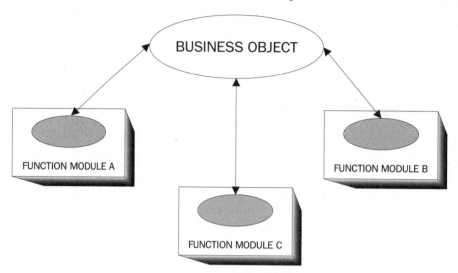

SAP R/3 took a top-down approach in defining its business objects and used all the existing functionality of SAP R/3. This approach allowed for minimum modifications to the existing function modules, and no modification to the existing data structures at all. This was very important for an application like SAP R/3 because of its complex data integrity implementation.

## SAP R/3 Business Object Structure

The following diagram shows the structural layout of an SAP R/3 business object:

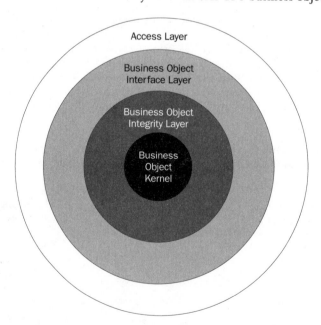

As you may notice this diagram presents a view of an abstract business object implemented in SAP R/3. If we use Microsoft terminology it is rather an object-model layout. It does not define the particular business object; rather it offers the SAP R/3 standard implementation of a business object, similar in concept to the COM standard for ActiveX objects.

> *The word similar in the previous sentence should not be interpreted as a suggestion that SAP R/3 uses COM to define its business objects. COM and CORBA are standards used to define reusable components by Microsoft and the Object Management Group respectively. SAP does not adhere to or use these standards for its SAP R/3 business objects. However, the SAP R/3 implementation of business objects does relate to COM and CORBA. At this moment the connection to COM is implemented fully and you can take advantage of it using Visual Basic and SAP supplied ActiveX components.*

Before we get into details on SAP R/3 business object implementation, let's concentrate on the above diagram:

> ➤ The first layer is the **Business Object Kernel**. This layer contains all the core business logic. It is shielded from any direct external access.

> ➤ The second layer wrapped around the Kernel is the **Business Object Integrity Layer**. This layer implements all the object-related constraints and business rules relevant to this object. For example, if you attempt to create a Customer using a non-existent Distribution Channel or Language, it will be intercepted at this layer. This layer is responsible for the communication with various check tables and function modules that perform validation and implement business rules. This layer is also shielded from any direct external access.

> ➤ The third layer is the **Business Object Interface Layer**. This layer contains all the methods, events and input/output control functionality. It is accessible externally using COM and handles the communication and business object related outbound messaging.

> ➤ The last layer is an **Access Layer** that implements different standards of access to the business object – COM, CORBA and Java. In this book we'll obviously be concentrating on the COM implementation of the Access Layer.

The above demonstrates how SAP has practically developed its own object architecture standard for business objects. SAP in its R/3 product had to devise a way to uniformly define business objects internally and yet expose their interfaces to external programming environments that are not aware of SAP R/3 specifics. If you think about it for a moment you will appreciate SAP's effort.

> **The list of platforms and programming languages capable of using SAP R/3 business object technology clearly indicates that SAP has created a cross-platform integration layer for the enterprise.**

We can justifiably say that, because you can implement SAP R/3 business objects from different platforms, using different binary systems and object standards, and still have consistent data and transactional implementation. You can have SAP R/3 implemented on Unix and connect to it from a Windows NT machine. Another part of your enterprise information system can connect to the SAP R/3 from anywhere else and the *Customer* business object will be the same in all parts of your system.

Another very important thing is that SAP R/3 business objects are defined only in SAP R/3 and have no other *external* implementation. This is very different from all other object libraries that Visual Basic programmers are used to working with. Traditionally, object libraries under Windows reside in some DLL file and all the objects are accessible via the standard COM mechanism. Windows knows everything about these DLLs and all the internal objects adhere to the COM standard.

This basically means you can use the Data Access Object (DAO) Library as long as you have Windows and a properly installed version of DAO. With SAP R/3 business objects it is a completely different story. There is no such COM, or any other object library, that includes the defined SAP R/3 business objects. In other words, there is no type library to reference in your Visual Basic project and you cannot have your favorite `Dim Customer As SAP.Customer` declaration.

# Business Objects and BAPIs

Methods defined in SAP R/3 business objects are those magic **BAPI**s or **Business Application Programming Interface** functions that everybody talks about.

> **BAPI technology is the core of the new business object paradigm for SAP R/3 external application development.**

SAP R/3 has created a well-defined set of functions for its business objects to implement the object's functionality. Every business object has a set of BAPIs defined within its structure.

> **The domain of BAPIs is the business object, *not* SAP R/3 in general.**

In other words, you cannot get to a BAPI without first creating a valid reference to a running instance of an appropriate business object. It's not a new concept for VB programmers. It's standard to first create an object instance and then access its methods.

Let's diverge for a moment and take a look at something familiar – the Data Access Object library (DAO).

Like all other data access technologies DAO shields the Visual Basic programmer from the specifics of database implementation and presents a common object hierarchy to be programmed against. All objects of this component are defined inside a DLL that we reference from a Visual Basic project. To gain access to any DAO functionality we have to first create a valid running instance of the object that encapsulates the functionality. In other words, to open a recordset we have to first have an instance of the Database object:

```
Dim daoDb As Database
Dim daoRs As Recordset

Set daoDb = OpenDatabase("C:\Biblio.mdb" , False)
Set daoRs = daoDb.OpenRecordset("Authors" , dbOpenDynaset)
```

If we attempt to use any method of an object without a valid running instance of that object we will get an error message. This little exercise illustrates one of the fundamental principles of object-oriented programming – methods belong to objects. There is no such thing as an orphan method in a library. Even if you do not explicitly create an instance of the object, VB may do it for you. For example, the `OpenDatabase` method that is defined in the Workspace object is created for us with a global class in Visual Basic. You do not have to explicitly create an instance of such a class; Windows will do it for you when you refer to the method or a property of such a class.

If we apply the same principle to SAP R/3 we may rephrase it this way:

> **Every BAPI should belong to some business object and cannot be invoked without first creating an instance of said object.**

## BAPI Parameters

Every BAPI implements a process of accessing data relevant to a business object or delivering data to a business object, via an internal SAP R/3 mechanism transparent to the external program. Like all functions, BAPIs have **parameters**. These parameters are also defined in SAP R/3 and are of three types:

> - **Fields**
> - **Structures**
> - **Tables**

You can think of these as data types that you can use from Visual Basic. Parameters are needed to supply data to a BAPI and transport data back. In SAP R/3 terminology, inbound parameters are considered **Import** and outbound parameters **Export**. Some parameters are bi-directional.

However, with SAP nothing is trivial. Yes there are only three types of data for parameters, but there is a much bigger list of parameters with a predefined structure in SAP R/3.

> **Every BAPI has a predefined set of parameters that it expects and it will not take anything less.**

The most important thing to understand is that it's the name of the parameter that SAP R/3 reacts to. Once a BAPI call "enters" SAP R/3, all kinds of necessary work are performed on it to execute the BAPI. It makes sure that the arguments supplied match with predefined parameters in both structure and content; it performs all types of validation and integrity checks and finally executes the call. SAP R/3 parses every parameter and compares its structure to a predefined template.

Another important thing to notice is that in SAP R/3, BAPIs may have the same parameters. This is understandable since we already know that all the business object related constructs are implemented internally in SAP R/3, together with the mechanism that connects them to physical data.

The following diagram will give you an idea of the sort of parameters a BAPI expects:

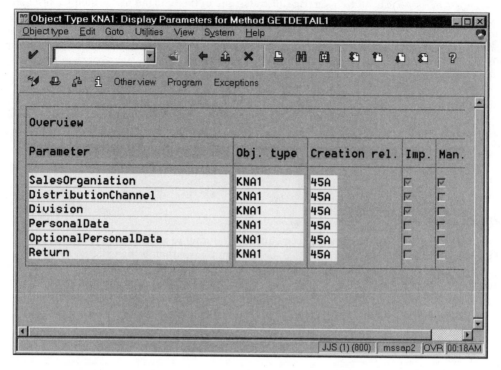

### The Field Parameter Type

This represents a single value that you pass to the BAPI, and corresponds to a Visual Basic String data type. Every Field parameter has a predefined length and you may be tempted to declare Visual Basic variables for Field types as fixed-length strings. You may do so, just bear in mind string initialization and manipulation specifics when handling fixed-length strings.

### The Structure Parameter Type

Structure represents a composite value that you pass to the BAPI, and corresponds to an Object data type in Visual Basic. Treat it as a single row table. Every named Structure has a predefined layout and field names. Beware of the fact that in every Structure there are fields that require values and those that do not. Moreover, the content of a Structure will be validated in SAP R/3 and in most cases you have no way of validating the content prior to loading it into SAP R/3.

> *In some cases you can restrict the content of the fields to the content of some known Check Table – an SAP R/3 internal table where fixed values are stored e.g. Country abbreviations.*

### The Table Parameter Type

This represents a table style data structure, and corresponds to an Object data type in Visual Basic. Treat it as a regular table. All the specifics outlined for a Structure apply to the Table parameter as well.

## *Exploring SAP R/3 Business Objects and BAPIs*

All this discussion warrants some SAP R/3 exploration. The place to go in SAP R/3 to explore business objects and their architecture is the **Business Object Builder**:

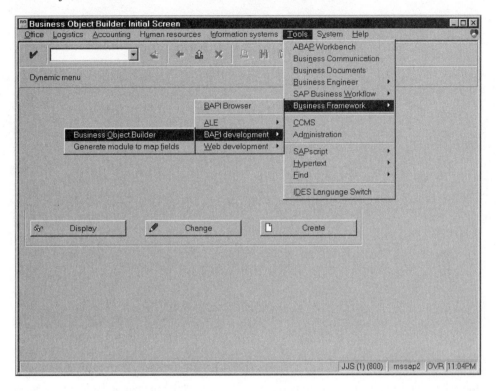

Select the menu item as indicated in the above screenshot and you will be presented with the Initial Screen of this utility:

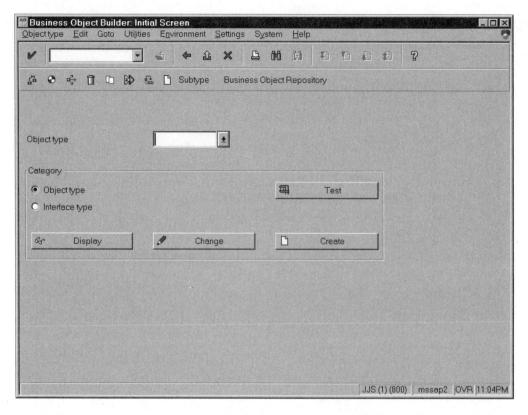

At this point we have to decide which business object we want to explore. I recommend the *Customer* business object because it has an intuitive interface and virtually every Visual Basic programmer has done something related to a Customer or Order Processing database application before.

> *Please also note, as I have repeatedly stressed, this book is not an SAP R/3 tutorial and should not be treated as such. All screenshots are for illustrative purposes only; provided to familiarize the Visual Basic developer with the SAP R/3 environment.*

Having clarified that, we can proceed to the exploration of the *Customer* business object. I first came across this object at the BAPI Browser page of the SAP web site. It maintains a list of business objects and provides some information on them. One such piece of data was the internal name for the *Customer* business object – KNA1 – and I set out to find it in SAP R/3. When I typed KNA1 into the Object type box provided and hit Display I got this intriguing picture:

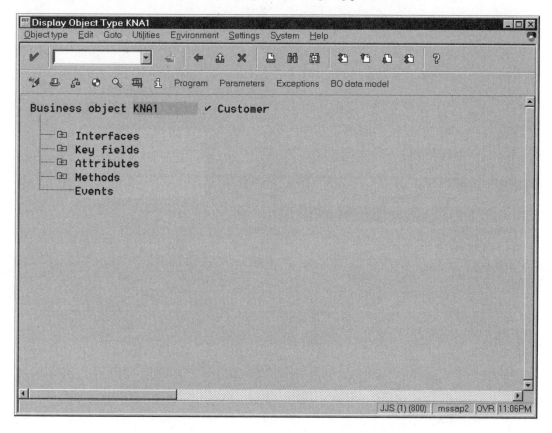

Now I could see something that looks familiar to the Visual Basic programmer – Methods. I selected Methods by double-clicking on them and I was presented with the following screen:

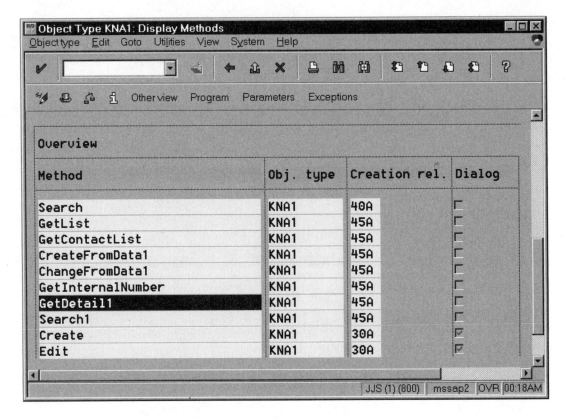

This picture was in synch with the web page that displayed the BAPIs for the *Customer* business object.

> *Please note that these screenshots are a representation of SAP R/3 release 4.5 - the latest and greatest. In this release additional BAPIs have been added and if you are looking at an earlier release you won't see as many BAPIs.*

The strategy of incrementally adding new BAPIs, instead of changing those already in existence, guarantees a stable function interface (parameters and their names). If SAP develops a new, better BAPI, it marks the old one as obsolete and recommends that you don't use it.

I continued my exploration by selecting the `GetDetail1` BAPI, because it seemed self-explanatory, and I was presented with the following screen:

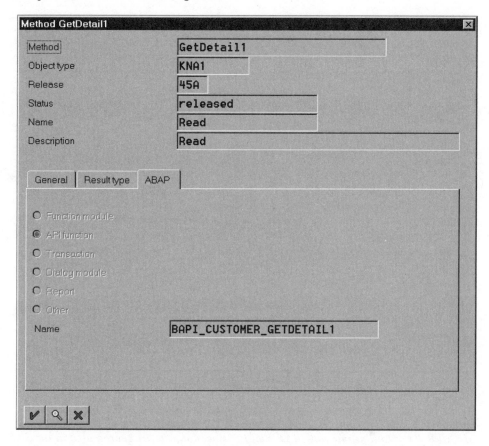

Now things get more interesting. We can see the 'real name' for the BAPI that is used in SAP R/3 – `BAPI_CUSTOMER_GETDETAIL1`. This should be conceptually familiar. You've used aliases for the API `Declare` statements in Visual Basic before.

Then I went on to explore the parameters or arguments for this BAPI by clicking on the Parameters button on the Display Object Type screen and I was presented with the following:

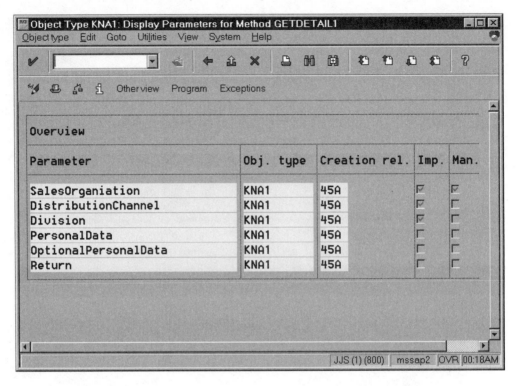

*Again, this is a representation of release 4.5. In release 4.5 new BAPIs have different parameters. However, our objective here is not to learn the differences in the releases of SAP R/3 but to illustrate how BAPIs and business objects are represented in the SAP R/3 repository.*

If we continue to drill down this BAPI, we can select one of the parameters – `SalesOrganiation` (not a typo – as it is in SAP R/3) – and see some details on it:

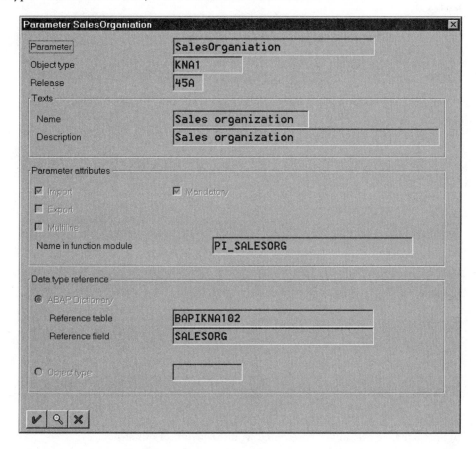

As you might have already noticed, SAP R/3 maintains at least two sets of names for all the entities involved in the business objects architecture:

> ➤ The name exposed from the business object level – `SalesOrganiation`
> ➤ The name as defined in the function module – `PI_SALESORG`

One more thing is that at the parameter level we can see the name of the database object or Reference table. If we continue to explore the reference table, by double-clicking on it, we will find the following:

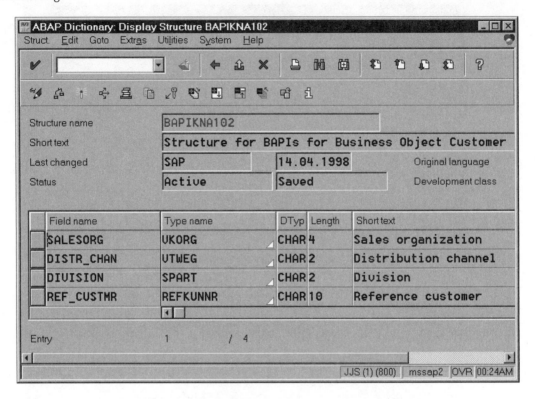

What we can learn from this screen is that this BAPI parameter is a `Structure` and it is a data entity of SAP R/3. We are, in fact, presented with the layout of this structure.

*You'll see why knowing the layout of a structure is important later.*

This is about as deep down the hierarchy as we are interested in going. We've reached the level of the fields of the data object that the BAPI parameters encapsulate.

Now it's time to confirm that every BAPI is a function defined in an SAP R/3 ABAP function module. If we select `BAPI_CUSTOMER_GETDETAIL1`, by double-clicking on it, on the initial Method screen, SAP R/3 will present us with this view:

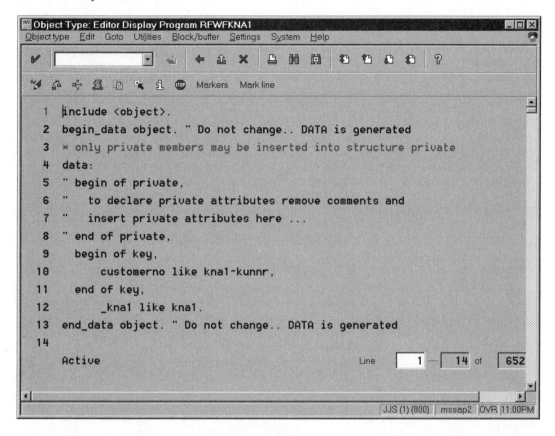

The code is rather long and doesn't make much sense to a VB programmer anyway, but I think the above screenshot confirms our statement that every BAPI is defined internally in SAP R/3.

Therefore, as with all methods, BAPIs serve the purpose of encapsulating access to data. However, instead of programming in ABAP using the SAP R/3 specific environment, SAP R/3 provides a collection of business objects that expose methods to external programs that manipulate the data relevant to the business object.

One of the objectives of SAP R/3 is to offer predefined solutions to virtually any business problem. This is possible only by making all complex business rules transparent to the external programmer and exposing high-level functions to implement SAP R/3 functionality. This means that this SAP R/3 BAPI technology presents a very clear and intuitive interface to program SAP R/3 applications. Something we'll spend the rest of the book examining how to do.

# Visual Basic Objects vs. SAP R/3 Business Objects

First, the quick and dirty Visual Basic oriented-definition for an object: An object has properties, methods and associated events.

SAP R/3 business objects have attributes, some of them reflecting the state of the business object, which are analogous to properties. SAP R/3 business objects also have methods and may publish and subscribe to event implementation.

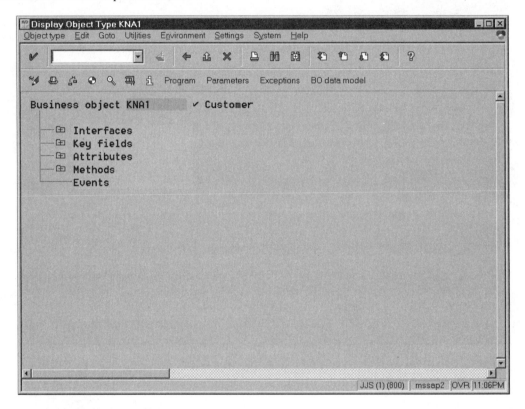

## *SAP R/3 Business Object Attributes*

Attributes may be directly linked to internal tables or be virtual, i.e. computed on demand each time they're invoked. Sounds very familiar except for one small thing.

> **The attributes of SAP R/3 business objects are not directly accessible.**

Let me clarify this statement. In the traditional Visual Basic environment if you get a valid reference to a running instance of an object, all of its public properties become available to you. You can get to them using the dot operator and treat them according to their data type. With SAP R/3's business objects it's a different story. Even if you successfully create a valid reference to an SAP R/3 business object, it's not possible to use its business data attributes directly.

*In the following chapters I will provide very clear code examples to illustrate this phenomenon.*

Before we get there it is imperative to understand the difference between **object attributes** and **object data attributes**.

### Data- and Object-Related Attributes

To better comprehend this difference let's revisit the DAO library. When we create an instance of a Recordset object, we can access the properties of the Recordset object itself and the data in it. In other words, we don't have to invoke specific functions to access the records or fields. Moreover, we can access the properties of the Recordset object not related to data.

With the SAP R/3 business object it is different. We can create an instance of an abstract *Customer* object. This will allow us access to some of the object's attributes. However, if we want to see something that relates to the business data, we have to create a specific instance of the business object and use a specific method, defined in the business object, to populate its business data-related attributes.

For example, if we want to examine the *Customer* business object as an abstract object we can create an instance of it using the **Business Object Repository (BOR)**. This will let us access the object-related attributes of the *Customer* business object. If we need an `Address` for a particular *Customer* object, we have to create an instance of a particular *Customer* object using specific key field attributes. The **key** is a value that uniquely identifies a particular business object, e.g. `CustomerNo` is the key for the *Customer* business object:

| Key field CustomerNo | | ☒ |
|---|---|---|
| Key field | CustomerNo | |
| Object type | KNA1 | |
| Release | 21A | |
| Status | released | |
| **Texts** | | |
| Name | Customer | |
| Description | Customer number | |
| **Data type reference** | | |
| Reference table | KNA1 | |
| Reference field | KUNNR | |
| Search help | | |

✔ 🔍 ✖

After that we can use methods defined in the *Customer* object to get the attribute that contains the needed information. Remember, if you simply create a reference to an abstract business object you won't have access to the functionality provided by a specific instance of the business object. For example, an abstract *Customer* object will let you search and list *Customer* objects, but will not give you the ability to get details on a particular customer. For now it is necessary to understand the fact that you cannot directly access business data-related attributes and object-related attributes using the same object reference.

Another by-design feature of SAP R/3 business objects is that we cannot use early binding. Remember there are no published type libraries for SAP R/3 business objects, so Windows, or Visual Basic for that matter, is unaware of the SAP R/3 business object implementation and therefore cannot provide browsing of the object interface.

# The SAP R/3 Remote Function Call – RFC

As we have already learned, every element of SAP R/3 that deals with data manipulation is channeled through a code module that is developed in ABAP. These modules comprise an internal *Application Layer* for SAP R/3 and there is no way to directly access the physical data. See the diagram earlier in the chapter.

Every function module is a function that can be called by name and is capable of accepting predefined parameters. These functions are rarely self-sufficient and can in turn call other functions and so on. The main point is this:

> **Every operation that SAP R/3 is capable of performing on data can be delegated to a well-defined function. SAP R/3 provides the mechanism to remotely invoke these functions that are appropriately named Remote Function Calls (RFC).**

The RFC mechanism is not new and has been used for a long time to communicate with SAP R/3. However, it lacks flexibility and has one major drawback. Like with the Windows API, although you can easily achieve a single task, it's tedious to use them to implement complex solutions. In other words, you can program the Windows API directly to manually create the tree view control, but it's not the most efficient way to program.

A single RFC will also let you accomplish a task but if you need to call multiple RFCs you need to know the order of calls to make. You are not provided with any kind of user exits or event handling. You can think of SAP R/3 functions and RFCs as synonymous to the Windows API. There are some functions that you can export and some that you cannot. This approach is no different from, say, developing OCX controls – you take multiple low-level system APIs and build a wrapper around them.

## SAP BAPIs and RFCs

RFCs are accessible externally and were present well before BAPIs came along with business objects, however, the following statement could best describe the relationship between BAPIs and RFCs:

> **Behind every BAPI is an RFC.**

We'll prove this statement in further chapters using tools provided by SAP, but for now it is important to understand that BAPIs and RFCs are related and have very much in common.

# Developing SAP R/3 Applications

SAP R/3 application development has always been uncharted territory for non-ABAP programmers. The architecture of SAP R/3 is very self-enclosed, which is not surprising given the main premise of SAP R/3:

> **Any enterprise can fully implement itself using SAP R/3 *alone*.**

This last statement, as with any extreme statement, is not 100% accurate. However, it's very close to being so.

The least attractive feature of SAP R/3 has always been its unfriendliness to external applications and systems. In comparison to any Microsoft product, we immediately notice the lack of external libraries or controls that implement the most commonly used features of SAP R/3. As VB programmers, we're used to looking up the References and Components dialogs after installing any software on our machines, because we can immediately see if we have gained any new ActiveX components to use in our programs.

Moreover, any software vendor that wants its software to be used packages its functionality into COM-compliant, or simply COM, components. Software vendors do this, not out of sheer admiration of Microsoft, but rather out of simple business sense. If the technology is accessible from the COM-compliant environment, it can be implemented on a wide range of applications. Another reason for every software vendor to implement its technology in COM is the open nature of Microsoft Windows, which allows the easy integration of different software packages. All these factors facilitate the COM-compliant component development for all vendors that want wide acceptance of their software and extensibility of their systems.

## Integrating SAP with Microsoft

SAP took a gradual approach to enabling Windows integration for their SAP R/3 product. First of all, they made it possible to run SAP R/3 with SQL Server as a back-end RDBMS. That enabled SAP R/3 to be installed and run entirely on a Windows platform.

This alone, however, does not solve the problem. SAP R/3 is a self-enclosed system, and no matter what environment it runs in, it still does not offer any integration by design. Another issue is that SAP R/3 is traditionally a non-Windows system, and to enable the integration of SAP R/3 into Windows applications, SAP had to resolve the ever-present Windows/Unix conflict. Fortunately, the SAP R/3 architecture naturally lends itself to the solution.

As we have already discussed, SAP R/3 is one of the few true client-server information systems with a well-designed communication mechanism. This mechanism allows for resolving conversions between different data types. To a certain extent, SAP R/3 acts like a cross-platform hub for data and functionality.

In addition, in SAP R/3 all data and data structures have the same representation, regardless of the underlying operating system. It therefore serves like a common denominator for different data representation schemas on heterogeneous binary systems. Yet another mechanism that has always been present in the SAP family of products is the Remote Function Call mechanism that provides a well-documented and solidly implemented mechanism for external function calls.

The above list of features comprises an SDK in its most primal form: a communication mechanism and format for API-style function calls. This however, is not the preferred development environment for Windows programmers and particularly for Visual Basic programmers. The strongest point of Visual Basic has always been its ability to relieve developers from the unsightly, low-level implementation details. The assumption that the entire world programs in C or C++ is not valid anymore. Java and Visual Basic programmers are used to implementing out-of-the-box components or packages. This means that for SAP to reach out to that group of programmers, it was necessary to implement integration functionality in a *component* based way.

## COM Integration

To solve all these problems, SAP came up with a set of COM-compliant components to be used from COM environments, with the traditional C++ SDK to provide programmers with the ability to roll their own components. This book's target audience is Visual Basic programmers, so I won't go into the details of the C++ SDK. We'll be exploring the possibilities offered by the OCX controls and DLL components supplied by SAP.

> *There's one more observation I would like to make. Although SAP packages its components as OCX controls, they do little beyond providing some rectangle or icon on the form. My recommendation is to treat them more like* reference libraries.

Another very important point is that SAP and Microsoft have announced their joint effort to make Visual Studio a *bona fide* development environment for SAP R/3 external application programming. This has at least the following consequences:

> ➢ Microsoft positions and promotes Visual Basic as a premier development language for business applications on the COM platform. This in turn means that SAP has to provide COM-compliant libraries and OCX controls so Visual Basic programmers can implement them out-of-the-box.

> ➢ SAP has to accommodate the developers that use Microsoft development tools and Visual Basic developers in particular. This means that SAP has had to realign its view of the software world and accommodate Windows NT/Windows 2000 and all components of Planet Microsoft – SQL Server, MTS, MSMQ, IIS, MS Office etc.

> ➤ Microsoft actively promotes its Universal Data Access strategy, which is based on OLEDB. The by-product of this is that ADO becomes a *de facto* standard in data access for Microsoft products. This forces all software vendors, including SAP, who wish to integrate their products with Microsoft development tools to enable any-to-ADO data converters or providers. We'll see one implementation of this integration with the DCOM Component Connector later in the book.

### SAP R/3 Business Objects and COM

Windows or any other platform knows nothing about how business objects are implemented in SAP R/3. But it's SAP R/3 and not Windows who manages these business objects, their attributes and functionality. External applications only connect to the SAP R/3 business object mechanism, marshall requests and get back results.

> **The differences are due to the fact that the domain for all SAP R/3 business objects is SAP R/3 itself.**

I would suggest thinking of SAP R/3 as an "operating system/environment" for its business objects. This approach allows SAP R/3 to be very flexible in terms of the integration of its business object technology into different environments, binary systems and programming languages. As long as any external program can invoke certain functionality, can dispatch data to, and accept data from SAP R/3, it can employ SAP R/3 business objects. That's why SAP is able to say it can seamlessly integrate into any standard. It has done so with COM, and is working on CORBA and Java implementations, without even touching its own business objects. All it is working on is essentially a *transport mechanism.*

This is a totally different approach to traditional Visual Basic programming. If it had followed that approach, SAP would have created COM-compliant DLLs that would contain definitions of its business objects and their hierarchy. We would connect to SAP R/3, create instances of these objects and manipulate them outside of SAP R/3, pretty much like we handle any database access using DAO or ADO. This would have been convenient for Windows programmers, but would have forced SAP to do at least two things:

> ➤ First, they would have had to step out of the box and start worrying about specific implementations on particular platforms for its internal functionality
> ➤ Second, they would have lost the many-to-one paradigm for SAP R/3, meaning that it runs the same on all platforms and implements its functionality in the same way

Moreover, it would have caused substantial modifications to SAP R/3's rock-solid function modules and internal data structure. Every time Microsoft or Sun got creative with their products SAP would have to had play catch-up with them. This is a sure recipe for disaster and it's no surprise that SAP has chosen a different strategy. SAP defined and implemented its business objects internally and provided only *external access* to them:

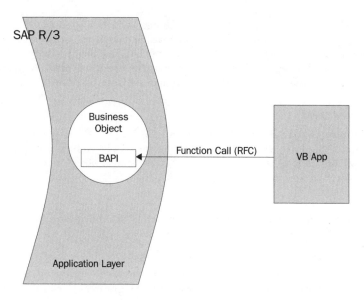

The SAP R/3 way of implementing its business objects provides another major advantage for both SAP R/3 and external accessing entities, in our case Visual Basic programmers: business object **implementation transparency**.

This means that if I have a program written in Visual Basic that implements the *Customer* business object and SAP R/3 internally changes the way its implements, it does not affect my code or application insofar as the object's interface does not change. In other words, the SAP R/3 implementation specifics for its business objects are *transparent* to an external application programmer. SAP made a commitment not to jeopardize the stability of its business object interfaces by promising not to remove existing methods or their parameters. This will guarantee at least one thing – your Visual Basic programs will not fail on you when something changes in SAP R/3.

# Summary

In this chapter we outlined most of the important concepts of SAP R/3 business objects and their implementation. We covered the necessary specifics of SAP R/3 itself and the way it implements an enterprise. We analyzed the differences and similarities in the SAP R/3 and COM object implementation, and started to outline the specifics of SAP R/3 programming from Visual Basic.

This chapter provides a basis to the understanding of a new paradigm of SAP R/3 business objects and how it relates to traditional Windows and Visual Basic programming. We have also learned the implementation specifics of BAPIs and their parameters.

In the next chapter we'll look at the first main tool for integrating Windows-based applications with SAP R/3: the SAP Automation Toolkit.

# 3

# The SAP Logon Control

In the previous chapters, we reviewed SAP R/3 as a system and gained some familiarity with SAP R/3 business objects. As we established, SAP R/3 business objects are defined within SAP R/3, and don't have any external implementation, unlike the objects that the VB programmer is accustomed to. We also discussed the difference between the way that conventional in-process COM servers (DLLs) and SAP R/3 business objects interact with the Visual Basic programming environment. Finally, we started to explore Business Application Programming Interface functions (BAPIs) and the listed parameter types that BAPIs have.

We'll now go on to analyze the specifics of BAPI implementation. Visual Basic programmers have been historically shielded from implementation details when it came to any external systems. To accomplish the same result SAP went the same way – they developed COM components that allow access to the SAP R/3 and invocation of BAPIs. What SAP didn't do is create any COM library to define its business objects, thereby providing a familiar means of using BAPIs as object methods.

To implement any given BAPI a programmer has to do the following:

- ➢ Establish a connection to the SAP R/3 system
- ➢ Create a running instance of the business object the BAPI belongs to
- ➢ Prepare necessary parameters for the BAPI
- ➢ Invoke the BAPI

In the following three chapters, we will analyze every item in this bulleted list. We'll detail the first item on our list later in this chapter. But first, we'll take a general look at the tools that allow external programmers access to SAP R/3.

# The SAP Automation Toolkit

SAP R/x has always been much more than just a big database application – it has traditionally been a very complex implementation of various business scenarios and functionality. SAP has built an enormous application layer around its physical data storage, which, unlike other conceptually similar systems, does not allow direct access to physical tables. Moreover, to ensure enterprise data integrity, SAP R/3 has a very complex set of business rules implemented at the application layer. This is much more than the usual ON INSERT triggers. Every action goes through rock-solid function-modules that perform necessary data validation and internal normalization.

For SAP R/3 to be integrated into Windows development, it has to provide a minimal set of functionality: connectivity, a remote function call mechanism and the ability to convert or map SAP R/3 data to COM compliant data types.

## SAP and Data Access

Visual Basic programmers will be familiar with providers that resolve the object to table mapping conflict. Good examples of this concept are Microsoft's OLEDB Data Providers, which work with the ADO Data control. The OLEDB Data Provider allows the mapping of proprietary and often exotic data objects to ADO Recordsets. It also enables external applications to communicate with the data store, as with a conventional relational database. The problem is that objects rely on the property/method paradigm and databases on column/row. Therefore, to implement the SQL view of data objects, we either have to have access to the physical data storage where those objects persist data, or to ask the RDBMS or ERP vendor to implement such functionality.

As we saw in previous chapters, SAP will not let anybody access its physical data storage, and it deliberately presents all data as objects. Therefore, for SAP to implement SQL functionality for an external data provider would be against its core architecture. This means that there will not be an SAP Data control that lets you execute SQL statements. Even if the data is presented in the ADO Recordset format, it does not reflect the physical data storage element. To phrase it differently, we're not likely to have an equivalent of ODBC API for SAP R/3.

This is a serious departure from the traditional database access technologies. Visual Basic programmers are used to tools that enable them to view and manage databases and their physical data storage objects – tables, queries, stored procedures, etc. Neither SAP R/3 nor any other tool will expose the SAP R/3 internal data structure.

## SAP R/3 Extensibility Tools

To achieve its integration goals, SAP created the **SAP Automation toolkit**. It has gone thorough several releases, patches and updates, and there are currently several major variations of this package: **SAP Automation**, **SAP Automation 4.5A** and the latest version, **SAP Automation 4.5B**.

The SAP R/3 Automation package comprises several tools, components and class libraries designed to enable access to the SAP R/3 system using popular, non-SAP programming environments, such as Microsoft Visual Studio or Semantec Visual Café. This package is available for free download from either www.saplabs.com or www.sap.com/bapi.

*We will abstract ourselves from the specifics of this package's technical implementation – that's beyond the scope of this book. Instead, we'll concentrate on the ready to use components and their functionality.*

A major part of SAP R/3 Automation is the **SAP Assistant**. This is an extremely useful utility for two reasons: it provides the ability to browse the SAP R/3 Business Object Repository metadata online and offline, and has great educational value.

As we've seen, the SAP R/x implementation approach has always met object-oriented design criteria, allowing access to data only via well-defined structures and their member functions. This allowed SAP to take their product to the next level and introduce the **Business Object Repository** (**BOR**).

The word "repository" will sound familiar to most Visual Basic developers, since Microsoft Repository is being heavily promoted as a common standard of component storage. Essentially, the SAP R/3 Business Object Repository is not different – it's intended for the purpose of storing business object definitions. These objects reflect the SAP view of an enterprise as implemented in the SAP R/3 system.

To expose objects and their interfaces to the developers of external applications, SAP developed **Repository Services**. The aim is to provide read-access to business objects' metadata and RFC function modules to programs that follow COM. To simplify usage of this class library, SAP developed the **Repository Browser ActiveX control**, which became a base component for the SAP Assistant itself.

This package includes many other controls and libraries, and we'll explore them in detail in the following chapters. Specifically, we will be implementing BAPIs using the SAP Logon control, SAP BAPI control, SAP Table Factory control, SAP Table View control and SAP RFC control.

The SAP Automation package also includes an SDK (Software Development Kit) that can be used to build custom solutions (that is, your own COM components) using C and C++. It also includes header files that can be useful as a learning tool (provided that you're familiar with C/C++).

Although a wide variety of tools exist for several languages (C/C++ and Java as well as Visual Basic), the only things that are ready to work out of the box are the OCX controls and COM libraries. This means that Visual Basic is well suited to be the most effective language to program SAP R/3 applications.

I am getting a little ahead of myself here, but just guess what SAP chose to be its metadata repository for the SAP Automation? The answer: Microsoft's Access database! Feels like home, doesn't it?

## *Working with the SAP Automation Controls*

Before we proceed, a word of advice – I recommend saving your work frequently. SAP related OCX controls are fairly stable. However, they can demonstrate some bizarre behavior, specifically under error conditions. Although I have experienced problems during design and debugging, they vanish once the code is stabilized. I don't like to speculate about why these things happen, but they do.

*One factor that may contribute to some of the problems I have experienced: my development workstations at work and at home have been through a few too many Install-Uninstall-Register-Unregister loops for the SAP related components and libraries to cope with.*

You may see the control disappear from the form, or even get my favorite message about the control not being registered. When you get this condition, the only way out is to close Visual Basic, not just reopen the project and refresh Windows by hitting *F5*.

You may also check for **SAPHLPPROC** in Task Manager, and if it's there, **End Task**. The process name is `HLPPROC.EXE`. This is a hacker style solution.

A more elegant and technically correct solution is to start programming with error handling routines to let the program end gracefully:

```
On Error GoTo ErrTrap

....

ErrTrap:

    MsgBox "Error # " & Err.Number & vbLf & Err.Description
```

## Getting Started with SAP Automation Tools

Now it's time to start some actual BAPI programming using the SAP Automation tools. The following is a quick checklist of what you will need to run the sample projects in this book, or to code yourself:

> ➤ A valid connection to an SAP R/3 release 4.0 or higher. It may be your LAN, WAN or dial-up.
> ➤ A properly installed SAP Automation 4.5 toolkit. This is available for download from the SAP and SAPLABS web sites – see Appendix C for details.
> ➤ A properly registered SAP Logon control.
> ➤ Visual Basic 6.0

I also recommend you have the SAP front-end GUI component installed on your development machine, so you can validate the information that you get using Visual Basic.

Recall our list of requirements for implementing BAPIs, from the beginning of this chapter. The first item on that list was:

> ➤ Establish a connection to the SAP R/3 system

We're going to investigate how to do this using one of the components that comes with the SAP Automation – the **SAP Logon control**.

# The SAP Logon Control

We are used to connecting to databases in an ordinary Visual Basic programming environment. In my opinion, DAO terminology did a little disservice in hiding all communication and connection related functionality. ADO, on the other hand, is much closer to reality. In ADO we have a Connection object, and this has a method, Open, that establishes a connection. You must then assign the instance of the Connection to the appropriate properties of other objects to perform any database-related functionality.

The same can be said about connecting to SAP R/3. We first have to establish a connection, and then we can get access to the functionality defined inside SAP R/3.

The sole purpose of the SAP Logon control is to connect to the SAP R/3 server, and to create a valid instance of the **Connection object**. This is used to enable the functionality of other SAP related controls and libraries, and the concept is similar to the ADO Connection object. You can create it separately and then use it to enable Recordset or Command objects to connect to the database.

The hierarchy of this control is very simple. The Logon control is the creatable object and it creates the Connection object. In other words, you cannot create the Connection object without having a valid instance of the Logon control object first.

The control's functionality can be used by either placing it directly on the form, or creating a reference to it using the CreateObject method. We will look at both of these approaches in this chapter.

The file name for the control is WDTLOG.OCX, and its location depends on your directory structure. The registry entry for the control's library is SAP.LogonControl.1.

*I want to make yet another clarification. I don't plan this book to be a reformatting of the help file available for the SAP Automation. It should provide you with complimentary material, beyond what you can find elsewhere. Therefore, I will detail only relevant and critical properties, events and methods of controls and classes.*

First, we are going to create a project that lets us logon to SAP R/3 using the SAP Logon control. The complete source code for the projects in the book is available from the Wrox Press web site.

# Connecting to SAP R/3 with the SAP Logon Control

First, we need to add the SAP Logon control to our project. Open a new Standard EXE project, and name it SAP_Connect. Then check SAP Logon Control in the Components dialog:

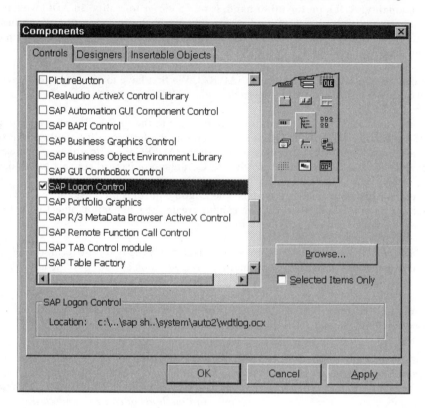

This will add the SAP Logon control to your toolbox:

Some of the SAP Automation controls don't have a run time GUI – just like the Visual Basic Timer control. However, the Logon control does have a run time GUI. Place a copy of the control onto the default form – it's an exact copy of the standard command button GUI:

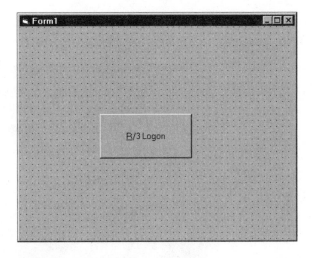

## Properties and Methods of the Logon Control

Before we begin programming this control, it's important to familiarize ourselves with some SAP R/3 specific terminology that is linked to the names of some properties and methods:

> **Application Server**
> The name of the server that the SAP R/3 instance is running at. Ask the SAP R/3 administrator or a fellow ABAP programmer. Make sure that you can "ping" that server. If you've never done this before, now is a good time to start. Go to the Start | Command Prompt and type ping followed by the server name or IP address of the server. If you're doing well, you'll see something like the following:

```
Microsoft(R) Windows NT(TM)
(C) Copyright 1985-1996 Microsoft Corp.

C:\>ping yahoo.com

Pinging yahoo.com [204.71.200.245] with 32 bytes of data:

Reply from 204.71.200.245: bytes=32 time=211ms TTL=244
Reply from 204.71.200.245: bytes=32 time=190ms TTL=244
Reply from 204.71.200.245: bytes=32 time=190ms TTL=244
Reply from 204.71.200.245: bytes=32 time=190ms TTL=244

C:\>
```

Otherwise, you'll see some negative message, such as `Bad IP Address` or `Host is unreachable`:

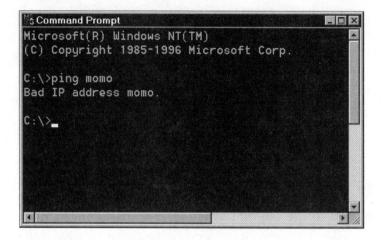

> **Client**
> The number that indicates the client for the SAP R/3. It has nothing to do with the user ID or name of you client workstation. Ask the same people.

> **System Number**
> The number for your SAP R/3 system. Ask the same people.

> **User ID and Password**
> Self-explanatory. If you don't have them you should get them, because you cannot program without them.

> **Language**
> Not the programming language, but the letter abbreviation defined in SAP R/3 and selected during installation. The value for English is `E` or `EN`.

If you have the SAP R/3 front-end GUI installed on your machine, you can use the System | Status menu item of the initial SAP R/3 screen to get values for these arguments:

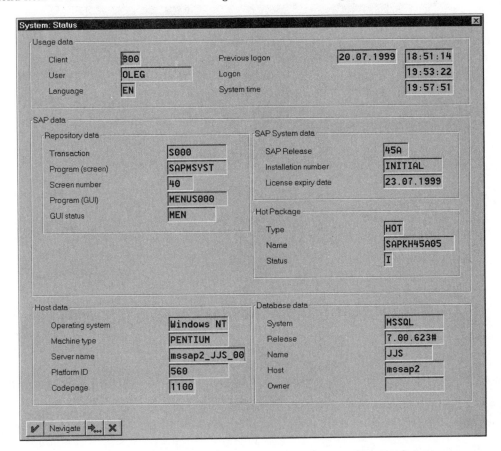

Let's view the SAP Logon control library in the Object Browser:

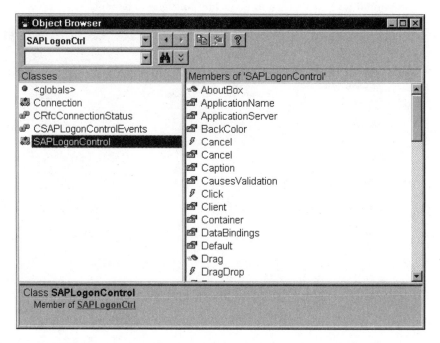

This allows us to examine the class structure.

Once we have gathered all the necessary information, we can begin assigning values to the appropriate properties of the Logon control. At this point, we have the choice of using Property Pages or code. I personally prefer assigning properties from code whenever possible, and that's the approach we'll take here. It's more flexible, and it also means I don't have to type into those tiny boxes. Fortunately, all the properties that we need for this exercise are not run-time read-only.

The following code snippet demonstrates property value assignment:

```
With SAPLogonControl1

    .ApplicationServer = "Your Server Name"
    .Client = "Your Client Number"
    .User = "Your User Name"
    .Password = "Your Password"
    .Language = "EN"

End With
```

## Connection and Logon

After we assign properties, we can attempt to logon. There are two types of logon implemented by this control – **silent** logon and **non-silent** logon. The silent logon will attempt to log you in without displaying the logon screen, just using the properties' values. If it fails, it won't let you know. A non-silent logon will pop up the logon screen that lets you enter all the information yourself, and it will produce an error message on failure:

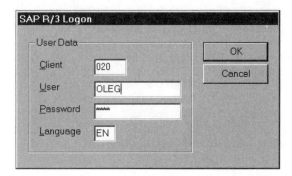

If your application always logs into the same SAP R/3 server using the same attributes, you may be better off using a silent logon. If you're logging into different servers, or give access to the same SAP R/3 to multiple users, implement a non-silent logon. The non-silent logon is the better bet in a multi-user environment for security reasons. Because the logon screen doesn't allow you to change the server name, you don't have the opportunity to use applications that you're not authorized to.

### The Logon Method

We can use the `Logon` method of the Connection object to log on to SAP R/3. Here's the caveat – to get a valid instance of the connection, we have to first set all the necessary properties of the Logon control. Only then can we use the control's `NewConnection` method. This way, all the values of the Logon control properties will be carried over to the Connection object.

In the `SAP_Connect` project, the code to do this is attached to the `Click` event of the control:

```
Option Explicit

Private msapConn As SAPLogonCtrl.Connection
```

```
Private Sub SAPLogonControl1_Click()

  With SAPLogonControl1

      .ApplicationServer = "Your Server name"
      .Client = "Your Client Number"
      .User = "Your User Name"
      .Password = "Your Password"
      .Language = "EN"

  End With

  Set msapConn = SAPLogonControl1.NewConnection

End Sub
```

Note that I prefer explicitly defining the ProgID for the object:

```
Private msapConn As SAPLogonCtrl.Connection
```

This may seem like overkill, but wait until you start using ADO – that also has a Connection object. These days I prefer explicit definitions.

Once you get a valid Connection object you can execute the `Logon` method of the connection. This method has the following definition as per the Object Browser (which I prefer to documentation while learning a new component or library):

```
Function Logon(hWnd, bSilent As Boolean) As Boolean
```

Where:

> ➤ hWnd is the Long window handle. Pass the hWnd property of the form that hosts the control.

> ➤ bSilent is a Boolean that determines the logon type. If you pass True it will execute a silent logon, if False, non-silent.

The return value of this function is True on successful logon and False on failure. A failed logon will not generate a run-time error, so this value is used to determine the status of the logon.

The following code executes a silent logon based on the values we passed to the properties of the Logon control earlier:

```
Set msapConn = SAPLogonControl1.NewConnection
```

```
If msapConn.Logon(Me.hWnd, True) Then
   'Do nothing
Else
   MsgBox "Connection Failed"
End If
```

A non-silent logon would be done this way:

```
Set msapConn = SAPLogonControl1.NewConnection

If msapConn.Logon(Me.hWnd, False) Then
   'Do nothing
Else
   MsgBox "Connection Failed"
End If
```

### A Warning

Be forewarned. The IntelliSense editor will list the Connection object in the member drop-down list when you hit the space bar after the New keyword, and the lines:

```
Dim x As SAPLogonCtrl.Connection
Set x = New SAPLogonCtrl.Connection
```

Will be completed in your code. However, any attempt to execute a reference to x, such as:

```
With x
     .Logon Me.hWnd, False
End With
```

Will result in a familiar **ActiveX component can't create object** error message.

Normally, Visual Basic will not display a class that can't be created with the New keyword in the IntelliSense's list. You won't see a Database class in the IntelliSense helper if you use the New keyword. However, it depends on how the particular class is defined in the library.

The only way to create a valid instance of the Connection object is via the NewConnection method of the SAPLogonControl class:

```
Dim x As SAPLogonCtrl.Connection
Set x = SAPLogonControl1.NewConnection
```

## The System Information Dialog

After we have successfully connected to the SAP R/3 system, we can perform all the manipulations we need: call BAPIs, browse object metadata, lookup data in the SAP R/3 tables and execute Remote Function Calls.

This little exercise aims to give you an idea of what any programming of the SAP R/3 application using Visual Basic will start from. As you've seen, the control itself is not very flashy in the GUI department – but it doesn't need to be. All it's supposed to do is to give you access to the SAP R/3 server.

However, it offers one more functionality that's very useful – the System Information dialog:

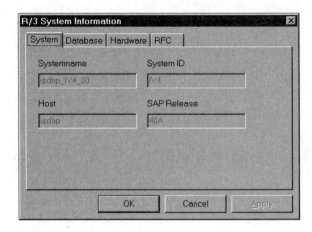

By selecting the tabs of this dialog, you can look up all the system information that you may need. This information should be fairly self-explanatory.

The syntax is:

```
Sub SystemInformation(hWnd)
```

This method requires one argument – the window handle of the host form.

## Events of the Logon Control

The Logon control implements some very useful events: Logon, Cancel and Error among others:

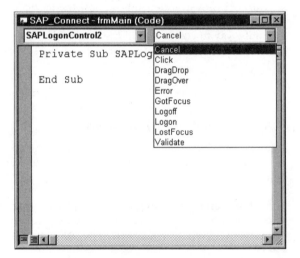

### The Logon Event

The Logon event is defined as shown below:

```
Event Logon(Connection As Object)
```

This event occurs upon successful logon and provides a reference for a valid Connection object. It is used for logon confirmations, obtaining system information or triggering processes that depend on successful logon:

```
Private Sub SAPLogonControl1_Logon(ByVal Connection As Object)

  Dim intResp As Integer

  intResp = MsgBox("Successfull Logon into the SAP Server" & vbLf & _
              "View SAP System Info?", vbYesNo + vbInformation)

  Select Case intResp

    Case vbYes
        msapConn.SystemInformation Me.hWnd
        Label1 = "Connected To SAP Server at " & Connection.ApplicationServer

    Case vbNo
        Label1 = "Connected To SAP Server at " & Connection.ApplicationServer

  End Select

End Sub
```

### The Error Event

The `Error` event occurs when an error happens in one of the objects of the library. It has the following definition:

```
Event Error(Number As Integer, Description As String, Scode As Long, _
        Source As String, HelpFile As String, HelpContext As Long, _
        CancelDisplay As Boolean)
```

The confusing thing about this event is that it does not indicate unsuccessful login. You can use it to display error information:

```
Private Sub SAPLogonControl1_Error(Number As Integer, Description As String, _
        Scode As Long, Source As String, HelpFile As String, _
        HelpContext As Long, CancelDisplay As Boolean)

  MsgBox Description & vbCrLf & "Error # " & Number & "Scode " & Scode

End Sub
```

### The Cancel Event

This event is defined as follows:

```
Event Cancel(Connection As Object)
```

It occurs when the user clicks the Cancel button on the logon screen when using a non-silent logon. We can use this to trap the user's refusal to connect.

### The Logoff Event

This event occurs when you log off from the SAP R/3 server using the `Logoff` method of the Connection object.

```
Private Sub SAPLogonControl1_Logoff(ByVal Connection As Object)

   MsgBox "Logged Off From The SAP Server at " & Connection.ApplicationServer
   Label1 = "Disconnected From The SAP Server at " & msapConn.ApplicationServer

End Sub
```

# Writing a Wrapper Class for the SAP Logon Control

That completes our description of how to use the Logon control by placing it on the form. This is convenient and straightforward. However, the needs of your development may dictate that you avoid having a form in your project. Ideally, you want to build a class to wrap the functionality of the Logon control and do some other things you cannot do using the control itself.

As it turns out, it's possible to use the controls library directly without adding the control to the project, by using the `CreateObject` function. This function has been upgraded in Visual Basic 6.0 and can now create objects on remote servers. The documentation for the SAP Automation Toolkit provides values for the first argument of `CreateObject`, but you can also look it up in the registry using the registry editor. For the SAP Logon control it is `"SAP.LogonControl.1"`:

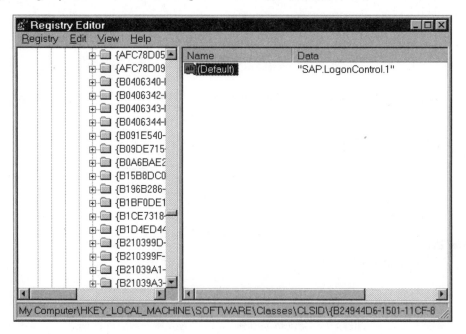

Let's implement the functionality of the SAP Logon control library using a class module. We will build a small ActiveX DLL component and implement the functionality of the SAP Logon control in the single class module of that component.

## Building the ActiveX Component

Start Visual Basic and select **ActiveX DLL** as project type. Change the name of its single class module to `clsSAPLogon` and the name of the project to `SAPSrv_Log`, and save the project.

We can now implement the Logon and Logoff functionality of the control. First of all, we have to create a valid reference to the Logon library. The logical place for this task is the `Initialize` event of the class module.

*Please note that because of Visual Basic specifics, we cannot pass any arguments into the Initialize event. In our case, we don't need to, but this point has to be noted.*

Firstly, we need to create a generic object type variable, because we cannot use any early binding in this case:

```
Option Explicit

Private mobjSapLogOn As Object
```

Now we can code the `Initialize` event:

```
Private Sub Class_Initialize()

   Set mobjSapLogOn = CreateObject("SAP.LogonControl.1")

End Sub
```

### Assigning Logon Control Properties

Upon successful initialization, we can start assigning values to relevant properties of the Logon control object. This task is implemented in a `Logon` function defined in the `clsSAPLogon` class, and it replicates the `Logon` method of the Connection object. To fully replicate the functionality of the `Logon` method, we will define the `Logon` function of the class to have an optional argument that defaults to `True` and determines the type of the logon – silent or not.

To ensure compatibility with the original Logon control, I defined several properties that are absolutely necessary to logon. I used the Class Builder utility of Visual Basic 6.0 to define these properties, and I did it using `Property Let/Get` pairs:

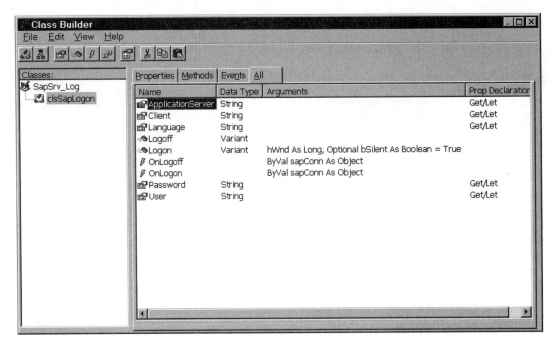

To reduce the chances of typos and improve code maintainability we will keep the names of the original properties:

```
Private mvarApplicationServer As String
Private mvarClient As String
Private mvarUser As String
Private mvarPassword As String
Private mvarLanguage As String

Public Property Let Language(ByVal vData As String)
  mvarLanguage = vData
End Property

Public Property Get Language() As String
  Language = mvarLanguage
End Property

Public Property Let Password(ByVal vData As String)
  mvarPassword = vData
End Property

Public Property Get Password() As String
  Password = mvarPassword
End Property

Public Property Let User(ByVal vData As String)
  mvarUser = vData
End Property

Public Property Get User() As String
  User = mvarUser
End Property
```

```
Public Property Let Client(ByVal vData As String)
  mvarClient = vData
End Property

Public Property Get Client() As String
  Client = mvarClient
End Property

Public Property Let ApplicationServer(ByVal vData As String)
  mvarApplicationServer = vData
End Property

Public Property Get ApplicationServer() As String
  ApplicationServer = mvarApplicationServer
End Property
```

We could have used public variables for properties instead of `Let`/`Get` pairs. Using public variables would have reduced the overhead associated with property referencing. However, using `Let`/`Get` property procedures allows us to implement any type of validation for the values being assigned. For example, we can validate user names prior to submitting them to SAP R/3, or implement default values for the `Language` property.

### Implementing Logon Control Events

What we are missing at this point are the SAP Logon control events. This is no problem at all. We can easily implement events using the `Event` keyword, keeping the event definitions the same as in the original library. I encourage readers to further elaborate on these events' definitions. For example, if you decide to use more than one instance of `clsSAPLogon`, you can add an argument for the `Index` value so you can keep track of them.

> *This part of the exercise has two objectives: to reinforce your skills in designing Class Modules in Visual Basic, and to demonstrate various approaches to working with SAP R/3 related ActiveX controls and relevant COM libraries.*

The necessary general declarations and event definitions are shown in the listing below:

```
Private msapConn As Object

Event OnLogon(ByVal sapConn As Object)
Event OnLogoff(ByVal sapConn As Object)
```

These events are raised using the `RaiseEvent` method from the `Logon` and `Logoff` functions defined in `clsSAPLogon`. We are now all set to code the `Logon` function:

```
Public Function Logon(hWnd As Long, Optional bSilent As Boolean = True)

  With mobjSapLogOn

    .ApplicationServer = Me.ApplicationServer
    .Client = Me.Client
    .User = Me.User
    .Password = Me.Password
    .Language = Me.Language
```

```
    End With

    Set msapConn = mobjSapLogOn.NewConnection

    If msapConn.Logon(hWnd, bSilent) Then
       RaiseEvent OnLogon(msapConn)
    Else
       MsgBox "Connection Failed"
    End If

End Function
```

And the code for the `Logoff` function is:

```
Public Function Logoff()

    msapConn.Logoff

    RaiseEvent OnLogoff(ByVal msapConn)

End Function
```

At this point, we are done with the server component of our project. We have in fact implemented all of the core functionality of the SAP Logon control library without using the control itself. We now have to program a client to test our ActiveX server.

## Building a Logon Client

The best way to do this is to use the Add Project functionality of the Visual Basic File menu. This will offer you the familiar choice for project types. Select Standard EXE and name the project SAPCli_Log.

> *I personally prefer naming server projects and client projects in such a way that Visual Basic will present them in the client then server order in the Project Explorer window. Knowing that Visual Basic displays projects in alphabetical order, this is not difficult at all. If you want to stay consistent with naming, use Cli and Srv suffixes for the same project name.*

Save the client project in a separate folder and save the Group file as well.

The GUI for the client will be very trivial and functionality-focused. We only need to add one label and two command buttons:

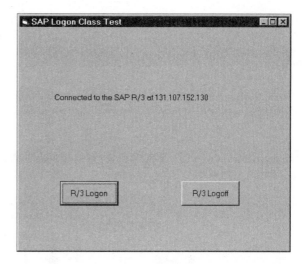

Now, open the **References** dialog – you will notice the name of the server project in the list of available references. This is a very nice feature of Visual Basic. You can reference ActiveX projects in the same Group (or workspace) as if they were a compiled DLL or EXE. This gives us the ability to debug client and server components without being forced to recompile the server component every time we change it.

> *This is possible because Visual Basic temporarily registers the ActiveX component under its umbrella and acts like a host. Other applications capable of using external references, such as Microsoft Access, will stay oblivious to these ActiveX projects because they are not compiled and registered with Windows.*

Make a reference to the server project:

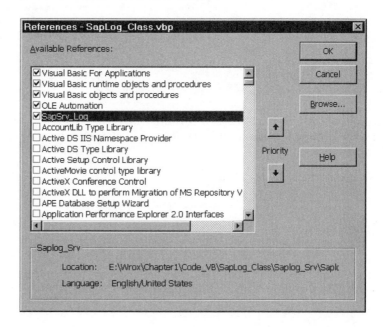

Then save the group and set the client project as <u>S</u>tartup. We are now ready to start programming the client.

To make sure of what we have in the referenced "library", bring up my favorite Visual Basic utility – the Object Browser.

*A word of advice – when working with project groups, always check which project is active before popping up the Object Browser, to avoid any confusion.*

The Object Browser should present you with the following:

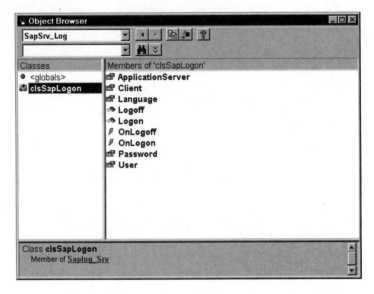

As you may see, all the functionality we programmed into the server component is available for the client. First let's define a variable for our class in the General Declarations section of the form:

```
Option Explicit
```

```
Private WithEvents mobjLogOn As clsSapLogon
```

Remember, you can't use the `New` keyword with the `WithEvents` keyword. That's why we have to create a running instance for the `clsSAPLogon` class elsewhere in the code. Usually the `Load` event is a good choice:

```
Private Sub Form_Load()

    Set mobjLogOn = New clsSapLogon

End Sub
```

Once we do this, we can program the client the same way we would if we had the SAP Logon control on the form. First, let's implement the logon functionality, by adding the following code to the `Click` event of the logon command button on the form:

```
Private Sub Command1_Click()

With mobjLogOn

    .ApplicationServer = "your R/3 server"
    .Client = "your client"
    .User = "your user name"
    .Password = "your password"
    .Language = "EN"

End With

mobjLogOn.Logon Me.hWnd, True

End Sub
```

The code above demonstrates a silent logon – the value `True` is passed into the second optional argument of the `Logon` method of the class. You can omit this argument because we implemented it as `Optional` with `True` for the default value. Alternatively, you can pass `False` and the Logon dialog will pop up.

The code for the `Logoff` method is even more trivial. Add the following code to the `Click` event of the second command button:

```
Private Sub Command2_Click()

    mobjLogOn.Logoff

End Sub
```

Because we used the `WithEvents` keyword, the `mobjLogOn` object is added to the object list and the events defined in the class module are available for programming. We can use these events to display confirmation information into the Label control on the form:

```
Private Sub mobjLogOn_OnLogoff(ByVal sapConn As Object)

    Label1 = "Disonnected from the SAP R/3 at " & sapConn.ApplicationServer

End Sub

Private Sub mobjLogOn_OnLogon(ByVal sapConn As Object)

    Label1 = "Connected to the SAP R/3 at " & sapConn.ApplicationServer

End Sub
```

# Summary

This chapter was devoted to the SAP Logon control – a member of the SAP Automation toolkit. I introduced two approaches to using this control, and we developed sample projects that implemented both techniques. First, we learned how to use the SAP Logon control out of the box. Then we used the Logon control library functionality without using the control itself. As a result of this exercise, we now have a reliable, reusable ActiveX component that we created based on the SAP supplied libraries. This allows us to connect to the SAP R/3 server. We can now move on to perform all other operations.

As you have seen, programming and using the SAP Logon control is rather straightforward and does not have any non-trivial caveats. In the following chapters I will provide detailed information, complete with narrated code snippets, of other ActiveX components and libraries available in the SAP Automation toolkit and DCOM Component Connector toolkit.

I will provide you with samples both using the control and using relevant libraries without controls. This is very important when it comes to developing your own ActiveX components that cannot or should not have GUIs.

In the next chapter, we'll examine the next step in BAPI programming: creating a running instance of an SAP R/3 business object.

# 4

# The SAP BAPI Control

Having learnt how to successfully connect to SAP R/3, we are now going to cover the first step in actually calling BAPIs. As you recall, the domain of a BAPI is a business object. Therefore, we need to learn how to create a valid instance of an SAP R/3 business object before we can invoke any BAPIs. In this chapter, I will introduce you to the SAP BAPI control, part of the SAP Automation toolkit, that allows you to do just this.

For reasons already outlined in previous chapters, using BAPIs and business objects to integrate with SAP R/3 has many benefits. Skeptics will argue that BAPIs do not implement every possible function of SAP R/3 and cannot therefore compete with ABAP/4 developed programs.

I don't like arguments where programming languages or platforms are positioned as being mutually exclusive or antagonistic. In my opinion, this is wrong both technically and conceptually. All programming languages and technologies have to be judged on how they deliver on their promises. If they succeed in their objectives then they can be considered a good language or technology.

In my opinion, BAPIs and ABAP/4 programming are *complementary* not mutually exclusive. SAP committed itself to the Business Object Framework, and more and more BAPIs become available with each release. At a certain point SAP will have released enough BAPIs to implement any functionality currently used by SAP R/3 customers, and they will eventually replace the current data exchange mechanisms.

## Introducing the SAP BAPI Control

This control, which resides in `WDOBAPI.OCX`, is one of my personal favorites. It is an enabling tool for the BAPI technology and is very powerful in terms of its functionality. This control alone encapsulates *all* you need to execute BAPI calls.

To use this control, select the SAP BAPI Control entry in the Components dialog in a Visual Basic project:

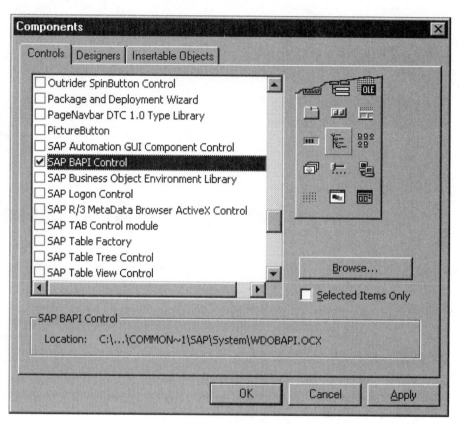

This will add the control to the toolbar:

The Object Browser presents us with the following view of this control:

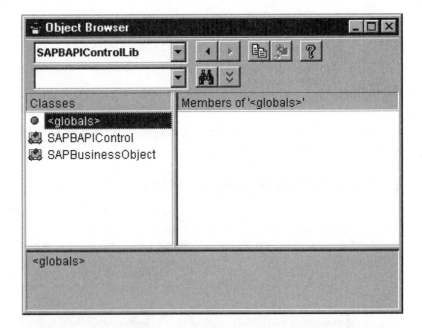

As you can see, the object hierarchy of this control is very simple. It comprises the SAPBAPIControl class itself and the oddly named SAPBusinessObject class – odd because looking at its members clearly indicates that it's a Collection in nature:

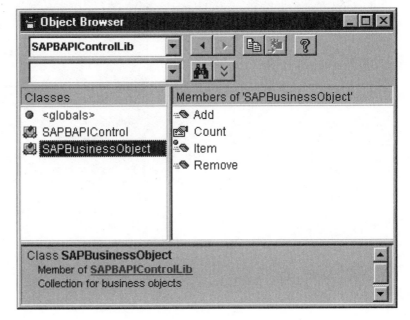

The SAP BAPI control provides the following functionality:

> Dimensions an abstract object as the parameter for a BAPI

> Creates instances of SAP R/3 business objects according to their definition in the SAP R/3 Business Object Repository

> Executes BAPI calls

This brief outline sums up the core functionality of the SAP BAPI control. We'll now start to explore this functionality in greater detail.

## SAP BAPI Control Properties

Let's develop a focused project to explore the functionality of the SAP BAPI control.

*To successfully run the sample projects, you will need a valid account and connection to SAP R/3 release 4.0 or higher, and a properly installed SAP Automation Toolkit. Look for detailed instructions on installation and configuration in Appendix C.*

Start a new **Standard EXE** Visual Basic project and add a SAP BAPI control to the form. The SAP BAPI control doesn't have a run-time GUI, just like the timer control. At design-time, you'll see the following icon appear on the form:

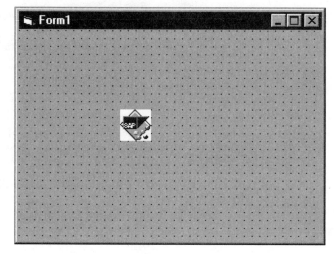

The SAP BAPI control has a custom property page with two tabs:

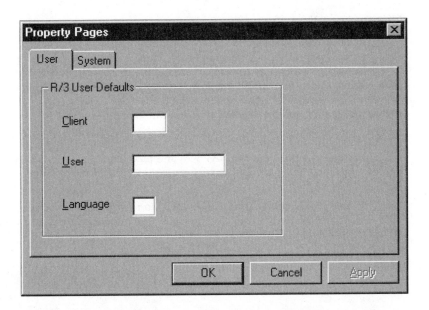

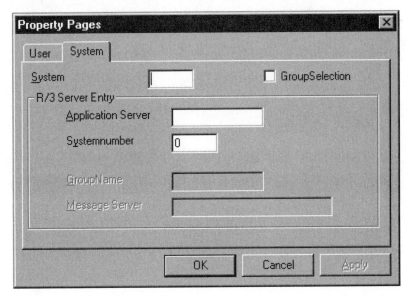

As we have already learned, to do anything with SAP R/3, we have to first connect to it, and these property pages allow you to enter values for the **connection attributes**.

## *The Connection Property*

The BAPI control has a `Connection` property that has to be set to a valid instance of a Connection object, or it returns the Connection object, depending on whether or not the BAPI control is already connected to SAP R/3. However, if we examine the BAPI control in the Object Browser, we won't find any property or method that is directly related to logon information. On the other hand, if we recall the Logon control, we remember having `User`, `Application Server`, `Logon` and other methods and properties relevant to logon functionality.

That being the case, our initial reaction would be to add an SAP Logon control, use it to create a Connection object, connect to SAP R/3 and pass the Connection object to the BAPI Control. This is in fact the recommended way of performing this task, provided that you put your code into forms.

> *However, this is not such a good idea, and I will discuss why later in the book. At this point, we are just introducing the SAP Automation controls and we can live with this limitation.*

Add the SAP Logon control to the form:

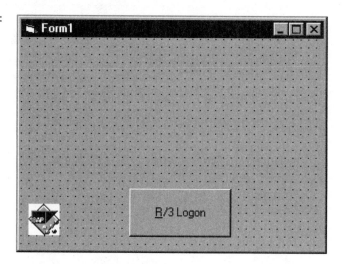

Now we can apply our knowledge of the SAP Logon control to get a valid connection:

```
Option Explicit

Dim msapConn As SAPLogonCtrl.Connection
```

> *Note that I purposely refer to classes using their library name. We may have many classes that are differently implemented in different libraries that have the same name, and the SAP Automation libraries are no exception.*

After we declare a connection variable, we can execute a non-silent logon to actually log into the SAP R/3 system and get a valid Connection object:

```
Private Sub SAPLogonControl1_Click()

   Set msapConn = SAPLogonControl1.NewConnection

   msapConn.Logon Me.hWnd, False

End Sub
```

Upon successful login, we have a valid Connection object that we can set the `Connection` property of the SAP BAPI control to:

```
Private Sub SAPLogonControl1_Click()

   Set msapConn = SAPLogonControl1.NewConnection

   msapConn.Logon Me.hWnd, False

   Set SAPBAPIControl1.Connection = msapConn

End Sub
```

### SAP Logon Configuration

You might have noticed that I didn't explicitly assign any logon-related values to the relevant Connection object properties in this project, as opposed to the project in Chapter 3. Instead, I've use the SAP Logon control.

If you select **SAPlogon**, for the front-end GUI, from the **Start** menu you will see its GUI component:

To add a profile simply click the <u>N</u>ew
button and the dialog opposite appears:

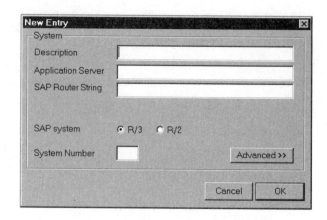

Enter values for the Description and the Application Server; select R/3 for the SAP system and enter
the System Number. After you've done this, hit OK, and you'll see a newly created icon in the main
window. The Description will be displayed in the label next to the icon.

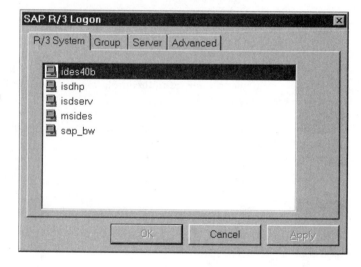

After you've completed this
exercise, the logon dialog that
appears when you use a non-silent
logon will have the first R/3 System
tab populated by icons from your
SAP Logon dialog:

All you have to do now is to double-click on the desired icon and enter Client, User, Password and
Language when prompted. If you use the SAP Logon to simply log into the SAP R/3 itself, it will
start the SAP front-end and you will enter your credentials from the SAP R/3 initial screen.

## Connection Object Logon Related Properties

You may find the following properties useful:

| Property | Access | Type | Description |
|---|---|---|---|
| ApplicationServer | Read/Write | String | Contains the name of the SAP R/3 server. |
| System | Read/Write | String | Contains the string value of the SAP R/3 system that you want to connect to. |
| SystemNumber | Read/Write | Long integer | Contains the value of the SAP R/3 System Number. |
| GroupName | Read/Write | String | Contains the string value of the SAP R/3 servers group |
| MessageServer | Read/Write | String | Contains the string value of the name of the Message Server of the R/3 System that performs load balancing. If you are not using load balancing, disregard this property. |

This definition of `ApplicationServer` needs some elaboration. The term "name" is somewhat ambiguous when applied to servers on the network. This property will reflect the information used at logon, and you can interchangeably use the IP address, URL (if you are connecting via the Internet) or some meaningful acronym that is the name of your server. For example, I can use `somesap.somecompany.com` or `111.111.11.1` to connect to SAP R/3. I will see the relevant values in the `ApplicationServer` property after logon.

If you use the SAP Router you need to populate or read the `SAPRouter` property value.

*Other relevant properties, such as* `Client, User` *and* `Password` *were discussed in Chapter 3.*

## Connection Information

At this point, I want to examine other informative properties of the Connection object that can be used in any development. These properties become populated upon successful logon and contain information on the system that you have connected to.

Of course, you can read this information off the dialog that is the result of the `SystemInformation` method of the Connection object. This however, won't let you access different portions of that information programmatically. Let's examine these properties by applying them to the project.

Add a list box control to the form and the following code to our logon routine:

```
Set SAPBAPIControl1.Connection = sapConn

List1.Clear

With msapConn

  If .IsConnected Then
     List1.AddItem "System " & .System
     List1.AddItem "Server " & .ApplicationServer
     List1.AddItem "Release " & .SAPRelease
     List1.AddItem "Client " & .Client
     List1.AddItem "Language " & .Language
  Else
     List1.AddItem "Not Connected"
  End If

End With

End Sub
```

If we execute our code now, the list box will be populated accordingly:

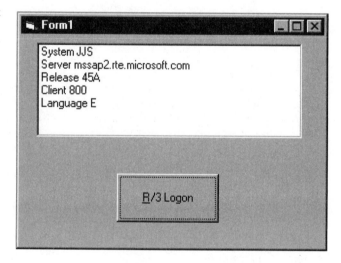

To better understand these values let's recall the SAP R/3 system status window. To get there start the SAP front-end, logon and select the **System | Status** menu item. You will be presented with the following screen:

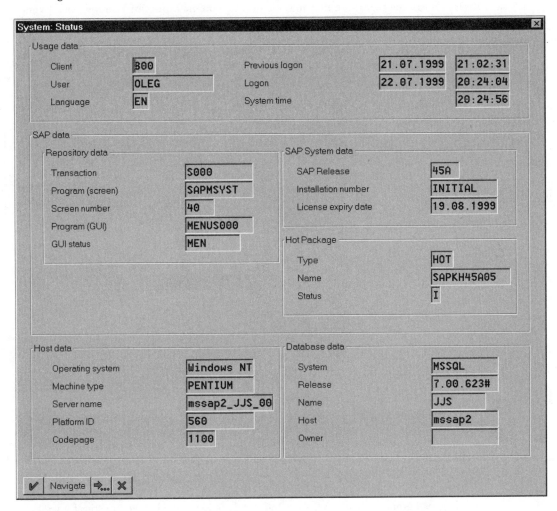

Now, if you compare these two screenshots, it becomes clear where the logon information related properties of the Connection object are coming from.

## The Log/Trace File Properties

The SAP BAPI control has another unusual aspect when compared to Visual Basic controls – it can create and populate a **trace file** based on selected options.

The history of trace files harks back to the days when you could not use a Debug window or any debugger at all. To monitor the flow of the program and to see intermediate outputs, applications included functionality to write values into some text file that you could analyze later. If we keep in mind that the SAP R/3 remains largely a black box to an external application development tool, such as Visual Basic, we can see that these files may be useful. You may think of Windows NT Event Viewer as a remote relative of the trace file functionality.

The SAP BAPI control has two design-time properties accessible at run-time that govern the log file functionality:

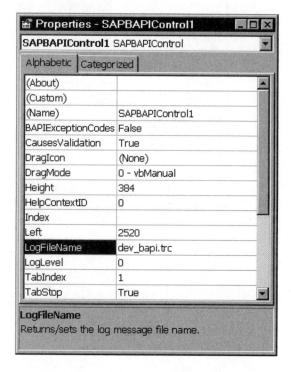

> The LogFileName property sets/returns the log file's name. As you may notice, this property has a default file name: dev_bapi.trc. Even if you specify a different file name complete with the path, the control will still create the zero-length dev_bapi.trc file, together with the file you specified. However, it will populate the file that you specified. Every time the program runs it will append new content onto the old file. If you don't specify the full path for the log file, it will create the dev_bapi.trc log file in the Visual Basic directory.

> The LogLevel property regulates the level of detail present in the log file. It varies from 0 to 9, with 9 being the most detailed.

Below is a fragment of a trace file:

```
dev_bapi.trc - Notepad
File  Edit  Search  Help

----------------------------------------------------
trc file: "dev_bapi.trc", trc level: 2, release: "45A"
----------------------------------------------------
Thu Apr 29 22:55:04 1999
SAP.BAPI up and running (version 4.5 A )
loaded from c:\PROGRA~1\COMMON~1\SAPSHA~1\system\auto2\wdobapi.ocx

        >>swo_set_environment(43698496, JJS.800)
        <<swo_set_environment(43698496, JJS.800) returns OK

----------------------------------------------------
trc file: "dev_bapi.trc", trc level: 3, release: "45A"
----------------------------------------------------
Thu Apr 29 22:56:08 1999
SAP.BAPI up and running (version 4.5 A )
loaded from c:\PROGRA~1\COMMON~1\SAPSHA~1\system\auto2\wdobapi.ocx

        >>swo_set_environment(62099304, JJS.800)
Thu Apr 29 22:56:09 1999
        <<swo_set_environment(62099304, JJS.800) returns OK
```

To set values for these properties use the following code:

```
Private Sub SAPLogonControl1_Click()

   Set msapConn = SAPLogonControl1.NewConnection

   msapConn.Logon Me.hWnd, False

   SAPBAPIControl1.LogFileName = App.Path & "\bapi_ctrl.log"
   SAPBAPIControl1.LogLevel = 3

   Set SAPBAPIControl1.Connection = msapConn

End Sub
```

The above code will force the control to create a new log file and log activities at level 3.

## *The TransactionID Property*

This property returns/sets the ID for an **SAP R/3 Transaction**. It is populated after a call to the `CreateTransactionID` method of the control.

> **A transaction is a single business task carried out by a user. It consists of a set of screens that users pass through to complete the task. – Using SAP R/3 (Special Edition), 3rd Ed.**

Please bear in mind that the very term transaction may be used more often in the business-oriented sense – as a logical unit of work. The transaction being discussed here is a SAP R/3 specific, GUI screen-based unit of work e.g. the creation of *Material*. To create new *Material* the SAP R/3 user would go through a series of screens on the SAP front-end in a predefined sequence.

The old SAP Assistant 2.1 included a tool to browse transaction screen fields online. The new SAP Assistant doesn't have this option. The screenshot below illustrates the previous release of the SAP Assistant with one of the custom transactions shown:

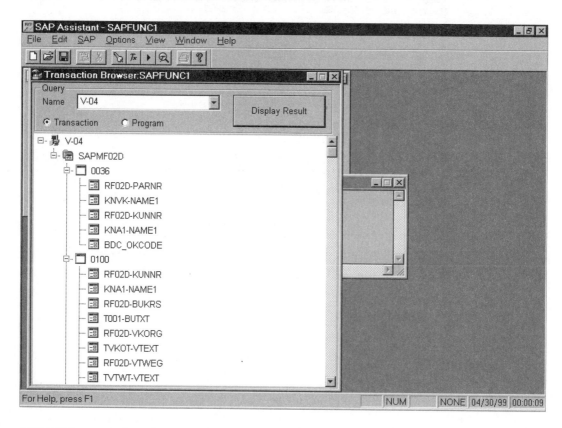

SAP R/3 has several mechanisms for external data exchange, namely **BDC** – Batch Data Communication and **IDoc**. The explanation of these mechanisms and the functionality behind them is well beyond the scope of this book. Moreover, SAP is seriously committed to BAPI technology, and BAPIs will become the preferred mechanism for external communications with SAP R/3.

*I'll give a more detailed account of transactions, related controls and the history of the technology later in the book.*

# Using the BAPI Control for BAPI Programming

All of the connectivity issues of the SAP BAPI control discussed earlier are secondary in importance to the core BAPI control functionality – creating running instances of business objects, thereby providing the ability to execute BAPIs. To fully comprehend this functionality let us briefly recap some of the basics of SAP business objects.

> ➢ Business objects encapsulate functionality relevant to the logical structure of the enterprise's implementation.

> ➢ Each business object has a predefined behavior and implementation.

> ➢ A business object implements its functionality via BAPIs (Business Application Programming Interface functions), which are defined as member functions of the business object. Therefore, a BAPI can and should be considered a method of a business object.

To call a BAPI we first need a valid running instance of the business object that the BAPI belongs to. Another factor is that SAP R/3 implements all its business objects internally and the SAP R/3 internal environment is anything but COM-compliant. To enable communications and provide COM-compliant object structures to the COM environment, SAP implemented several libraries and components that provide this needed functionality in a way familiar to Windows programmers.

> **The core component for BAPI programming is the SAP BAPI control.**

*As we have learned, this control has no GUI presence so should only really be used as an ActiveX control if you desire to put all the code in the form's code module.*

Another caveat is that even if the SAP R/3 business object behaves like a regular object, it's not defined in any COM-compliant library. Therefore, there's no way we can use early binding when dealing with SAP R/3 business objects. All that the BAPI control library does is provides functionality analogous to the `CreateObject` function of Visual Basic. It creates a COM-compliant interface for the business object proxy. In the background, this library maintains a connection with SAP R/3, marshalls all requests to it, and provides bi-directional exchange. That's why we cannot have a 'disconnected' reference to an SAP R/3 business object.

Having refreshed our memory, we can now start looking at an actual business object and its BAPIs. We shall use the *Customer* business object. To ensure concurrency, I will first find an existing customer in SAP R/3 itself, and then create a business object of the *Customer* type using the BAPI control library, and utilizing the attributes of the existing object.

*I believe in maintaining this form of concurrency scenario when you are learning BAPI technology or building any kind of prototype.*

I also recommend starting from the outbound applications where data is coming from SAP R/3. Although inbound samples may look more impressive, I'd rather pull data *out* of SAP R/3 than attempt to put it *in*.

*Another factor is that inbound BAPIs require more SAP R/3 specific knowledge, something that the VB programmer learning external SAP R/3 development normally lacks. This book is about the technology, not SAP R/3 as a business application. Nevertheless, I will try to balance inbound and outbound samples.*

# Exploring the Customer Business Object

To preserve consistency, let's build this project off the BAPI control project from earlier in the chapter. We'll build a project that will open the connection to the SAP R/3 server and provide customer data based on the Customer Number.

We already have the code that enables us to connect to the SAP R/3 system. Just remember to use release 4.0 or greater. The first thing we need to learn is the method of the SAP BAPI control library that creates running instances of regular Visual Basic objects based on SAP R/3 business objects.

## *The GetSAPObject Method*

This method of the SAPBAPIControl class returns a regular object based on the required object type and optional object keys. It has the syntax:

```
Function GetSAPObject(ObjType As String, [ObjKey1], [ObjKey2], [ObjKey3], _
                    [ObjKey4], [ObjKey5], [ObjKey6], [ObjKey7], [ObjKey8], _
                    [ObjKey9], [ObjKey10]) As Object
```

The required parameter ObjType is expected to have a value of the SAP R/3 business object type that can be found in the SAP Business Object Repository. We'll explore the Business Object Repository itself, and the tools that enable external access to it, a little later. For now, we'll just use *Customer* as the given object type.

As you can see, this method allows for up to 10 optional **object key** values to be passed to it. The concept of the object key is very understandable. If you want to look up a particular customer, it would be logical to use some unique identifier for the object. Every business object in SAP R/3 that implements a particular data structure has at least one key. Some business objects require more than one key to provide data. For example, the *APAccount* business object has two keys – CompanyCode and Vendor.

You may wonder why the keys are optional. There are two reasons:

> ➢ Firstly, not all business objects have keys, because they don't implement any retrieval functionality, or at least not yet.

> ➢ Secondly, if you want to create a new object, like a *Customer*, you may not have the ID at the moment of calling the GetSAPObject method. I say "may", because it depends on the configuration of your system: it may assign customer numbers itself or require you to assign one yourself.

*As you may notice, even the most straightforward looking method or technique brings up many issues that at first glance are not relevant to Visual Basic programming.*

## *Making the Connection*

We are now armed with enough knowledge to start programming. First, open a new Standard EXE Visual Basic project and add the SAP BAPI control and the SAP Logon control to the default form. I

also added a command button (with the caption Get Customer) and the Status Bar control (with 3 panels) to display the status of the logon process:

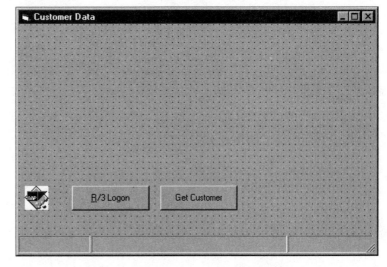

Define the variable for the Connection object in the General Declaration part of the form's module:

```
Option Explicit

Private msapConn As SAPLogonCtrl.Connection
```

Add the already familiar code to the SAP Logon control's Click event:

```
Private Sub SAPLogonControl1_Click()

    Set msapConn = SAPLogonControl1.NewConnection

    msapConn.Logon Me.hWnd, False

    SAPBAPIControl1.LogFileName = App.Path & "\bapi_ctrl.log"
    SAPBAPIControl1.LogLevel = 3

    Set SAPBAPIControl1.Connection = msapConn

    With msapConn

        If .IsConnected Then
            StatusBar1.Panels(1).Text = "System " & .System
            StatusBar1.Panels(2).Text = "Server " & .ApplicationServer & _
                                        " " & "Release " & .SAPRelease
            StatusBar1.Panels(3).Text = "Client " & .Client & " " & _
                                        "Language " & .Language
```

```
      Else
          StatusBar1.Panels(1).Text = "Not Connected"
      End If

  End With

End Sub
```

This code will prompt you for the logon attributes using the **Logon** dialog of the SAP Logon control. Upon successful connection, you should have the panels of the status bar reflect your system attributes:

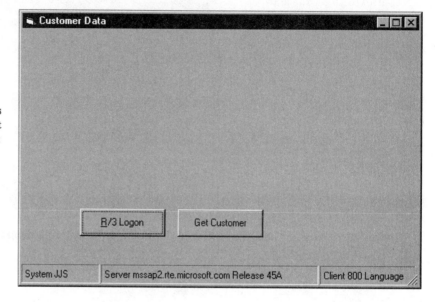

Before we can start programming with the GetSAPObject method, we need to look up the values for the Customer Number in SAP R/3 itself. If you don't have the SAP R/3 front-end, ask your ABAP programmers to give you a ten-character long Customer Number. If you do have the SAP R/3 front-end software (strongly recommended), do the following.

## Obtaining the Customer Number

Launch the SAP front-end and logon. Select the <u>A</u>ccounting | <u>F</u>inancial Accounting | A<u>c</u>counts Receivable menu items.

On the Accounts Receivable screen select Ma<u>s</u>ter Records | D<u>i</u>splay:

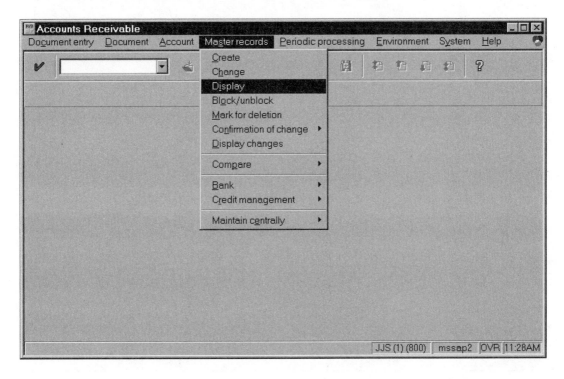

After you do all that, you'll be presented with the Display Customer screen:

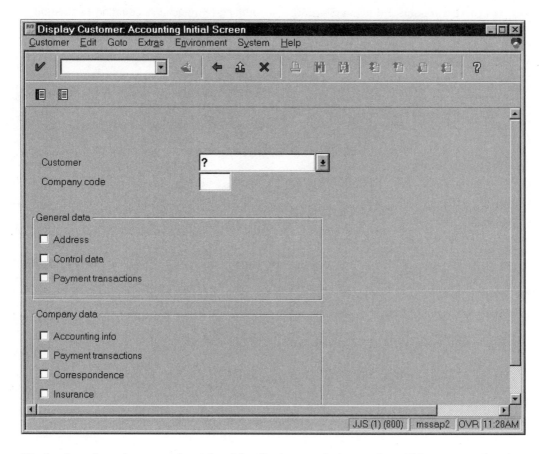

Hit the drop-down button to the right of the Customer edit box and you'll be presented with a variation of a search dialog:

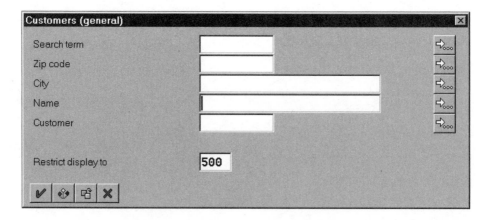

Click on the green check button without entering any selection criteria, and you'll see the list of all customers.

*Note that when it comes to actual values, screenshots in this book will reflect values in the SAP R/3 system that I connect to, and you will have something different.*

I selected INTERBANK and its number now appears in the Customer field:

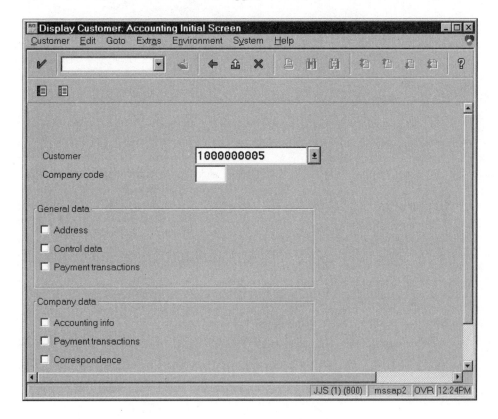

Now select some processing options related to what part of the customer data you want to see - I selected **Address** and **Control data**:

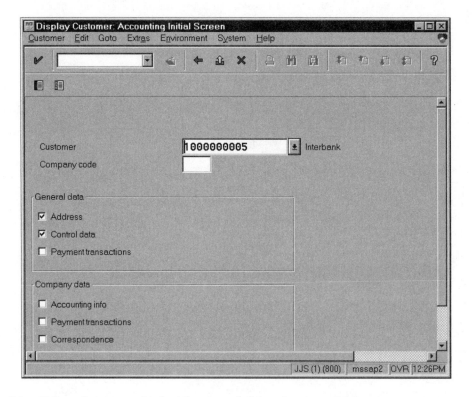

After this, click on that green check at the upper left-hand corner of the screen.

You will get the customer data screen. It is very understated in appearance to say the least, but it presents you with all you wanted to see. The gray background of edit fields conveys that you can't alter these values from this screen:

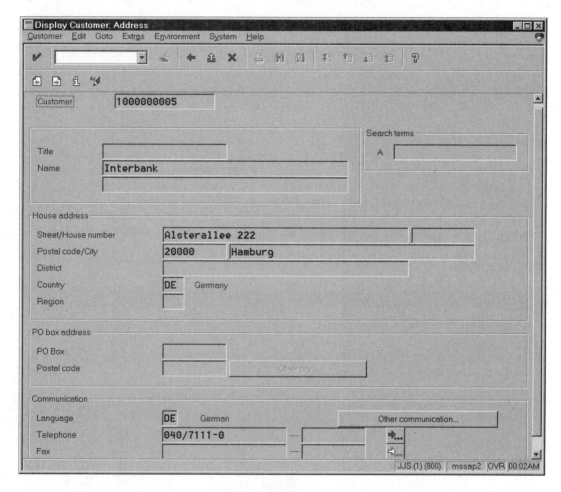

We now have the Customer Number that we needed for the GetSAPObject method and the place in SAP R/3 to go to compare the values in the SAP database against the values that we are going to get from our Visual Basic program.

## Retrieving the Object

Add a label to the form and attach the following code to the command button's Click event:

```
Private Sub Command1_Click()

   Dim sapCustomer As Object

   Set sapCustomer = SAPBAPIControl1.GetSAPObject("Customer", "1000000005")
```

```
    If sapCustomer Is Nothing Then
       Label1 = "Failed to create the Customer Object"
    Else
       Label1 =  "Customer " & sapCustomer.Name & " createssfully"
    End If

    Set sapCustomer = Nothing

End Sub
```

As you may notice, I dimension the variable for the *Customer* object as an abstract `Object` type as we discussed earlier. I also pass the type `Customer` and the value of the Customer Number that we got from SAP R/3.

> *I trap un-initialized objects with the* `Is Nothing` *condition. This is very convenient when you have a function that will not generate a run-time error if it fails to return the object. Un-initialized objects will evaluate to* `Nothing` *while returning true for* `IsObject` *and evaluating into* `Object` *for the* `VarType`.

Now run the project. Hit the **Logon** button to logon into the SAP R/3, and after you have all the attributes of your R/3 system correctly displayed in the status bar, click on the **Get Customer** button. As a result, you should see a message that the customer has been created successfully:

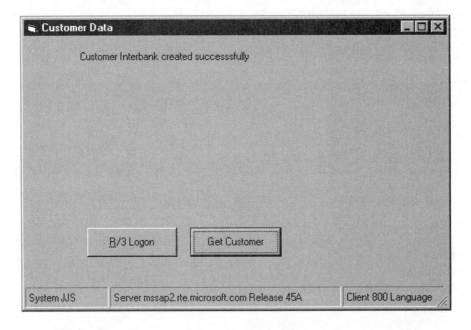

> *Be aware that the response time depends on many factors. Your network may sometimes be a little slow or the server a little too busy. If you connect remotely via dial-up then you should factor in the modem speed. I suggest creating some progress indicators for the GUI, even something as simple as toggling from a normal to hourglass cursor.*

So far, we've created a valid reference to a specific *Customer* object, as defined in SAP R/3, and accessed the data it encapsulates. If we recall earlier chapters, we'll see that every business object has attributes. These attributes are best compared to an object's properties. We have already seen one attribute/property at work – the `Name` attribute of the *Customer* object.

# Creating Collections

If you wish to create an empty collection to hold business objects, you can use the `CreateCollectionOfSAPObjects` method of the **SAP BAPI** control's `SAPBAPIControl` class.

> The `CreateCollectionOfSAPObjects` method creates an empty, zero-based collection that can store **SAP R/3** business objects.

When you execute this method, you get an empty collection that you can add business objects to using the `Add` method, and retrieve business objects from using the `Item` method. Use indices only when retrieving business objects, because the `Add` method will not accept a second argument for the key.

Add a new command button (**Get Customer Collection**) plus a list box to the form and add the following code to the new command button's `Click` event:

```
Private Sub Command2_Click()

    Dim sapCustomer1 As Object
    Dim sapCustomer2 As Object
    Dim sapCustomer3 As Object

    Dim tmpCustomer As Object
    Dim colSapCust As Object

    Me.MousePointer = vbHourglass
    List1.Clear

    Set sapCustomer1 = SAPBAPIControl1.GetSAPObject("Customer", "1000000005")
    Set sapCustomer2 = SAPBAPIControl1.GetSAPObject("Customer", "1000000006")
    Set sapCustomer3 = SAPBAPIControl1.GetSAPObject("Customer", "1000000010")

    If sapCustomer1 Is Nothing Or sapCustomer2 Is Nothing Or _
        sapCustomer3 Is Nothing Then

        Label1 = "Failed to create a Customer object"
        Exit Sub

    Else

        Set colSapCust = SAPBAPIControl1.CreateCollectionOfSAPObjects

        colSapCust.Add sapCustomer1
        colSapCust.Add sapCustomer2
        colSapCust.Add sapCustomer3
```

```
    End If

    Label1 = colSapCust.Item(2).Name

    For Each tmpCustomer In colSapCust
       List1.AddItem tmpCustomer.Name
    Next

    Me.MousePointer = vbNormal

    Set sapCustomer1 = Nothing
    Set sapCustomer2 = Nothing
    Set sapCustomer3 = Nothing
    Set tmpCustomer = Nothing
    set colSapCust = Nothing

End Sub
```

Because of this feature, I suggest you treat this collection as an array. This fits the bill, since an array is an indexed set of items of the same kind.

You can also totally disregard this collection and use the regular Visual Basic Collection or Dictionary object. The code below represents using a regular VB collection:

```
Private Sub Command2_Click()

    Dim sapCustomer1 As Object
    Dim sapCustomer2 As Object
    Dim sapCustomer3 As Object

    Dim tmpCustomer As Object
    Dim regVbColl As New Collection

    Me.MousePointer = vbHourglass
    List1.Clear

    Set sapCustomer1 = SAPBAPIControl1.GetSAPObject("Customer", "1000000005")
    Set sapCustomer2 = SAPBAPIControl1.GetSAPObject("Customer", "1000000006")
    Set sapCustomer3 = SAPBAPIControl1.GetSAPObject("Customer", "1000000010")

    If sapCustomer1 Is Nothing Or sapCustomer2 Is Nothing Or _
       sapCustomer3 Is Nothing Then

       Label1 = "Failed to create the Customer Object"
       Exit Sub

    Else

       regVbColl.Add sapCustomer1, sapCustomer1.CustomerNo
       regVbColl.Add sapCustomer2, sapCustomer2.CustomerNo
       regVbColl.Add sapCustomer3, sapCustomer3.CustomerNo

    End If

    Label1 = regVbColl.Item("1000000005").Name
```

```
For Each tmpCustomer In regVbColl
  List1.AddItem tmpCustomer.Name
Next

Me.MousePointer = vbNormal

Set sapCustomer1 = Nothing
Set sapCustomer2 = Nothing
Set sapCustomer3 = Nothing
Set tmpCustomer = Nothing
set regVbColl = Nothing

End Sub
```

When you execute either of the above code segments, the list box will be populated with customers' names:

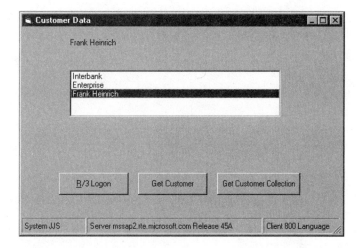

You can change which customer is selected. In the BAPI control collection code segment, I used the index in the collection, and in the VB collection fragment, I assigned keys and retrieved the customer by the key value (which I selected to be different for illustrative purposes).

# Summary

In this chapter, we started using the SAP BAPI control, which is a main component in BAPI programming.

We also started learning how to explore the SAP Business Object Repository using the SAP R/3 front-end. This chapter should have given you sufficient information to be able to independently explore the inner implementation of the SAP R/3 Business Framework.

SAP provides a robust technology that abstracts the external software developer from the specifics of the internal implementation of SAP business objects. While it is possible to be ignorant of the internal implementation of SAP business objects and develop a functioning application using BAPI technology and Visual Basic, this is not the way to become proficient in this very promising area of software development. Therefore, we'll be exploring SAP R/3 in a bit more detail over the course of the book and I'll be sprinkling in tidbits of useful information.

In the next chapter, we'll complete the BAPI invocation process now we know how to create a valid instance of a business object.

# BAPI Parameters and Invoking BAPIs

In this chapter, we'll learn how to handle BAPI parameters. The process of preparing BAPI parameters prior to calling a BAPI, and extracting meaningful data from them after the BAPI has executed, requires special care and attention. SAP integration technology is all about how to access and manipulate data in SAP R/3. Like with any data processing technology we need a mechanism that will allow us to define, populate, and read data. Therefore, it has to provide the means to process the data in the same way as all other data access technologies do.

For example, in ADO we can use the Recordset object defined in the ADODB library to define a variable, use the `AddNew` method to add records, and access records in the recordset. We also have navigation and searching functionality for the ADO Recordset.

We have described the functionality of the SAP BAPI control to the extent of creating and accessing instances of the SAP R/3 business objects. Before we plunge into the SAP R/3 internal business object definition, let's summarize what we have learned so far:

> The functionality of the SAP Logon control

> How to connect to SAP R/3

> The Connection object and its functionality

> How to connect the SAP BAPI control to SAP R/3

> How to create running instances of SAP R/3 business objects

The next logical step is to understand where to get all the object types, attribute names and so on. For example, in the project at the end of the previous chapter, we used the `Name` property and the `CustomerNo` property of the *Customer* business object.

To see where it all comes from let's explore SAP R/3 business objects using the SAP front-end.

# Finding BAPI Parameters Using the SAP Front-End

*Although SAP tries to abstract the external programmer from its implementation details, I strongly recommend that you use SAP R/3 to better understand BAPI technology.*

Launch the SAP R/3 front-end and logon to SAP R/3. Select the Tools | Business Framework | BAPI Development | Business Object Builder menu item:

After you select this menu item you should see the following screen:

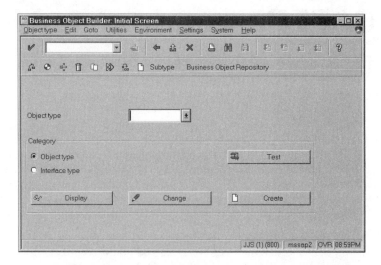

Click on the Business Object Repository button on the toolbar. The following dialog will pop up:

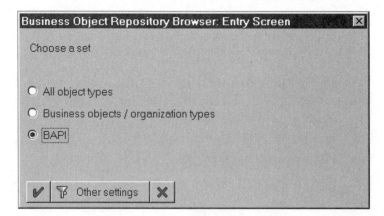

Select the **BAPI** option and hit the green check button. You should see a rudimentary variation of the tree view control:

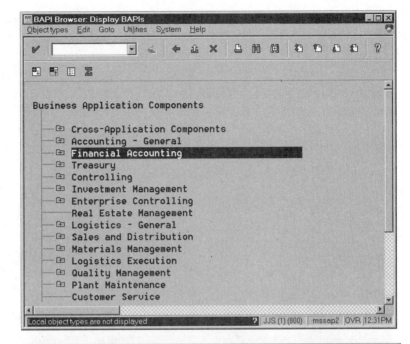

Now click to expand the Financial Accounting node and drill down this path: Financial Accounting | Accounts Receivable | Basic Functions. You should see our familiar Customer among other nodes:

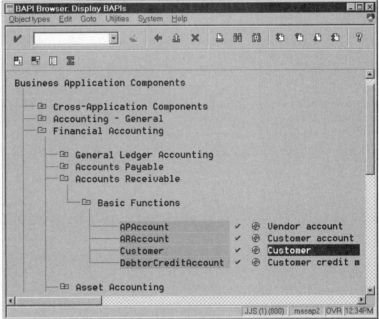

Double-click on
either Customer
and you should see
the following:

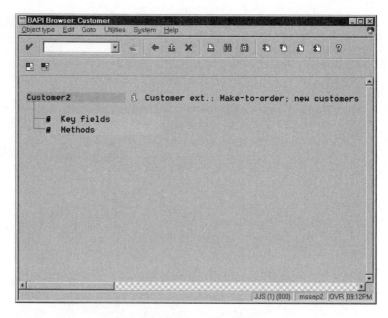

If you expand Key fields and Methods you will see Customer Number as a key field and a list
of BAPIs implemented for the *Customer* business object. Now we have to continue our search for the
attributes.

> *Please note that in your system you may see just* Customer, *not* Customer2 – *it*
> *depends on configuration and customization.*

If you double-click
on Customer2 (or
Customer) the
following screen
comes up:

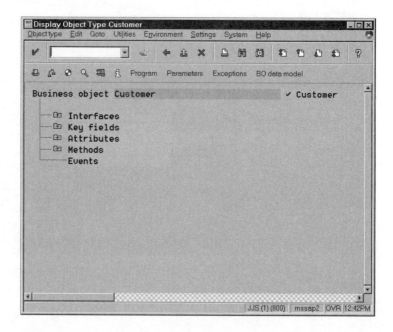

Now we have
access to its
`Attributes`.
Expand the
`Attributes`
node:

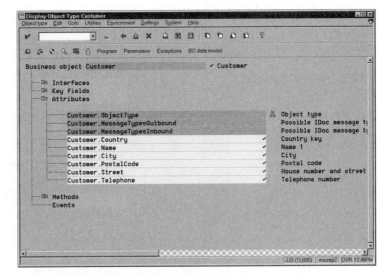

Now we can see where I got the properties for the *Customer* object. Highlighted in red are those attributes not exposed via the business object.

> *Note that this approach is not a 'suggested' one. SAP assumes that the Visual Basic programmer will not venture this far and will stay only with BAPIs. Honestly, I cannot convince myself that using attributes for BAPI programming can be that useful. However, this exercise helped me to better understand SAP business object technology and I hope it will help you too.*

The only one
thing I would
like you to note
is that if you
double-click on
`Customer` in the
above screen you
will see the
following:

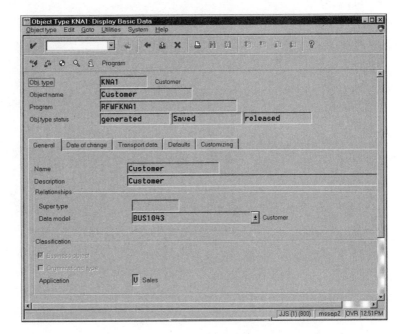

This screen is useful because it reveals the object type - KNA1 - for the *Customer* object. You will see analogies with this when we use the SAP Assistant in Chapter 6. Then, you'll already know where the data is coming from and what it means.

# BAPI Implementation

Now is the time to go back to the **Display Object Type** screen. Expand the `Key fields` node:

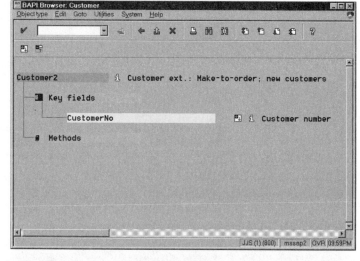

We can now see the key field for the *Customer* business object – `CustomerNo`. We used the value of this key to create an instance of a particular customer. If you continue to drill down the nodes, you will see the following:

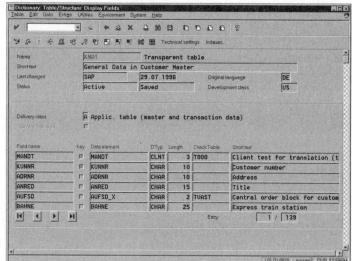

This latest series of screenshots had one major objective – to show that a business object is internally defined in SAP R/3 and it encapsulates the data stored in a table or tables in the SAP R/3 database.

If we go back and expand the `Methods` node, we'll see all the BAPIs defined for the *Customer* business object:

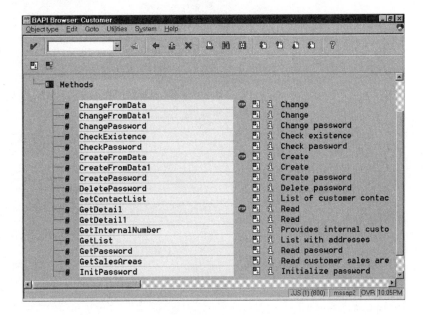

*Note that BAPIs with the STOP sign next to them are obsolete for the SAP R/3 release I am using. Your picture may be different depending on your system.*

If you expand any of these implemented BAPIs you will see their parameters.

*You should be familiar by now with the SAP implementation of the drill-down GUI and you shouldn't be surprised if you have to double-click on the word in the middle of the text to get help, or get to another screen that has more details on that item.*

BAPI parameters are no different from any other function arguments. The only problem with these parameters is that they are not of any Visual Basic data type. They are Field, Structure and Table in the SAP R/3's interpretation. Let's explore the BAPI that we are going to implement for our first BAPI project. In this project, we will create a simple GUI that is going to display the customers in SAP R/3.

## The GetList BAPI

The BAPI that we need is called `GetList`.

*Please note that this BAPI is enabled with release 4.5. I will later show another way to list customers, should you have an earlier release of SAP R/3.*

Expand the GetList
BAPI's node from the list
of methods, and you will
see the following:

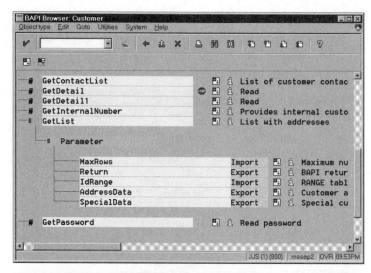

Now we know what
parameters this BAPI
expects. Any method may
have mandatory and
optional parameters. To
find out whether a
parameter is mandatory
or optional, place the
mouse pointer over the
small rectangle to the left
of the letter i. The mouse
pointer will turn from an
arrow into a hand. Click
on IdRange and
AddressData:

It is very clear now if a parameter is mandatory or not.

> *Also note the* Import *and* Export *labels. We'll come back to what these represent shortly.*

Another very important thing to find out is the data type of these parameters. Depending on their type we will have to handle them differently. Structures and Tables are similar but have different approaches to data retrieval/population and it is important to know which you're using in advance.

# The BAPI Interface

> The BAPI Interface is the set of Parameters and Parameter properties that are exposed for external programming.

As with virtually everything with SAP R/3, there's no straightforward way to find out the data type of BAPI parameters from the BAPI Browser: Customer screen. Remember that SAP R/3 implements essentially the same functionality in several ways and displays it from different angles. To find what we need, we have to recall that any functionality in SAP R/3 is implemented via internal functions that reside in function modules. Every function should therefore be available for browsing, including the function's interface.

Remember how we accessed the business objects by selecting BAPI in the Business Object Repository Browser: Entry Screen? Let's go there and instead select the Business objects / organization types option. Expand the same set of nodes as we did before to drill-down to the Customer node. We will see the following:

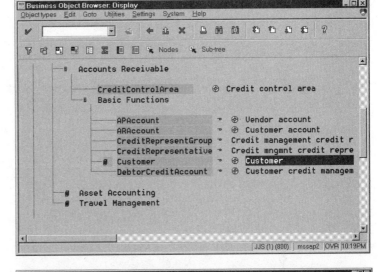

Drill down the Customer node and we will get the list of methods:

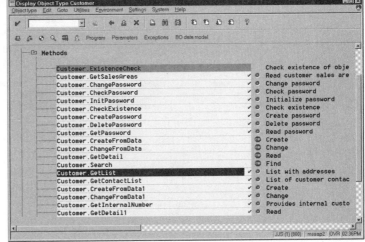

If we scroll to GetList and
double-click on it, you will be
presented with a screen
resembling our familiar
property pages:

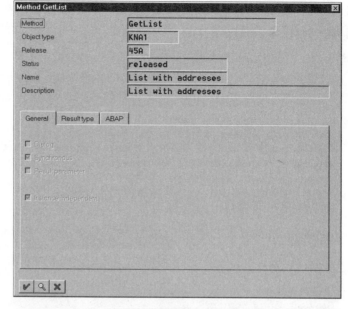

Click on the ABAP tab and
you will see the following:

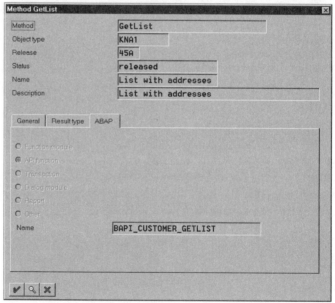

The purpose of this exercise was to get the real name of the BAPI. For the `GetList` BAPI, it is `BAPI_CUSTOMER_ GETLIST`. Double-click on `BAPI_CUSTOMER_ GETLIST` – you will see the code on the screen. Select the Goto | Interface menu item as shown:

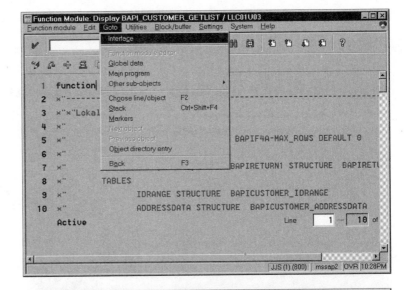

After you select it, you should see this screen reflecting the BAPI. Browse the different tabs to familiarize yourself with the BAPI.

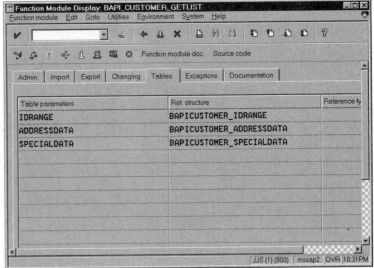

Let's summarize our explorations of this BAPI's parameters:

> `RETURN` is a Structure

> `MAXROWS` is a Field

> `IDRANGE` is a Table

> `ADDRESSDATA` is a Table

> `SPECIALDATA` is a Table

The above list reflects all the information found on the SAP GUI screen and represents the BAPI interface – i.e. the BAPI interface is comprised of parameters only. The question now is, how are we going to define these data types in Visual Basic?

# The SAP BAPI Control – DimAs Function

The SAP BAPI control has an unusual method for a VB component – DimAs. However, it has a familiar name and it's not too difficult to guess what it does – it dimensions the SAP R/3 structures as Visual Basic compatible data types.

> **You should always use this method to create BAPI Parameters of the Structure or Table type. Do not use it for Field types.**

The DimAs function has the following syntax:

```
Function DimAs(Object As Object, Method As String, Parameter As String) As Object
```

The DimAs function returns a valid reference to the Parameter object of a Structure or Table type, as required for the BAPI method. This means that after you execute the DimAs function you will have empty, yet valid, parameters for the BAPI. It is a generic function and it requires the following arguments:

> ➤ Object – A valid reference to the SAP R/3 business object created using the GetSAPObject method

> ➤ Method – String value of the BAPI's name. Note that it expects the BAPI's name, not the underlying function name, i.e. GetList not BAPI_CUSTOMER_GETLIST

> ➤ Parameter – String value of the BAPI Parameter's name

In the code it looks like this:

```
Dim sapCustomer As Object
Dim sapAddrData As Object

Set sapCustomer = SAPBAPIControl1.GetSAPObject("Customer")
Set sapAddrData = SAPBAPIControl1.DimAs(sapCustomer, "GetList", "ADDRESSDATA")
```

The above code will result in having a valid reference to the Parameter object derived from the ADDRESSDATA parameter of the GetList BAPI of the *Customer* business object.

If you use it for a Field parameter type you will get a run-time error. For example, if you try the following code:

```
Dim sapCustomer As Object
Dim sapMaxRows As Object

Set sapCustomer = SAPBAPIControl1.GetSAPObject("Customer")
Set sapMaxRows = SAPBAPIControl1.DimAs(sapCustomer, "GetList", "MAXROWS")
```

The result will be as shown below:

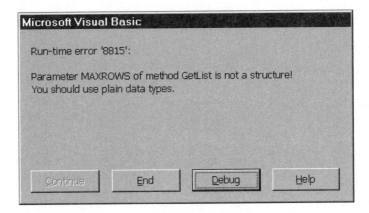

## Using the DimAs Method

Create a new **Standard EXE** project, add a tree view control, image list control, status bar with 2 panels, SAP Logon control and SAP BAPI control to the project and place them on the form. I populated the image list with some pictures, which you can find in the source code, and I set tree view's **Style** property to tvwTreelinesPlusMinusPictureText and the **LineStyle** property to tvwRootLines.

For illustrative purposes, we are going to invoke the BAPI from a separate command button, so add one to the form. Your design-time GUI should look similar to this one:

Add this to the **General Declarations** part of the form's code module:

```
Dim msapConn As SAPLogonCtrl.Connection
```

Set up the controls in the Form's `Load` event:

```
Private Sub Form_Load()

  Dim sapNode As Node

  Command1.Enabled = False
  StatusBar1.Panels(1).Text = "Not Connected"

  Set sapNode = TreeView1.Nodes.Add(, , "topsap", "SAP R/3", 4)
  Set sapNode = TreeView1.Nodes.Add("topsap", tvwChild, "custs", _
                                      "Customers", 2)

  Set sapNode = Nothing

End Sub
```

Add this to the SAP Logon control's `Click` event:

```
Private Sub SAPLogonControl1_Click()

  Set msapConn = SAPLogonControl1.NewConnection

  If msapConn.Logon(Me.hWnd, False) Then
      StatusBar1.Panels(1).Text = "Connected to " & msapConn.ApplicationServer
      Command1.Enabled = True
    Else
      StatusBar1.Panels(1).Text = "Not Connected"
      Command1.Enabled = False
    End If

  Set SAPBAPIControl1.Connection = msapConn

End Sub
```

Nothing radical here – just our traditional connectivity code. Now let's get into the `DimAs` implementation. We know all the values we need to implement for all the attributes.

Add this code to the `Command1_Click` event:

```
Private Sub Command1_Click()

  Dim sapCustomer As Object

  Dim sapAddrData As Object
  Dim sapReturn As Object
  Dim sapIdRange As Object

  Me.MousePointer = vbHourglass

  Set sapCustomer = SAPBAPIControl1.GetSAPObject("Customer")
```

```
    Set sapAddrData = SAPBAPIControl1.DimAs(sapCustomer, "GetList", "ADDRESSDATA")
    Set sapReturn = SAPBAPIControl1.DimAs(sapCustomer, "GetList", "RETURN")
    Set sapIdRange = SAPBAPIControl1.DimAs(sapCustomer, "GetList", "IDRANGE")

    Me.MousePointer = vbNormal

    Set sapCustomer = Nothing
    Set sapAddrData = Nothing
    Set sapReturn = Nothing
    Set sapIdRange = Nothing

End Sub
```

Suppose we added the following code after the Parameter objects had been initialized:

```
Debug.Print sapAddrData.Name
Debug.Print sapReturn.Name
Debug.Print sapIdRange.Name
```

Now if you ran the project, logged on and hit the command button, the output in the **Immediate** window would look like this:

The **Immediate** window's output confirms that we did create valid references to the Parameter objects. Now it is time to populate these parameters with data. SAP R/3 defines BAPI parameters in one of two ways to describe how it expects the parameter to be used:

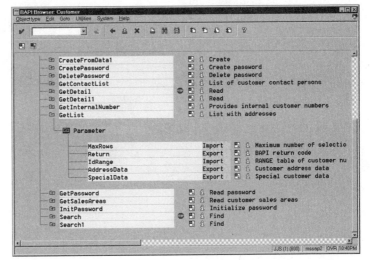

- ➤ Parameters expected to be *passed to* SAP R/3 are marked as `Import`

- ➤ Parameters that are expected to be *populated by* SAP R/3 are marked as `Export`

In order to successfully execute the BAPI we have to not only correctly dimension the BAPI's parameters but also populate them with the required data, and correctly interpret that data from SAP R/3. Let's use our project to elaborate on this.

# The SAP Table Factory Control

As with the BAPI control, it's much better to treat the **SAP Table Factory control** like a library rather than a control. It does not have a run-time GUI and its design-time properties are irrelevant to its core functionality. This library holds, among other things, definitions for the Structure and Table Parameter objects used for BAPI calls.

As we have already illustrated, all BAPI related entities are defined in SAP R/3. They are ABAP structures that Visual Basic has no idea how to handle. To enable the Windows programming of BAPIs, SAP supplies libraries that map ABAP data structures to COM-compliant objects. We can always define Structure and Table parameters as `Object` in Visual Basic, as we saw when I demonstrated the `DimAs` method. However, this approach prevents the use of IntelliSense and type checking. It is particularly painful to process data using just methods and properties of objects. To resolve this, SAP developed the SAP Table Factory control:

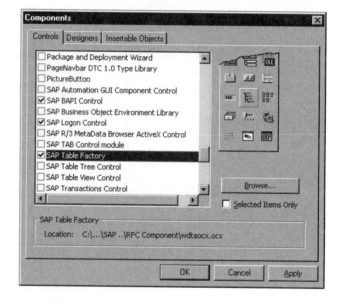

This control resides in `WDTAOCX.OCX`, and when you add it to the toolbox it displays the following icon:

A quick look at the Object Browser gives a good idea of the functionality and architecture of the Table Factory library:

For now, we are interested in the Structure and Table objects that are represented by their namesake classes in the Table Factory library and the `SAPTableFactory` class itself.

# The SAPTableFactory Class Methods

This class has the following methods:

> `AboutBox` – Will display an About Box

> `NewStructure` – Will create a Structure object

> `NewTable` – Will create a Table object

> `NewTables` – Will create a Tables Collection object

These three `New*` methods allow us to create valid objects that are both expected by the BAPI library and suitable for Visual Basic, which can treat them as objects of a certain type. Referencing of the SAP Table Factory Control library makes it possible to use IntelliSense in your programming, because we can define variables as Tables and Structures. The code below illustrates this:

```
Dim sapAddrData As SAPTableFactoryCtrl.Table
Dim sapIdRange As SAPTableFactoryCtrl.Table
Dim sapReturn As SAPTableFactoryCtrl.Structure
```

*Please fully reference objects with possibly ambiguous class names, by including the library name itself. It will save you some sanity if you have the SAP Table Factory, DAO and ADO libraries referenced in the same project.*

Although it is possible to declare parameters as a Structure or Table, I recommend defining variables for BAPI parameters as objects in Visual Basic code. I don't have access to the system documentation or source code of the creators of the libraries that we use here, and as you can see, there are many different implementations of the transformation of the SAP business objects into COM-compliant objects. The whole SAP Automation Toolkit is 'living' code with patches and updates arriving almost monthly. Given this dynamism, I would advise following the most generic variable definition and something that I refer to as the logical path of execution. For example, if we are about to call the BAPI and we need to prepare parameters using the `DimAs` method, don't use anything to preprocess the parameter. Rather hand it over to the `DimAs` method as a generic `Object` type.

Now we are fully prepared to learn how to populate BAPI parameters should the need arise. First of all let us analyze the `Table object`. As its name suggests, it has to have some functionality to input and read data. The same can be said about the Structure object.

*As I have noted before, I will give detailed information only on those methods and properties that are most useful, stable and implementation friendly from the Visual Basic perspective.*

# The Table Object

The Table object implements all the functionality necessary to access and manipulate Table type parameters for BAPIs. It is conceptually analogous to the TableDef object in DAO.

## Properties

The Table object has the following properties:

| Property | Description |
|---|---|
| Name | String data, contains the name for the Table as defined in the SAP Business Object Repository. |
| Columns | Object data, returns the reference to the Columns collection object. |
| ColumnCount | Long data, returns the number of columns in the Table. |
| Data | Variant data, returns/sets the two-dimensional Variant array containing data in the Table. Use to quickly initialize the array with the Table's data. |
| Rows | Object data, returns the reference to the Rows collection object. |
| RowCount | Long data, returns the number of Rows (records) in the Table. It is analogous to the `RecordCount` property of the ADO Recordset. Use it to see if you have any records in the Table. |
| Value | Variant data, returns the value of the cell, expects ordinal values for the row and the column. |

| Property | Description |
|----------|-------------|
| Views | Object data, returns all views that are enclosed in the Table object. It's used to bind the Table object to the Table View control (we'll explore this later). This functionality is conceptually analogous to the data grid-data control tandem functionality. |

Let's see these properties in action in some simple illustrative code. We'll assume that we managed to get the data from the BAPI call, (we'll see how to do this shortly), and we have the Table object that contains the customer data:

```
Dim sapAddrData As SAPTableFactoryCtrl.Table
Dim intCounter As Integer

Debug.Print "Table - " & sapAddrData.Name & " contains:"
Debug.Print "Columns - " & sapAddrData.ColumnCount
Debug.Print "Rows - " & sapAddrData.RowCount

Debug.Print "Column Names Are:"

For intCounter = 1 To sapAddrData.ColumnCount
    Debug.Print sapAddrData.Columns(i).Name
Next
```

The above code will result in the following content of the Immediate window:

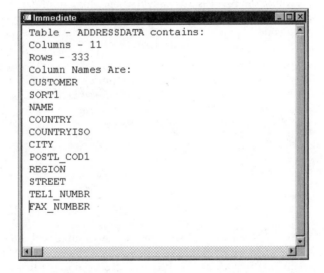

```
Table - ADDRESSDATA contains:
Columns - 11
Rows - 333
Column Names Are:
CUSTOMER
SORT1
NAME
COUNTRY
COUNTRYISO
CITY
POSTL_COD1
REGION
STREET
TEL1_NUMBR
FAX_NUMBER
```

You may be curious as to why I didn't use the ColumnName property, that can supposedly return me a name for the column, based on the ordinal number. The answer is simple – it did not work. The call didn't fail, but equally it didn't return any values. This property is also missing from the Help's list of properties. Bear in mind that any future release – I used the 4510.4.0.7 version of the Table Factory control – may enable this functionality. Another thing to beware of is that the Columns collection is a regular Visual Basic style collection in the sense that it is one-based for the Item method.

## Methods

The Table object has the following methods.

### The AppendRow Method

This appends an empty row (record) to the already defined table. You have to execute it prior to any data assignment. It is analogous to the `AddNew` method of the ADO Recordset.

### The Create* Methods

These are a group of methods that create Table objects using various techniques and input parameters. These methods are used when you want to create an SAP R/3 BOR compliant table without calling any BAPIs to prepare or manipulate data. It is vaguely analogous to disconnected ADO Recordsets. These methods are not necessary for BAPI calls, because we can get all we need using the `DimAs` method.

> *Another advantage of the `DimAs` method is that it creates the structure of the BAPI parameter based on the internal BOR definitions. It relieves the Visual Basic programmer who is not intimately familiar with the internal SAP R/3 data model from being forced to learn it.*

These methods can be very useful for the creation of generic routines that dynamically define tables in certain scenarios where the BAPI is not known at the moment of data preparation. These situations don't normally occur in client-specific applications, where BAPIs are implemented statically. Below you can find a simple code fragment for one of the `Create*` methods.

> *Please note that some of those methods are annotated as Not Documented and do not have any reflection in the documentation. My sample is based on a tested and working method. I supply the name for the Structure as defined in the SAP R/3 Data Dictionary (it can be accessed from the Object Repository Browser – KNA1 for Customer data) and some name that I want to refer to the new table by.*

```
Dim sapTable As SAPTableFactory1.Table
Dim blnRetval As Boolean

Set sapTable = SAPTableFactory1.NewTable
blnRetval = sapTable.CreateFromR3Repository(msapConn, "KNA1", "MYTABLE")
```

After execution of this code, we will have a valid formatted table with no data in it. We can then use the `Create*` methods when we do not have any business objects created but need the Tables corresponding to their BAPIs' parameters. We may also need to get the Table that is not a parameter for any BAPI but can be a parameter for an RFC.

### The SelectTo*Methods

These are a group of methods that provide views on the table's data that satisfies the `key-value` criteria pair for the specific dimension of the table – where the Key is the name for the field, and the Value is the value. The result of these methods is the `Matrix` object. They are substitutes for SQL functionality that is unavailable with Table objects.

> You cannot execute any SQL statements against SAP Table Factory derived Tables.

This means that SQL-related lookup, such as Find, Seek and all other SELECT…FROM…WHERE based functionality is absent from the SAP Automation family of products.

> *The DCOM Component Connector Toolkit offers a more familiar architecture, generically converting all Table and Structure objects into ADO Recordsets. This solution is superior from the Visual Basic and DCOM perspective. The SAP Automation SDK solution is more generic and can be implemented on different platforms using C++ or Java.*

The best possible scenario for use of the SelectTo* methods is writing a macro to integrate Table object content into an Excel workbook. Otherwise, all this vector/matrix-based logic is too cumbersome to implement – you are far better off manipulating arrays.

Here is an example for calling one of the Select* methods – SelectToMatrix. This method has the following syntax:

```
Function SelectToMatrix(RowVector, RowAssocIndex As Long, ColumnVector, _
                ColumnAssocVector As Long, DataAssocIndex As Long) _
                As Object
```

Where:

> RowVector is an array of values for the first dimension of the returned matrix

> RowAssocIndex is the index of the table column with which the RowVector values are to be compared

> ColumnVector is an array of values for the second dimension of the returned matrix

> ColumnAssocIndex is the index of the table column with which the ColumnVector values are to be compared

> DataAssocIndex is the index of the table column from which the desired data is to be taken

All the index values mentioned above refer to the one-based ordinal position of the column in the Table object – in our case in the ADDRESSDATA Table. For example, if I want to extract Customer Numbers for customers located in Berlin, Germany, I should use DE for the Country field – ordinal position 4 of the ADDRESSDATA Table; and 11 for the Region field – ordinal position 8. These two columns will provide the data for the RowVector and ColumnVector parameters respectively. The column for the Customer Number has ordinal position 1. Armed with this knowledge we can code the call for the method:

```
Dim objMatrix As Object
Dim arrRowVector(1)
Dim arrColumnVector(1)

arrRowVector (0) = "DE"
arrRowVector (1) = "DE"
arrColumnVector (0) = "11"
```

```
arrColumnVector (1) = "11"

Set objMatrix = sapAddrData.SelectToMatrix(arrRowVector, 4, _
                                   arrColumnVector, 8, 2)
```

The result will be a two dimensional array containing two Customer Numbers.

> **Note that this method will not return you all the customers that satisfy the selection criteria but only as many as the number of selection criteria you supplied – we supplied just two value pairs and we got just two Customer Numbers.**

It's very primitive and inconvenient. That is why instead of concentrating on this methodology, alien to data access technologies used in Visual Basic and other Microsoft products, I decided to implement the functionality that will bring this low-level data array manipulation mechanism to the level of ADO.

> *I also suspect that MS Excel was the first Microsoft product that SAP wanted the Automation package to be integrated with. If it were Access, they would have come up with some more DAO/ADO-related data manipulation techniques. Treating a table as a two-dimensional matrix is correct technically, after all a table is a matrix. However, the approach is very Excel minded. We'll see a different approach in the DCOM Component Connector, which is ADO based.*

The good thing about these `SelectTo*` methods is that they allow the business analyst to easily input values for 'data slicing' implementation. As I have already stated, the SAP Automation Toolkit is an SDK. The programmer has to decide which functionality to use. The toolkit is great for connectivity to SAP R/3 and BAPI/RFC execution. However, it lacks substantial functionality in the data representation and manipulation areas. We'll elaborate on these topics in later chapters. At this point, it's time to go back to the Table object.

## *Adding Records to the Table Object*

As we have already learned, there is an `IDRANGE` parameter of the `GetList` BAPI that we have to pass to the BAPI, and it expects certain values to be entered before the call. This parameter acts like a criteria table.

> *For the sake of the structural clarity of the book, I will not embark on looking up predefined values for parameters in SAP R/3. I will provide detailed samples for this very important part of the SAP R/3 related development in following chapters, using both the SAP Automation Toolkit and the DCOM Component Connector. In this chapter, we will rely on values as given.*

A look at the structure of the `IDRANGE` Table reveals that it has four columns:

> ➢ The `SIGN` column is a single character column and can have either "I" for Inclusive or "E" for Exclusive, predefined values.

> ➤ The OPTION column can have more predefined values, but we will select "NP" for No Pattern. Note that all these values are defined in SAP R/3. You can use your newly gained skills and explore SAP R/3 or read on until you reach the discussion and code for something called **help values** in SAP R/3.

> ➤ The LOW and HIGH columns are criteria columns that expect Customer Numbers for the low and high end range of customers that interest us. We will populate them with empty strings because we need data for all customers.

Before we assign any of these values, we have to add a row to the IDRANGE Table object. We will use the AppendRow method of the Table object. As you already know this method simply adds a new record to the Table object. Add this line after the sap* objects have been initialized:

```
Set sapReturn = SAPBAPIControl1.DimAs(sapCustomer, "GetList", "RETURN")
Set sapIdRange = SAPBAPIControl1.DimAs(sapCustomer, "GetList", "IDRANGE")

sapIdRange.AppendRow
```

A new empty row is created. Because this row obviously inherits the Table's structure, we can use named references to each column in the Columns collection of the Table:

```
Set sapReturn = SAPBAPIControl1.DimAs(sapCustomer, "GetList", "RETURN")
Set sapIdRange = SAPBAPIControl1.DimAs(sapCustomer, "GetList", "IDRANGE")

sapIdRange.AppendRow

sapIdRange.Columns("SIGN").Value(1) = "I"
sapIdRange.Columns("OPTION").Value(1) = "NP"
sapIdRange.Columns("LOW").Value(1) = ""
sapIdRange.Columns("HIGH").Value(1) = ""
```

I could have used the Value property of the Table object using ordinal numbers for every cell, but I like the convenience of a named reference.

> *Note that the Value property of the Column object behaves predictably differently from the Table's Value property. The column's Value property requires only one ordinal number for the row from which we want to get/set the data. We have only one row (record) in the IDRANGE Table and we pass 1 to the Value's Index of the Column object.*

After successful parameter setup, we are ready to actually call the BAPI.

# Calling an SAP R/3 BAPI

We already know that a BAPI is a method of a business object. As such, it is handled as a regular method of an object in Visual Basic, adhering to the ObjectName.MethodName convention.

> *Remember that business objects are defined as generic objects and you will not see any drop-down list of methods. Therefore, be particularly careful with spelling.*

The calling of a BAPI is also somewhat special. SAP recommends using `named arguments` when calling BAPIs. The most obvious reason for Visual Basic programmers is that we cannot use the IntelliSense functionality to learn the correct order of BAPI arguments.

A more fundamental reason is that the use of named arguments in external programs allows SAP to change its implementation specifics without breaking the external application's code. Yet another reason is that there is no way an external programmer can learn the order of positioning of the BAPI parameters, programmatically, using any of the SAP Automation libraries.

The only problem with using named arguments is that you cannot build them dynamically. It means many hard coded functions in your application. Any attempt to build a generic BAPI execution wrapper in Visual Basic may become very problematic.

In our case, we are not building any generic BAPI wrappers and we can simply implement the BAPI call as suggested. Add this line after the `IdRange.Columns` code in the `Command1_Click` event:

```
sapCustomer.GetList RETURN:=sapReturn, ADDRESSDATA:=sapAddrData, _
                    IDRANGE:=sapIdRange
```

If we execute this BAPI and Visual Basic does not generate any run-time errors, the only way to learn if the BAPI was executed successfully is to look at the values in the RETURN argument.

## The BAPI RETURN Argument

Another specific of a BAPI is that it has a RETURN argument that contains status information on the BAPI's execution. If the BAPI fails, it will provide an error indicator, number and description. If the BAPI fails because it is called incorrectly, Visual Basic will raise a run-time error. If the BAPI fails because you used an invalid parameter value, the BAPI control library will not generate an exception for the Visual Basic run-time to intercept. It will instead return the status and the error description in the RETURN BAPI parameter. If a BAPI call is successful, it will populate the RETURN argument with a success type of result.

For example, if you are creating customers using the relevant BAPI, and you enter 4 digits into the field that contains a zip code in the ADDRESSDATA argument. The BAPI call will fail in SAP R/3, and the RETURN structure's message field will contain a string telling you that the zip code field should have 5 or 10 positions. In the wide variety of BAPI arguments, the RETURN argument is one that does not change its layout from one BAPI to another. Therefore, we can present its structure and use it in our code:

Properties of RETURN

General | Data Types | Value Info | Documentation

| Name | Internal Name | Length | Deci | Description |
|---|---|---|---|---|
| TYPE | TYPE | 1 | 0 | Message type:S success, E error, W warning, I information |
| ID | ID | 20 | 0 | Message ID |
| NUMBER | NUMBER | 3 | 0 | Message number |
| MESSAGE | MESSAGE | 220 | 0 | Message text |
| LOG_NO | LOG_NO | 20 | 0 | Application log: log number |
| LOG_MSG_NO | LOG_MSG_NO | 6 | 0 | Application log: message serial number |
| MESSAGE_V1 | MESSAGE_V1 | 50 | 0 | Message variable |
| MESSAGE_V2 | MESSAGE_V2 | 50 | 0 | Message variable |
| MESSAGE_V3 | MESSAGE_V3 | 50 | 0 | Message variable |
| MESSAGE_V4 | MESSAGE_V4 | 50 | 0 | Message variable |

We already know how to access Structures and Tables. We can add the following code right after the BAPI call:

```
If sapReturn("TYPE") = "E" Then
    MsgBox "BAPI Failed " & vbCrLf & sapReturn("MESSAGE")
    Exit Sub
End If
```

The logic is very simple. We check for the success value of the TYPE field of the RETURN structure. If it is an "E" that indicates error, we display a message box with the value of the MESSAGE field of the RETURN structure. To test this, let's deliberately set the SIGN field of the IDRANGE table to "O", which is not an allowed value, and execute the code:

```
sapIdRange.Columns("SIGN").Value(1) = "O"
sapIdRange.Columns("OPTION").Value(1) = "NP"
sapIdRange.Columns("LOW").Value(1) = ""
sapIdRange.Columns("HIGH").Value(1) = ""
```

The BAPI control library will dutifully dispatch the call to SAP R/3, and it will fail the check that SAP R/3 performs on values prior to execution. From the Visual Basic standpoint, everything is fine and no error is raised. However, our trap for the RETURN structure reveals that the BAPI failed, and displays our custom error message:

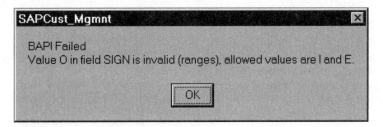

If we reverse the IDRANGE values back to normal, the BAPI will not fail.

Alternatively, if the BAPI does not fail, it may bring an empty result parameter. It is also easy to implement a check for this scenario. We know in advance the type of the informative BAPI parameter. In our case, we are interested in the ADDRESSDATA Table. As we already know, a non-zero value of the RowCount property indicates the presence of the data:

```
If sapAddrData.RowCount = 0 Then
    MsgBox "No Records Retrieved"
    Exit Sub
End If
```

After we confirm the success of the BAPI call and that we have retrieved results, we can begin exploring ways of displaying the data from SAP-specific data objects.

# Data Display

Let's load the tree view control with a list of customers. All we need to do is loop through the `sapAddrData` Table and display the Customer Names in nodes of the Tree View. We can use the unique Customer Numbers for key values of the nodes:

```
For intRowCount = 1 To sapAddrData.RowCount

    Set cusNode = TreeView1.Nodes.Add ("custs", tvwChild, _
                "CUST" & sapAddrData.Columns("CUSTOMER").Value(intRowCount), _
                sapAddrData.Columns("NAME").Value(intRowCount), 1)

Next
```

> *You will need to add two more local variables to the routine:* `intRowCount` *and* `cusNode`.

This code goes right after we get the data from the BAPI call and uses a simple `For...Next` loop to step through every cell of the `sapAddrData` Table parameter using the `Value` property of the Column object. I use the `Value` of the `CUSTOMER` column for the node key value because it contains unique Customer Numbers and this uniqueness is guaranteed by SAP R/3. The result of this code is shown opposite:

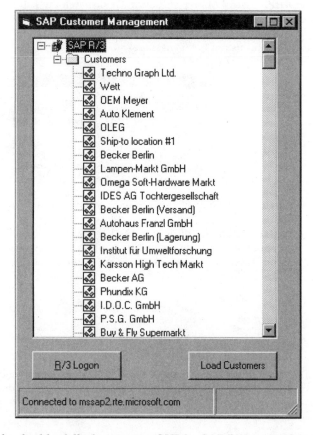

We can now say that we have managed to build a fully functioning GUI for SAP R/3 using Visual Basic and BAPI technology.

Before we start the next topic, I would like to summarize what we have achieved so far. We have learned:

> How to connect to SAP R/3 using the SAP Logon control

> How to set up the SAP BAPI control and connect it to SAP R/3

> How the SAP BAPI control library enables BAPI functionality

> How to create instances of the SAP R/3 BOR objects

> How to explore the structure and definition of the business object, BAPI and the parameters of the BAPI

> How to create instances of valid BAPI parameters

> What data types are used for the BAPI parameters and how to use the Table type parameter

> How to use the SAP Table Factory control to work with Table objects

> How to call a BAPI

The above list looks impressive. However, there is one important thing that is missing from it. The problem is that we retrieved specific data structures defined in SAP R/3 and 'shoe-horned' them into the COM-compliant objects for Visual Basic to work with them. However, every time any VB programmer deals with business data, the first thing that they will think of is how it all fits into the familiar Microsoft Data Access technologies. In other words, how can we apply existing Data Access technology, such as ADO, to BAPI programming? If you traverse the Object Browser you will not find any kind of "convert to ADO recordset" functionality readily available in the SAP Table Factory control library or in any other library that we have used so far. There is no control in the SAP Automation Toolkit that implements this type of operation.

# Enter ADO

The solution would have been very cumbersome prior to ADO. The help comes from my favorite feature of ADO – disconnected recordsets. As we all know, ADO Recordsets can be created, populated and manipulated without having a connection to any database at all. This means that we are able to dynamically create an ADO Recordset based on the structure of the BAPI parameter we are interested in, and populate it with the data. After that, we can treat our data as a regular ADO Recordset.

Teaching ADO is beyond the scope of this book and I'll assume that you are familiar with ActiveX Data Objects. There are plenty of books on ADO and I am sure that you will find one for yourself.

Add the reference to the ADO library in the References dialog for our project.

> *Please note that I use the ADO 2.1 library not ADO 2.0 that ships with Visual Basic 6. You can get the new ADO 2.1 as part of the Microsoft Data Access Components download from Microsoft's web site.*

Add the following code to the General Declarations of the form:

```
Option Explicit

Dim msapConn As SAPLogonCtrl.Connection
Dim mrecCustomers As New ADODB.Recordset
```

We now have a valid Recordset object. Please beware of ambiguous class names. ADO and the SAP Logon library both have a `Connection` class defined in them, ADO and SAP Table Factory both have `Field` classes. Use the `libname.classname` reference convention.

After we have a valid reference to the BAPI argument that we are interested in – `sapAddrData` – we can start creating fields for our ADO Recordset. Let's create a generic routine that accepts the reference to the SAP Table Factory control library's Table object, creates fields for the ADO recordset based on the structure of the Table, and populates the ADO Recordset with Table data.

I have created the `MapAdoRs` routine to be called after populating the tree view that has a single argument – the SAP Table Factory type `Table`:

```
MapAdoRs sapAddrData


Public Sub MapAdoRs(parCustTable As SAPTableFactoryCtrl.Table)

    Dim sapColumn As SAPTableFactoryCtrl.Column
    Dim intRowCount As Integer
    Dim intColCount As Integer

    For Each sapColumn In parCustTable.Columns

        mrecCustomers.Fields.Append sapColumn.Name, adChar, sapColumn.IntLength

    Next
```

Nothing unusual here. The routine accepts the populated Table object after a successful BAPI call, and for each Column in that Table creates a Field in the ADO Recordset, creating in fact the mirror of the Table object. It uses the same names for the ADO Recordset `Fields` as in the Table object.

For the sake of simplicity and code clarity, I don't use any logic to map the SAP Table Factory Field types to the corresponding ADO Field types. For this sample, I simply create Character type fields that have the same length as in the source Table object. To do that I use the SAP Table Factory library Column object's `Name` and `IntLength` properties:

```
mrecCustomers.Fields.Append msapColumn.Name, adChar, msapColumn.IntLength
```

After the above code fragment executes, we have a readily available ADO Recordset with a structure that mirrors the BAPI table argument structure. Because of this design, our function can populate this ADO Recordset using ordinal numbers for Fields and Columns, not names. Just do not forget to open our ADO Recordset. Remember it is valid but disconnected:

```
mrecCustomers.Open

For intRowCount = 1 To parCustTable.RowCount
    mrecCustomers.AddNew

    For intColCount = 1 To parCustTable.ColumnCount
        mrecCustomers.Fields.Item(intColCount - 1) = _
                    parCustTable.Rows(intRowCount).Value(intColCount)
    Next

mrecCustomers.Update
```

```
    Next

    Set sapColumn = Nothing

  End Sub
```

This fragment uses nested For…Next loops to correspond the Row of the Table object to the Record of the ADO Recordset, and to then set values of Fields of the ADO Recordset to values of Columns of the Table object. It is nothing more than navigating a two-dimensional array – something that any Visual Basic programmer can do blindfolded.

To test our new function, add the Microsoft DataGrid Control 6.0 (OLEDB) to our project and add it to our form. I selected this grid because it can use ADO Recordsets as its Data Source directly without any additional data controls. In addition, this particular grid control is the only grid control that allows you to edit its data directly.

Add this code to the Load Customers button that kicks it all off:

```
    Set DataGrid1.DataSource = mrecCustomers

  ' Scroll data grid to top
    DataGrid1.Scroll -1 * (DataGrid1.LeftCol), -1 * (DataGrid1.FirstRow)

    StatusBar1.Panels(2).Text = "Retrieved " & mrecCustomers.RecordCount _
                        & " Records"
```

That is it. We can now see it all in action:

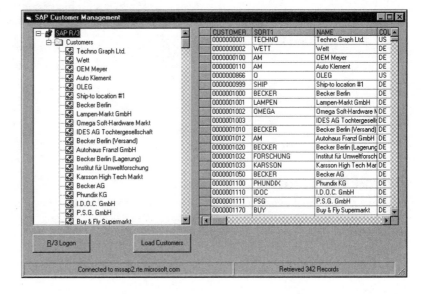

We have now come full circle. Our code connects to SAP R/3, creates an instance of one of the SAP R/3 Business Object Repository defined business objects – *Customer* – then prepares parameters and executes a BAPI of that business object – GetList. It then checks for the return value of the BAPI – RETURN argument – and whether or not we got any data – RowCount property of the Table object. It then creates a disconnected ADO Recordset that mirrors one of the BAPI arguments with data – ADDRESSDATA – and populates it with data for the BAPI argument. And we did it all with the most trivial technology available from Visual Basic.

# Component Implementation

To stay true to the form of this book, after we learn some new functionality of the SAP Automation Toolkit using OCX controls, we shall create a reusable ActiveX component that implements the very same functionality. This way, by the end of the book, you will have a complement of Visual Basic generated ActiveX components that can be readily implemented into any SAP R/3 related project development.

In this case, I have created a BAPI executing ActiveX component that implements the same functionality as our previous sample – retrieve customers from the SAP R/3 system and return them in the form of an ADO Recordset. I also decided to reuse the Logon component that we created in Chapter 3. Additionally, I augmented the functionality of the proposed server component with user-defined events that will notify the client application of important occurrences, such as when the Logon is completed, the BAPI executed and the records retrieved.

Create a new **ActiveX DLL** project and call it SAPSrv_BAPI, and change the name of the default class to clsBAPI. Make a reference to the ADO library and add the Logon class from Chapter 3:

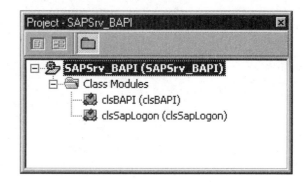

The only thing I changed in the Logon component is that I made the msapConn variable globally available by changing its declaration to Public, so now my BAPI component can access it.

## *General Declarations*

I have added some event definitions to clsBapi to reflect the status of the BAPI and data access functionality of the component:

```
Option Explicit

Event FetchInProgress(lngRecord As Long, blnCancel As Boolean)
```

lngRecord is the number of the record that has been added to the recordset and blnCancel can be set to True in the calling application to stop the retrieval process:

```
Event FetchComplete(lngRecords As Long)
```

This event is fired after the recordset is completely created and the value of the lngRecords is set to the number of records in the recordset.

```
Event BAPIStatus(strType As String, strMessage As String)
```

This is raised upon execution of the BAPI and it returns the type of error and message for the error if it occurs. These values are from the RETURN structure as in the previous project.

I also defined several member variables:

```
Private WithEvents msapLogon As clsSapLogon
Private msapBAPILib As Object
Private mrecCust As ADODB.Recordset
Private mblnLog As Boolean
Private mstrAppSrv As String
```

The value for the CreateObject method to create an instance of the BAPI control library's root class is "SAP.BAPI.1". The code to do it resides in the clsBapi Initialize event:

```
Private Sub Class_Initialize()

    Set msapLogon = New clsSapLogon
    Set msapBAPILib = CreateObject("SAP.BAPI.1")

End Sub
```

The BAPI component has three methods: GetCustomers, LogonToSAP and MapAdoRs, plus an event handler.

## The LogonToSAP Method

The LogonToSAP method calls the Logon method of the old clsSapLogon class. After a successful logon, it returns to the client application the value of the ApplicationServer property of the Connection object and a Boolean value that corresponds with the success/failure of the logon:

```
Public Function LogonToSAP(hwnd As Long, rtval As Boolean, rtAppSr As String)

    msapLogon.Logon hwnd, False

    rtval = mblnLog
    rtAppSr = mstrAppSrv

End Function
```

## The GetCustomers Method

As you can see the code is almost 100% reused from Command1_Click event of the previous project. It accepts two arguments: one for the recordset to be populated and one to determine the maximum number of rows to be returned. This MaxRows parameter is the number of Customer records to get that is passed to the MAXROWS parameter of the GetList BAPI. If an empty string is passed for this parameter, the component gets all the records:

```
Public Sub GetCustomers(recCustomers As Recordset, strMaxRows As String)

    Dim sapCustomer As Object

    Dim sapAddrData As Object
    Dim sapIdRange As Object
    Dim sapReturn As Object

    Dim intColCount As Long
    Dim intRowCount As Long

    On Error GoTo ErrTrap

    Set mrecCust = New ADODB.Recordset

' Create the reference to the Customer business object
    Set sapCustomer = msapBAPILib.GetSAPObject("Customer")

' Create valid objects of the BAPI parameters type and structure
    Set sapAddrData = msapBAPILib.DimAs(sapCustomer, "GetList", "ADDRESSDATA")
    Set sapReturn = msapBAPILib.DimAs(sapCustomer, "GetList", "Return")
    Set sapIdRange = msapBAPILib.DimAs(sapCustomer, "GetList", "IDRANGE")

' Populate IDRANGE parameter
    sapIdRange.AppendRow
    sapIdRange.Columns("SIGN").Value(1) = "I"
    sapIdRange.Columns("OPTION").Value(1) = "NP"
    sapIdRange.Columns("LOW").Value(1) = ""
    sapIdRange.Columns("HIGH").Value(1) = ""

' Call BAPI usning named arguments
    If strMaxRows = "" Then
        sapCustomer.GetList RETURN:=sapReturn, ADDRESSDATA:=sapAddrData, _
                        IDRANGE:=sapIdRange
    Else
        sapCustomer.GetList RETURN:=sapReturn, ADDRESSDATA:=sapAddrData, _
                        IDRANGE:=sapIdRange, MAXROWS:=strMaxRows
    End If

' Analyze return BAPI parameter
    If sapReturn("TYPE") = "E" Then
        RaiseEvent BAPIStatus(sapReturn("TYPE"), sapReturn("MESSAGE"))
        Exit Sub
    Else
        RaiseEvent BAPIStatus("Success", "The BAPI Executed!")
    End If

' Check if we got any Rows (records) in the table
    If sapAddrData.RowCount = 0 Then
        MsgBox "No Records Retrieved"
        Exit Sub
    End If

' Call the function to crete the ADO Recordset and populate it
    MapAdoRs sapAddrData, mrecCust

' Return the recordset
    Set recCustomers = mrecCust
```

```
    RaiseEvent FetchComplete(mrecCust.RecordCount)

    Set sapCustomer = Nothing
    Set sapAddrData = Nothing
    Set sapIdRange = Nothing
    Set sapReturn = Nothing

    Exit Sub

ErrTrap:

    RaiseEvent BAPIStatus("E", Err.Description)

End Sub
```

## The MapADORs Method

The MapADORs routine also became a method of the clsBapi class. The only additions to this routine are the RaiseEvent statements:

```
Public Sub MapAdoRs(parCustTable As Object, recCustomers As ADODB.Recordset)

    Dim sapColumn As Object
    Dim intRowCount As Long
    Dim intColCount As Integer
    Dim blnCancel As Boolean

    On Error GoTo ErrTrap

' Append fields to the ADO Recordset
    For Each sapColumn In parCustTable.Columns

        recCustomers.Fields.Append sapColumn.Name, adChar, sapColumn.IntLength

    Next

' Set values for the Recordset
    recCustomers.CursorLocation = adUseClient

' Open the Recordset
    recCustomers.Open

' Nested loops to set values of the Table's Rows
' Outer loop steps Rows/Records, inner loop - Columns/Fields
    For intRowCount = 1 To parCustTable.RowCount
        recCustomers.AddNew

        For intColCount = 1 To parCustTable.ColumnCount

            recCustomers.Fields.Item(intColCount - 1) = _
                        parCustTable.Rows(intRowCount).Value(intColCount)

        Next

        recCustomers.Update
        RaiseEvent FetchInProgress(intRowCount, blnCancel)
```

```
        If blnCancel Then Exit Sub

   Next

   Set sapColumn = Nothing

   Exit Sub

ErrTrap:

   MsgBox Err.Description

End Sub
```

## The OnLogon Event Handler

We also need to set some variables when we are notified of a successful logon attempt by the OnLogon event of the clsSapLogon class:

```
Private Sub msapLogon_OnLogon(ByVal sapConn As Object)

   Set msapBAPILib.Connection = sapConn
   mblnLog = True
   mstrAppSrv = sapConn.ApplicationServer

End Sub
```

The only thing of note here is that we set the Connection property of our BAPI control library object to the Connection object returned from our custom msapLogon object.

A view of clsBAPI in the Object Browser is presented below:

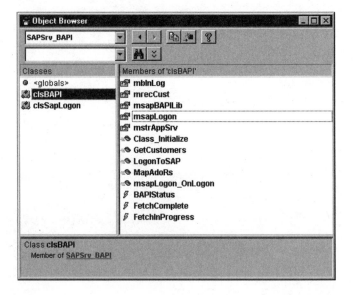

## The Client

To modify the client project to use our component instead of the SAP Automation controls, remove the controls from the project and instead add a reference to our new BAPI component. You should also add a text box to the form to allow you to enter values for the MaxRows argument. The client now simply calls methods in clsBapi and displays the results:

```
Option Explicit

Dim WithEvents msapBapiSrv As SAPSrv_BAPI.clsBAPI
Dim mstrType As String
Dim mstrMessage As String

Private Sub Command1_Click()

   Dim blnSuccess As Boolean
   Dim strAppSrv As String

   msapBapiSrv.LogonToSAP Me.hWnd, blnSuccess, strAppSrv

   If blnSuccess Then
      StatusBar1.Panels(1).Text = "Connected to SAP R/3 at " & strAppSrv
      Command2.Enabled = True
   End If

End Sub

Private Sub Command2_Click()

   Dim cusNode As Node
   Dim sapNode As Node
   Dim recSapCustomers As New ADODB.Recordset

   recSapCustomers.CursorLocation = adUseClient

   msapBapiSrv.GetCustomers recSapCustomers, Text1

   If mstrType <> "E" Then

      recSapCustomers.MoveFirst

      If TreeView1.Nodes("custs").Children > 0 Then

         TreeView1.Nodes.Clear
         Set sapNode = TreeView1.Nodes.Add(, , "topsap", "SAP R/3", 4)
         Set sapNode = TreeView1.Nodes.Add("topsap", tvwChild, "custs", _
                                           "Customers", 2)

      End If

      Do Until recSapCustomers.EOF

         Set cusNode = TreeView1.Nodes.Add("custs", tvwChild, "CUST" & _
                                  recSapCustomers![CUSTOMER], _
                                  recSapCustomers![Name], 1)
         recSapCustomers.MoveNext
      Loop
```

```
       Set DataGrid1.DataSource = recSapCustomers

   Else

     MsgBox mstrMessage

   End If

   Set recSapCustomers = Nothing

End Sub


Private Sub Form_Load()

   Dim sapNode As Node

   Set msapBapiSrv = New SAPSrv_BAPI.clsBAPI

   Command2.Enabled = False
   Text1 = ""

   StatusBar1.Panels(1).Text = "Not Connected"
   Set sapNode = TreeView1.Nodes.Add(, , "topsap", "SAP R/3", 4)
   Set sapNode = TreeView1.Nodes.Add("topsap", tvwChild, "custs", "Customers", 2)

End Sub


Private Sub msapBapiSrv_BAPIStatus(strType As String, strMessage As String)

   mstrType = strType
   mstrMessage = strMessage

End Sub


Private Sub msapBapiSrv_FetchComplete(lngRecord As Long)

   StatusBar1.Panels(2).Text = "Retrieved " & lngRecord & " Records"

End Sub


Private Sub msapBapiSrv_FetchInProgress(lngRecord As Long, _
                                        blnCancel As Boolean)

   If lngRecord < 10 Then
     'Debug.Print lngRecord
   Else
     'blnCancel = True
   End If

End Sub
```

The clsBAPI class offers a very handy framework you can improve upon. This group of projects will
provide you with reusable components that encapsulate the SAP Logon functionality and a BAPI
execution process. This is important because with BAPI programming pre- and post-processing
operations are necessary to ensure a successful call and meaningful results. SAP R/3 business objects
do not offer any direct support for events as of now. I simply used the ADO event structure as an
example because it is well designed and has a very logical model.

# Summary

In this chapter, we learned the major part of the SAP R/3 integration technology – calling BAPIs. We have learned how to prepare and handle parameters for a BAPI and what libraries and controls from the SAP Automation toolkit to use for it.

In addition we developed reusable components that implement calling BAPIs and generating ADO recordsets for resultant BAPI parameters. This allows us to fully integrate our existing data processing Visual Basic applications and MS Office based applications with SAP R/3.

# 6

# SAP Assistant 3.0

In the previous three chapters, we introduced the SAP Automation toolkit. We learned how to connect to SAP R/3 and implement BAPI functionality using the controls it provides. In the following three chapters, we're going to change track slightly, and concentrate on how SAP Automation helps us to learn more about BAPIs.

This chapter will be devoted to learning the functionality and utilization of the SAP Assistant 3.0. This tool and its core components are an essential part of the SAP Automation toolkit. The main purpose of the SAP Assistant is to provide users with the ability to browse the SAP R/3 Business Object Repository in online mode, and to be able to save all necessary BOR metadata into a local Access database to browse offline.

Another benefit of the SAP Assistant is its educational value. Using SAP Assistant will help anyone unfamiliar with SAP R/3's inner structure to understand, or at least get a sense of, what the business objects and BAPIs are. Additionally SAP Assistant has an intuitive user-friendly GUI that looks and behaves like a regular Windows explorer style application. This means that any Visual Basic programmer or business analyst not trained to handle the arcane SAP front-end GUI can be analyzing the SAP R/3 business object metadata right after they install the SAP Automation tools.

> **I want to stress that the Repository Browser should be used like the Object Browser in Visual Basic. You do not program from the Object Browser, you learn what is available for you.**

# Using SAP Assistant

For this chapter, you will need:

> ➢ An installed SAP Automation toolkit
> ➢ A connection to SAP R/3 release 4.0 or higher system
> ➢ The SAP R/3 front-end (preferred)

*Please bear in mind that SAP Assistant, as well as the whole SAP Automation toolkit, is a work in progress. If you monitor the SAP Labs and SAP web sites, you will see updates, patches and new versions being released quite frequently, with several releases being hosted at the same download page. However, new versions are unlikely to have any breakthrough innovations and technologies incorporated, and you should have absolutely no problems working with updated releases of SAP Assistant after reading this chapter.*

Start the SAP Assistant from the SAP Automation group. It will appear as shown below:

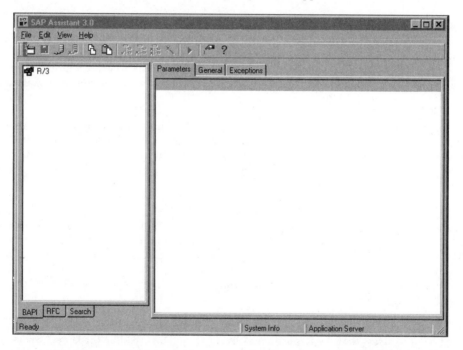

Before we can start working with this tool, it's necessary to logon to an SAP R/3 server. You can do this either by selecting the Logon menu item from the File menu, or by clicking on the logon button on the toolbar. In either case, you will get the familiar Logon screen. Enter your usual settings:

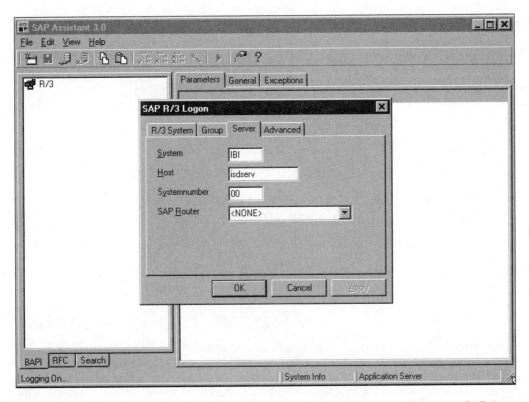

This functionality is the same as that of the SAP Logon control. After successful logon, SAP Assistant will automatically begin loading metadata from the BOR. It can take several minutes if you're on the LAN or have a really fast connection. If you're using the dial-up connection with a conventional USR 56 bps modem, it can take much longer, especially if you're using your regular ISP. I don't recommend using your AOL account for it.

Also make sure that you have sufficient memory available at your box. Performance becomes sluggish on RAM deprived workstations. One more word of advice – close other memory and communication intensive applications such as Lotus CC Mail or MS Access. It's also not advisable to download files off the Internet while using the SAP Assistant. Not because it is going to stop working or behave incorrectly, it will simply work very slowly.

# Application Hierarchies and Business Objects

Upon a successful load, you
should see the populated
explorer component:

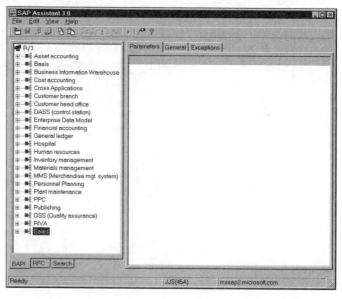

In the tree view section, we can see the first level of the hierarchical Business Object Repository. SAP R/3 is an enterprise system that fits practically any business structure. To reflect that, SAP came up with a logical view of its business objects by grouping them into **Application Hierarchies**. Every Application Hierarchy acts as host for a collection of Business Objects. This may remind Visual Basic developers of Data Access Object structure.

To drill down the structure, click and expand any node – try clicking on Sales. This will display any Business Objects associated with that Application Hierarchy.

Next click on Customer in
the left side of the browser,
and observe the values on the
right-hand side:

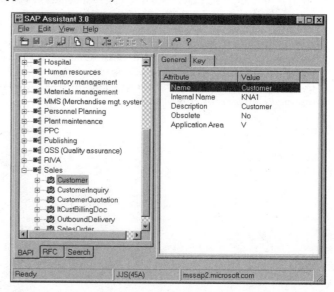

*Beware – what you see in the browser varies greatly depending on the source SAP R/3 release. The screen shots in this chapter were taken using the SAP Assistant connected to an SAP R/3 4.5 system. Connect to 4.0 or 3.0 and you're going to see different content in the browser. SAP adds business objects and BAPIs with every release, and you can monitor this process using the SAP Assistant to make sure that your applications adapt accordingly.*

This is a reassuring view for Visual Basic developers and ABAP developers who learn Visual Basic. Even the icons for objects are the same as VB class module icons.

At this point, Visual Basic developers might find it useful to ask SAP ABAP programmers some questions if they really want to know what these values are. Remember, SAP is a German company and all abbreviations are very Teutonic – no CUSTNUM here. By the way, if you're serious about learning SAP R/3, get yourself a German – English / English – German dictionary.

Watch out for the Obsolete flag. SAP will not remove objects that you shouldn't use, but it will mark them as obsolete. Also note that the value Internal Name has nothing to do with the value Name. In this particular situation KNA1 is a table that stores Customer data. From the object-design standpoint, the Customer object encapsulates access to data.

Let's click on the KEY tab. We will see the name of a **key** for the object.

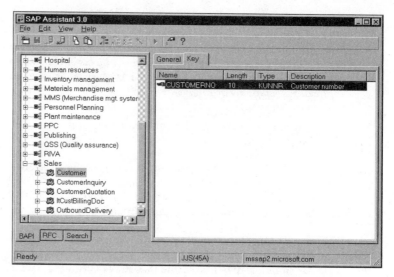

The term key is very familiar to anyone who has ever worked with any RDBMS – a field that uniquely identifies a record. Therefore, CUSTOMERNO uniquely identifies the Customer. As we will see later, the key is used to search for or create an instance of the Customer object.

We have already seen the key for the business object during our exploration of the SAP R/3 Business Object Repository. In fact, we have actually seen most of what you can find using the SAP Assistant in SAP R/3 directly.

# Browsing BAPIs

Now it's time to see some BAPIS. One more time, BAPIS are member functions or methods of business objects. Therefore, in order to see BAPIS, it is logical to expand a Business Object. So expand the Customer node, and you'll see something like this:

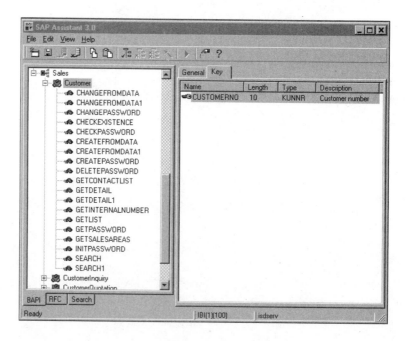

The previous screen shot represents BAPIs that belong to the Customer business object. SAP correctly claims that you don't have to be intimately familiar with internal BAPI implementation, as long as you stay within the Business Object Framework paradigm.

> **To avoid confusion, I advise you to always think of BAPIs as methods of business objects.**

The above screen shot also follows the visual pattern of the Visual Basic IntelliSense editor, using the same icon for BAPIs as for methods. You can now browse all BAPIs that belong to the Customer business object. SAP does a good job naming BAPIs consistently and meaningfully – it doesn't take long to figure out what the CHANGEPASSWORD function is for.

From this point, you can start thinking about how you would fit these things into your business solution needs. Hype and buzz aside, we are doing nothing more than getting some data from point A to point B, and applying some transformations in the process.

## Exploring a BAPI

Let's analyze a single BAPI, to try to develop our understanding of both BAPIs and the Repository Browser. We'll use our familiar GETLIST BAPI here. Click on GETLIST and observe the right side of explorer:

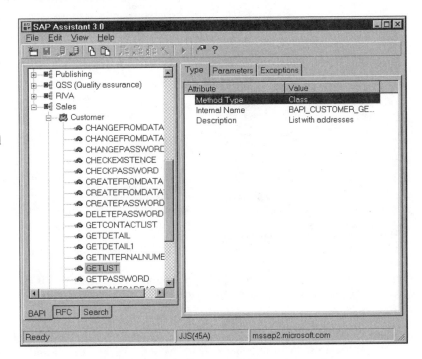

The first thing to notice is the fact that the internal name is always different from what you see exposed. I advise you to get used to it, because there is no alternative. SAP R/3 already had a well-developed naming convention and internal structure when business objects came to life, and this causes a naming dualism throughout the entire object library.

Internal names are shown here on purpose. You can query function module interfaces, read documentation and look up definitions in SAP R/3 directly. Moreover, ABAP programmers in your team may already be familiar with the business functionality of function modules and can help you with them.

*One more side note: programming external applications for ERP systems is a big departure from traditional OLTP or Decision Support applications. Please always consult somebody on the specifics of SAP R/3 implementation. You may implement a BAPI absolutely perfectly, but find that it doesn't work because you were not aware of a specific configuration of your particular R/3 instance.*

### BAPI Parameters

Click on the
Parameters
tab:

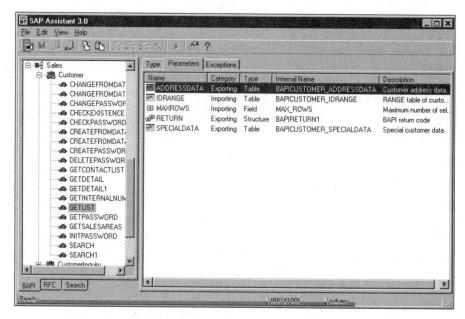

We are presented with **parameters**, or rather **arguments**, of the selected BAPI. The official term for these is parameter. However, to adhere to Visual Basic terminology I will routinely call them arguments. This argument/parameter dualism is also very indicative of their relationship. As I've mentioned before and will illustrate later, behind every BAPI stands an RFC. In the RFC universe, it is a parameter, not an argument that is passed to a function module. Luckily, this is all a matter of semantics.

Another very important characteristic of an argument is its directionality. This is reflected in the Category column. Importing means that SAP R/3 expects the argument to be passed inbound to SAP R/3, Exporting means that SAP R/3 will return information in this argument back to the BAPI call.

> **Reminder: BAPI calls are synchronous.**

One more critical piece of information is in the **Type** column. In the BAPI world, there are only three types of parameters: Field, Structure and Table. All this is also not totally unfamiliar – we have already seen parameters for BAPIs in the SAP R/3 Business Object Repository. The internal implementation of the SAP R/3 business object is very complex, and what we see in the SAP Assistant is only part of the picture. You may argue that this is all you need, but this argument is only as valid as claiming that you don't have to understand Jet as long as you can use the VisData, and this is sufficient to become a professional Visual Basic programmer.

Let's recap some information on the Field, Table and Structure parameters.

### Field

**Field** is equivalent to the string data type in Visual Basic. The internal data type is CHAR. When passing values or expecting values back, use the string data type in Visual Basic.

Don't associate this Field type with the Field object of ADO. The Repository Library's field does not belong to any table visible to a Visual Basic programmer. In other words, a Field belongs to the business object, not to any Table object. This is again due to SAP R/3's fortress-like application layer that completely hides physical data storage.

### Structure

**Structure** is a composite data type – think of it as of a single record table. Every Structure is uniquely named and defined. A BAPI expects Structures to be populated prior to call, should these Structures be of an import type. Moreover, every field of a Structure will be validated against complex rules, and the entire call will fail if you provide incorrect data. This could be a language abbreviation that doesn't exist in some check table, or a four-digit zip code.

Another twist is that some values in a Structure are required and some are not. To explore a Structure in the Assistant, click on the Structure name (with the magnifying glass type cursor) and you will get a property page similar to the following:

Properties of RETURN

General | Data Types | Value Info | Documentation

| Name | Internal Name | Length | Decimal Positic | Description |
|---|---|---|---|---|
| TYPE | TYPE | 1 | 0 | Message type:S success, E error, W warning, I information |
| ID | ID | 20 | 0 | Message ID |
| NUMBER | NUMBER | 3 | 0 | Message number |
| MESSAGE | MESSAGE | 220 | 0 | Message text |
| LOG_NO | LOG_NO | 20 | 0 | Application log: log number |
| LOG_MSG_NO | LOG_MSG_NO | 6 | 0 | Application log: message serial number |
| MESSAGE_V1 | MESSAGE_V1 | 50 | 0 | Message variable |
| MESSAGE_V2 | MESSAGE_V2 | 50 | 0 | Message variable |
| MESSAGE_V3 | MESSAGE_V3 | 50 | 0 | Message variable |
| MESSAGE_V4 | MESSAGE_V4 | 50 | 0 | Message variable |

As we can see, every field of the Structure has a defined name, decimal position and length. This certainty makes it easy to populate or read a Structure, either using field names or numeric positioning for the fields.

A structure is interpreted as an object in the BAPI class library. Therefore, Structure fields can be referred to either explicitly – StructName ("FieldName") – or implicitly – StructName (n), where n is a position number. You can also use the Fields collection of the Structure object. Do not use the bang operator (!), as you would to refer to a field in a Recordset object.

Click on the **Data Types** tab and you will see another property page, exposing data types for every individual field of the Structure:

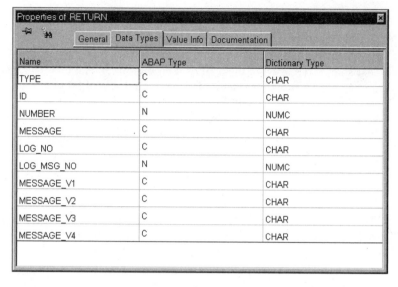

This does not tell you much, except for making you aware that there are ABAP data types and Data Dictionary data types defined internally in SAP R/3. This page is useful to map Visual Basic data types to these data types.

A more interesting tab is **Value Info**. To show you the functionality of this tab in full, I selected another BAPI Parameter – ADDRESSDATA:

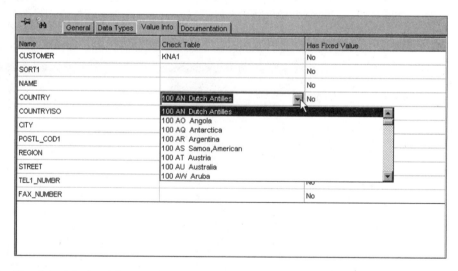

If you click on the **Check Table** drop down field, the SAP Assistant will produce (after some heavy breathing) a list of values predefined in your configuration of the R/3 server. This is extremely important when you design external applications to interface R/3. You can query these values (I will show you how in later chapters) and create a mirror selector in a Visual Basic generated GUI. Moreover, this can be a dynamic process. In other words, you can always query Check Table on startup if needed, to detect any changes.

### Table

**Table**, like structure, has a predefined layout, field length and data type. The only difference is that a Table may have more than one row. Do not even think of trying to slip a DAO or ADO table to BAPI. SAP R/3's understanding of a table and that of Jet and OLEDB are very different. Remember that you're in a COM-compliant environment, not in yet another OLEDB data provider library. Tables can be populated in a Visual Basic program and passed to a BAPI, or received from a BAPI call and parsed on the receiving end. This fits well into the disconnected ADO Recordset's technique of ADO 2.0 supplied with Visual Basic 6.0.

Another implementation is to wrap BAPI Tables or Structures into Data Providers or Data Consumer classes in Visual Basic 6.0. Throw in ADO and user defined events, and you just got yourself a real-time interface to and from SAP R/3. Just don't try to subclass any of the SAP R/3 supplied objects. We saw detailed code for this developmental concept in Chapter 5.

Although not displayed on the property pages, every parameter has a Boolean `IsMandatory` property that indicates whether this parameter is optional or not. This piece of information is critical to correctly call BAPIs.

Every BAPI has a `RETURN` parameter. This can be a Structure or a Table depending on the BAPI. The `RETURN` parameter is obviously of an Export type and it will bring you error information from SAP R/3. Sometimes you may call a BAPI correctly, but supply values that are not acceptable to SAP R/3. You can use the information in the `RETURN` parameter to find out what you're doing wrong.

# RFCs

SAP Assistant also offers you an RFC option. Select the **RFC** tab on the left-hand side, and you will get the following screen:

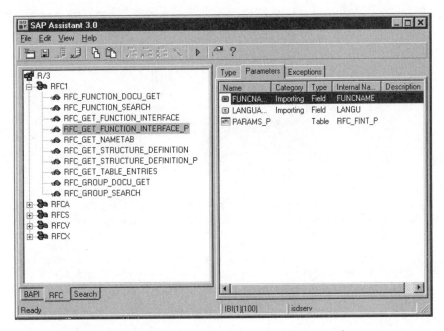

As you may see, this is very similar to what we have already explored. However, there are no business objects for RFCs to belong to. Recall that a Remote Function Call executes an SAP R/3 function module remotely. The RFCs exposed from the SAP Assistant are function calls that do not logically belong to any business object. Otherwise, they would have been turned into BAPIs.

Both RFCs and BAPIs are internally defined in function modules, and because of that, they behave similarly. They both need arguments to be passed to and returned from them. Unlike BAPIs however, RFCs do not need an instance of any object to be created. They are not defined as member functions of any object. This makes it possible to call an RFC directly from the SAP Assistant.

Let's use `RFC_GET_FUNCTION_INTERFACE_P` to explore two things at once. First, we are going to call an RFC. Second, we are going to illustrate my earlier statement about RFCs being behind BAPIs.

Before we actually call an RFC, we need to learn the list of parameters. You can view parameters for RFCs just like you did for BAPIs.

## Calling an RFC from SAP Assistant

To call an RFC, select it from the browser and click on the **Execute RFC** button on the toolbar. You will see the following:

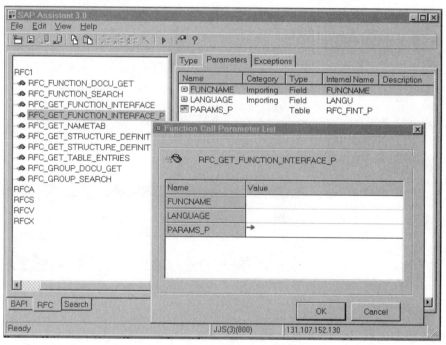

To continue, you have to fill the Function Call Parameter List where required. The red arrow indicates a return or export parameter – don't type anything there. It's obvious that we have to supply the function name in the FUNCNAME parameter – the name of the RFC we want to see an interface of. Now the question is, what name to type in?

Let's return to the BAPI property page. Recall that BAPIs have two names – the name that we saw in the browser and the internal name that we saw on the right-hand side. This is where we see the difference. RFC calls are not business object method calls, and therefore they need real names for functions, not their object interface aliases. That's the reason why we should type in the internal name of the BAPI.

Let's use the `GETLIST` BAPI of the Customer object – its internal name is `BAPI_CUSTOMER_GETLIST`. Notice the distinctive naming convention: RFC and BAPI prefix the relevant functions. This is used to tell the difference between them.

You may also type in a value for
**Language** – just remember to use
expected values:

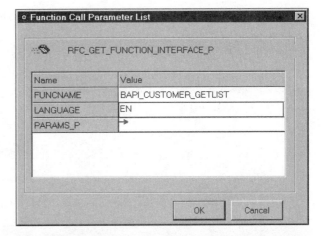

Click **OK**
and the
result will
look like
this:

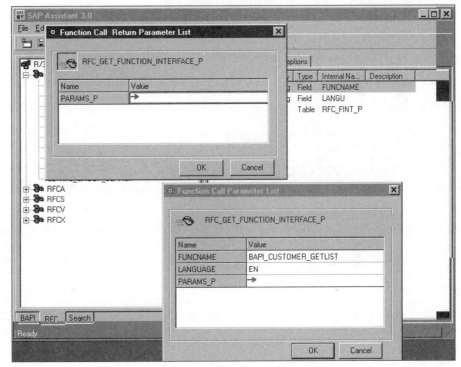

To view the results, select the red arrow or **OK**, and you will get the contents of the return parameter:

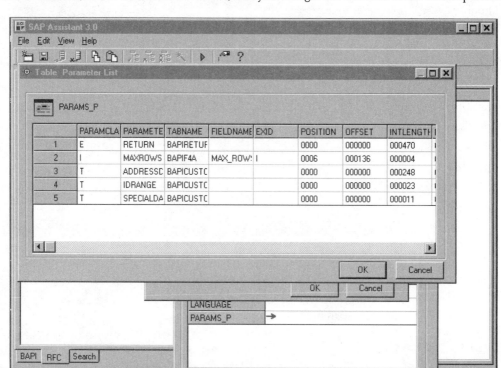

If you now compare the results with the screen we saw in the BAPI Parameters section, you'll see that this is exactly the interface for the `GETLIST` BAPI of the Customer object. This confirms our previous statement that BAPIs will effectively call an RFC behind the scenes. It also provides us with a handy tool to use when we need to programmatically query the BAPI interface.

You can freely experiment with this exciting feature of the SAP Assistant. You should see many interesting results. You can also go straight to `RFC_CUSTOMER_GET` and see how it duplicates the `GETLIST` BAPI of the Customer object. `GETLIST` was not available in release 4.0 of SAP R/3, and `RFC_CUSTOMER_GET` was the RFC to use to list customers. From release 4.5, SAP R/3 added this very useful functionality as a BAPI.

# The SAP Assistant Metadata Repository

Another useful feature of the SAP Assistant is its ability to generate an MDB database (fully accessible from MS Access) and save all the Business Object Repository metadata in it. This means that you can browse the metadata repository working offline. It also offers you incremental saves – so if all you're interested in is the SalesOrder object, you can save just that object.

The mechanism is very simple: retrieve the metadata, browse to the desired object, select it and click the **Save Node** icon on the toolbar. If you want the complete metadata, click on the top node and save it. Beware – this is a long process, no matter how fast your connection. It also hangs the SAP Assistant and bogs down the whole box.

Another annoyance is that if you have several SAP R/3 installations of different versions, and you want to create a separate database for each one, you have to do some extra work. The SAP Assistant will dump everything into one database, making distinctive key entries for multiple systems. However, your database may grow too large for you to be able to save it into any database you like.

You can do two things to get around this. First you can relocate or rename the database that you already have. The SAP Assistant saves the path and name of the database into the Repository and looks it up every time you ask it to save any metadata. The second option is to manually delete the key value in the registry. While tinkering with the registry strangely appeals to many programmers, I recommend the renaming option.

> *For those who like the Registry, it is in the key* `HKEY_USERS ... Software\VB`
> `and VBA Program Settings\SAPAssistant\Options` *in the* `DBFile` *value.*

When you have successfully imported and saved your metadata, you get an Access database without any specified relations or referential integrity – you only have meaningfully named tables. Because this database has no referential integrity rules defined, it's very easy to migrate it to any other RDBMS without being forced to create triggers to replicate the functionality.

If you open the SAP Metadata Repository database in Access, you'll see the following:

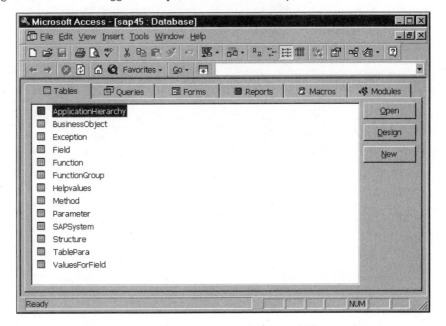

Every table has an AutoNumber field that ensures the uniqueness of entries. SAP provides a Repository Services library for online and offline that encapsulate the functionality of data manipulation for this database. However, should you need to work with this database directly, you would like to know what fields to use to build relations.

The first thing that your management and ABAP programmers will ask you is most likely to be "Can you get me the list of all the... BAPIs?" What they really mean is that they need a report that lists all the BAPIs grouped by Application Hierarchies and Business Objects. This is no problem at all.

## The SAP Metadata Repository Database

Open the database in Access and select Query, New and Design View. Recreate the query as shown below:

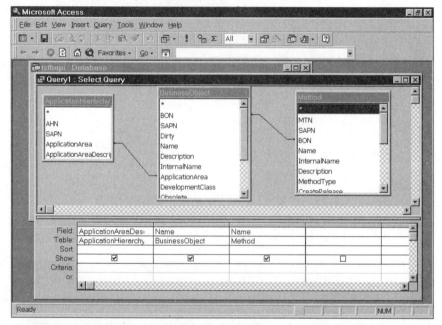

Executing this query will give you the desired results. To generate a printable report, start the Report Wizard, and use grouping by ApplicationArea and Name for the Business Objects. Adjust the design to your requirements, and you're finished. You should see something similar to the following:

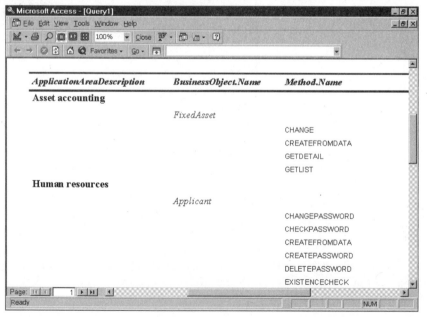

# The SAP Assistant Code Generator

As we have already discussed, SAP aims to create a mechanism for seamless integration of the business object technology into a modern programming environment. Providing the programmer with a tool that enables BAPI programming is a good start, but SAP did not stop there. It created the functionality to dynamically generate C++ and Java code based on the metadata. This is done via the **Code Generator**.

This functionality, integrated into the SAP Assistant, provides the ability to generate proxy business objects using C++ or Java. You can then use these components in your programming. The code generator maps ABAP data types to the selected language and wraps business objects into classes. You can then compile the C++ code and turn it into an ActiveX DLL that's going to hold definitions for business objects, BAPIs and parameters.

I will describe this feature briefly, because the regular Visual Basic programmer has little use for C++ source code anyway. However, it does give you the ability to automate code generation for your fellow C++ or Java programmers. The DCOM Component Connector offers friendlier implementation of this technology, actually compiling the source code and creating a COM DLL to be readily used in Visual Basic.

## Using the Code Generator

Start the SAP Assistant and logon. You can either logon to R/3 in online mode, or work offline, provided that you have your metadata saved in a database.

Drill down to the Business Object you want to generate code for. Using the toolbar or pop-up menu, mark it for code generation:

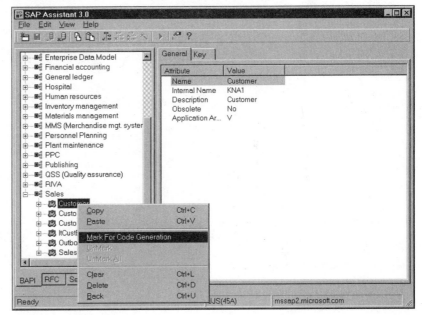

Once marked for code
generation, the Business
Object will change its icon:

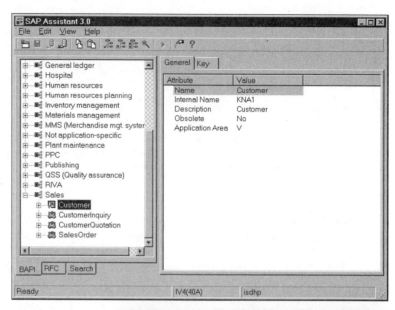

Repeat this selection for all the objects you
require code for. Then start the code creation
using either the File | Generate Code menu
item or the toolbar button. You will be
presented with a choice for the programming
language:

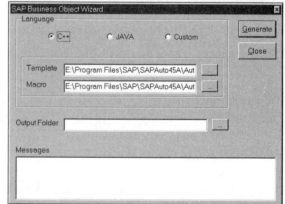

Note that this dialog points to the Template and
Macro directory. It also provides the Custom
option (not recommended). These features let
you modify existing templates and create your
own. You can create your own templates in
Visual Basic and generate code dynamically
using your favorite language. You also have to
specify the directory for the source code to be
saved into. When you've done all that, click the
Generate button and wait for the confirmation
message in the message area:

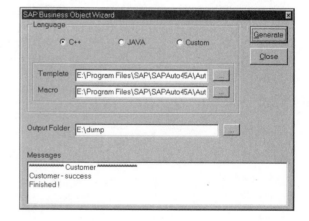

The target directory will contain a folder named after the Business Object, and this will hold the source code:

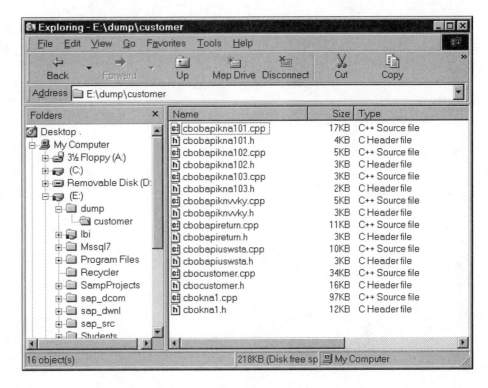

# Summary

In this chapter, we explored the functionality of the SAP Assistant and demonstrated how to use it as a stand-alone tool to browse SAP R/3 business object, BAPI and RFC metadata. We have also developed our understanding of the key components of the Business Object Framework.

In the following chapters, I will introduce the SAP Browser Control combined with the SAP Repository Services library. I will also introduce the Remote Function Call control. Essentially, we're going to learn how to replicate and extend SAP Assistant's functionality programmatically, and incorporate it into Visual Basic applications.

# The SAP R/3 Business Object
# Repository Service

We have already started to explore the SAP R/3 Business Object Repository using the SAP R/3 front-end software and the SAP Assistant. These exercises were supposed to familiarize you with some specifics of the SAP R/3 BOR. In this chapter, we'll move on to explore the possibilities of performing the same tasks *programmatically*.

The SAP R/3 Business Object Repository metadata is vital for any business object related programming. Remember that business objects are not defined in COM libraries, and therefore we cannot look up their properties and methods in the Object Browser in Visual Basic. We require some tool, or technique, that will allow us to discover SAP R/3 business objects, complete with their BAPIs and parameters, before we can start programming. We also have to know the layout of the BAPI parameters, their type and the data that they expect.

All these factors call for a reliable mechanism that would allow dynamic metadata extraction from the SAP R/3 Business Object Repository. Before we begin, let's recap the object hierarchy for the SAP R/3 Business Object Repository:

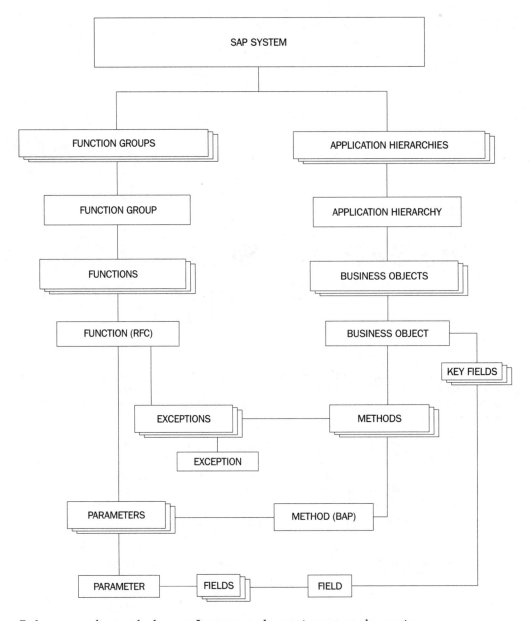

Before we explore each element, I want to make one important observation.

> **All object names are consistent with their class implementation in the SAP Repository Services Library, which in turn reflects their hierarchy in the SAP R/3 BOR.**

Another rather interesting observation is that in the SAP R/3 Business Object Repository the elements seem to have some dualism in their implementation. When we access the SAP R/3 BOR using tools provided in the SAP Automation Toolkit, we get the SAP understanding, and implementation, of the business objects for *external access*. However, if we go directly into SAP R/3 using the front-end application, we see a different picture.

A good example of this is when we went into the SAP R/3 BOR directly, we never saw the *SALES* Application Area, but when we used the SAP Assistant, there was a *SALES* Application Area. These discrepancies are due to the implementation specifics of the external tools – the core SAP R/3 BOR architecture does not change.

To avoid redundancy, I will combine the discussion on the above diagram with an exploration of the SAP Repository Services Library located in `rsonline.dll`. This library does not have any OCX or any other GUI implementation; you need only reference it to access its functionality, just like with ADO. By elaborating on the SAP Repository Services library, we will automatically understand the above diagram too.

# The SAP Repository Services Library Structure

Add the reference to the SAP Repository Services Type Library to a Standard EXE project and take a look in the Object Browser:

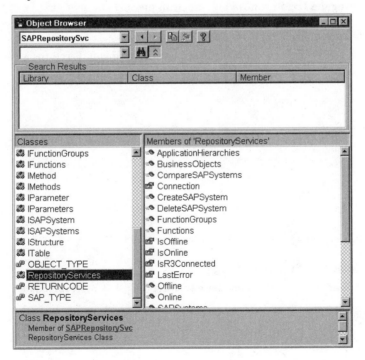

The most important functionality of this library is the implementation of the SAP R/3 BOR. For every structural component of the SAP R/3 BOR, the Repository Services library has a namesake interface to implement. For example, the Business Object element is implemented by the `IBusinessObject` class.

However, the Repository Services library's object hierarchy reflects two different sides of exploring the BOR. It implements the hierarchy of BOR elements – Application Hierarchies, Business Object, Functions, Parameters etc. Additionally it has to implement some mechanism to access the BOR – the `RepositoryServices` class. Therefore, technically speaking, the top-most class is `RepositoryServices`. However, the top-most class of the BOR side of implementation is `ISAPSystems`.

# Repository Services

The **Repository Services object** is the root of the library – it contains collections for all the other members of the BOR, i.e. Application Hierarchies, Business Objects, Function Groups and Functions.

You can create an instance of it using either the `New` keyword or the `CreateObject` method using the `"SAP.RepositoryServices.1"` progID.

This class is also responsible for connecting to SAP R/3 using the familiar Connection object created with the SAP Logon control library. To establish the connection to the SAP R/3 system, create a valid Connection object using the Logon control and then call the `Online` method.

### Function Online(aConnection As Object) As Long

`aConnection` – is a valid Connection object after a successful logon. It returns a value that corresponds to a non-zero value if successful, and 0 if failed.

```
Dim sapRepServ As RepositoryServices
Dim sapConn As Object
Dim sapLog As Object

Set sapLog = CreateObject("SAP.LogonControl.1")
Set sapConn = msapLog.NewConnection

sapConn.Logon 1, False

sapRepServ.Online sapConn
```

Interestingly this class has another connectivity-related method – `Offline`.

### Function Offline(aDatabase As String) As Long

`aDatabase` – is a full name of an MDB database that the SAP R/3 BOR metadata is stored in.

```
Dim sapRepServ As RepositoryServices

sapRepServ.Offline App.Path & "\sap45.mdb"
```

This method allows for implementing offline functionality. The ability to work offline is important for at least two reasons:

> - Firstly, it allows you to browse the metadata much faster than you could even on a LAN, and reduces network traffic.

> - Secondly, you don't need a connection to SAP R/3 whatsoever, so you can design programs that use the metadata information while being disconnected from SAP R/3.

*There is a group of* `Write*` *methods that save the metadata into the local repository database and we will see them in action later in this chapter.*

# SAP System

The SAP system is the top-most object of the BOR implementation in the hierarchy. It contains attributes that identify the SAP System. These are all familiar from the SAP Logon control properties:

> - `ApplicationServer`
> - `System`
> - `SystemNumber`
> - `SAPRelease`
> - `HostName`
> - `Name`

To get a reference to this object we have to call the `SAPSystems` method of the `RepositoryServices` class:

### Function SAPSystems() As ISAPSystems

This method returns a reference to the `ISAPSystems` collection object. Like any other collection this one has `Count` and `Item` properties that allow you to retrieve a reference to a particular `ISAPSystem`:

```
Dim sapSystems As ISAPSystems
Dim sapSystem As ISAPSystem

Set sapSystems = sapRepServ.sapSystems
Debug.Print "Systems Count " & sapSystems.Count

Set sapSystem = sapSystems.Item(1)
Debug.Print "System Name " & sapSystem.Name
```

This would result in the following:

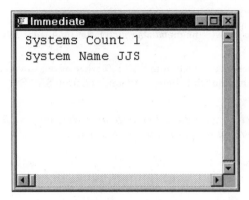

```
Immediate
   Systems Count 1
   System Name JJS
```

You may also use the `ItemByName` property and pass the name of the SAP R/3 system if you know it in advance, or the `ItemByIndex` property passing the index value. These two are just an added convenience:

```
Dim sapSystems As ISAPSystems
Dim sapSystem As ISAPSystem

Set sapSystems = sapRepServ.sapSystems
Debug.Print "Systems Count " & sapSystems.Count

Set sapSystem = sapSystems.ItemByName("JJS")

' Or

'Set sapSystem = sapSystems.ItemByIndex(1)

Debug.Print "System Name " & sapSystem.Name
```

The results of these two code fragments will be the same as before.

# Application Hierarchies

The next step in the object hierarchy would be the **Application Hierarchies collection**. This collection contains references to the **Application Hierarchy objects** that implement the logical areas in the SAP R/3 BOR that group together into business objects.

To access the Application Hierarchies collection, we can call the namesake method of the Application Hierarchies collection. This method call will return a reference to the `IApplicationHierarchies` collection object also defined in the Repository Services library.

### Function ApplicationHierarchies() As IApplicationHierarchies

The `IApplicationHierarchies` collection object implements the same collection relevant properties as the `ISAPSystems` collection:

```
Dim sapSystems As ISAPSystems
Dim sapSystem As ISAPSystem

Dim sapAppHs As IApplicationHierarchies
Dim sapAppH As IApplicationHierarchy

Set sapSystems = sapRepServ.sapSystems
Debug.Print "Systems Count " & sapSystems.Count

Set sapSystem = sapSystems.ItemByName("JJS")
Debug.Print "System Name " & sapSystem.Name

Set sapAppHs = sapRepServ.ApplicationHierarchies
Debug.Print "Number of Application Hierarchies " & sapAppHs.Count

For Each sapAppH In sapAppHs
  Debug.Print sapAppH.ApplicationArea & " " & _
              sapAppH.ApplicationAreaDescription
Next
```

This would produce the following results:

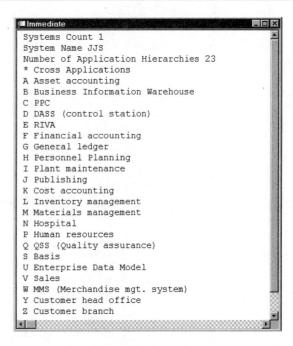

```
Systems Count 1
System Name JJS
Number of Application Hierarchies 23
* Cross Applications
A Asset accounting
B Business Information Warehouse
C PPC
D DASS (control station)
E RIVA
F Financial accounting
G General ledger
H Personnel Planning
I Plant maintenance
J Publishing
K Cost accounting
L Inventory management
M Materials management
N Hospital
P Human resources
Q QSS (Quality assurance)
S Basis
U Enterprise Data Model
V Sales
W MMS (Merchandise mgt. system)
Y Customer head office
Z Customer branch
```

Using the Application Hierarchies collection we can access each individual member – the Application Hierarchy object – that is implemented in the `IApplicationHierarchy` class. To create a valid reference to one of the available Application Hierarchy objects we can use any of the `Item*` properties of the Application Hierarchies collection. After we do that, we can then access all the individual properties and methods of the Application Hierarchy object.

# Business Objects

To continue our exploration of the SAP R/3 Business Object Repository, we have to go down one level to **Business Objects**. The domain of the Business Object is the Application Hierarchy. It is therefore logical that the Application Hierarchy object has the `BusinessObjects` method that returns a reference to the `IBusinessObjects` class that implements a collection of Business Objects.

### Function BusinessObjects() As IBusinessObjects

This collection includes all Business Objects that logically belong to the particular Application Hierarchy. This is a robust model because it allows SAP to implement the logical view of the enterprise in a hierarchical fashion. Once we have a reference to the collection of Business Objects, we can use one of the familiar `Item*` properties of the `IBusinessObjects` class to get a reference to a particular member of this collection, thus getting a reference to a particular Business Object:

```
Dim sapSystems As ISAPSystems
Dim sapSystem As ISAPSystem

Dim sapAppHs As IApplicationHierarchies
Dim sapAppH As IApplicationHierarchy

Dim sapBusObjs As IBusinessObjects
Dim sapBusObj As IBusinessObject

Set sapSystems = sapRepServ.sapSystems
Set sapSystem = sapSystems.ItemByName("JJS")

Set sapAppHs = sapRepServ.ApplicationHierarchies
Set sapAppH = sapAppHs.ItemByName("S")
Debug.Print sapAppH.ApplicationAreaDescription

Set sapBusObjs = sapAppH.BusinessObjects
For Each sapBusObj In sapBusObjs
  Debug.Print sapBusObj.Name
Next
```

This would give the following results:

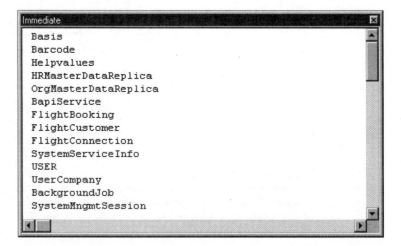

```
Immediate
    Basis
    Barcode
    Helpvalues
    HRMasterDataReplica
    OrgMasterDataReplica
    BapiService
    FlightBooking
    FlightCustomer
    FlightConnection
    SystemServiceInfo
    USER
    UserCompany
    BackgroundJob
    SystemMngmtSession
```

As we see, we can now access individual Business Objects of the Business Objects collection of the Application Hierarchy object.

> *Note that I arbitrarily selected the* `Basis` *Application Hierarchy to browse its Business Objects and I got the name for it,* `"S"`*, from the results of the previous code snippet.*

Now we can apply the same logic to the separate Business Objects and extract metadata for their members – Key Fields and BAPIs. To gain access to a particular Business Object we have to use one of the `Item*` properties of the `IBusinessObjects` class. Let's select the *Helpvalues* object. This object is very useful for BAPI programming and we'll see its application in a little while. At this point, we will simply use it as a test object.

# Key Fields and Methods (BAPIs)

To continue our exploration, we have to establish a reference to a Business Object and then list its members. Once we get the metadata on the Business Object's members, we can start drilling down to the BAPI and Field level. The Field level is the lowest in the object hierarchy. Consider the code below:

```
Dim sapAppH As IApplicationHierarchy
Dim sapBusObj As IBusinessObject
Dim sapKeyFields As IFields
Dim sapField As IField
Dim sapMethods As IMethods
Dim sapMethod As IMethod

Set sapAppH = sapRepServ.ApplicationHierarchies.ItemByName("S")
Set sapBusObj = sapAppH.BusinessObjects.ItemByName("Helpvalues")

Set sapKeyFields = sapBusObj.KeyFields

If Not sapKeyFields Is Nothing Then

    For Each sapField In sapKeyFields
        Debug.Print sapField.Name
    Next

End If

Set sapMethods = sapBusObj.Methods
For Each sapMethod In sapMethods
  Debug.Print "BAPI " & sapMethod.Name
Next
```

The result of this code will be the name of the single BAPI that belongs to the *Helpvalues* Business Object – GETLIST:

> *Note that I minimized the code by eliminating the creation of separate references for the collection object and simply referenced the objects that I needed directly. I also purposely postponed elaborating on the properties and methods of the classes that we discuss. It's imperative to review the object hierarchy of the SAP R/3 Business Object Repository first and then we can have a detailed look at the classes.*

This Business Object does not have any Key Fields and to avoid any run-time errors, I do the usual check for the Key Fields collection in the Is Nothing condition. The two methods that are used in the above code fragment are KeyFields and Methods. These methods return collections that contain **Key Fields** and **Methods** of the Business Object.

### Function KeyFields() As IFields

The Repository Services library does not have a separate class to implement the Key Fields collection. Because Key Fields are, by nature, regular fields, the library implements them in the generic IFields class:

```
Set sapKeyFields = sapBusObj.KeyFields
```

### Function Methods() As IMethods

The collection of methods is implemented in the IMethods class. These methods are BAPIs.

```
Set sapMethods = sapBusObj.Methods
```

# BAPI Parameters

The next step is to explore the BAPI metadata. You should recall from previous chapters that the BAPI is essentially a function that has arguments or parameters. These parameters can be of three types only – Field, Structure and Table.

If we use the same logic for the **Method object** of the Methods collection, it has to have some method that is going to return a reference to the Parameters collection. The IMethod class that implements the Method object has a method Parameters that returns a reference to the IParameters class.

### *Function Parameters() As IParameters*

Therefore, we can continue building our code using the same logic:

```
Dim sapAppH As IApplicationHierarchy
Dim sapBusObj As IBusinessObject
Dim sapParameters As IParameters
Dim sapParameter As IParameter

Set sapAppH = sapRepServ.ApplicationHierarchies.ItemByName("S")
Set sapBusObj = sapAppH.BusinessObjects.ItemByName("Helpvalues")

Set sapParameters = sapBusObj.Methods.ItemByName("GETLIST").Parameters
For Each sapParameter In sapParameters
  Debug.Print sapParameter.Name
Next
```

This code would result in the following:

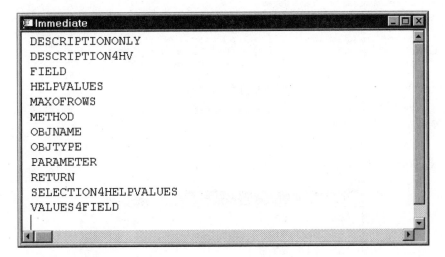

> **Please note an important characteristic of the `ItemByName` property.** *It is case sensitive.*

You have to enter the name for the method exactly as you receive it from the `Name` property of the `IMethod` class. Note that the `"Helpvalues"` entry is mixed-case and that is exactly the way the `Name` property returned it from the `IBusinessObject` class. We are now one step away from getting access to the atomic object of the BOR – the **Field**.

If we recall the possible parameter types, we see that the only possible options are Field, Structure and Table. Structure and Table comprise fields. However, we do have a generic **Parameter object** and it would help if we could somehow learn its type. Therefore, we need some mechanism that will allow us to learn the type of the parameter. A quick look at the Object Browser reveals three properties of the IParameter class that will do the trick for us:

> ➢ IsField
> ➢ IsStructure
> ➢ IsTable

If we examine their values, the property corresponding to the Parameter's type will have a value of 1. The other properties will be set to 0. Consider the code fragment below:

```
Dim sapAppH As IApplicationHierarchy
Dim sapBusObj As IBusinessObject
Dim sapParameters As IParameters
Dim sapParameter As IParameter

Set sapAppH = sapRepServ.ApplicationHierarchies.ItemByName("S")
Set sapBusObj = sapAppH.BusinessObjects.ItemByName("Helpvalues")
Set sapParameters = sapBusObj.Methods.ItemByName("GETLIST").Parameters

Set sapParameter = sapParameters.ItemByName("HELPVALUES")

Debug.Print "IsField is " & sapParameter.IsField
Debug.Print "IsStructure is " & sapParameter.IsStructure
Debug.Print "IsTable is " & sapParameter.IsTable
```

After execution it would produce the following results:

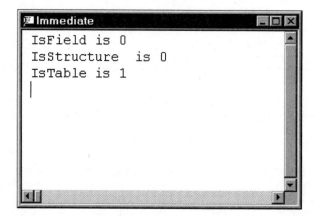

As we may now see, the Parameter HELPVALUES of the GETLIST BAPI that belongs to the *Helpvalues* Business Object is of the type Table. This technique gives us a way to find the Parameter's data type and this is critical for any BAPI related programming.

## *The Parameter Object and Fields Collection*

The next step would be to explore the Parameter object. We should be able to create a valid instance of the Parameter because we already know how to determine its type and browse the Fields collection of the Structure or the Table parameter. Keep in mind that a Structure is best understood as a single-row (one-record) table. If we simply browse the Fields collection of the Parameter, we gain access to each **Field object** that is implemented in the `IField` class of the Repository Services library. This library also includes the Fields collection implemented in the `IFields` class in the library. We can get the Fields collection of the Table or Structure objects by using the `Fields` method of the Table or Structure objects.

### *Function Fields() As IFields*

As you may notice in Visual Basic's Object Browser, the `IParameter` class does not have a `Fields` method. This is correct because the parameter may be the Field itself. However, the Parameter object has the ability to return the Structure or Table objects. This is enabled via the `Table` and `Structure` methods of the `IParameter` class:

> ➢ `Parname.Table` – Returns the `ITable` type object – Table Object
>
> ➢ `Parname.Structure` – Returns the `IStructure` type object – Structure Object

We should use the `IsStructure` and `IsTable` properties of the `IParameter` class to determine which method to use. If the parameter is a field itself, determined using the `IsField` method of the `IParameter` class, then we can use the `Field` method implemented in the `IParameter` class to get a reference to the `IField` class that is going to encapsulate the `Field` object.

# A Simple Online Business Object Browser

Now that we have discussed the SAP Online Repository Services, seen some code snippets and how to code against it, it would be useful to illustrate those techniques in a more practical manner. I have decided against elaborate GUI implementations for two main reasons:

> ➢ Firstly, the SAP Assistant does a good job illustrating the structure of the SAP R/3 Business Object Repository and lets you navigate the BOR and save its content into the metadata repository database.
>
> ➢ Secondly, creating an elaborate Explorer style GUI does nothing beyond familiarizing readers with the tree view control. Developing an Explorer style GUI is a good exercise by itself but it would add volume not value to the book. I would rather provide my readers with working functionality than pontificate on looping though the Nodes collection.

Considering the above, I set out to create a simple application that includes an ActiveX DLL component encapsulating the core functionality. I also wanted to combine the functionality to work online and offline. This is important specifically if you are going to design an application for remote users.

A typical scenario would be your business analyst who travels and wants to use his laptop while away from the luxury of the LAN. True, you can logon from the SAP Assistant using an Internet connection or dial-up to your company server. The problem is that your typical connection will work very, very slowly. On the other hand, if you supply your remote user with the repository database that you created in your home office, and offline Repository Services functionality, your user will enjoy a very fast application using the same data.

As we already know, the SAP R/3 BOR cannot change by itself, and normally changes from release to release. The SAP Assistant lets you work online by design. However, the need to customize or integrate its functionality will force you into using the SAP Online Repository library, instead of simply relying on the SAP Assistant.

# Considerations for Building the Component

Based on the above discussion, we have to design a component that will combine the ability to work offline with the ability to work online in a generic fashion using a minimal set of the library's functionality. The reason for the minimalist approach is that the SAP Automation toolkit is a very dynamic SDK – I went through at least five downloads and patches whilst writing this book. It is to a certain extent a beta product. Some functionality may disappear from future releases; some may be added.

For example, as long as there is a collection there will be an `Item` method whereas `ItemByName` may disappear. That is why I decided to navigate collections using the ordinal number for members rather than names. Another decision was to avoid passing Repository Services library objects by reference from the calling application to the server component.

The client application in this sample does not have a reference to the Online Repository Services library at all. Communication is handled using pipe-delimited strings. All we need are string values for the objects' properties that are defined in the Repository library which you can display as you wish. This library will not provide you with the business object proxy for you to execute BAPIs like the BAPI control library.

# The ActiveX Component

Therefore, we will build an ActiveX DLL component capable of supplying string values for various properties of objects defined in the Repository library. This functionality will be implemented using generic methods to retrieve names for Application Hierarchies, Business Objects, BAPIs, Parameters and Fields. The only thing that the component will implement differently is the online logon and the offline browsing.

Start a new **ActiveX DLL** project and call it `SAPSrv_Browser`. Add a reference to the **SAP Repository Services Type Library**, and name the default class `clsSapBrowser`. Note that because we have agreed to avoid direct OCX usage you do not have to add the SAP Logon control to the project.

> *A word of caution. If you do not add the control to the project you have to make sure that you include relevant libraries with the distribution package.*

## Declarations

We will need a series of member variables to hold references to the upper levels of the BOR hierarchy:

```
Option Explicit

Dim msapSystems As ISAPSystems
Dim msapSystem As ISAPSystem
Dim msapAppHs As IApplicationHierarchies
Dim msapAppH As IApplicationHierarchy
Dim msapRepServ As SAPRepositorySvc.RepositoryServices

Dim msapLog As Object       'SAPLogonControl
Dim msapConn As Object      'SAPLogonCtrl.Connection
```

> *Note that variables for the Logon control object and Connection object are defined as a generic* `Object`. *This is because we don't have links to the libraries at design time and therefore we can't access the definitions in the SAP Logon control library.*

Initialize the Repository Services object in the `Class_Initialize` event:

```
Private Sub Class_Initialize()

   Set msapRepServ = New RepositoryServices

End Sub
```

## Online and Offline Functionality

As you recall the `RepositoryServices` class implements two methods:

- ➢ `Online` to work connected to SAP R/3
- ➢ `Offline` to use the Metadata Repository

The Metadata Repository can be created using the SAP Assistant or programmatically using the group of `Write*` methods of the `RepositoryServices` class.

> *Note that* `Write*` *methods will either populate the MDB that you already have, or generate a new database if the one specified does not exist.*

### Creating an Offline Repository Database

Every `Write*` method has one common argument – `aSAPSystem As ISAPSystem`. This should be a reference to the particular SAP R/3 system that you are connected to. The most convenient and sound approach is to connect one instance of `RepositoryServices` to one SAP R/3 system.

The `Write*` methods do not have any arguments to hold the name and path for the repository database. It is handled from the `Offline` method of the Repository Services object. The `Offline` method has a single argument for the full path to the repository database. To use the `Offline` method to specify the repository database we can code the following fragment:

```
msapRepServ.Offline App.Path & "\" & "sap45.mdb"
```

This fragment will set the Repository Services object – `msapRepServ` – to the offline repository database, `sap45.mdb`, located in the root directory of the project. If this database already exists, the Repository Services object will use it to store SAP R/3 BOR metadata; if it doesn't exist, the Repository Services object will create a new repository database with all necessary tables.

After you specify the repository database, it is necessary to create a valid reference to the SAP System object. To do so we have to use the following methodology:

```
Dim msapSyst As ISAPSystem
Dim msapRFC As IFunction

Set msapSyst = msapRepServ.SAPSystems(1)
```

Because we know in advance that we are connected to only one SAP R/3 system, we can use "1" for the index of `SAPSystems`. After we get the SAP System object, we have to get a reference to the object we want to save into the repository. Let's save the RFC metadata. First, we need to get a valid reference to the particular Function object:

```
Set msapRFC = msapRepServ.Functions("BAPI_CUSTOMER_GETLIST").Item(1)
```

The above line will get us the reference to the valid Function object that uses the `BAPI_CUSTOMER_GETLIST` RFC. Now we have all the necessary ingredients to call one of the `Write*` methods – `WriteRFC`. Below I present the code for a small routine that will save the metadata of the `BAPI_CUSTOMER_GETLIST` RFC into the repository MDB database:

```
Dim msapSyst As ISAPSystem
Dim msapRFC As IFunction

Set msapSyst = msapRepServ.SAPSystems(1)
Set msapRFC = msapRepServ.Functions("BAPI_CUSTOMER_GETLIST").Item(1)

msapRepServ.Offline App.Path & "\" & "sap45.mdb"

msapRepServ.WriteRFC msapSyst, msapRFC
```

Every `Write*` method behaves the same way and you will not have any problems using all of them to save different members of the SAP R/3 BOR into the local repository. For example, if you want to save all of them using one method, use `WriteAppHierarchies`. It will take some time, even on a fast network, but it will save the entire metadata for Application Hierarchies, Business Objects with Key Fields, BAPIs, BAPI parameters and their Fields. Just pass a reference to an Application Hierarchies object.

## Offline Functionality

To implement the offline functionality, I first saved the metadata for the SAP R/3 release 4.5 into the MDB database using the SAP Assistant, as described in Chapter 6.

Then I implemented the `Offline` method of the `RepositoryServices` class:

```
Public Sub OpenMetaRepository(strDataBase As String)

  msapRepServ.Offline strDataBase

  Set msapSystems = msapRepServ.SAPSystems

  msapRepServ.SetSAPSystem msapSystems(1)

  Set msapAppHs = msapRepServ.ApplicationHierarchies

End Sub
```

The first line is simple. I simply pass the full path to the repository database and execute the `Offline` method. The following two lines of code require some explanation. Because you are working with the repository database, it is unknown, at the beginning, which SAP R/3 system the metadata is coming from. The SAP Assistant allows you to save the metadata from different SAP R/3 systems into the same database. Therefore, you have to select which one you are going to use. First, it is necessary to get a reference to the SAP Systems object using the `SAPSystems` property of the `RepositoryServices` class. After we have this collection, we can use the name, or ordinal number, to get the particular item. I have only one set of metadata in my repository so I can use this line of code:

```
msapRepServ.SetSAPSystem msapSystems(1)
```

The `SetSAPSystem` method of the `RepositoryServices` class sets the current system. Each instance of the Repository Services object may work with only one system. The last line of code in this routine is very simple:

```
Set sapAppHs = msapRepServ.ApplicationHierarchies
```

It gets the instance of the Application Hierarchies collection.

### Online Functionality

The `Logon` function implements the online functionality:

```
Public Function Logon()

  Set msapLog = CreateObject("SAP.LogonControl.1")
  Set msapConn = msapLog.NewConnection

  msapConn.Logon 1, False

  If msapConn.IsConnected Then
     MsgBox "Connected to " & msapConn.ApplicationServer
     msapRepServ.Online msapConn
     Set msapAppHs = msapRepServ.ApplicationHierarchies
  End If

End Function
```

As you can see, there is nothing here that we have not already used before.

From this point on there is no difference between online and offline functionality.

## Retrieving Data from the Repository

Then I created functions to retrieve the members of the repository. These functions rely heavily on ordinal numbers of collection items. This means that if I store the retrieved values without breaking their natural order by any sorting, I will always have the value for the ordinal number.

To achieve this, I designed all my functions to build pipe-delimited strings using values for necessary properties – mostly the names for the objects. It is less elegant and intuitive than passing ADO Recordsets or XML structures but string manipulation works for every conceivable OS and programming language.

> *Just beware of memory limitations and inefficiency of string manipulation in Visual Basic. I don't 'suggest' building delimited strings of data, it is mostly for illustrative purposes.*

Visual Basic 6.0 includes new string manipulation functions and my personal favorite is the `Split` function that returns an array of strings sans the delimiter when you pass a delimited string to it. Microsoft recognizes the potential need for Visual Basic developers to handle the whole lot of character delimited strings – the minimum common denominator for data exchange among heterogeneous applications running on different operating systems. The pipe is traditionally selected for a delimiter because it is unlikely that it is going to be a meaningful character. You also have to collaborate with some legacy COBOL or C code that manipulates delimited text files. On the other end of the spectrum sit the new Java applications that are not the most COM friendly of things.

The first set of data we want to retrieve is a list of the Application Areas.

### Application Areas

```
Public Sub GetAppHs(strAppHsName As String, strAppHsRealName As String)

   Dim intCount As Integer

   On Error GoTo ErrTrap

   For intCount = 1 To msapAppHs.Count

       strAppHsName = strAppHsName & "|" & _
                      msapAppHs.Item(intCount).ApplicationAreaDescription

       strAppHsRealName = strAppHsRealName & _
                          "|" & msapAppHs.Item(intCount).ApplicationArea

   Next

   Exit Sub

ErrTrap:

   MsgBox Err.Description

End Sub
```

This function populates two arguments with values from the `ApplicationArea` and `ApplicationAreaDescription` properties of the Application Hierarchy object.

Another function will retrieve Business Objects based on the Application Area:

## Business Objects

```
Public Function GetBusObjs(intAppArea As Integer, blnNoObj As Boolean) _
            As String

   Dim sapBusObjs As IBusinessObjects
   Dim intCount As Integer

   On Error GoTo ErrTrap

   Set sapBusObjs = _
            msapRepServ.ApplicationHierarchies.Item(intAppArea).BusinessObjects

   If sapBusObjs Is Nothing Then
      blnNoObj = True
      Exit Function
   Else

      For intCount = 1 To sapBusObjs.Count
         GetBusObjs = GetBusObjs & "|" & _
         sapBusObjs.Item(intCount).Name
      Next

      Set sapBusObjs = Nothing
      blnNoObj = False

   End If

      Set sapBusObjs = Nothing

   Exit Function

ErrTrap:

   MsgBox Err.Description

End Function
```

The specific of this function is that I use the ordinal number for the Application Area, that I pass from the client, to retrieve the Business Objects attached to that Application Area. Once I have the Business Objects collection, I loop through it building the pipe-delimited string populated with names of the Business Objects.

The other functions are also very direct:

## BAPIS

```
Public Function GetBapis(strBusObj As String) As String

   Dim sapBapis As IMethods
   Dim intCount As Integer

   On Error GoTo ErrTrap

   Set sapBapis = msapRepServ.BusinessObjects(strBusObj).Item(1).Methods

   If sapBapis Is Nothing Then
      Exit Function
   Else
```

```
        For intCount = 1 To sapBapis.Count
            GetBapis = GetBapis & "|" & sapBapis.Item(intCount).Name
        Next

    End If

        Set sapBapis = Nothing

    Exit Function

ErrTrap:

    MsgBox Err.Description

End Function
```

This function gets the name for the Business Object and returns the string populated with BAPI names for this Business Object.

## BAPI Parameters

```
Public Function GetBapiParams(strBo As String, intBapi As Integer) As String

    Dim sapParams As IParameters
    Dim intCount As Integer

    On Error GoTo ErrTrap

    Set sapParams = _
        msapRepServ.BusinessObjects(strBo).Item(1).Methods.Item(intBapi).Parameters

    For intCount = 1 To sapParams.Count
      GetBapiParams = GetBapiParams & "|" & sapParams(intCount).Name
    Next

        Set sapParams = Nothing

    Exit Function

ErrTrap:

    MsgBox Err.Description

End Function
```

Again, I pass the ordinal number for the BAPI and the name for the Business Object. As you may notice, the call to get an instance to the collection in question gets longer:

```
Set sapParams = _
    msapRepServ.BusinessObjects(strBo).Item(1).Methods.Item(intBapi).Parameters
```

*You can easily see how we are going down the internal object hierarchy in the Repository Services library with these calls.*

After we have the BAPI's parameters we then need the Fields:

### Parameter Fields

```
Public Function GetParamFields(strBusObj As String, intBapi As Integer, _
                        intParam As Integer) As String

    Dim intCount As Integer
    Dim sapParam As IParameter

    Dim sapStruct As IStructure
    Dim sapTable As ITable
    Dim sapField As IField

    On Error GoTo ErrTrap

    Set sapParam = msapRepServ.BusinessObjects(strBusObj).Item(1). _
                Methods.Item(intBapi).Parameters.Item(intParam)

    If sapParam.IsStructure Then

        Set sapStruct = sapParam.Structure
        For intCount = 1 To sapStruct.Fields.Count
            GetParamFields = GetParamFields & "|" & _
                        sapStruct.Fields.Item(intCount).Name
        Next

    ElseIf sapParam.IsTable Then

        Set sapTable = sapParam.Table
        For intCount = 1 To sapTable.Fields.Count
            GetParamFields = GetParamFields & "|" & _
                        sapTable.Fields.Item(intCount).Name
        Next

    ElseIf sapParam.IsField Then

        Set sapField = sapParam.Field
        GetParamFields = "|" & sapField.Name

    End If

        Set sapParam = Nothing
        Set sapStruct = Nothing
        Set sapTable = Nothing
        Set sapField = Nothing

    Exit Function

ErrTrap:

    MsgBox Err.Description

End Function
```

This function is longer but logically the same. Pass the name for the object and ordinal numbers for the BAPI and the Parameter. Based on this, I can use the corresponding Field, Structure and Table methods of the Parameter object to create the correct parameter.

## Field Attributes

```
Public Function GetFieldAttributes(strBusObj As String, _
                                   intBapi As Integer, _
                                   intParam As Integer, _
                                   intField As Integer) As String

    Dim sapField As IField
    Dim sapParam As IParameter

    On Error GoTo ErrTrap

    Set sapParam = msapRepServ.BusinessObjects(strBusObj).Item(1). _
                Methods.Item(intBapi).Parameters.Item(intParam)

    If sapParam.IsStructure Then

        Set sapField = msapRepServ.BusinessObjects(strBusObj).Item(1). _
                    Methods.Item(intBapi).Parameters.Item(intParam). _
                    Structure.Fields.Item(intField)

        With sapField
            GetFieldAttributes = "|" & "ABAP Type " _
                                & .ABAPType & "|" & "Length " & .Length
        End With

    ElseIf sapParam.IsTable Then

        Set sapField = msapRepServ.BusinessObjects(strBusObj).Item(1). _
                    Methods.Item(intBapi).Parameters.Item(intParam) _
                    .Table.Fields.Item(intField)

        With sapField
            GetFieldAttributes = "|" & "ABAP Type " _
                                & .ABAPType & "|" & "Length " & .Length
        End With

    ElseIf sapParam.IsField Then

        Set sapField = sapParam.Field

        With sapField
            GetFieldAttributes = "|" & "ABAP Type " _
                                & .ABAPType & "|" & "Length " & .Length
        End With

    End If

        Set sapField = Nothing
        Set sapParam = Nothing

    Exit Function

ErrTrap:

    MsgBox Err.Description

End Function
```

*You can build a more complete attribute string using all the properties of the Field object. The core code will not change.*

## The Client

I have already said I'm not interested in building a sophisticated GUI for this project, so I'm only going to incorporate as much functionality as we need.

The data retrieval functions all rely heavily on using the ordinal numbers to locate items within the various collections. Therefore, I implemented the GUI component using a series of list box controls. This control is ideal for the task because of its ListIndex property.

There are six data retrieval functions that we coded into our server component, so start a new Standard EXE project and add six list boxes to the form with appropriate labels:

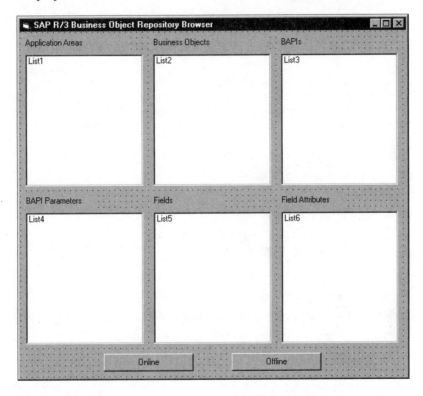

Also add two command buttons to the form. One to enable online browsing; the other offline browsing.

Before we can enable any of the browsing functionality we need a reference to the server component. Add the following line to the General Declarations for the form:

```
Option Explicit

Dim msrvRep As New clsSapBrowser
```

Then, to enable offline browsing I placed the following code behind the appropriate command button:

```
Private Sub Command1_Click()

   Dim strAppHs As String
   Dim strRealNames As String

   msrvRep.OpenMetaRepository App.Path & "\sap45.mdb"
   msrvRep.GetAppHs strAppHs, strRealNames

   FillListBox strAppHs, List1

End Sub
```

*You may have to change the name and/or path to your copy of the database.*

This routine simply calls the `OpenMetaRepository` method of our server component, passing in the path to the database. Then we call the `GetAppsHs` function to return the list of Application Areas. This list is returned as a pipe-delimited string, so before we can load the first list box we need to separate out the different elements. To do this I created a separate function called `FillListBox`:

```
Public Sub FillListBox(astrValues As String, objListBox As ListBox)

   Dim arrValues
   Dim intCount As Integer

   arrValues = Split(astrValues, "|")

   For intCount = 1 To UBound(arrValues)
      objListBox.AddItem arrValues(intCount)
   Next

End Sub
```

Nothing creative here. Just straightforward array manipulation.

The **Online** command button is almost identical to the **Offline** one, except that we call the `Logon` method instead of `OpenMetaRepository`:

```
Private Sub Command2_Click()

   Dim strAppHs As String
   Dim strRealNames As String

   msrvRep.Logon
   msrvRep.GetAppHs strAppHs, strRealNames

   FillListBox strAppHs, List1

End Sub
```

The next step is to fill the second list box with the related Business Objects. To do this, I coded the DblClick event of the first list box:

```
Private Sub List1_DblClick()

   Dim strBusObjs As String
   Dim blnFlag As Boolean

   Me.MousePointer = vbHourglass
   List2.Clear

   strBusObjs = msrvRep.GetBusObjs(List1.ListIndex + 1, blnFlag)

   If blnFlag Then
      Me.MousePointer = vbNormal
      Exit Sub
   Else
      FillListBox strBusObjs, List2
   End If

   Me.MousePointer = vbNormal

End Sub
```

*Note that we have to add 1 to the* List Index *property. This is because the* ListIndex *property is zero-based, whereas the BOR collections are one-based.*

Rather than passing in a series of nested ListIndexes each time, I defined several member variables in the form to hold the ListIndex value for the list boxes:

```
Option Explicit

Dim srvRep As New clsSapBrowser
Dim mstrBufferBo As String
Dim mintBufferBapi As Integer
Dim mintBufferParam As Integer
Dim mintBufferField As Integer
```

They are needed because I drill down the hierarchy and I depend on ordinal numbers from all the list boxes involved in the chain. I need the name for the Business Object and the ordinal numbers for the BAPI, the Parameter and the Field. Every time I make my selection by double-clicking on the item, these variables are updated.

The remaining DblClick event handlers are essentially the same as the one above, except each one calls a different function of the server component:

```
Private Sub List2_DblClick()

   Dim strBapis As String

   Me.MousePointer = vbHourglass
   List3.Clear
```

```
   mstrBufferBo = List2.List(List2.ListIndex)
   strBapis = msrvRep.GetBapis(mstrBufferBo)

   FillListBox strBapis, List3

   Me.MousePointer = vbNormal

End Sub

Private Sub List3_Click()

   Dim strParams As String

   Me.MousePointer = vbHourglass
   List4.Clear

   mintBufferBapi = List3.ListIndex + 1
   strParams = msrvRep.GetBapiParams(mstrBufferBo, mintBufferBapi)

   FillListBox strParams, List4

   Me.MousePointer = vbNormal

End Sub

Private Sub List4_DblClick()

   Dim strFields As String

   Me.MousePointer = vbHourglass
   List5.Clear

   mintBufferParam = List4.ListIndex + 1
   strFields = msrvRep.GetParamFields(mstrBufferBo, mintBufferBapi, _
                                   mintBufferParam)

   FillListBox strFields, List5

   Me.MousePointer = vbNormal

End Sub

Private Sub List5_DblClick()

   Dim strFieldAttrs As String

   Me.MousePointer = vbHourglass
   List6.Clear

   mintBufferField = List5.ListIndex + 1
   strFieldAttrs = msrvRep.GetFieldAttributes(mstrBufferBo, mintBufferBapi, _
                                      mintBufferParam, mintBufferField)

   FillListBox strFieldAttrs, List6

   Me.MousePointer = vbNormal

End Sub
```

The end result of this modest, yet powerful, exercise is shown below:

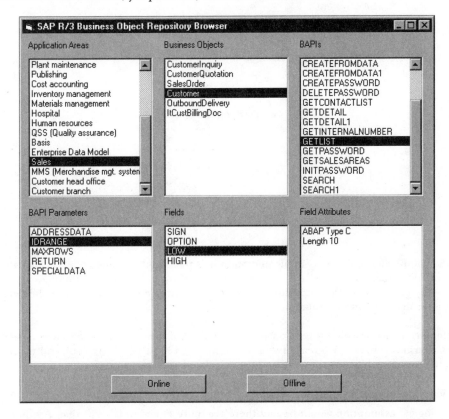

You may expand this project quantitatively and qualitatively, adding more information and more functionality. Because all the information is handled in delimited strings and arrays, you can easily build a GUI of any complexity. If you do not like ordinal referencing, you can use the Dictionary object, which is more powerful than a collection. However, you now have the core component that you can use as is or as a framework for your development.

# The Remote Function Call and the BOR

As we already know, everything we are dealing with in SAP R/3 is implemented via Function Modules. A Function Module is an ABAP written program that performs a particular functionality. Some of these functions are exposed to the Remote Function Call facility that allows these functions to be called from external applications.

The RFC mechanism is older than BAPI, and there are many more RFC functions than there are BAPIs. Moreover, as we have already seen, behind every BAPI stands an RFC. Considering the importance of RFCs, and the abilities these functions would bring to external applications, it is logical that SAP developed the same object-oriented mechanism for the external RFC access as it did for BAPIs.

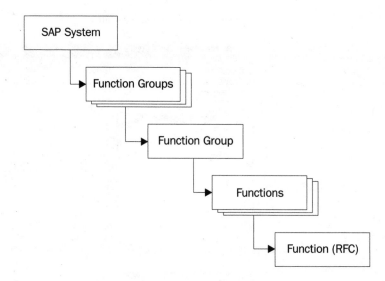

Given the complexity of the RFC implementation let's put together some code to calculate the total number of RFC functions available for external access. Having already programmed against the Business Object portion of the Repository Services it will not be difficult to notice the very same paradigm for the RFC implementation.

The difference is that for the `FunctionGroups` method of the Repository Services object there is a **Search Criteria** argument. Whereas, if you recall the `ApplicationHierarchies` method of the Repository Services object, there were no criteria-related arguments.

### Function FunctionGroups(aSearchCriterion As String) As IFunctionGroups

The only logical assumption would be that there are more Function Groups than Application Hierarchies, which they are analogous to.

Every time there is a string argument for search criteria my first reaction is to pass the * wildcard to it and to see what happens. Consider the code fragment below:

```
Dim sapFunctionGrs As IFunctionGroups

Dim intCount As Integer
Dim lngFCount As Long

Set sapFunctionGrs = sapRepServ.FunctionGroups("*")

Debug.Print sapFunctionGrs.Count

For intCount = 1 To sapFunctionGrs.Count

   lngFCount = lngFCount + sapFunctionGrs(intCount).Functions.Count

Next

Debug.Print "Total Number of Functions: " & lngFCount
```

The result of this code would be:

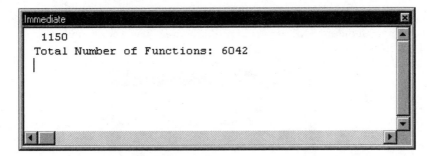

As you can see there are almost twelve hundred Function Groups that include Functions. This means that we have the potential of dealing with thousands of Functions that allow us to perform various operations in SAP R/3.

The **Function Groups object** is implemented in the `IFunctionGroups` class in the Repository Services library. This class is typical for this library with the `Item*` family of properties. The **Function Groups object** is implemented in the `IFunctionGroups` class that has a `Functions` method. This method returns the **Functions collection** that belongs to each Function Group. As you may easily notice, the architecture is absolutely the same as for Business Objects and BAPIs. I simply decided to add up the values of the `Count` properties of the Functions collections.

After the above code completed, the result that I got for the number of Functions was 6042. This is an impressive number. Reassuringly, the code fragment below returns the same number:

```
Dim sapFns As IFunctions

Set sapFns = sapRepServ.Functions("*")

Debug.Print sapFns.Count
```

It demonstrates that Function Groups act like Application Hierarchies. That is why the `BusinessObjects` method of the Repository Services object also has a search criteria argument and will return a collection of Business Objects based on that search criteria. The Function object obviously lacks a parent object, unlike a BAPI that always has a Business Object parent object.

# The RFC Browser

To further explore the RFC functionality, we will build a small demo project to browse the RFC objects. Start a new Standard EXE project and add the tree view, command button and image list controls to the default form:

The presentational functionality of this project is very simple. It uses a tree view control to present the data. The reason for using this control is that it is very illustrative and intuitive for presenting hierarchical data. Additionally, it is well known to Visual Basic developers and the Explorer style GUI has became a *de facto* standard for majority of applications.

> *To avoid overloading with GUI features irrelevant to this project's core functionality, I try to keep my code and interface to the necessary minimum. It will allow you to easily reuse the code for your own projects.*

As you may notice, I try to develop all the projects using the controls supplied with Visual Basic and use the SAP controls as libraries rather than GUI OCXs. The reason is that you cannot do anything without the core functionality of those libraries, but you may want to expand your existing code and knowledge of Visual Basic. If you have an Explorer style application that presents data and you want to integrate SAP R/3 into it, you need the functionality of the SAP Automation controls, not their GUI. Another, more serious, reason is that the emphasis of Visual Basic development shifts the business logic layer to server-side development. These components do not normally have any front-end at all.

Add a class module to your project, called clsRFCServ. This class module will encapsulate two things:

> Drive the tree view control

> Include the SAP related functionality

*This is not the most elegant solution because you are far better off to implement the above functionality in two separate class modules, thereby separating the presentation from the business logic. I have cut these types of corners for the sake of brevity.*

Add the reference to the **SAP Repository Services Type Library** to the project. Then add the following code to the **General Declarations** section of the class module:

```
Dim msapConn As Object        'SAPLogonCtrl.Connection
Dim msapLogon As Object       'SAPLogonControl
Dim msapRepServ As SAPRepositorySvc.RepositoryServices

Dim mastrFields() As String
Dim mastrStrs() As String
Dim mastrTabls() As String

Dim mblnFlIsData As Boolean
Dim mblnStIsData As Boolean
Dim mblnTbIsData As Boolean

Dim WithEvents xTree As TreeView
```

The last variable is the reference to the tree view control, dimensioned using the WithEvents keyword. We need that because event handling will be performed from the class module, not from the form. This technique allows you to reuse the same component to control different complex controls on different forms. It gives you the framework for the generic tree view control handling class.

# Initialization

The only annoyance is that you cannot pass the reference to the particular tree view control to the Initialize event of the class module, because the definition of this event does not allow for any arguments. I make another shortcut here hard coding the name of the tree view control in the Initialize event. If you need a totally generic class, create a method or property procedure to accept the reference to the particular tree view in an argument, and call it first. In my case the Initialize event looks like the one below:

```
Private Sub Class_Initialize()

  Set msapRepServ = New RepositoryServices
  Set msapLogon = CreateObject("SAP.LogonControl.1")
  Set msapConn = msapLogon.NewConnection
  Set xTree = frmMain.TreeView1

End Sub
```

This event will fire and create valid instances for the Repository Services object, Logon object, and the Connection object. This event will also cause the tree view related variable to be set to the valid tree view control on the form. The next step would be to establish a connection to the SAP R/3 system:

```
Public Function Logon(hw As Long) As Integer

   On Error GoTo ErrTrap

   msapConn.Logon hw, False

   If msapConn.IsConnected Then
      msapRepServ.Online msapConn
      Logon = 1
   Else
      MsgBox "Connection Failed"
      Logon = 0
      Exit Function
   End If

   Exit Function

ErrTrap:

   MsgBox Err.Description & vbCrLf & "From Logon"

End Function
```

Nothing unusual here. We use the familiar `NewConnection` method to create a valid instance of the Connection object. We then use a non-silent logon.

> *Please note that the* `Logon` *requires the window handle argument regardless of where it is used.*

This may pose an interesting question. What if we develop an ActiveX component that does not have any GUI and therefore cannot have a window handle parameter?

I did some experimentation on this matter and I have found that the `Logon` method will happily take any long integer including zero.

> **Please beware that this is not a supported or recommended approach and SAP does not indicate this in the help file or any other documentation.**

Moreover, the documentation makes an explicit statement on the argument in question being the window handle of the parent window for the Logon control. I do not have access to the SAP's source code or any other "insider" information and I cannot really explain why it works this way. Therefore, consider this to be one of those "unsupported features" we get used to in Visual Basic.

Notes aside, the next thing to do is to pass the Connection object to the Repository Services object. The line of code included below performs this task:

```
msapRepServ.Online msapConn
```

The process of passing the Connection object to the Repository Services object takes some time and you will notice it regardless of the speed of your connection.

# Data Retrieval

After the Repository Services object gets the valid connection to SAP R/3 we can begin loading the RFC metadata. To do so I have created a method of our class to perform the loading of the Function objects:

```
Public Function GetRfc(strFuncGroup As String, retRFC() As String)

   Dim sapFgs As IFunctionGroups
   Dim sapFg As IFunctionGroup
   Dim sapF As IFunction
   Dim intCount As Integer

   On Error GoTo ErrTrap

   Set sapFgs = msapRepServ.FunctionGroups(strFuncGroup)

   For Each sapFg In sapFgs

      intCount = intCount + 1
      ReDim Preserve retRFC(intCount)
      retRFC(intCount) = sapFg.Name

      For Each sapF In sapFg.Functions
         retRFC(intCount) = retRFC(intCount) & "|" & sapF.Name
      Next

   Next
      Set sapFgs = Nothing
      Set sapFg = Nothing
      Set sapF = Nothing

   Exit Function

ErrTrap:

   MsgBox Err.Description & vbCrLf & "From GetRfc"

End Function
```

The above code combines the extraction and metadata processing functionality. To extract the metadata we have to first create a valid instance of the `IFunctionGroups` object. We do it using the `FunctionGroups` method that accepts the criteria parameter for the name of the Function Groups we are interested in. This parameter can be created using wildcard characters. In our case, I pass the value `RFC*` for that argument. The result will be all the Function Groups whose names begin with RFC.

*This mechanism is understandable considering the amount of RFCs defined in the BOR. Using a value for the criteria allows avoiding unnecessary data.*

After we get a valid collection of Function Groups, we can loop through it and get names of all the Functions. The following nested `For...Next` loops does the trick:

```
For Each sapFg In sapFgs

  intCount = intCount + 1
  ReDim Preserve retRFC(intCount)
  retRFC(intCount) = sapFg.Name

  For Each sapF In sapFg.Functions
    retRFC(intCount) = retRFC(intCount) & "|" & sapF.Name
  Next

Next
```

The above code fragment populates the dynamic array to be passed back to the calling function. This is a string array with every new member beginning with the name of the Function Group followed by a pipe-delimited list of Functions.

After we populate the string array with the necessary information we can pass it back to the function that populates the tree view. Remember that we have all the code for the tree view control handling in the class module. Therefore, it makes perfect sense to include the tree view population routine into the same class module. This approach also lets you define as many handling routines as you need:

```
Public Function PopTree(hw As Long)

  Dim aretString() As String
  Dim intCount As Integer
  Dim intCount2 As Integer
  Dim ndX As Node
  Dim dummy As Node
  Dim retval As Integer
  Dim varSplitResult As Variant

  On Error GoTo ErrTrap

  retval = Logon(hw)

  If retval Then

    GetRfc "RFC*", aretString()

    For intCount = 1 To UBound(aretString)

      varSplitResult = Split(aretString(intCount), "|")

      Set ndX = xTree.Nodes.Add("topnode", tvwChild, "grp" _
                              & varSplitResult(0), varSplitResult(0), 2)

      For intCount2 = 1 To UBound(varSplitResult)

        Set ndX = xTree.Nodes.Add("grp" & varSplitResult(0), tvwChild, _
                                "rfc" & varSplitResult(intCount2), _
                                varSplitResult (intCount2), 4)
        Set dummy = xTree.Nodes.Add("rfc" & varSplitResult(intCount2), _
                                tvwChild, "dum" & "rfc" & _
                                varSplitResult(intCount2))
```

```
        Next

        Erase varSplitResult

    Next

  Else

    MsgBox "Load Aborted"
    Exit Function

  End If

  Exit Function

ErrTrap:

  MsgBox Err.Description & vbCrLf & "From PopTree"

End Function
```

This procedure also relies on nested For...Next loops that are logical mirrors of the similar loops that populated the string array in the previous procedure.

Our structure for the array element is that the first value in the array element is the name of the Function Group followed by names of the Functions that belong to this group.

You may be curious about the "dummy" node that is being created and then removed throughout this and many other sample projects in this book. This is a standard trick used by the Windows Explorer itself and many other GUI elements that include hierarchical interface elements.

The problem is that it is often a long process that populates the whole hierarchy, and it is unknown whether the parent element has any child elements. The choice would be either to bite the bullet and let the users wait until you populate the whole hierarchy, or to create the parent elements first and populate their child elements on demand. Because users have come to expect to find some child elements if there is a "plus" on the left of the element in the tree view control, I simulate that by using a temporary dummy node that I remove when the user requests child elements. If there are no child elements the user will be presented with the parent node with no plus sign, if there are child elements the user will see them without any dummy nodes.

The Node_Click event of the tree view control triggers the procedure that requests parameters for the RFC. This functionality is implemented in the following procedure:

```
Public Function GetParams(strRFCName As String)

  Dim sapFs As IFunctions
  Dim sapPars As IParameters
  Dim sapPar As IParameter
  Dim sapFld As IField
  Dim sapStruct As IStructure
  Dim sapTable As ITable

  Dim intFl As Integer
  Dim intSt As Integer
  Dim intTb As Integer
```

```
      On Error GoTo ErrTrap

      Set sapFs = msapRepServ.Functions(strRFCName)
      Set sapPars = sapFs(1).Parameters

      For Each sapPar In sapPars

        If sapPar.IsField Then

            Set sapFld = sapPars.ItemByName(sapPar.Name).Field
            intFl = intFl + 1
            ReDim Preserve mastrFields(intFl)
            mastrFields(intFl) = sapFld.Name
            mblnFlIsData = True

        ElseIf sapPar.IsStructure Then

            Set sapStruct = sapPars.ItemByName(sapPar.Name).Structure
            intSt = intSt + 1
            ReDim Preserve mastrStrs(intSt)
            mastrStrs(intSt) = sapStruct.Name
            mblnStIsData = True

        ElseIf sapPar.IsTable Then

            Set sapTable = sapPars.ItemByName(sapPar.Name).Table
            intTb = intTb + 1
            ReDim Preserve mastrTabls(intTb)
            mastrTabls(intTb) = sapTable.Name
            mblnTbIsData = True

        End If

      Next

          Set sapFs = Nothing
          Set sapPars = Nothing
          Set sapPar = Nothing
          Set sapFld = Nothing
          Set sapStruct = Nothing
          Set sapTable = Nothing

      Exit Function

  ErrTrap:

      MsgBox Err.Description & vbCrLf & "From GetParams"

  End Function
```

The above function accepts the Function name and then uses this code to get the reference for the collection of Function objects:

```
Set sapFs = msapRepServ.Functions(strRFCName)
```

It uses the `Functions` method of the Repository Services object to get all the functions, in our case just one, from the SAP R/3 BOR. Because we are absolutely sure that we are going to get only one function – we are passing the exact name to the `Functions` method above – the following line is a valid solution:

```
Set sapPars = sapFs(1).Parameters
```

It uses the `Parameters` method of the Function object to get the collection of Function parameters. Once we get the collection of Function parameters we have to evaluate the type that they belong to – Field, Structure or Table. It is necessary to adequately present them in our tree view. The logic behind this evaluation is based on the `IsField`, `IsStructure` and `IsTable` properties of the Parameter object. These properties return 1 if the Parameter belongs to the relevant type. Therefore it is easy to write the following code:

```
For Each sapPar In sapPars

  If sapPar.IsField Then

      Set sapFld = sapPars.ItemByName(sapPar.Name).Field
      intFl = intFl + 1
      ReDim Preserve mastrFields(intFl)
      mastrFields(intFl) = sapF.Name
      mblnFlIsData = True

  ElseIf sapPar.IsStructure Then

      Set sapStruct = sapPars.ItemByName(sapPar.Name).Structure
      intSt = intSt + 1
      ReDim Preserve mastrStrs(intSt)
      mastrStrs(intSt) = sapStruct.Name
      mblnStIsData = True

  ElseIf sapPar.IsTable Then

      Set sapTable = sapPars.ItemByName(sapPar.Name).Table
      intTb = intTb + 1
      ReDim Preserve mastrTabls(intTb)
      mastrTabls(intTb) = sapTable.Name
      mblnTbIsData = True

  End If

Next
```

Note that we use our familiar `ItemByName` method to extract elements from collections. It is also important to understand the logic behind the use of the `Field`, `Structure` and `Table` methods of the Parameter object. Note that I dimensioned relevant variables as `IField`, `IStructure` and `ITable`. That gives me all the benefits of early binding and hence the ability to use the IntelliSense editor. To avoid any type mismatches I therefore needed to explicitly set these variables to the appropriate object. To enable this, SAP created the `Field`, `Structure` and `Table` methods for the Parameter object. They return the corresponding objects provided that you apply them to the correct parameter. You will get a run-time error if you try to get the `Structure` out of the `Field` parameter. To present parameters differently in the GUI, I assign different pictures to nodes depending on the type of the parameter.

## Tree View Events

The only thing left is the fact that I manage the tree view events from the same class module that handles the BOR related functionality. The code for the tree view events is presented below:

```
Private Sub xTree_Collapse(ByVal Node As MSComctlLib.Node)

    If Left(Node.Key, 3) = "grp" Then
        Node.Image = 2
    End If

End Sub
```

```
Private Sub xTree_Expand(ByVal Node As MSComctlLib.Node)

    Dim ndX As Node
    Dim sapFl As IField
    Dim sapSt As IStructure
    Dim sapTb As ITable
    Dim intCount As Integer

    On Error GoTo ErrTrap

    If Left(Node.Key, 3) = "grp" Then
        Node.Image = 3
    End If

    Select Case Left(Node.Key, 3)

      Case "rfc"
          GetParams Node.Text
          xTree.Nodes.Remove "dum" & Node.Key

          If mblnFlIsData Then
              For intCount = 1 To UBound(mastrFields)
                  Set ndX = xTree.Nodes.Add(Node.Key, tvwChild, Node.Key & _
                                          mastrFields(intCount), _
                                          mastrFields(intCount), 5)
              Next
          End If

          If mblnStIsData Then
              For intCount = 1 To UBound(mastrStrs)
                  Set ndX = xTree.Nodes.Add(Node.Key, tvwChild, Node.Key & _
                                          mastrStrs(intCount), _
                                          mastrStrs(intCount), 6)
              Next
          End If

          If mblnTbIsData Then
              For intCount = 1 To UBound(mastrTabls)
                  Set ndX = xTree.Nodes.Add(Node.Key, tvwChild, Node.Key & _
                                          mastrTabls(intCount), _
                                          mastrTabls(intCount), 7)
              Next
          End If

    End Select
```

```
    mblnFlIsData = False
    mblnStIsData = False
    mblnTbIsData = False

    SetsapFl = Nothing
    SetsapSt = Nothing
    SetsapTb = Nothing

    Exit Sub

ErrTrap:

    MsgBox Err.Description & vbCrLf & "From " & "xTree_NodeClick"

End Sub
```

## The Form

Now we have to add the minimal code to the form.

The code is executed by the single command button:

```
Private Sub Command1_Click()

    mobjRfc.PopTree Me.hWnd

End Sub
```

Where `mobjRfc` is the reference for the class module, added to the **General Declarations** section of the form:

```
Option Explicit

Dim mobjRfc As New clsRFCServ
```

The only other line is in the form's `Load` event to add the top-most node to the tree view control:

```
Private Sub Form_Load()

    TreeView1.Nodes.Add , , "topnode", "SAP R/3 BOR", 1

End Sub
```

You can expand nodes and the screen will look like the one below at its maximum detail:

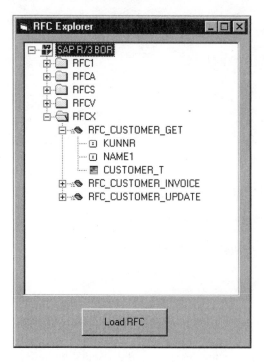

You can augment this project with many additional niceties but the core functionality is presented here. You can reuse the class module from this project for your own development. The primary objective for sample projects in this book is to be an extension to the SDK presented in the SAP Automation Toolkit targeted at Visual Basic programmers.

# Summary

This chapter was devoted to the SAP R/3 Business Object Repository and the tools from the SAP Automation Toolkit built to work with the BOR. Unlike the previous chapter, we were interested in those tools that gave us *programmatic* access to the BOR. We saw that there are two distinct parts to the BOR – Business Objects and RFCs.

We built browser applications for both the RFC and Business Objects. These components were small, yet powerful. They implemented all the necessary functionality and allowed for future expansion. I tried to reinforce the compatibility of all the tools discussed with the familiar Visual Basic development paradigm.

The next chapter will be devoted to the task of BAPI programming and RFC programming. You will see the RFC control in action and the BAPI control again. We will also continue exploring ways to integrate the SAP Automation Toolkit's component functionality into existing, and future, Visual Basic and Office applications.

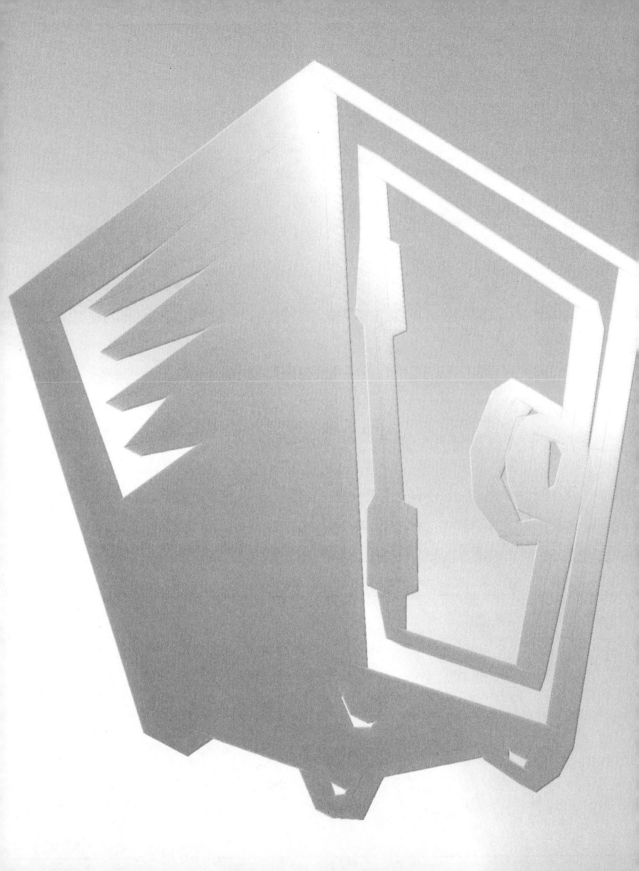

# 8

# Calling RFCs and BAPIs

In this chapter, we'll finish our exploration of the core functionality of the SAP Automation toolkit. That is, those components that are relevant to BAPIs and RFCs.

This chapter consists of two parts:

> The first part describes the SAP RFC control, its functionality and application.

> The second part is essentially an SAP R/3-specific, problem-solving project that uses controls that we already know – the SAP Logon control and the SAP BAPI control – to explore a particularly useful business object called *Helpvalues*.

As we have come to expect, SAP wrapped the access to its numerous RFCs, that comprise the functional core of SAP R/3, into a COM/VB friendly library. This is the **SAP Remote Function Call control**.

## The SAP RFC Control

The SAP Remote Function Call (RFC) control is contained in the WDTFUNCS.OCX file. The purpose of this control is to execute RFC calls – it does not provide any RFC browsing capabilities. This control, like many others in this series, doesn't have any run-time GUI.

*You may wonder why these components are implemented as controls rather than DLLs, when they don't have any run-time interface. I'm afraid I can't throw any light on this – I don't know the rationale behind SAP's decision to go with OCX controls.*

One possibility is that, once placed on the form, the controls expose their functionality plus they provide property pages. This particular control, however, has more functionality than regular property pages. It provides the ability to logon to SAP R/3 and retrieve the interface for an RFC, provided you already know the correct name of the RFC.

## The SAP RFC Control Hierarchy

The object hierarchy of this control is presented in the following diagram:

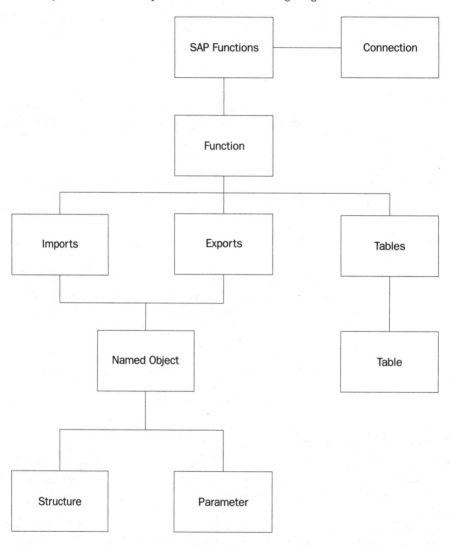

This diagram illustrates the structure of the SAP RFC control and provides a reference to follow as we discuss the control.

*The presence of the familiar Connection object illustrates the fact that, like with all other controls that connect to SAP R/3 directly, the RFC control needs a valid connection provided via the Connection object from the SAP Logon control library.*

# Setting Up the RFC Control

Add the SAP Remote Function Call Control to a new Standard EXE project (RFC_OCX). We don't need the Logon control this time round as the RFC control can implement its own connectivity:

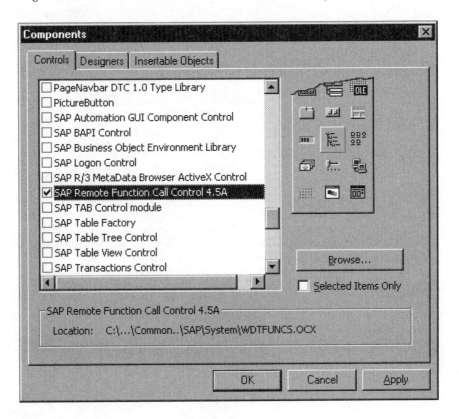

The Object Browser presents you with this view of the SAP RFC control:

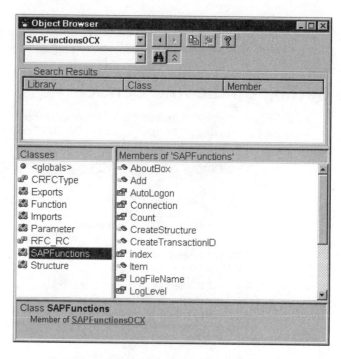

The Logon functionality is needed to provide the Connection object and to set up the connection to SAP R/3. The concept is the same as in ADO – to connect a Recordset to a database you need to supply the Recordset with a valid connection.

As usual, we will first do everything using OCX controls. We'll begin by placing the SAP RFC control on the form:

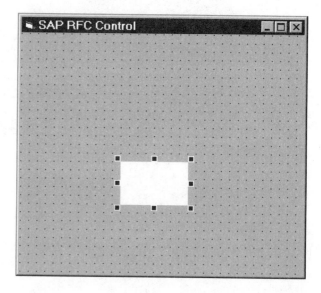

Now we will explore the **Property Pages** for the RFC control. Go to the **Property Pages**, using the *F4* function key or by double-clicking on the **(Custom)** property. The following dialog will be presented:

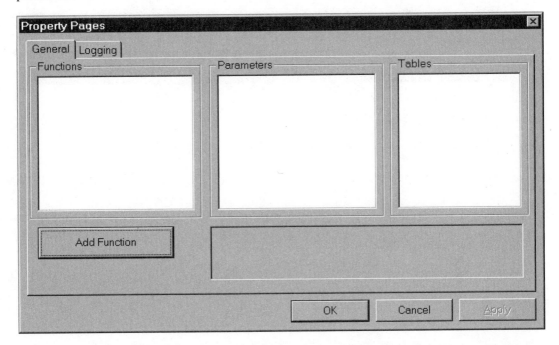

This dialog allows you to load the required RFC and retain the connectivity information without having to use a Logon control explicitly.

Click on the **Add Function** button. The result will be the following input box:

Let's type in some familiar RFC – RFC_CUSTOMER_GET – and click **OK**.

*Please note that this control does not provide any BOR browsing functionality.*

The Logon dialog will pop up, and after a successful logon, the RFC interface metadata will be loaded into the Property Pages:

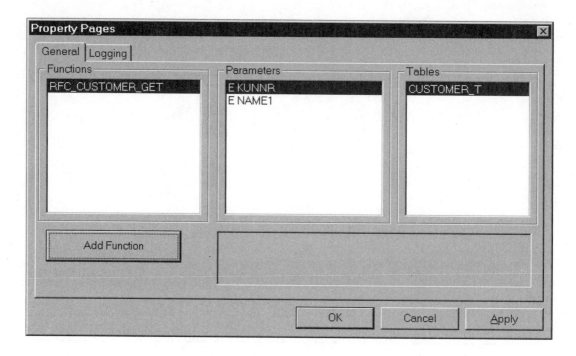

*Clicking on the parameters will produce an abbreviated description for each of them.*

Should you need trace file functionality, you can go to the Logging tab of the Property Pages and specify the trace file name and the trace level, as we did for the BAPI control:

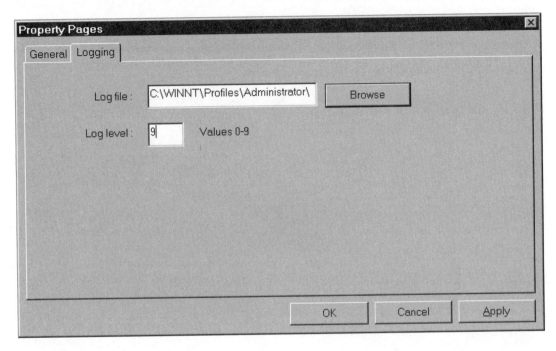

Click Apply followed by OK and save the project. Now the RFC control is set to logon to SAP R/3 and to execute the RFC on our command. Although we connected to SAP R/3 and loaded all the metadata, we still need some code to actually execute the RFC and retrieve the results.

## Programming the RFC Control

The logic behind this control is quite simple. You need to supply Import and Export (inbound and outbound) parameters, call the function and evaluate the results. The first point is to differentiate between **Import** and **Export** Table parameters.

## *Import or Export?*

Fire up the SAP Assistant, go to <u>V</u>iew | <u>O</u>ptions and make sure that the dialog that you see has the following values:

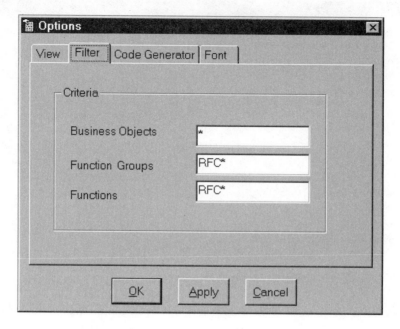

Logon and go to the **RFC** tab. Double-click on the **R/3** node if you don't have anything displayed. You will be presented with a familiar view. Now, expand the **RFCX** Function Group and click on RFC_CUSTOMER_GET:

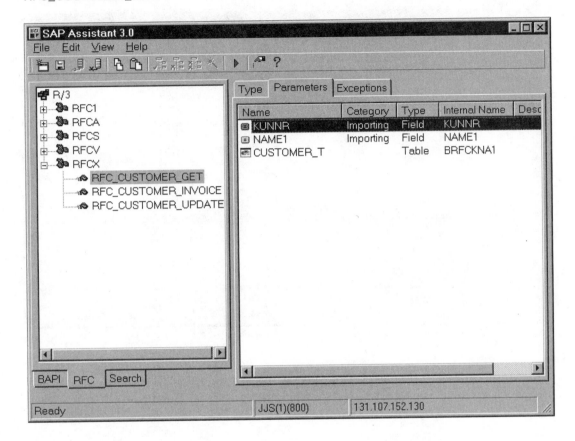

Observe the Category values in the right-pane of the browser for each parameter, and compare this view to the one from the RFC control's property pages:

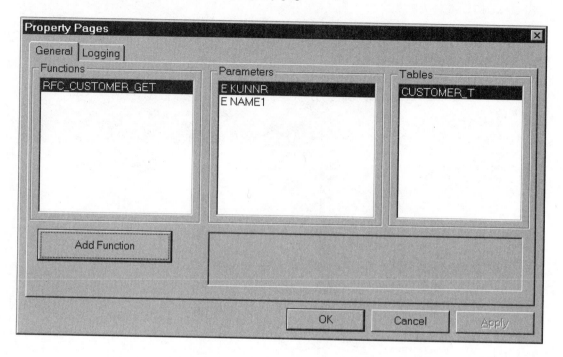

Look at the letters to the left of the parameter name. You will see E for Export next to the KUNNR parameter on the property page, but it is categorized as Importing in the SAP Assistant. This can be attributed to semantics, but it is an unpleasant difference to have.

To clarify such a discrepancy, let's go to the source. In this case, that means going to the SAP R/3 front-end and logging in. Then go to the familiar System | ABAP Workbench | Function Builder. Type RFC_CUSTOMER_GET into the Function module box and you should see the following screen:

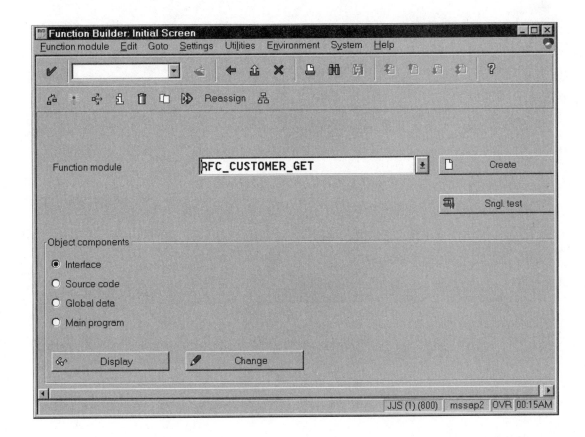

Select Interface, click on Display and observe the results:

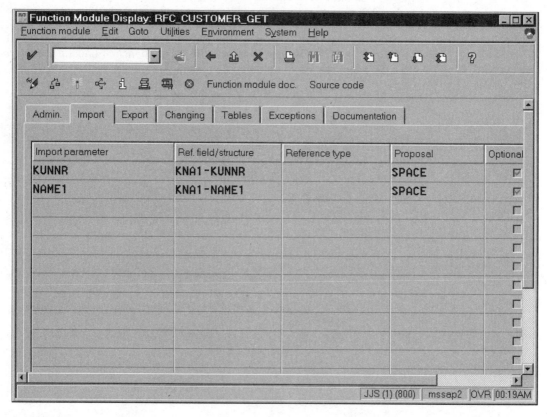

This conforms to the view presented by the SAP Assistant showing KUNNR as an Importing parameter. Is it a bug in the RFC control? I don't think so. Apparently, it's a change of perspective.

> The RFC control *exports* (supplies) the KUNNR parameter and SAP R/3 *imports* (gets) the KUNNR parameter.

It would have been better to have consistent terminology, but for me, the most important thing is that it all works, and it does. The main inconvenience is that you cannot use values from your Metadata Repository database or the SAP Assistant directly.

## Executing the RFC Control

Now, it's time for some coding. Looking at the object structure of the RFC control, and at the Object Browser, it's clear that before we can do anything, we have to first get an instance of the Function object. This is because parameters are accessible via the Function object. We can create a reference to the object using the Item method of the RFC control. In this instance, I can use an index of 1 because there is only one RFC added to the control.

Add a command button to the form in our project and add the following code to the button's `Click` event:

```
Private Sub Command1_Click()

  Dim sapRFC As SAPFunctionsOCX.Function

  Set sapRFC = SAPFunctions1.Item(1)

  Debug.Print sapRFC.Name

  Debug.Print sapRFC.Exports(1).Name
  Debug.Print sapRFC.Exports(2).Name

  Set sapRFC = Nothing

End Sub
```

The first thing you might notice is that the SAP Functions object does not have a Functions collection. This is because it implements the Functions collection directly, and therefore has an `Item` method. Since we populated the control with only one RFC, the command:

```
Set sapRFC = SAPFunctions1.Item(1)
```

Will correctly return a reference to the RFC in question. After executing the code fragment above, the Immediate window presents the following:

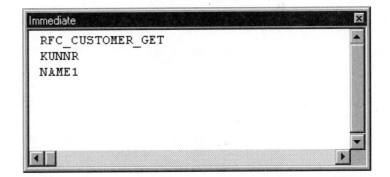

```
Immediate
RFC_CUSTOMER_GET
KUNNR
NAME1
```

## Setting Parameter Values

Because our Export parameters are fields, we can simply set them to the required values. We can learn what KUNNR and NAME1 are from the SAP R/3 Function Builder or the SAP Assistant. Either way, we will find that KUNNR is a Customer Number and NAME1 is the Name. Let's get all the customers with names that satisfy the A* criterion, i.e. all customers whose name starts with the letter "A". Because we are searching by a wildcard criterion for the name, we do not need to supply a value for the KUNNR.

Add the following code to the above fragment:

```
Private Sub Command1_Click()

    Dim sapRFC As SAPFunctionsOCX.Function
    Dim KUNNR As SAPFunctionsOCX.Parameter
    Dim NAME1 As SAPFunctionsOCX.Parameter
    Dim CUSTOMER_T As Object

    Set sapRFC = SAPFunctions1.Item(1)

    Debug.Print sapRFC.Name

    Debug.Print sapRFC.Exports(1).Name
    Debug.Print sapRFC.Exports(2).Name

    Set NAME1 = sapRFC.Exports(2)
    Set CUSTOMER_T = sapRFC.Tables(1)

    NAME1.Value = "A*"

    sapRFC.Call

    Debug.Print "Record count - " & CUSTOMER_T.RowCount

    Set sapRFC = Nothing
    Set KUNNR = Nothing
    Set NAME1= Nothing
    Set CUSTOMER_T = Nothing

End Sub
```

We can safely set the reference for the table using an ordinal of 1, because we know that there is only one table: CUSTOMER_T.

> *Note that I name the parameter variables after the real RFC parameters simply for better code readability and nothing else.*

Now execute the above code and observe the results:

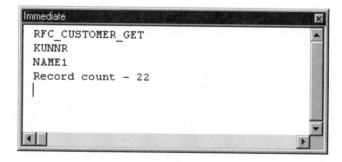

228

## *Utilizing Additional Controls*

I did not have to add the Table Factory control to my project to use the property of the Table object, CUSTOMER_T.RowCount, because all Parameter type objects are reused for all controls. However, I will add the Table Factory control so that we can declare appropriate arguments as Table type.

Add the Table Factory Control to the project and declare CUSTOMER_T as Table. This will also enable the IntelliSense features of the VB IDE:

```
Dim CUSTOMER_T As SAPTableFactoryCtrl.Table
```

The Call method of the Function object does not require any arguments, and simply executes the RFC. However, if your objective is to quickly display results, you will need the **SAP Table View control**. Every Table object exports the **Views collection**. If we add the Table View's Object property value to the Views collection, we would establish a connection between the Table View and the Table object.

Add the SAP Table View control to the project, put it on the form and add the following line of code. It's imperative to add this code at the right place – before the RFC call is executed:

```
Set NAME1 = sapRFC.Exports(2)
Set CUSTOMER_T = sapRFC.Tables(1)

NAME1.Value = "A*"
CUSTOMER_T.Views.Add SAPTableView1.Object

sapRFC.Call
```

The result will be similar to a quick implementation of the Data Bound Grid:

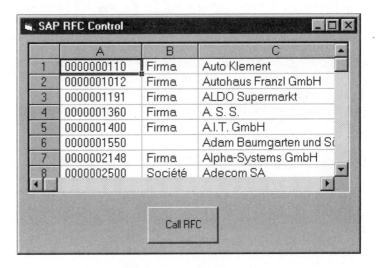

Another way of using the RFC control is to set all necessary values at run-time, thereby avoiding any persistence for names and connections.

# Using the RFC Control Library Without the Control

Create a new **Standard EXE** project, `RFC_Run`, with a single form and one class module. We can now start programming using the progID for the RFC control library. Add the following declaration to a class module called `clsRFC`:

```
Option Explicit

Private msapRFC As Object
Private msapRFCC As Object
```

And in the `Class_Initialize` event, we create an instance of the `SAPFunctions` class:

```
Private Sub Class_Initialize()

   Set msapRFCC = CreateObject("SAP.Functions")

End Sub
```

Note that we had to define the variable `msapRFCC` as the generic `Object` type because we don't have a reference to the RFC control. Do not forget to clean up in the `Terminate` event:

```
Private Sub Class_Terminate()

   Set msapRFCC = Nothing

End Sub
```

After we create the reference to the `SAPFunctions` class, we have to add the RFC itself. The `SAPFunctions` class implements the `Add` method, which requires a String parameter containing the correct RFC name:

```
Function Add(functionName As String) As Object
```

This method returns a reference to the Function object. Note that we don't create any Connection object, because we don't have to. The `Add` method will trigger the logon activity and the RFC library will query the SAP R/3 BOR. To create more generic code, we will use names for parameters instead of their ordinal position.

Create a routine that will add the RFC to the Functions collection and return a reference to it:

```
Public Sub Add(strRFCName As String)

   Set msapRFC = msapRFCC.Add(strRFCName)

End Sub
```

## Setting Parameter Values at Run-Time

Once we have reference to the Function object, we can create another function to set up the parameters:

```
Public Function SetParams(strKunnr As String, strName As String)

    Dim KUNNR As Object
    Dim NAME1 As Object
    Dim CUSTOMER_T As Object

    Set KUNNR = msapRFC.Exports("KUNNR")
    Set NAME1 = msapRFC.Exports("NAME1")

    Set CUSTOMER_T = msapRFC.Tables("CUSTOMER_T")

    NAME1.Value = strName
    KUNNR.Value = strKunnr

    msapRFC.Call

    Set KUNNR = Nothing
    Set NAME1 = Nothing
    Set CUSTOMER_T = Nothing

End Function
```

This code is very similar to the code from the previous project, except that the parameters are named rather than referred to by their ordinal position. You can easily expand this routine by passing not only values for parameters, but also their names and their directionality, to add them correctly to `Imports` or `Exports`. For the present sample, this semi-generic code will be just right.

## Using ADO Recordsets

The `MapAdoRs` function, which we built in Chapter 5, creates a disconnected ADO Recordset based on the structure of a Table object and populates it with the contents of the table. Copy this function and the event declarations from `clsBapi` into `clsRFC`. Now add the `MapAdoRs` function call to the `SetParams` method of our class, modified to return the resultant Recordset:

```
Public Function SetParams(strKunnr As String, strName As String) As Recordset

    Dim KUNNR As Object
    Dim NAME1 As Object
    Dim CUSTOMER_T As Object

    Set SetParams = New ADODB.Recordset

    Set KUNNR = msapRFC.Exports("KUNNR")
    Set NAME1 = msapRFC.Exports("NAME1")

    Set CUSTOMER_T = msapRFC.Tables("CUSTOMER_T")

    NAME1.Value = strName
    KUNNR.Value = strKunnr

    msapRFC.Call
```

```
     MapAdoRs CUSTOMER_T, SetParams

   Set KUNNR = Nothing
   Set NAME1 = Nothing
   Set CUSTOMER_T = Nothing

 End Function
```

*Don't forget to add the reference to ADO 2.1 to your project.*

Remember that we also implemented events in the class in Chapter 5. Do not forget to use the WithEvents keyword when declaring the variable for our class module. The following line of code goes into the **General Declarations** of the form:

```
 Dim WithEvents mobjRFC As clsRFC
```

The Load event should look like the one below:

```
 Private Sub Form_Load()

   Set mobjRFC = New clsRFC

 End Sub
```

After all these coding efforts, add the Data Bound Grid control to our project and place it on the form. The following code will display our results in the grid:

```
 Private Sub Command1_Click()

   On Error GoTo ErrTrap

   mobjRFC.Add "RFC_CUSTOMER_GET"

   Set DataGrid1.DataSource = mobjRFC.SetParams("", "A*")

   Exit Sub

 ErrTrap:

   MsgBox Err.Description

 End Sub
```

The end result will look very familiar:

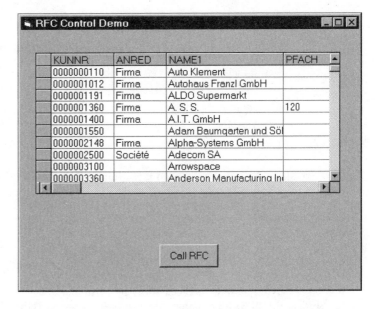

This small project illustrates how to work with the RFC control's library without using the control itself. The only component you should have is the Data Grid and the only reference should be to the ADO Library. This approach simplifies ActiveX component development.

ActiveX components do not usually support a GUI, therefore making it impossible to work with SAP Automation controls directly. These controls don't actually provide any GUI-related value anyway so you're not losing out by using them simply as libraries.

There are some other more subtle reasons. SAP frequently upgrades its controls, and if you always download and install the latest version, you will get ActiveX control compatibility issues. Moreover, in the case of abnormal termination of your program, these controls may become unstable. I frequently run into **ActiveX Control is not registered** messages, curable only by closing Visual Basic and restarting it.

> **The safest way to work with these controls is to treat them as libraries and use the `CreateObject` function of Visual Basic.**

# SAP BAPI Help Values

Before we conclude our discussion on the SAP Automation Toolkit, I want to demonstrate how to solve a problem that belongs to the "SAP R/3 essentials" category. Some things are inevitable for any external programmer developing SAP R/3 integration applications. These are:

> ➢ The Logon process
> ➢ BOR navigation
> ➢ BAPI/RFC execution

We have already learned how to do these things. The remaining problem from the "must do" list is to look up fixed values for certain fields of BAPI parameters.

As we discussed in earlier chapters, SAP R/3 has very complex data validation functionality, and there are some fields that can only contain a **fixed value**. For example, the Currency, Region and Language fields will only accept a value that is predefined in SAP R/3. These fixed values are stored internally in different **Check tables**.

It is obviously impossible to successfully perform any data validation from an external program, prior to calling a BAPI, without being able to look-up what these fixed values are.

The SAP Assistant can generate a metadata database that has a **Helpvalues** table, but unfortunately, the `HelpvaluesCount` field is not populated in the current release (3.0) of this tool. Moreover, if you want to use that database, or the functionality of the Repository Services library, to determine if a field has a Check table – an indicator that it has look-up values – it will not present you with the information in a very intuitive manner.

For example, let's use our familiar OPTION field from the IDRANGE table parameter of the GETLIST BAPI that belongs to the *Customer* business object. Start MS Access and open your SAP R/3 Metadata database, created using the SAP Assistant. Create a new query to determine the name of the Check table for the given field:

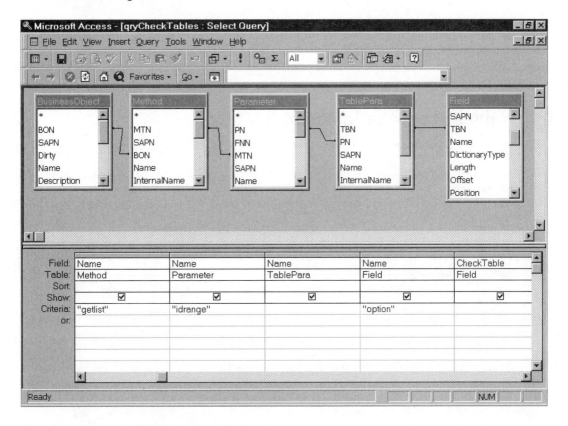

Please consider the full SQL statement below:

```
SELECT BusinessObject.Name, Method.Name, Parameter.Name, TablePara.Name,
       Field.Name, Field.CheckTable, Field.HasFixedValues,
       Field.HelpvaluesCount, Field.ValuesForFieldCount

FROM (((BusinessObject INNER JOIN Method ON BusinessObject.BON = Method.BON)

INNER JOIN Parameter ON Method.MTN = Parameter.MTN) INNER JOIN TablePara ON
                 Parameter.PN = TablePara.PN) INNER JOIN Field ON
                 TablePara.TBN = Field.TBN

WHERE (((BusinessObject.Name)="customer") AND ((Method.Name)="getlist") AND
       ((Parameter.Name)="idrange"));
```

Enter appropriate values and execute the query. If you test for the Check table it will not display anything in the CheckTable field, but it will populate the HasFixedValues field with 1, indicating that there are fixed values.

On the other hand, the REGION field of the PERSONALDATA parameter of the CREATEFROMDATA1 BAPI of the *Customer* business object will show zero for the HasFixedValues field. But the CheckTable field now has a "T005S" entry, which is the name of the internal SAP R/3 table where the values are.

I call this counterintuitive, because there is no single flag-style property, or table entry, to clearly indicate if a field of a BAPI Parameter has help values. In any case, the Helpvalues table remains empty, and that means that, for at least this release of SAP Assistant, the Visual Basic programmer has to either ask his ABAP counterpart, or create some SAP R/3 querying tool to locate internal help values.

## Help Values From the Inside of SAP R/3

To continue our tradition, we'll first look at the SAP R/3 BOR from the SAP front-end directly.

Fire up the front-end and logon. Follow the familiar path Tools | Business Framework | BAPI Browser and locate the Customer business object. Then drill down Methods | Parameters | IdRange. Expand IdRange and double click on the BAPICUSTOMER_IDRANGE icon. You should get the following picture:

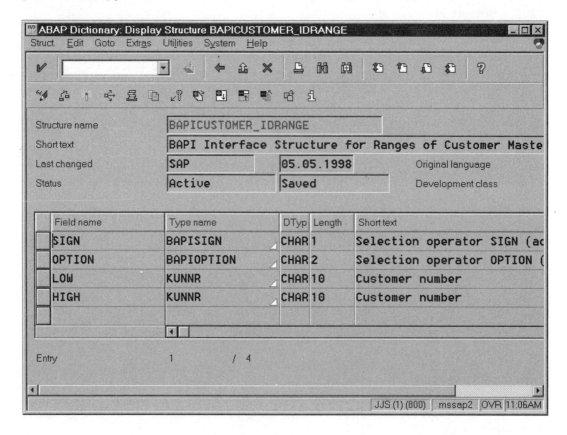

Double-click on BAPIOPTION and you should get the screen like the one below:

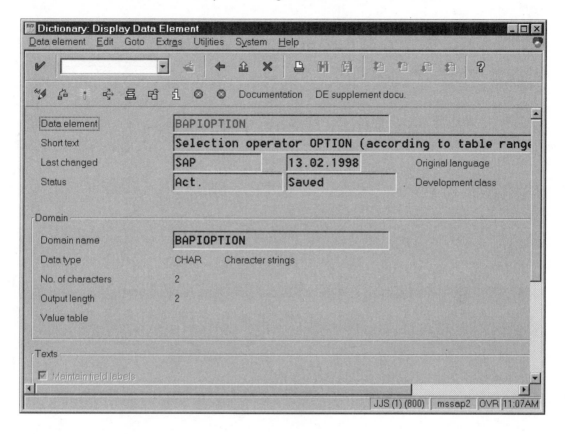

Dictionary: Display Data Element

Data element   Edit   Goto   Extras   Utilities   System   Help

Documentation     DE supplement docu.

| | |
|---|---|
| Data element | BAPIOPTION |
| Short text | Selection operator OPTION (according to table range |
| Last changed | SAP          13.02.1998       Original language |
| Status | Act.          Saved       Development class |

Domain

| | |
|---|---|
| Domain name | BAPIOPTION |
| Data type | CHAR     Character strings |
| No. of characters | 2 |
| Output length | 2 |
| Value table | |

Texts

☑ Maintain field labels

JJS (1) (800)   mssap2   OVR   11:07AM

Double-click on the BAPIOPTION located in the **Domain name** box of the **Domain** frame. You will get the following:

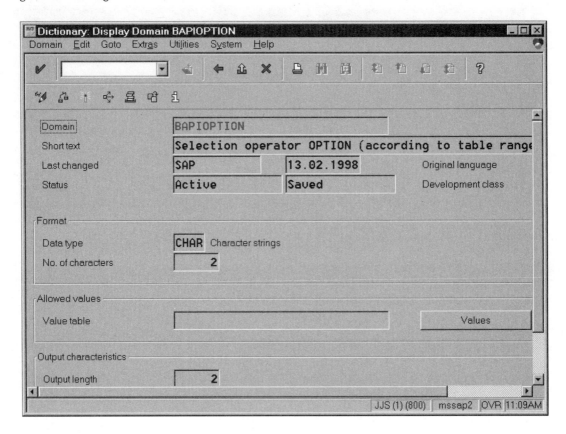

Now click on the **Values** button and you will be presented with the screen with values for this field:

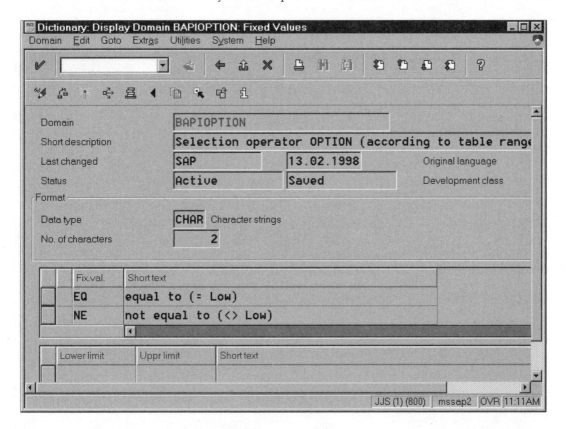

Scroll down to see all the values. These are the help values in question. Now go back to the BAPI Browser and drill down the REGION Field of the PERSONALDATA Parameter. You should get to the screen below:

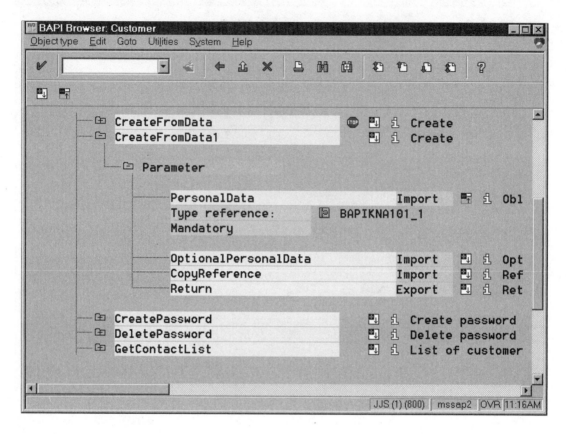

Double-click on BAPIKNA101_1 and you will see the following screen:

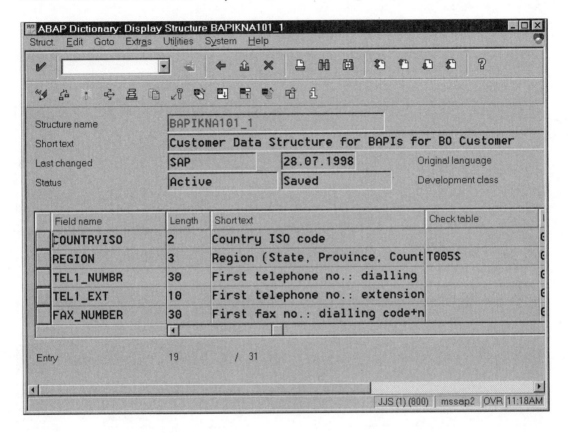

Scroll to see the Check table for the REGION Field and double-click on the T005S to get the following screen:

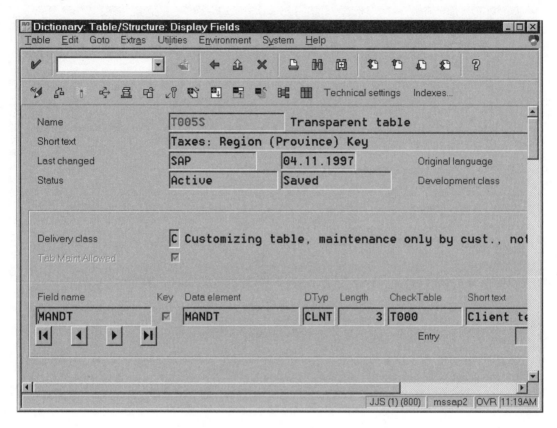

Now go to the Utilities | Table contents menu item, and you will be presented with the following screen:

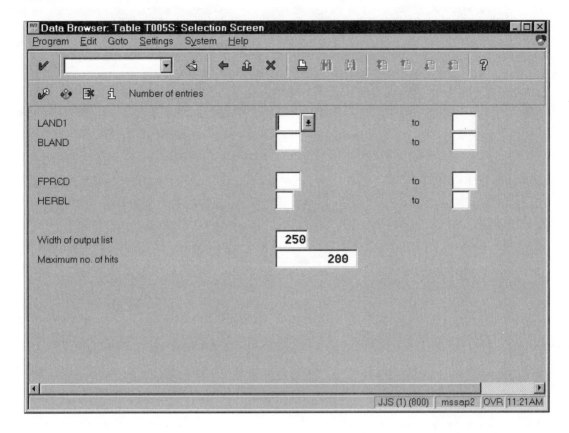

Hit the cherry-check button to get all the available help values and you will see the following:

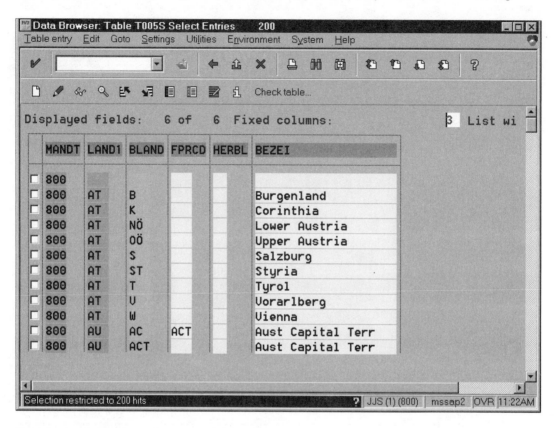

Now that we know the real source of help values, we can start looking and comparing it to the mechanism available to us from Visual Basic using BAPIs.

# Help Values From the Outside of SAP R/3

Fire up the SAP Assistant, or any other applications that you have built by now that browse the SAP R/3 Business Object Repository. Expand the Basis Application Hierarchy. Then expand the Helpvalues object:

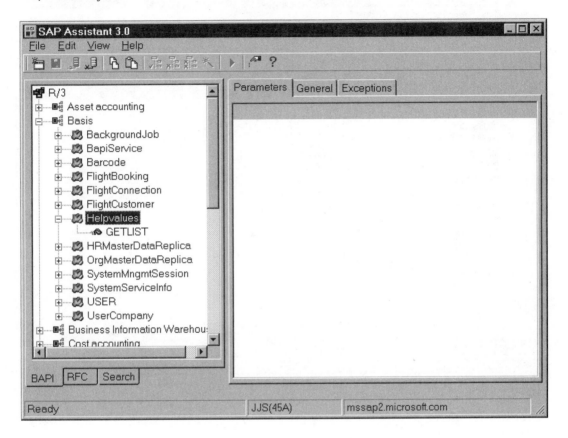

Firing up SAP R/3 implements the generic *Helpvalues* business object that allows you to view all help values for a field of a BAPI parameter. The *Helpvalues* object has a single method – the GETLIST BAPI. A look at the parameters of this BAPI reveals the following picture:

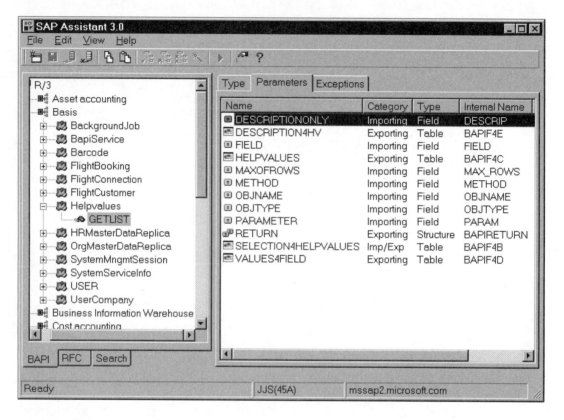

This BAPI works very logically. It accepts the business object name and/or business object type, Method (BAPI name), Parameter name and Field name. It will return you the following:

> ➢ HELPVALUES – The Table that contains composite values – one field with all the info

> ➢ VALUES4FIELD – The Table that contains only help values themselves without any descriptive characteristics

> ➢ DESCRIPTION4HV – The Table that contains the structure for the HELPVALUES records

I will now explain why we have so many return parameters and how to process them.

# Helpvalues Return Parameters

A record from the HELPVALUES table comprises a single 255-character long field. This field contains a cumulative value that includes not only the help values, but also detail and description information. For example, it might be US NY New York, where the actual help value itself is just NY.

Therefore, to enable dynamic record parsing for the HELPVALUES field we need another table that will bring us the layout for the help values record, which will change for every field. The DESCRIPTION4HV table does just that. Every record in the DESCRIPTION4HV table contains information on a meaningful unit of information in the HELPVALUES table. The structure of the DESCRIPTION4HV table is very self-explanatory:

| Name | Internal Name | Length | Decimal Positi | Description |
|------|--------------|--------|----------------|-------------|
| TABNAME | TABNAME | 30 | 0 | Table name |
| FIELDNAME | FIELDNAME | 30 | 0 | Field name |
| LANGU | LANGU | 1 | 0 | Language key |
| POSITION | POSITION | 4 | 0 | Position of the field in the table |
| OFFSET | OFFSET | 6 | 0 | Offset of a field in work area |
| LENG | LENG | 6 | 0 | Length (no. of characters) |
| FIELDTEXT | FIELDTEXT | 60 | 0 | Short text describing R/3 Reposit |
| REPTEXT | REPTEXT | 55 | 0 | Heading |
| SCRTEXT_S | SCRTEXT_S | 10 | 0 | Short field label |
| SCRTEXT_M | SCRTEXT_M | 20 | 0 | Medium field label |
| SCRTEXT_L | SCRTEXT_L | 40 | 0 | Long field label |

*Properties of DESCRIPTION4HV — General | Data Types | Value Info | Documentation*

The most important things needed to parse a record in the HELPVALUES table are the **OFFSET** and **LENG** values. Combined, they will allow us to get values for every virtual field in the HELPVALUES record.

The VALUES4FIELD table brings us only help values sans description data e.g. NY only. This is fine if the only things you need are help values. However, the full record in HELPVALUES contains descriptions and collateral information such as the country for the region.

The MAXROWS parameter of the GETLIST BAPI lets you limit the number of records that you are going to get from the BAPI call in the HELPVALUES table.

Another mechanism that you may use to narrow your search to specific values is the SELECTION4HELPVALUES table. It's normally used when you know a certain value in advance. For example, if you only want those regions that belong to a particular country. This is possible because of hierarchical relationships between the values. This table is similar to the IDRANGE table for the GETLIST BAPI of the *Customer* object. It has fields SELECT_FLD, which lets you specify the name of the field for the criterion, and SIGN, which is either the Include (I) or Exclude (E) flag.

The `OPTION` field has values for comparisons just like in `IDRANGE`. I will list these values here because they are generic:

> ➢ EQ – Equal
> ➢ NE – Not Equal
> ➢ GT – Greater Than
> ➢ LT – Less Than
> ➢ LE – Less than or Equal
> ➢ CP – Contains Pattern (wildcard type of criterion)
> ➢ NP – Does not contain Pattern
> ➢ BT – Between
> ➢ NB – Not Between

The `LOW` field of the `SELECTION4HELPVALUES` table lets you specify the beginning value to compare with, or the start of the comparison range; and the `HIGH` field is either empty or contains the end of the comparison range.

Because `SELECTION4HELPVALUES` is a table, you can have multiple rows, enabling you to specify multiple criteria. With multiple criteria, the question is always how this implements AND and OR logic. If, in SQL, I want to have multiple criteria, I can use `AND/OR` in the `WHERE` clause. For the `SELECTION4HELPVALUES` table the logic goes this way:

> **If you have the same field name for multiple rows in `SELECT_FLD`, it will implement the OR logic. If you have different field names AND logic will be implemented.**

To get a grip on this selection criteria implementation needs practice.

The `DESCRIPTIONONLY` parameter is a single fixed value flag. If set to `X` it will cause the `GETLIST` to return only `DESCRIPTION4HV` and the other tables will stay empty.

On top of all this, there is the standard `RETURN` structure that returns the status of the BAPI.

We can now develop a reusable component you can use in your development. To continue our tradition of presenting tabular data of fixed layout in the form of ADO Recordsets, I will develop a more generic `MakeAdoRs` function. This will return ADO Recordsets based on the Table parameters as defined in the SAP Table Factory control.

# Building the Help Values Project

Create a new project group and add
two projects named `Client_BH` and
`Srv_BH` – one **Standard EXE** for the
test client and an **ActiveX DLL** for the
help values server component:

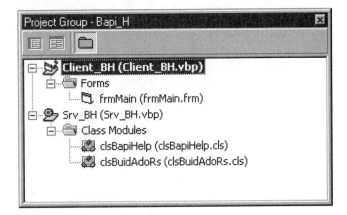

Because we use class modules, we cannot use the SAP Automation controls directly and don't have to
add them to the projects. However, both client and server components will need a reference to the
ADO library.

This project is built for a single desktop. However, you can easily implement the server component as
an ActiveX EXE and place it on a server. You can then modify both components for the server to
pass Strings, String arrays or XML structures to the client and for the client to parse them.

# The Server Project

First, we will develop a server component. This component has to perform the following:

> First, it should logon to the SAP R/3 of our choice

> It then has to prepare parameters for the BAPI call and call the BAPI

> Upon successful execution of the BAPI call, it has to convert Table parameters into ADO
Recordsets, preserving the structure of the initial Table parameter

This will allow us to integrate our BAPI related component into any MS tool that is capable of
working with ADO Recordsets, any Visual Studio application and any Internet application. It will
also allow us to save recordsets in either proprietary Microsoft or XML format.

Our component responsible for ADO conversions should not have any knowledge of the BAPI or the
BAPI Parameter it has to process, making it a truly generic SAP Automation Table–ADO Recordset
converter.

Based on this information, I decided to have two class modules in my server component. One will
implement connectivity and BAPI execution. This component, `clsBapiHelp`, will have hard-coded
business object information. This is no problem, because it is being built specifically to handle the
`GETLIST` BAPI of the *Helpvalues* business object.

The second class module in this component, clsBuildAdoRs, will implement the Table–ADO Recordset conversion. We will implement a minimal amount of functionality in this sample, to give you enough information to start your own more elaborate development.

## Connectivity and BAPI Execution – clsBapiHelp

We will first implement the familiar Logon functionality in the clsBapiHelp class module. To do so, we have to declare a variable for the Connection object. We will rely on the SAP BAPI control library functionality – it implements the Connection object, alleviating the need to use the SAP Logon control:

```
Option Explicit

Private msapConn As Object
Private msapBapi As Object
```

Before we do anything, we have to have a valid instance of the BAPI control object:

```
Private Sub Class_Initialize()

   Set msapBapi = CreateObject("SAP.BAPI.1")

End Sub
```

This is also a familiar technique. Because we define all our variables as abstract Objects, we cannot rely on the IntelliSense editor. The next step will be to logon to SAP R/3:

```
Public Function Logon()

   Set msapConn = msapBapi.Connection
   msapConn.Logon 1, False

End Function
```

This will implement a non-silent logon, prompting the user to enter attributes for the SAP R/3 logon.

### Preparing BAPI Parameters and Calling the BAPI

Once done, we can go on and implement all the BAPI related functionality. We need a function that prepares all the parameters for the GETLIST BAPI, calls it, checks for the return status and kicks off the ADO Recordset generation routines. This function is GetObject and accepts the following arguments:

```
Public Function GetObject(pObjName As String, pObjType As String, _
                    pMethod As String, pParam As String, _
                    pField As String, retHelpValues As ADODB.Recordset, _
                    retDescr4HV As ADODB.Recordset, _
                    retVals4Field As ADODB.Recordset, _
                    retResult As ADODB.Recordset, errMessage As String)
```

As we have already discussed in earlier chapters, the SAP BAPI control library offers all the necessary functionality for us, making the choice of tool obvious. In the course of my BAPI programming, I have developed some coding habits that save me time and effort. I will outline them for you here.

First, I always look up the list of parameters for the BAPI I will call and determine what parameters are mandatory. I always go to SAP R/3 itself because tools such as the SAP Assistant don't tell you whether or not a parameter is mandatory. SAP maintains the BAPI Catalog on their www.sap.com/bapi site where you can look up business objects with BAPIs. If you select a business object, you can get the help file that is going to list the Parameters without any specific information. That is why I always try to look it up in the SAP R/3 BOR directly.

Then I normally declare object variables for the business objects and all the BAPI parameters:

```
Dim sboHelpVals As Object
Dim bprHelpVals As Object
Dim bprDescripts As Object
Dim bprVals4Field As Object
Dim bprReturn As Object
```

- ➢ sboHelpVals is a variable for the *Helpvalues* business object
- ➢ bprHelpVals is a variable for the HELPVALUES Table parameter of the GETLIST BAPI
- ➢ bprDescripts is a variable for the DESCRIPTION4HV Table parameter of the GETLIST BAPI
- ➢ bprVals4Field is a variable for the VALUES4FIELD Table parameter of the GETLIST BAPI
- ➢ bprReturn is a variable for the RETURN structure parameter of the GETLIST BAPI

I don't want to invent any variable naming conventions for BAPI programming, but you may find it useful to keep certain standards. A three-letter prefix always serves me right, and it is consistent with traditional VB coding practices. Parameter names as defined in the BOR lend themselves naturally to variable names too. I always either copy them or truncate them if they are getting too long.

- ➢ sap – SAP Automation Toolkit library objects, e.g. sapLogon for the Logon object, sapConn for the Connection object.
- ➢ sbo – SAP Business Object
- ➢ bpr – BAPI Parameter
- ➢ bfl – BAPI Parameter Field
- ➢ bok – SAP Business Object Key Field
- ➢ bap – BAPI Object

*This is by no means any type of SAP or Microsoft "supported", "suggested" or "approved" naming convention. It's just to make the code more readable.*

After we declare all the variables, we can start using the SAP BAPI control library to create instances of the relevant objects. To do that, we will use the familiar `GetSAPObject` and `DimAs` methods of the `SAPBAPIControl` class, that we already have using the `CreateObject` function earlier in the project:

```
Set sboHelpVals = msapBapi.GetSAPObject("HelpValues")

Set bprHelpVals = msapBapi.DimAs(sboHelpVals, "GETLIST", "HELPVALUES")
Set bprDescripts = msapBapi.DimAs(sboHelpVals, "GETLIST", "DESCRIPTION4HV")
Set bprVals4Field = msapBapi.DimAs(sboHelpVals, "GETLIST", "VALUES4FIELD")
Set bprReturn = msapBapi.DimAs(sboHelpVals, "GETLIST", "RETURN")
```

*Remember that business object names are case-sensitive.*

After the instance of the business object is created, we execute the `DimAs` method to obtain valid running instances of Parameter objects for the BAPI. We now have all the necessary objects to actually call the BAPI:

```
sboHelpVals.GETLIST RETURN:=bprReturn, HELPVALUES:=bprHelpVals, _
                    VALUES4FIELD:=bprVals4Field, _
                    DESCRIPTION4HV:=bprDescripts, OBJNAME:=pObjName, _
                    METHOD:=pMethod, Parameter:=pParam, Field:=pField
```

We're using named arguments here, as suggested by SAP. It makes perfect sense, since we don't have any way of determining the ordinal numbers for the BAPI parameters. However, be careful with the spelling of the BAPI parameters.

After we call the BAPI, and it does not give us a run-time error, we have to check the `RETURN` structure to determine the status of the BAPI call:

```
If bprReturn("TYPE") = "E" Then
    errMessage = bprReturn("MESSAGE")
    Exit Function
End If
```

The logic behind the above routine is simple. I just check the content of the `TYPE` field of the `RETURN` structure. If it contains `"E"`, indicating an error during the BAPI's execution in SAP R/3, I assign the value of the `MESSAGE` field of the `RETURN` structure to the argument to be returned to the calling routine.

## Table to ADO Recordset Conversion – clsBuildAdoRs

If the BAPI call was successful, we can start our ADO conversion routines. To perform a very elementary but truly generic Parameter table to ADO Recordset conversion I developed the `MakeAdoRs` function, defined as a method of the `clsBuildAdoRs` class.

The General Declarations for the `clsBuildAdoRs` class module reads as presented below:

```
Option Explicit

Private Const RfcChar = 0
Private Const RfcNum = 6
```

The function itself looks like this:

```
Public Function MakeAdoRs(pXTab As Object, adoRet As ADODB.Recordset)

    Dim adoFld As ADODB.Field
    Dim bapFld As Object

    Dim intCols As Integer
    Dim intRows As Integer

    On Error GoTo ErrTrap

    For Each bapFld In pXTab.Columns

        Select Case bapFld.Type
          Case RfcChar
            adoRet.Fields.Append bapFld.Name, adChar, bapFld.IntLength
          Case RfcNum
            adoRet.Fields.Append bapFld.Name, adChar, bapFld.IntLength
        End Select

    Next

    adoRet.Open

    For intRows = 1 To pXTab.RowCount
      adoRet.AddNew

      For intCols = 1 To pXTab.ColumnCount
        adoRet.Fields(pXTab.Columns(intCols).Name) = _
                    pXTab.Value(intRows, intCols)
      Next

      adoRet.Update
    Next

    Set adoFld = Nothing
    Set bapFld = Nothing

    Exit Function

ErrTrap:

    MsgBox Err.Description & vbCrLf & "From clsBuildAdoRs - MakeAdoRs"

End Function
```

The logic of this function is simple. This function is passed an object argument for the Table parameter of the BAPI call, pXTab, and the variable for the resultant ADO recordset, adoRet. The resultant ADO Recordset has to have a structure that mirrors the structure of the Table parameter. This is similar to the routine in the previous project, RFC_RUN:

```
For Each bapFld In pXTab.Columns

   Select Case bapFld.Type
     Case RfcChar
       adoRet.Fields.Append bapFld.Name, adChar, bapFld.IntLength
     Case RfcNum
       adoRet.Fields.Append bapFld.Name, adChar, bapFld.IntLength
   End Select

Next
```

In the above code segment, we simply loop through the Columns collection of the Table object, the same as the one defined in the SAP Table Factory control library. Here, we also make a modest attempt to map the RFC Data Types to the ADO Field types.

As you may remember in the previous project, we simply mapped all RFC data types to the Character field type in the ADO recordset. This will work, but it will not provide you with the ability to treat the ADO Recordset as data and will not be the structure's mirror. If that is what you need, you have to expand the switch routine, adding all the RFC data types and corresponding ADO Field types.

> *You can find values for the RFC data types in the Enum CRFCType defined in the SAP Table Factory control library. You can then use these to define your constants just like in this project. Do not take the names of the RFC types literally. One would assume that RfcNum would translate into the Integer or Long data type. It does not. It is a character field that can contain only numeric characters.*

After the ADO Recordset is created, we populate it by iterating through the 2-dimensional Value property of the Table object:

```
adoRet.Open

For intRows = 1 To pXTab.RowCount
  adoRet.AddNew

  For intCols = 1 To pXTab.ColumnCount
    adoRet.Fields(pXTab.Columns(intCols).Name) = _
               pXTab.Value(intRows, intCols)
  Next

  adoRet.Update
Next
```

This is easy to do, because the structures of both the Table and the Recordset are the same. However, to prevent any ordinal conflicts, I refer to the ADO Recordset Fields by name. We now have a regular ADO Recordset that has the layout of the BAPI Table parameter and the data from it.

I have to call this function for all the Table parameters I wish to convert into ADO Recordsets, and I do that upon successful execution of the BAPI in the `clsBapiHelp`'s `GetObject` function:

```
If bprReturn("TYPE") = "E" Then
    errMessage = bprReturn("MESSAGE")
    Exit Function
End If
```

```
madoMake.MakeAdoRs bprHelpVals, retHelpValues
madoMake.MakeAdoRs bprDescripts, retDescr4HV
madoMake.MakeAdoRs bprVals4Field, retVals4Field
```

where `madoMake` **is a reference to** `clsBuildAdoRs`:

```
Option Explicit

Private msapConn As Object
Private msapBapi As Object

'reference to the ADO converter
Private madoMake As clsBuildAdoRs


Private Sub Class_Initialize()

    Set msapBapi = CreateObject("SAP.BAPI.1")
    Set madoMake = New clsBuildAdoRs

End Sub
```

## Structuring the Recordset

If we stop at this point in our project, we will have the Help Values table, the Description For Help Values table and the Values for Field table. This is very useful, but it still does not give us a structured recordset that contains parsed values of the help values records, and has the structure described in the Description for Help Values table.

Additionally, if you want to save help values in some lookup table in your RDBMS, it is much more intuitive to use a single ADO Recordset with all the values and their structure.

To do this, I have developed another routine that takes the Help Values table and Description For Help Values table, and creates a resultant recordset that has the structure defined in Description For Help Values. This recordset is populated by values that I get by parsing the `HELPVALUES` field of the Help Values table according to the Description For Help Values table content. This routine is `MakeResultsRs` and is called at the end of `GetObject` function:

```
madoMake.MakeAdoRs bprHelpVals, retHelpValues
madoMake.MakeAdoRs bprDescripts, retDescr4HV
madoMake.MakeAdoRs bprVals4Field, retVals4Field

retDescr4HV.MoveFirst

MakeResultRs retResult, retDescr4HV, retHelpValues
```

```
      Set sboHalpVals = Nothing
      Set bprHelpVals = Nothing
      Set bprDescripts = Nothing
      Set bprVals4Field = Nothing
      Set bprReturn = Nothing

      Exit Function

ErrTrap:

   MsgBox Err.Description & vbCrLf & "From clsBapiHelp - GetObject"

End Function
```

The main point here is that content or structure does not relate these two tables – there is no point in joining them. One table describes the layout of the values in the other table. The number of *Records* in the Description for Help Values table determines the number of *Fields* in the resultant recordset. Because this routine is very specific to Help Values we will define it in the `clsBapiHelp` class:

```
Public Function MakeResultRs(retResultM As ADODB.Recordset, _
                             retDescr4HVM As ADODB.Recordset, _
                             retHelpValuesM As ADODB.Recordset)

   Dim aintLen() As Integer
   Dim aintOffset() As Integer

   Dim intCount As Integer
   Dim intArrayCount As Integer

   On Error GoTo ErrTrap

' Builds a disconnected ADO recordset based on description table
   Do Until retDescr4HVM.EOF
      ' Uses SCRTEXT_S for field names and LENG for length
      retResultM.Fields.Append retDescr4HVM![SCRTEXT_S], adChar, _
                             retDescr4HVM![LENG]

      ' Increments arrays subscript
      intArrayCount = intArrayCount + 1
      ' Creates new array elements
      ReDim Preserve aintLen(intArrayCount)
      ReDim Preserve aintOffset(intArrayCount)

      ' Populates arrays with values
      ' Could use the DefinedSize property of the ADO field to determine
      ' the length during parsing but need array for offset anyway
      ' - two synch arrays more intuitive code
      aintLen(intArrayCount) = CInt(retDescr4HVM![LENG])
      aintOffset(intArrayCount) = CInt(retDescr4HVM![Offset])

      retDescr4HVM.MoveNext

   Loop

   retHelpValuesM.MoveFirst

   retResultM.Open
```

```
' Populate the result recordset
Do Until retHelpValuesM.EOF

    With retResultM
        .AddNew

        For intCount = 1 To retDescr4HVM.RecordCount
            .Fields(intCount - 1) = _
            Mid(retHelpValuesM![HELPVALUES], _
            IIf(aintOffset(intCount) = 0, 1, aintOffset(intCount)), _
                aintLen(intCount))
        Next

        retResultM.Update
    End With

    retHelpValuesM.MoveNext

Loop

retHelpValuesM.MoveFirst

retResultM.Open

' Populate the result recordset
Do Until retHelpValuesM.EOF

    With retResultM
        .AddNew

        For intCount = 1 To retDescr4HVM.RecordCount
            .Fields(intCount - 1) = _
            Mid(retHelpValuesM![HELPVALUES], _
            IIf(aintOffset(intCount) = 0, 1, aintOffset(intCount)), _
                aintLen(intCount))
        Next

        retResultM.Update
    End With

    retHelpValuesM.MoveNext

Loop


    Exit Function

ErrTrap:

    MsgBox Err.Description & vbCrLf & "From clsBapiHelp - MakeResultRs"

End Function
```

The function takes *two* ADO Recordset arguments that bring in the ADO Recordset containing the help values, retHelpValuesM, and the Recordset containing the description for help values, retDescr4HVM. It returns the resultant Recordset, retResultM, that is structured and populated as described above.

First, we have to create the resultant recordset:

```
Do Until retDescr4HVM.EOF
    ' Uses SCRTEXT_S for field names and LENG for length
    retResultM.Fields.Append retDescr4HVM![SCRTEXT_S], adChar, _
                            retDescr4HVM![LENG]

    ' Increments arrays subscript
    intArrayCount = intArrayCount + 1
    ' Creates new array elements
    ReDim Preserve aintLen(intArrayCount)
    ReDim Preserve aintOffset(intArrayCount)

    ' Populates arrays with values
    ' Could use the DefinedSize property of the ADO field to determine
    ' the length during parsing but need array for offset anyway
    ' - two synch arrays more intuitive code
    aintLen(intArrayCount) = CInt(retDescr4HVM![LENG])
    aintOffset(intArrayCount) = CInt(retDescr4HVM![Offset])

    retDescr4HVM.MoveNext

Loop
```

We iterate through the Description for Help Values recordset and create one field in the result recordset for each record in the Description for Help Values recordset. We use the value of the SCRTEXT_S field of the Description for Help Values recordset for the name of fields in the resultant recordset, and the value of the LENG field for the length of the field. All fields are of the Character type.

In the same loop, I also populate two dynamic arrays – one to hold values for OFFSET and another for LENG. To correctly parse the HELPVALUES field, I need both the offset and the length, and I have no other way of getting them except from the Description for Help Values Table. It is algorithmically illogical to try doing it directly in the parsing routine, and that is why I have created two synchronized arrays. I could have gotten fancier with collections or Dictionary objects, but arrays are just fine here – minimum overhead, ease of ordinal synchronization and minimum resource consumption.

After I'm done with creating the resultant recordset, I can start populating it:

```
retHelpValuesM.MoveFirst

retResultM.Open

Populate the result recordset
Do Until retHelpValuesM.EOF

    With retResultM
        .AddNew

        For intCount = 1 To retDescr4HVM.RecordCount
            .Fields(intCount - 1) = _
            Mid(retHelpValuesM![HELPVALUES], _
            IIf(aintOffset(intCount) = 0, 1, aintOffset(intCount)), _
                aintLen(intCount))
        Next
```

```
        retResultM.Update
    End With

    retHelpValuesM.MoveNext

  Loop
```

The core of this fragment is the Mid function. It gets part of the HELPVALUES field based on the OFFSET for the start and LENG for the length. These values come from the arrays I described earlier. The caveat here is that if the value for the offset is zero, and it is for the first field, the Mid function will generate an **Invalid Function Call** run-time error. To avoid this, I use the IIF statement, that will let me use 1 if the offset is zero and its value when it is not.

Upon execution of the whole function, we will have a well-structured ADO Recordset that has all the values from the HELPVALUES table. We have in fact built an ActiveX DLL component that you can use as a framework to build your own component or reuse as is.

# The Client Project

To test it, we will create a very simple client project, CLIENT_BH with a single form and the following GUI:

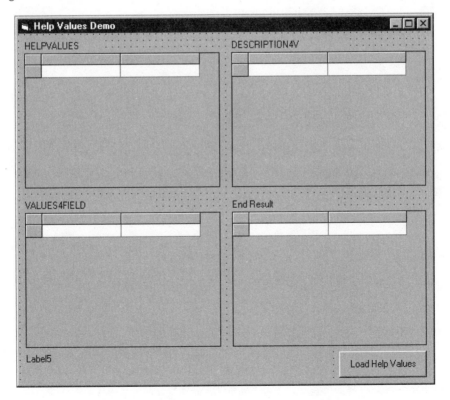

It has four Microsoft Data Grid controls that can be dynamically bound to a disconnected ADO Recordset. They will display all BAPI Table parameters and the resultant recordset so we can visualize our results.

Add the following code to the **General Declarations** section of the form:

```
Option Explicit

'Reference to the help values server component
Private mobjBapiHelpSrv As New clsBapiHelp
```

The single command button sets it all in motion:

```
Private Sub Command1_Click()

   Dim adoHelpValues As New ADODB.Recordset
   Dim adoDescr4Values As New ADODB.Recordset
   Dim adoVals4Field As New ADODB.Recordset
   Dim adoEndResult As New ADODB.Recordset

   Dim sapObjName As String
   Dim sapObjType As String
   Dim sapMethod As String
   Dim sapParameter As String
   Dim sapField As String
   Dim errVal As String

   On Error GoTo ErrTrap

   mobjBapiHelpSrv.Logon

   sapObjName = "Customer"
   sapObjType = ""
   sapMethod = "CREATEFROMDATA1"
   sapParameter = "PERSONALDATA"
   sapField = "REGION"

' Commented code shows different values for the BAPI parameters
' mobjBapiHelpSrv.GetObject "Customer", "KNA1", "CREATEFROMDATA1", _
'                           "PERSONALDATA", "REGION", adoRs, adoRsd, ret

' mobjBapiHelpSrv.GetObject "", "KNA1", "CREATEFROMDATA1", _
'                           "PERSONALDATA", "REGION", adors, adorsd, ret

   mobjBapiHelpSrv.GetObject sapObjName, sapObjType, sapMethod, _
                       sapParameter, sapField, adoHelpValues, _
                       adoDescr4Values, adoVals4Field, adoEndResult, _
                       errVal

   If Trim(errVal) <> "" Then
     MsgBox "BAPI Error - " & errVal
     Exit Sub
   End If

' display hardcoded values
   Label5 = "Business Object - " & sapObjName & " BAPI - " & sapMethod & _
            " Parameter - " & sapParameter & " Field - " & sapField
```

```
      Set DataGrid1.DataSource = adoHelpValues
      Set DataGrid2.DataSource = adoDescr4Values
      Set DataGrid3.DataSource = adoVals4Field
      Set DataGrid4.DataSource = adoEndResult

      Set adoHelpValues = Nothing
      Set adoDescr4Values = Nothing
      Set adoVals4Field = Nothing
      Set adoEndResult = Nothing

      Exit Sub

   ErrTrap:

      MsgBox Err.Description & vbCrLf & "From Command1_Click"

   End Sub
```

First, we define variables for the ADO Recordsets that the `GetObject` method of the `clsBapiHelp` class expects. Then we declare variables for the other arguments of the `GetObject` method.

> *Note that I included three variations of the call to the `GetObject` method. They are different only in regards to the Object Name and Object Type arguments. The `GETLIST` BAPI of the `HelpValues` business object allows you to pass either the name of the Business Object – `Customer` – or the Type – `KNA1`. It is more intuitive to deal with names, just bear in mind that they are case-sensitive.*

Then we call the `Logon` method of the `clsBapiHelp` class and set variables:

```
   mobjBapiHelpSrv.Logon

   sapObjName = "Customer"
   sapObjType = ""
   sapMethod = "CREATEFROMDATA1"
   sapParameter = "PERSONALDATA"
   sapField = "REGION"
```

I then test for the status of the BAPI call:

```
   If Trim(errVal) <> "" Then
     MsgBox "BAPI Error - " & errVal
     Exit Sub
   End If
```

If everything is OK, I assign ADO Recordsets to the appropriate grid controls:

```
   Set DataGrid1.DataSource = adoHelpValues
   Set DataGrid2.DataSource = adoDescr4Values
   Set DataGrid3.DataSource = adoVals4Field
   Set DataGrid4.DataSource = adoEndResult
```

The result for the values that I hard-coded (business object – *Customer*, BAPI – `CreateFromData1`, Parameter – `PERSONALDATA`, Field – `REGION`) is as follows:

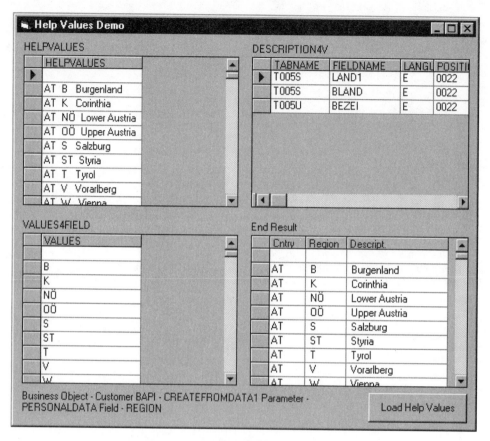

As you may now observe we have completed our task of reliably getting help values from SAP R/3. From this point, you can adorn this demo project with Explorer style browsing to look-up all the fields that have help values, and do many other things. However, the core functionality will not change.

# Summary

This chapter is very rich on code, and I have tried to give it a meaningful ending. SAP R/3 BOR browsing is very important, and we have learned how to do it. It is possible to bypass the SAP Repository library and do it all using direct RFC calls. However, that requires a much deeper knowledge of the SAP Business Object Framework. The problems with the current library and the SAP Assistant are performance, and some very important values that they do not provide – such as the mandatory indicator for BAPI parameters, ordinal number for BAPI parameters and help values.

The good news is that you can do it all yourself using the RFC control library. As you get more exposure to the enormous wealth of the SAP R/3 RFC and business object functionality, you will not only respect this software more, but you will be able to create your own components, performing tasks similar to the SAP Automation controls.

The help values type of project will become a staple for all SAP R/3 integration books. It provides needed functionality and illustrates the viability of the BAPI related technology. Another powerful example you might want to implement is to create customers in SAP R/3 from your RDBMS using a BAPI. You have all the tools necessary for it: logon, create an instance of the business object, prepare parameters for the BAPI, populate the Table or Structure parameters, call the BAPI and analyze the RETURN argument.

This chapter also concludes our review of the SAP Automation Toolkit. The following chapters will be devoted to the Microsoft DCOM Component Connector and the opportunities that this tool opens for the integration of SAP R/3 into existing information systems.

# 9

# Retrospection

It's very useful at some point of a serious undertaking to step aside and reflect on what you have done. This book is structured to have three logical parts:

> ➢ A general SAP R/3 overview
> ➢ Visual Basic programming using the SAP Automation toolkit
> ➢ Using the SAP DCOM Component Connector

We have already covered the first two items on this list.

## The SAP Automation Toolkit Reviewed

We've just been discussing the SAP Automation toolkit in reasonable detail. I tried to introduce all the major components of this toolkit. We discussed the main aspects of SAP R/3 programming using Visual Basic, starting from how you connect to SAP R/3, all the way to getting data out of it. We also investigated the architecture and purpose of the SAP R/3 Business Object Repository, and how SAP's implementation of objects relates to COM's.

To lay the foundation for our future development, we created some proof of concept type of projects. These projects were created with the principle of reusability in mind, giving you the opportunity to either use them as they are, or as a framework for your components.

Probably our single most important achievement is that we were able to prove that Visual Basic is very suitable for SAP R/3 programming. It gives programmers of the Microsoft domain an enormous advantage. We can all treat SAP R/3 as just another complex back-end component with transparent integration. This is conceptually similar to the OLEDB and ODBC technology – the intricacies of the RDBMS are transparent to the Visual Basic programmer.

This provides us with the ability to integrate SAP R/3 into our familiar programmatic paradigm without any significant effort. All we have to do is learn yet another set of controls and libraries. We have to laud the SAP effort in enabling practically seamless integration of its flagship product into the COM environment.

The discussion on the SAP Automation package would be incomplete without one simple statement – it is a **Desktop Integration SDK**. It includes more than the OCX components and COM compliant DLL components that we used. It also includes a traditional SDK for C++ and Java programmers.

However, we've concentrated on the components that are readily usable from Visual Basic. Those components provide us with a focused functionality that we can use to extend them and build complex applications.

Each component by itself does not solve an application domain problem. In other words, it does not offer an end-to-end solution. And that's exactly how the components are supposed to behave – provide encapsulated functionality to be used in conjunction with other components. All needs that the Visual Basic programmer may have are addressed through some SAP Automation component – we can connect to SAP R/3, browse the BOR, save metadata into a local Jet database, get data out of SAP R/3 and load data in.

# SAP Automation Toolkit Shortcomings

As with all SDK, the SAP Automation toolkit requires considerable programming effort to create a working and meaningful application. If we abstract ourselves from the cosmetic features of the toolkit, all it does is provide the bridge between RFC standards and COM standards. It also resolves conflicts between the RFC communication mechanism and the COM communication mechanism, including data types, communication protocols etc.

What it does not do is provide components that could have acted as proxies to SAP R/3 business objects out of the box. It provides you with the mechanism to implement the functionality yourself.

One issue that is not intuitively addressed in SAP Automation is data representation. The Table Factory control is a great tool, but it does not offer the data objects that Visual Basic and other programmers have come to expect: namely a Recordset object. The results of a BAPI call are returned in the Table object, and to use them we had to resort to multi-dimensional array handling antics. Moreover, the Table object of the Table Factory has no commonalties with the DAO Table or the ADO Table. And this feature renders the data handling code that you already have in your Visual Basic applications obsolete. The only choice you have is to create a functionally symmetrical but algorithmically different data handling layer.

Another inconvenience is that you can't reference an SAP R/3 business object in your applications directly to define variables as BOR objects. You have to declare the variable as an abstract object and then instantiate it using methods of the BAPI control library.

It's also difficult to look up methods and properties of the business object. You have to either use the SAP Assistant or build you own tool to look up BAPI names, parameters, fields etc.

C or Visual Basic programmers may feel compelled to write a wrapper around similar looking BAPI calls. This will be fine, until you try to dynamically generate BAPI calls – every BAPI has a different number of arguments, there is no logic behind the number or ordinal position of these arguments, plus SAP suggests you use named arguments. The situation gets worse if you consider the fact that SAP has already enabled hundreds of externally accessible BAPIs and RFCs. This number will grow with every release, and playing catch-up with it could prove difficult. Additionally, you are responsible for all data type mapping and transformation.

This is by no means a complete list of the SAP Automaton toolkit's shortcomings. But it's not supposed to do everything. It offers the enabling technology and a wide selection of well-designed components that let you create any application. The only thing that limits you is SAP R/3's internal constraints.

# DCOM Component Connector

The next logical progression would be to create a tool or technology that provides us with ready to use components encapsulating SAP R/3 business object functionality. It should also take care of all data conversions and integrate the RFC table data with the OLEDB representation of it. This should be done intuitively and generically – independent from the SAP R/3 release and the flavor of Windows you are using.

All this is implemented in the **DCOM Component Connector – DCOM CC**. It's advisable to download this tool from the `www.sap.com/bapi` COM section – that way you'll get the latest version of it. The DCOM CC is not an SDK, but rather an extension to the SDK. And this is what makes it a ready to use tool that produces focused results, rather than functionality.

The rest of this book will be devoted to the DCOM CC – its configuration, functionality and application.

# 10

# Introducing the DCOM Component Connector

This part of the book introduces the **DCOM Component Connector (DCOM CC)**. This is an SAP R/3 – Microsoft Windows integration tool, developed by the SAP middleware team with support from Microsoft. At the moment of writing, it's the only integration technology developed by SAP itself for the native integration of SAP R/3 into any operating system or programming environment. This fact itself makes Microsoft Windows a bona fide environment for integration of SAP R/3. From my perspective, it's an indicator that this technology is the one I would use to integrate SAP R/3 into my applications.

We have already discussed in depth the problems of integration, and why the Windows OS is especially suited to the purpose. We've also seen the implementation of the SAP Automation Desktop Integration SDK, and explored the functionality of its core components. The SAP Automation toolkit enables you to execute BAPI and RFC calls, and to explore the SAP R/3 Business Object Repository in online and offline modes.

As we demonstrated in previous chapters, SAP has implemented a robust RFC communication mechanism so that external applications can communicate with SAP R/3. This mechanism is enabled in the SAP Automation toolkit through the BAPI control and the RFC control libraries.

It's important to remember that SAP R/3 implements its own data formats and internal data exchange. The mechanism of loading data into and getting data out of SAP R/3 has historically been robust and cumbersome at the same time. The internal implementation of the SAP R/3 Application Server is indeed robust and very solid. The RFC communication mechanism is also well designed. The problem is that the format that SAP R/3 expects you to exchange data with is anything but easily integrated into any existing IT infrastructure. This was probably the most powerful factor that motivated SAP to implement the business object framework.

# The DCOM CC

The SAP Automation toolkit provided us with programmatic and infrastructure components to integrate SAP R/3 into conventional Windows data-processing systems. The target architecture for such integration would be as follows:

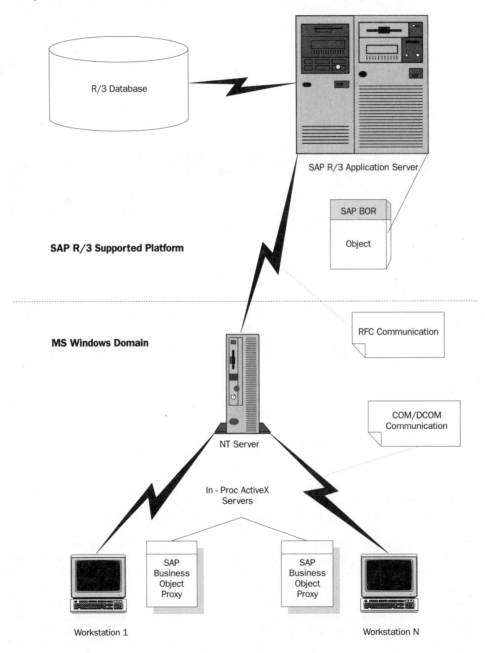

The NT Server on the above diagram may play two roles:

> The ordinary NT Server, without any SAP related implementation
> The host for SAP related components that applications on client workstations can use

The difference in implementation will not change the SAP R/3 – Windows applications integration strategy. The main idea behind that strategy is to give Windows application developers (and as far as this book is concerned, Visual Basic developers) the ability to treat SAP R/3 business objects as native COM components. And this is what the DCOM CC is all about.

# DCOM CC – Problem Statement

To successfully build and implement any software solution it's imperative to first have a clear outline of what problems the software has to address, and what should be implemented as a solution. I have found that problem analysis is a very productive place to start in learning any new technology. So let's list the areas that a tool such as the DCOM CC has to address, and then move on to exploring how the DCOM CC does it.

> To provide a seamless integration of SAP R/3 into any platform or software, it's imperative to first pinpoint what exactly will be integrated. A system of the complexity of SAP R/3 can't simply be used as a back-end RDBMS or data-processing application.

> Moreover, it is necessary to have functionality provided by the software vendor (in our case SAP) which allows you to programmatically use the functionality of their tool externally.

> The tool must provide a single uniform environment for SAP R/3 business object programming. The environmental configuration is always a tedious undertaking, especially for application programmers. It should be basically this way: if I have a connection to SAP R/3 and Visual Studio on my workstation, I can program any business object available in the SAP R/3 BOR.

> Finally, we have to address the issue of converting RFC tables and structures into the standard Windows data representation technology. At the moment, this would be OLEDB/ADO. We have already performed this operation on a rudimentary level in samples for previous chapters – we created disconnected ADO Recordsets based on the RFC table or structure metadata and then populated them.

The answer to the first part of our problem lies in the business need of such an integration. What we need from SAP R/3 is its Application Server functionality. External applications should not be aware of the SAP R/3 internal implementation specifics. They have to use a relatively high level of abstraction dealing with the SAP R/3 functionality. This is exactly what the SAP Open Business Framework is all about – SAP exposed its core application functionality via business objects and BAPIs.

To draw a very conceptual analogy, if SAP R/3 is Windows then the BAPIs are Win32 APIs. This analogy is obviously technically inaccurate. But BAPIs simply enable the use of services provided by some system externally. If we look one level deeper, we can recall that behind every BAPI is an RFC that does not belong to any business object. And the analogy SAP R/3 RFC – Win32 API becomes clearer. There's nothing conceptually new here. In fact, Visual Basic was built around the idea of alleviating programmers from low-level Windows API programming by encapsulating a logical sequence of API calls into reusable components.

The logical progression from this discussion would be to state that the first problem that the DCOM CC has to address is to implement the SAP R/3 business objects as COM components. Recall our initial discussion on how to program SAP R/3 from Visual Basic. Remember, you cannot reference any library or control and get a reference to a COM implementation of the business object from the SAP Automation toolkit. And this is the area that has to be addressed first.

The implementation of business objects as COM components eliminates the biggest chunk of problems that the Visual Basic programmer faces in integrating SAP R/3 into regular applications. Remember, it's not about building applications that perform BAPI calls, it is about integrating SAP R/3 functionality into your existing applications or productivity tools without any paradigm shifts.

The SAP Automation SDK offers a set of components that you need to employ simultaneously to program against SAP R/3 business objects. This means an increase in the number of referenced components and therefore potential failure points in your applications. Plus, you have to master all of the different components. However, this does not diminish the importance of the SAP Automation SDK. Remember, the SAP Automation is an SDK and the DCOM CC is a logical progression of the SAP Automation. DCOM CC is an extension to the RFC SDK built for a specific purpose – to provide proxy components for SAP R/3 business objects. It is therefore more robust in that area. The SAP RFC SDK, the SAP Automation Desktop SDK, and the DCOM CC are mutually complementary and relate to each other.

## Implementation of the DCOM CC

Let's move on to address the physical implementation of the COM proxies for the SAP R/3 business objects. There is a very clear choice – the ActiveX in-process server (DLL).

First of all, the component we need has to be natively accessed and integrated into Microsoft tools and applications. Native access means that the Visual Basic developer should be able to simply reference the component as a library and get access to all its functionality. An alternative choice could have been to develop an API-style DLL with exportable functions, but while this may be easier to implement technically, it violates the COM nature of the component.

The choice of a DLL as opposed to an out-of-process server is a logical one. These components have to be implemented without some sort of a client application. They are proxies after all. That's why implementing them as out-of-process components would not make much sense. Also, a DLL is a native implementation of a component when it comes to Microsoft Transaction Server or SQL Server. Normally, you implement the component as an out-of-process server (EXE component) if it has to be used remotely or has to be a stand-alone application. None of these applies to the SAP business object proxies.

This fits in with the whole idea of the SAP R/3 business object. SAP implemented its functionality as business objects based on its internal proprietary component definition standards. Regardless of their unique implementation, those components adhere to the rules of object-oriented programming and implement logical abstraction to data access. In Windows, the standard governing the analogous issue is COM. Therefore, if we could map RFC components to COM components, our problem would be solved. The diagram below shows the structural layout of this concept:

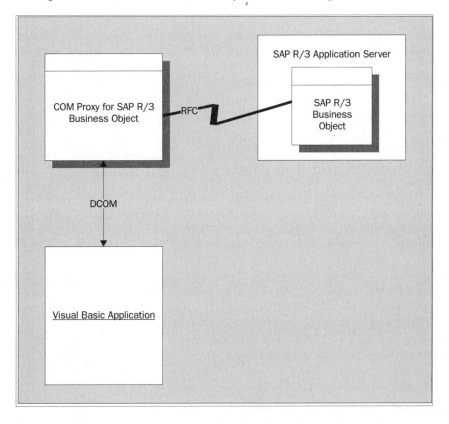

To summarize our introduction, we can say that SAP R/3 can be integrated into the Windows environment via COM business object proxies. Therefore, any tool that provides integration functionality has to be capable of generating COM business object proxies in the form of ActiveX DLLs.

# SAP DCOM Connector Component Implementation

As I mentioned at the beginning of this chapter, the DCOM CC is an SAP creation. SAP bundles it with its front-end 4.5, and SAP stands behind this product as it does for the rest of the SAP product family. I stress this because tools of the complexity of SAP R/3 can have a substantial impact on the mission-critical data of your enterprise – we are all better off with original SAP produced software.

Remember that SAP R/3 is very proprietary in terms of internal implementation. Every attempt by an external software vendor to implement SAP R/3 related, but not SAP provided, functionality would amount to some sort of reverse engineering of SAP R/3. I may contradict my nature as a software developer here, but I do not recommend that you try 'figuring out' SAP R/3. You may guess right for some things, but one wrong move and invaluable data or your reputation goes up in smoke. SAP guarantees data integrity of its supported and implemented functionality. The best result that you can achieve with SAP R/3 is when you work with it, not against it.

On the other side of the DCOM CC is Microsoft. Microsoft developers supported the SAP middleware team in their efforts to create the DCOM CC, and there's no need to question the COM and OLEDB/ADO expertise of Microsoft. In other words, you have a tool that implements the technology created, supported and recommended by SAP and Microsoft.

# Summary of Functionality

The DCOM CC is built on the top of the SAP R/3 RFC SDK, and relies on the `LIBRFC32.DLL` that implements all the connectivity functionality. This DLL is part of the SAP RFC SDK. The DCOM CC is implemented as a set of ActiveX DLLs that are created by the installation routine of the DCOM CC.

The DCOM CC itself is available as part of the SAP RFC SDK 4.5A or as an unrestricted download from the `www.sap.com/bapi` COM Section. Note that, unlike the SAP Automation, it is not available from the `www.saplabs.com` as Version 4.6 A.

> *I strongly recommend reading "Expanding the Reach of Your SAP Business Processes", also available from the* `www.sap.com/bapi` *COM Section. It will further expand your knowledge of the DCOM CC in areas that are beyond the scope of this book. In addition, you are welcome to frequent the DCOM CC Q & A area.*

The system requirements for the DCOM CC are:

- Microsoft Windows NT 4 with SP 3 or greater, Win95 or Win98
- Microsoft Data Access Components MDAC 1.5 or greater
- Microsoft Transaction Server – MTS 2.0 (Although not actually necessary it is recommended that you have MTS installed)
- Microsoft Windows Scripting Host
- Microsoft Internet Explorer IE 4.1 or greater
- IIS or Personal Web Server
- Microsoft Visual C++ 5.0 or 6.0 to use the Object Builder

After you download or otherwise install the SAP RFC SDK, you should see the following directory structure:

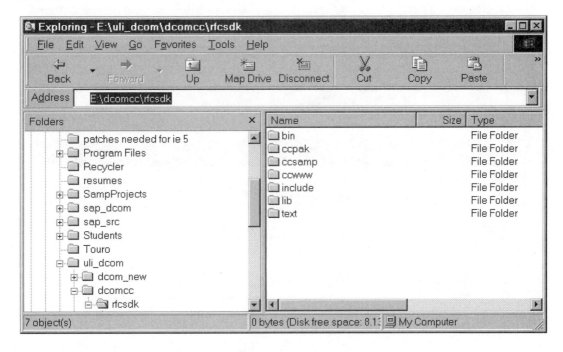

*The main DLL that implements all needed functionality for DCOM CC is the LIBRFC32.DLL, and it gets installed into the Winnt\System32 directory. If you had an old version of this DLL from RFC SDK or a previous version of the DCOM CC, I recommend unregistering and renaming it prior to a new installation. If you had the old version of the DCOM CC, delete all relevant components from MTS and then unregister them prior to the new installation. You may consider creating a small BAT file for environmental setups.*

You may question why SAP implement a browser-based GUI for the DCOM CC. This is done to emphasize the ability to employ the IIS to work with this tool remotely via the Internet or intranet.

# Installation and Configuration

To start using the DCOM CC go to the CCWWW folder and locate the DEFAULT.HTM file. You may consider creating a shortcut to this file for future use. Double-click on it:

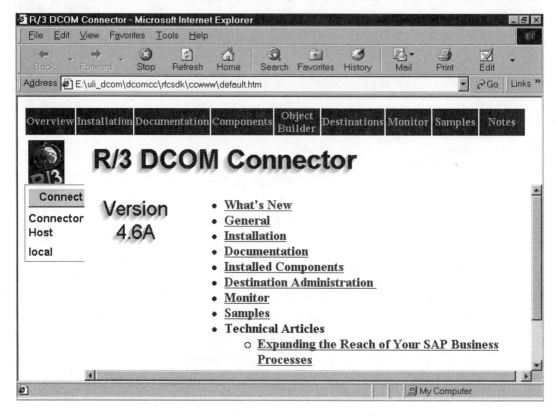

This is a main or start page for the DCOM CC and you can find all the functionality and support materials from this page.

The next step would be to click on `Installation`:

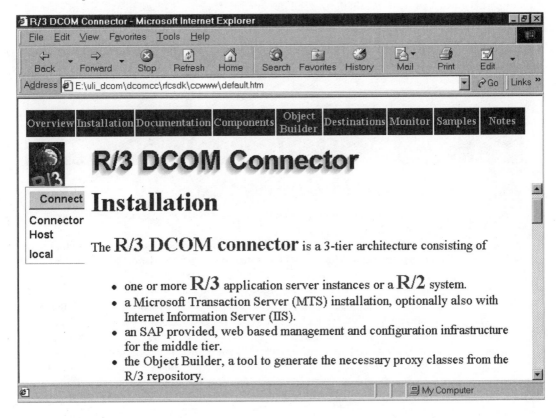

This page contains some very useful system and configuration related information and I recommend reading it. To proceed with installation, scroll down and locate the `Installation of the RFC SDK` fragment. Scroll down some more, and you'll see the following:

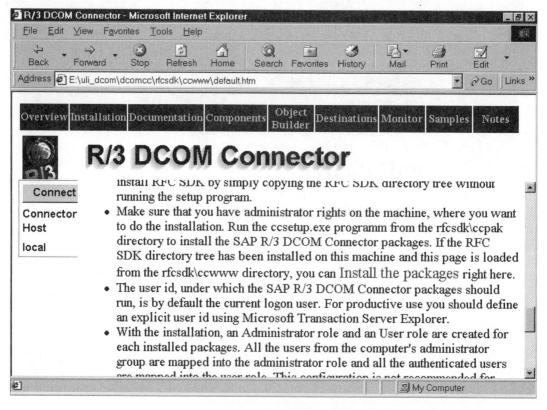

Click on `Install the packages` and observe the results. You'll see the prompt asking your permission to run ActiveX components:

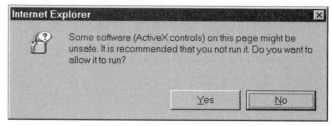

Answer <u>Yes</u> for all such prompts while working with the DCOM CC. The following screen will appear:

Heed the notification about MTS. If you have MTS installed, the installation routine will install all components that comprise the DCOM CC as MTS components. If MTS is not installed, it will install them as ordinary DLLs. Note that you can't deselect **Administration Components**, while you can opt not to install **Sample Components** and **Object Builder Components**. Leave them all selected and click **Setup**. After a successful installation, you will get the confirmation message:

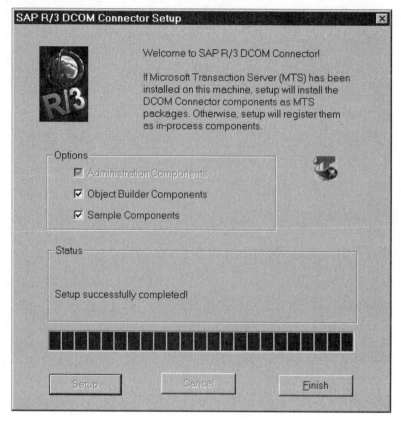

Click <u>F</u>inish, and you are ready to proceed with the DCOM CC.

The installation process registers the following DLLs, located in the CCPAK directory of the RFC SDK:

> ccadmin.dll – Implements the administrative functionality for the DCOM CC

> proxygen.dll – Implements the connectivity and component generation functionality

> ccgen.dll – Implements the DCOM CC object builder functionality

The executable for the installer itself is the file ccsetup.exe.

Let's take a look at the MTS components. You should see the following picture in the MTS Explorer:

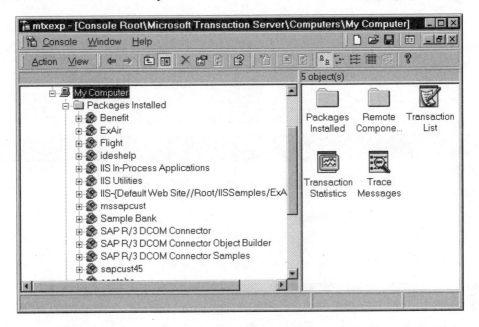

Note the components with names that start **SAP R/3 DCOM Connector**. If you have all three of them as shown, this is a good indicator of a successful configuration and setup.

So far, we have been installing components of the DCOM CC without much explanation of what they should do. Before we start exploring it, recall the purpose of the DCOM CC – to build COM proxies to the SAP R/3 business objects and implement them as in-process components.

# DCOM CC Functionality

If you have got this far into this book, then you have most likely developed a good sense of the functional paradigm of all tools that extend or integrate SAP R/3 functionality. And you should not have any problems predicting the functionality of the DCOM CC. At the very minimum it has to connect to SAP R/3, and browse the Business Object Repository for business objects and RFC functions. All other DCOM CC specific functionality should follow from here.

The DCOM CC implements connectivity to SAP R/3 somewhat similarly to ODBC connection strings, introducing the concept of a **destination**. A destination is best understood as a named data structure that includes all the necessary attributes for an SAP R/3 connection – client, user ID, password, host server and language. This approach allows for maintaining different sets of connectivity attributes for different SAP R/3 systems.

## Creating Destinations

To see destinations, click on the `Destinations` panel of the DCOM CC start page:

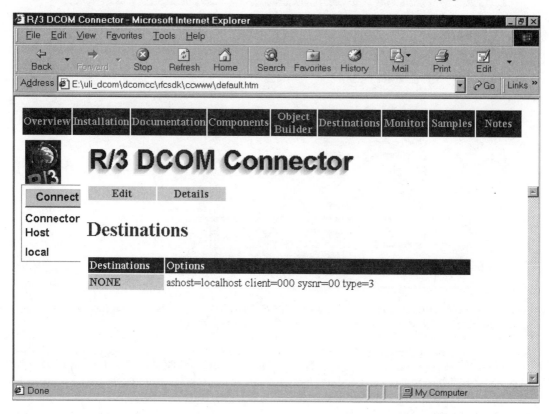

This presents you with the default destination – that's not very meaningful. What we need to do is walk through the process of creating a new working destination.

First, click on the Edit button:

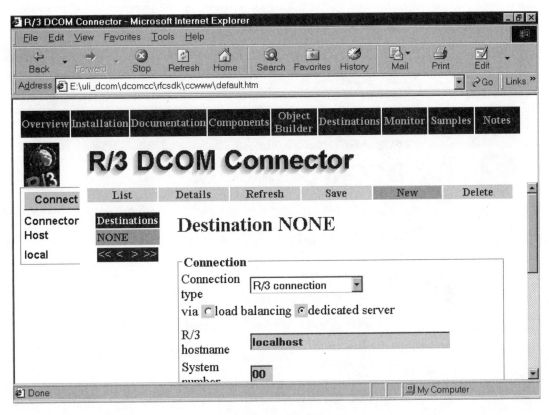

Then click on New, and enter some meaningful name for the destination:

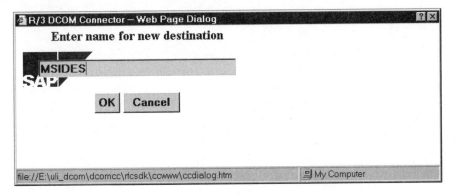

Click **OK**. The new Destination will be added to the list. To set the necessary values, click on your new destination name, in my case `MSIDES`. This will activate the edit screen for the destination:

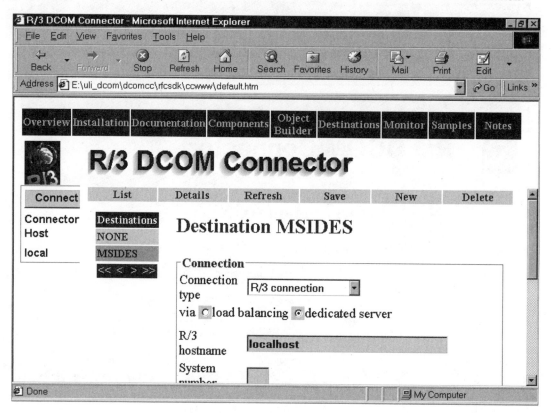

Accept the default value for the `Connection type`, because we will be connecting to the SAP R/3 system. Select the `dedicated server` option if you do not use load balancing. If you do connect to the SAP R/3 via load balancing, select the `load balancing` option and fill in the fields presented:

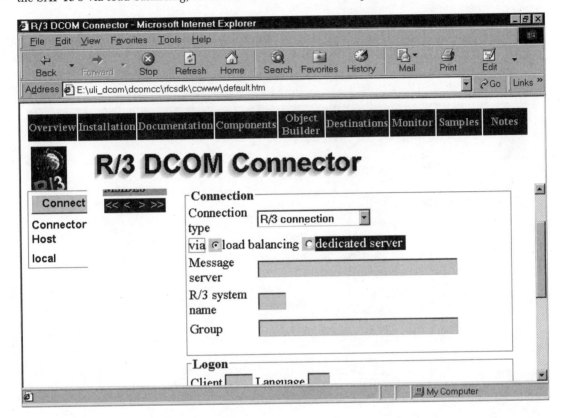

I will stay with the default option – dedicated server – and need to enter the IP address or host name into the R/3 hostname field. Remember that you can never go wrong with an IP address. If you use the host name – like IDES45A – make sure that your machine can resolve it into an IP address. Enter the System Number, Client and Language as well:

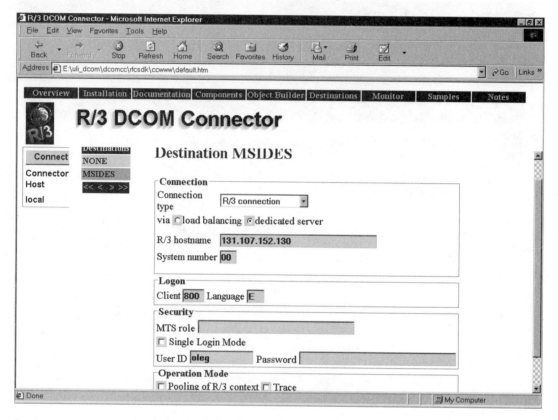

In the Security attributes section, you need to enter User ID and Password. If you want to use the users group defined in MTS, enter it here. If not, you can select the single logon mode or leave it not selected at all. The configurations for the initial design and deployment of components implemented in MTS are very different and depend on your particular setup scenario. For the purposes of learning the DCOM CC it's irrelevant. Refer to MTS documentation or texts to help design a better deployment scenario.

The Pooling of R/3 context option will let SAP R/3 3.x systems reuse (pool) connections. This will improve performance, because it will not enforce closing the connection after the RFC call. The word context may raise a few questions if you are not familiar with the concept. A very sketchy analogy would be a thread. This term context will become increasingly popular with the arrival of Windows 2000 and COM+. For our purposes, the documentation states that you do not have to select this option for 4.x systems at all.

The Trace option is self-explanatory – select it and watch the trace file grow. I would not recommend keeping it on without any legitimate reason.

When you are done entering attributes, hit the Save button and the information will be retained.

## DCOM CC Object Builder

We are now ready to start using the metadata browsing functionality of the DCOM CC. Click on the Object Builder button from the main page of the DCOM CC. You'll be presented with the following:

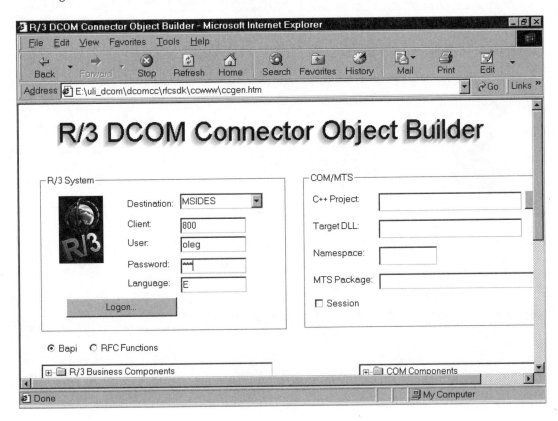

Enter the password and click on the Logon button. After a successful logon, you should see
something similar to the screen below:

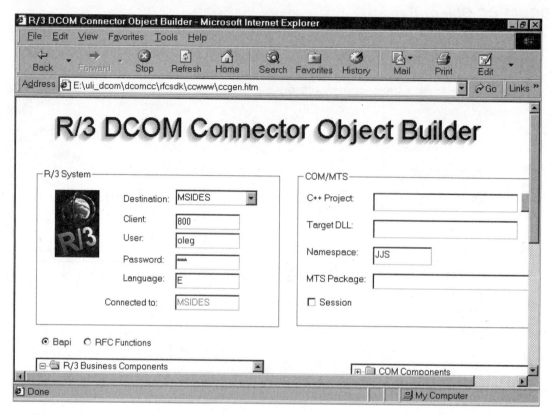

Scroll down to see the tree view populated with Application Hierarchies:

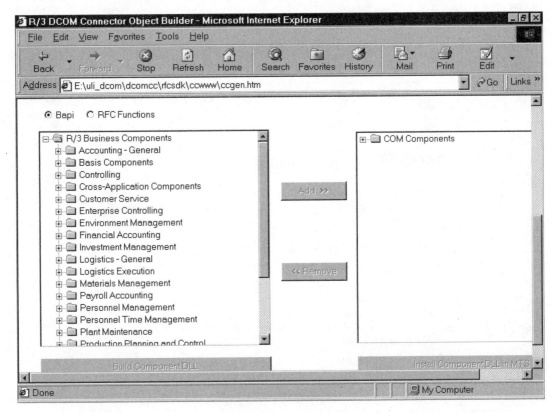

*Note that the time necessary to perform this operation is considerably less than the time needed for the similar functionality of the SAP Assistant or the SAP Online Repository library.*

What you will notice is that the view of Application Hierarchies is somewhat different from the one presented in SAP Assistant or via the SAP Online Repository library. This view is analogous to the one presented in the SAP R/3 BAPI Browser itself:

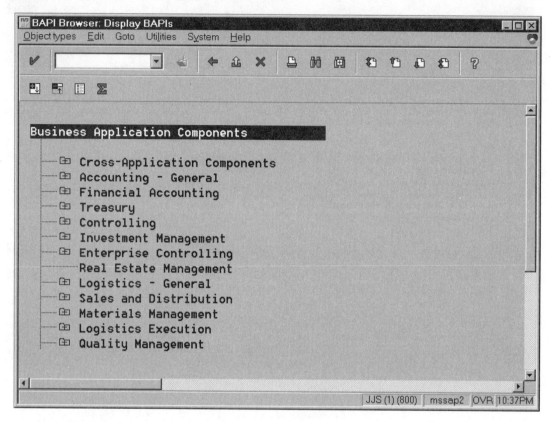

If we look at this discrepancy analytically, it becomes clear that the business objects are still the same, and the only thing that has actually changed is how they have been logically grouped for visual representation. Application Hierarchies do not have any object implementation or functionality. They simply present labels with business objects' names. To do anything meaningful with SAP R/3 you have to learn certain things – where and how to look for business objects is one of those things. We spent considerable time covering the SAP R/3 Business Object Repository, and this should be a no-brainer for you by now.

Expand an Application Hierarchy node and you'll see the business objects (if there are any):

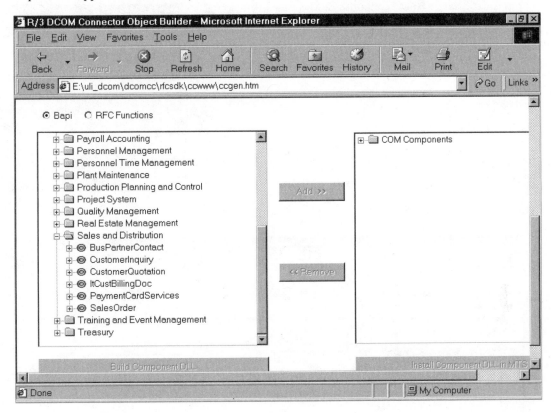

You can also select **RFC Functions**. You will be prompted with a dialog for the selection criteria. This is similar to the SAP Assistant – just enter some familiar values:

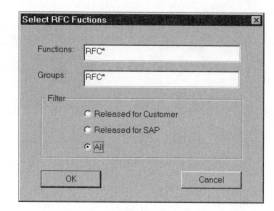

And you will get the RFCs:

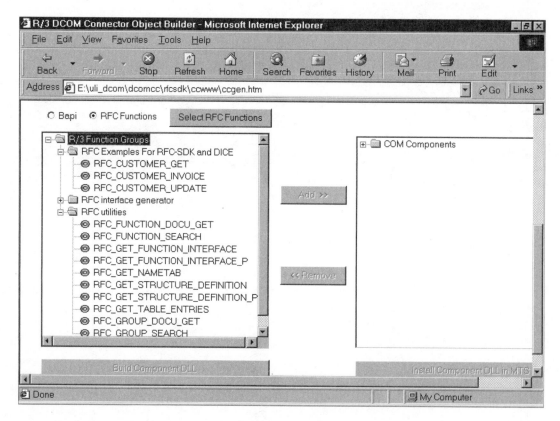

To me, the DCOM CC presentation of the SAP R/3 metadata is closer to the internal SAP R/3 implementation and presentation.

## Generating COM Components using DCOM CC

Now that we know how to navigate the BOR from the DCOM CC, it's time to turn our attention to the right-hand side of the Object Builder interface. Take a look at the COM/MTS group of controls:

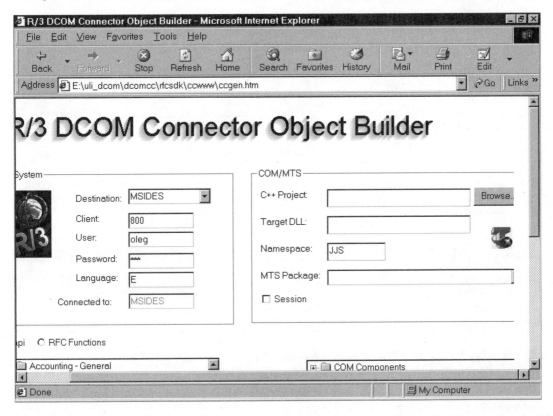

This is where the real fun begins. First you will notice that the Namespace is already populated with the system name. The namespace in DCOM CC is a prefix of up to four-letters used to annotate the names of future components, in order to better organize them. Obviously, a space is not allowed. You can use whatever makes more sense to you, because you will in fact be establishing company standards. I will use WROX for this value. There is one more reason for the namespace – it is used to avoid potential naming conflicts of BAPIs or RFCs with the same name.

The C++ compiler to build the component will use the C++ Project field's value. The **BROWSE** button helps to get to the desired location. Create a new directory for your components, and inside that directory create a new folder for every component. This is not mandatory, it will just preserve your sanity. I decided to use the familiar Helpvalues business object to replicate the functionality from the project in Chapter 8:

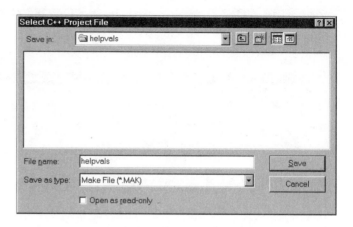

After you hit <u>S</u>ave you will see a picture similar to the one below. If we want to implement this component as an MTS package, we should either select an existing package or type in a name for the new package. To explore the full functionality of the Object Builder, I will use the MTS implementation. It would be logical to create a new package, which we'll call **HELPVALS**:

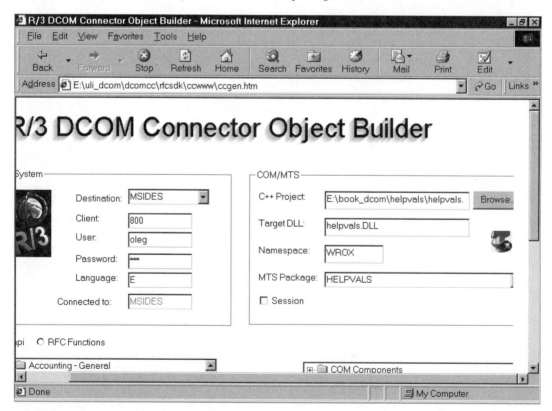

Locate the Helpvalues business object in the tree view – you'll find it in Cross-Application Components. Click on it, then click on the Add button. You'll see the following results:

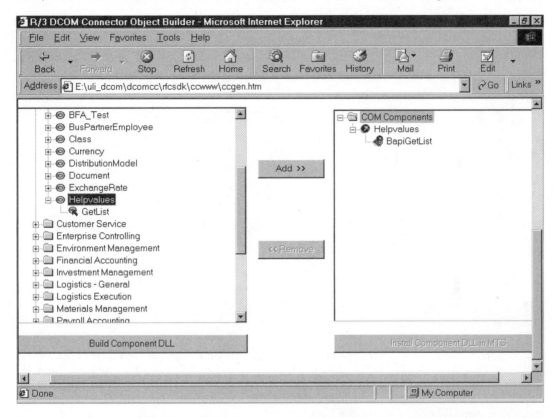

Note that the previously disabled Build Component DLL button has became enabled – click on it. The DCOM CC Object Builder will generate all the necessary C++ project files needed to build a COM DLL and automatically compile them, presenting you with the ready-to-use SAP business object proxy. Upon successful completion of this process you will be notified:

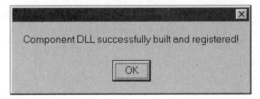

Accept the notification, and the Install Component DLL in MTS button will become enabled. Before we proceed with MTS, take a look in the directory you selected for the component:

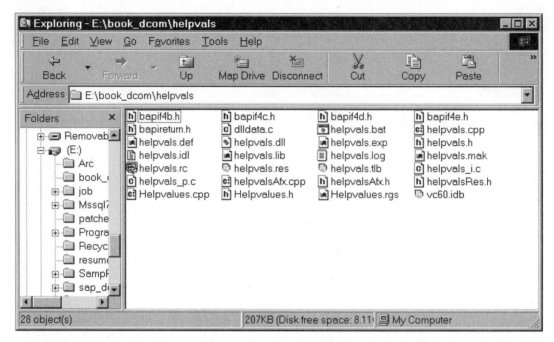

At first sight, this is not a pleasant picture for a Visual Basic programmer with no C++ background. We could get the C++ and header files from the code generation feature of the SAP Assistant. What we could not get is the fully compiled and ready to use DLL that implements all the functionality of the SAP R/3 business object – but that is what DCOM CC provides. You can delete all other files except for the DLL, because you don't need them.

*I did not provide the C++ specifics involved in this process because they are outside the scope of this book. If you need this information, you should refer to the DCOM CC documentation.*

## Using DCOM CC Generated Components

Fire up Visual Basic and take a look at the References dialog:

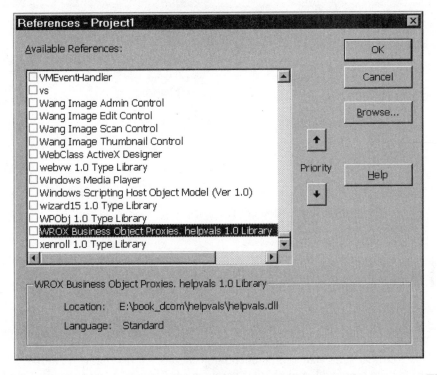

As you can see, the DLL that we have just created is already a fully registered component. The DCOM CC generates the name for the component automatically, using the namespace value and the version number.

You may now install the component in MTS if you want to. In this release of the DCOM CC it's not required. All components can be used as regular in-process servers, and you can always import components into MTS later if you need to. However, if you want to take advantage of MTS features, you should install your components in MTS. To do so, simply click on Install Component DLL in MTS in the Object Builder. After you click on the button, the component will be installed in MTS and you will get the confirmation:

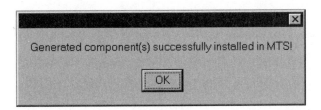

Take a look at the MTS Explorer:

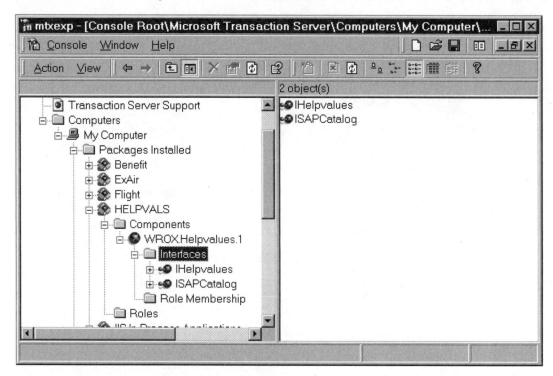

The Object Builder generated a fully functioning component that has two interfaces or classes as would have been presented in the Visual Basic Object Browser. You can easily see now how the namespace fits into the naming convention.

# Analyzing the Business Object Proxy

We will come back for more on MTS specific topics, such as role implementation, later in this chapter. What I want to do first is to go to the tool we are more familiar with – Visual Basic – and analyze the newly created component.

Fire up Visual Basic and create a new **Standard EXE** project. Then open the **References** dialog and add a reference to the DLL that we just created. Finally, save the project and bring up the Object Browser. It will display a view of the SAP business object proxy:

As we can see, the DCOM CC Object Builder has created three classes in this library. Two of them – **ISAPCatalog** and **ISAPConnector** – are interfaces derived from other DLLs.

Visual Basic does an excellent job in visually separating different kinds of classes. Just type the keyword New, and only those classes that you can instantiate will appear in the drop-down box of the IntelliSense editor. The DCOM CC implements these interfaces to enable functionality of the main component – in our case the **Helpvalues**. Take a look at this class in the Object Browser:

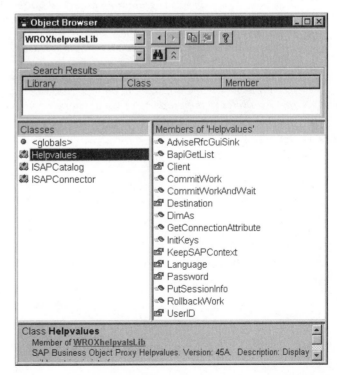

## Standard Methods

One advantage of choosing the *Helpvalues* business object is that it has only one BAPI. Therefore, we know that all the other methods we see have been added by the internal logic of the DCOM CC. There is nothing else in the Business Object Repository to implement, just the `GetList` BAPI.

To list the standard methods and properties that are added to the metadata definition of the COM proxy to the SAP business object, take a look at the Object Builder and the DCOM CC documentation.

### PutSessionInfo

Syntax:

```
Sub PutSessionInfo([Destination As String], [UserID As String], _
                   [Password As String], [Language As String], [Client As String])
```

All arguments for this method should already be familiar from the discussion on the Logon control, except for the `Destination` that I described earlier in this chapter. Supply all values to this method and you will connect to SAP R/3.

Note one significant difference from the Connection object setup for the Logon control or BAPI control. As you may remember you had to set each value individually, and every time you used *dot* operator in Visual Basic you made a trip to the object reference. Across a slow network, this can add up to a noticeable delay. In DCOM CC, SAP developers adhere to the old rule – better one function call with n parameters than n references to the properties.

> *A general Visual Basic programming observation: there is no hard rule on when to define functionality as a property or method. It is mostly a matter of choice or taste. From the Class Builder Utility perspective, it's to have many properties and then enjoy IntelliSense features. This is fine on a single workstation, or when you're set to debate object-oriented programming concepts. Scale up your components, and performance and network throughput start to count. No matter how many arguments your function has, it pushes them all to stack in one motion, whereas you cause a round trip every time you refer to the property of your remote component.*

### AdviseRfcGuiSink

Syntax:

```
Sub AdviseRfcGuiSink(pIRfcGuiSink As Object, AbapDebug As Integer, _
                     UseSapGui As Integer)
```

This method will return a reference to the SAP RFC GUI sink. If you set `AbapDebug` and `UseSapGui` to non-zero integers, and provided that you have an SAP front-end installed, you will get it up and running, plus you will get into the ABAP function modules.

I can't think up a scenario where a Visual Basic programmer would go this far. Additionally, you can't modify the RFC code, and looking at the ABAP Function Modules is exactly what the whole SAP Business Object Framework is all about. It would be analogous to stepping through the C++ code of the ADO DLL as you invoke its methods.

### CommitWork

Syntax:

```
Sub CommitWork()
```

This method has a self-explanatory name. Its use depends on the BAPIs that you work with. Some BAPIs in the 4.x releases require additional COMMIT calls to commit changes. This call will also implicitly call the SetComplete method of MTS.

### GetConnectionAttribute

Syntax:

```
Function GetConnectionAttribute([AttrName As String])
```

This method will get you the value of the connection attribute. The documentation produces the following list of attributes:

| Attribute | Description |
| --- | --- |
| PROCID | Process ID |
| HANDLE | RFC handle to identify the RFC connection |
| CALLS | Number of calls in the R/3 target system |
| STATE | Status of resource pooling |
| DESTINATION | Name of the RFC destination |
| SYSID | ID of the R/3 target system |
| PARTNER_HOST | Name of the R/3 application server |
| SYSTNR | System number of the R/3 target system |
| NT_USERID | Windows NT user |
| USER | User ID for the R/3 target system |
| OWN_CODEPAGE | Codepage number to integrate character sets in the client system |

*Table Continued on Following Page*

| Attribute | Description |
|---|---|
| PARTNER_CODEPAGE | Codepage number in the R/3 target system |
| PARTNER_REL | System release number of the R/3 target system |
| OWN_REL | Release number of the RFC library in the client system |
| TRACE | Name of the trace file containing recordings of the RFC communication |
| CPIC_CONVID | Conversation ID of the CPI protocol |
| LAST_FUNCTION | Name of the last called RFC function |

If you don't specify the name of the attribute, this method will return an ADO Recordset containing all the attributes as fields. If you do specify the name, you get the string value of the attribute. This method is rather statistical and does not directly relate to BAPI programming. However, you may use it to log information on RFC connections.

### RollbackWork

Syntax:

```
Sub RollbackWork()
```

As the name suggests, this method rolls back a transactional BAPI. It will also trigger SetAbort in MTS.

### InitKeys

Syntax:

```
Sub InitKeys (key1, ..., keyn)
```

This method sets values for keys of persistent business objects, such as existing Customer. Note that the Object Builder detects the presence and number, or absence of keys in the business object definition, and defines InitKeys accordingly. This means that the function signature of this method will differ from business object to business object.

A convenient feature of the Object Builder is that it puts the names of keys in the definition of InitKeys. For example, compare the way it is defined for the *Customer* business object proxy, that has a single key:

```
InitKeys(CustomerNo As String)
```

And for the *Helpvalues* object proxy, that doesn't have any keys:

```
InitKeys()
```

The most important characteristic of this method is that it just initializes (sets values for) keys. It does not perform any existence check validation. This is different from the `GetSAPObject` method that we saw in the BAPI control library. That method had keys for arguments, and if you supplied the wrong value for the key it returned a run-time error.

Luckily SAP implements some sort of Check Existence BAPI for business objects that have keys and therefore can be persistent. It would be good practice to check the existence prior to calling a retrieval BAPI, or passing the value for the key of one object to the BAPI of another object that needs more than one related key.

### DimAs

Syntax:

```
Sub DimAs(Method As String, Parameter As String, pRS)
```

This looks familiar. You pass the name of the `Method` (BAPI) and name of the BAPI `Parameter`, and in return you get the object formatted using the parameter's metadata. True – but with one significant difference. It returns you an ADO Recordset that has the structure of the RFC parameter. We have already done that programmatically. DCOM CC implements it natively, so we don't have to jump through hoops to do it.

This is what native integration is all about. The BAPI parameters are presented as disconnected ADO Recordsets, which makes them very easy to populate, browse and integrate into any Microsoft tool. And starting from ADO 2.1, it's possible to save the Recordset in XML format, so that any non-Windows or browser based application may read it.

There's even more to it. If you are familiar with MSMQ, you know that MSMQ accepts anything for the body of the message, as long as it evaluates into a Variant data type. The ADO Recordset does. And this gives you an opportunity to take advantage of guaranteed delivery and asynchronous message processing – areas traditionally dominated by IBM MQ Series. Put together MTS, MSMQ and DCOM CC and you get a very scalable distributed implementation and deployment environment.

One more important characteristic of `DimAs` – it is case-sensitive.

> *Side note. During my tenure as a Visual Basic programmer and vocal advocate for the Windows environment, I have experienced a great deal of prejudice towards the ability of Windows and Visual Basic to be the environment for enterprise development. I have also been involved in the development environment selection process, and I had to prove that Visual Basic is not a kiddy language and Windows NT 4.0 is not just a colorful picture on the top of DOS. You would be surprised how many non-Windows programmers and IT managers still think that remote method invocation is impossible for Visual Basic to implement. That's why I sprinkle this book with bits of information you can use to successfully argue in favor of Visual Basic as a development tool, and Windows as a platform, when it comes to SAP R/3 integration.*

## Standard Properties

The following are the standard properties added by DCOM CC:

| Property | Description |
|----------|-------------|
| Destination | This is a String type property that accepts the value of the named connection. |
| UserID | User ID for the SAP R/3 that you are connecting to (String). |
| Password | Password for the SAP R/3 logon (String). |
| Language | Value for language (String). |
| Client | Value for the Client (String). |
| KeepSAPContext | Boolean type. Defaults to True. If True, it will force the RFC connection to be kept open after the BAPI call. If set to False, it will cause the connection to be closed after every BAPI call. Use for transaction BAPIs and stateful method invocations. You would normally issue CommitWork at the end of a transaction that used a pooled connection. |

We have now seen the standard methods and properties that the DCOM CC Object Builder includes into every business object proxy it generates. The rest are BAPIs that are defined in the business object.

This part is very important to understand. As we can see, every business object proxy generated by the DCOM CC Object Builder contains functionality to connect to the SAP R/3 and implement all necessary functionality for the business object. This feature makes the component self-sufficient. It may seem redundant, but the alternative would have been to generate a sort of Connector object, and that would bring us back to the component dependency. You can also bundle many objects into a single proxy component, thus creating a logical unit of SAP R/3 functionality that you want to integrate into your system.

As you may notice, RFC functions are treated the same way as business objects. You can select RFC functions and build a proxy based on their metadata. The only difference would be that you do not get InitKeys for proxies generated for the RFC function.

# BAPI Transaction Related Functionality

The DCOM CC (starting from the 4.6 release) implements the **Session** option on the Object Builder. This option allows you to elect for the Session class to be generated for the proxy DLL. This functionality addresses the issue of transactional processing for BAPIs.

The word transaction is used to describe many different things. As far as BAPIs are concerned, every BAPI prior to release 4.0A had a Commit statement called at the end of the BAPI function module. Starting from 4.0A, the BAPIs are implemented without explicit commits in their code. It therefore becomes the job of the client program.

This requires more elaboration. To better understand the concept, think in terms of the Logical Unit of Work (LUW). For example, you want to integrate your existing Order Entry system – clichéd but familiar to many Visual Basic programmers. At some point, data processing may be grouped – you create a Customer, then generate Sales Order, then generate Invoice and then you may update Inventory. These four operations may be implemented as different BAPIs that belong to different business objects. However, the LUW will span these processes. It would make sense to have one commit on successful completion of the LUW, and rollback if anything goes wrong. If you're familiar with the design of stored procedures in SQL Server using Transact SQL, this is similar. This implementation of BAPIs gives external programmers more control over processes in SAP R/3.

Another important consideration is connection pooling and contexts. It does not make any sense to reconnect to SAP R/3 for every RFC call – BAPI execution. What would make a lot of sense is if we could keep the connection and the client's context for the duration of the LUW. And that's where the Session object comes in. If you select the Session option on the DCOM CC Object Builder it will generate a Session class in the proxy component. If we look at this class using the Visual Basic Object Browser, we are going to see the following:

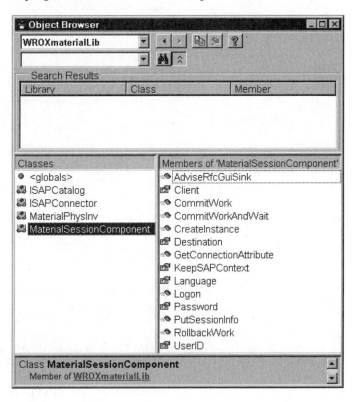

*Note that the DCOM CC will generate the name for the Session object class automatically.*

This class inherits its functionality from the `LIBRFC32.DLL` and implements the concept of Session. It has all the commit/rollback functionality, but also has a `CreateInstance` method:

```
CreateInstance(ProgID As String, [InterfID As String]) As Object
```

Note that the `KeepSAPContext` value is critical for transaction control. If `KeepSAPContext` = TRUE, the SAP R/3 will keep the user context until the object goes out of scope, or commit or rollback are invoked.

This `CreateInstance` method is similar to the `CreateInstance` method of the MTS Context object. It creates a running instance of the business object based on the ProgID and keeps them in one context. It does that because of the `Destination` attribute. You create the Session based on the connection to SAP R/3, hence `PutSessionInfo` and all related properties are defined in the Session class. So instead of connecting to SAP R/3 using the functionality of the business object class, it can be done once from the Session class: set the `KeepSAPContext` to `True` and create the business object within the context of the Session object. The pseudo-code style sample is provided below:

```
Dim sapSession as New SessionComponent
Dim sapObject1 As BusObjOne
Dim sapObject2 As BusObjTwo

sapSession.Destination = "SomeDest"
sapSession. KeepSAPContext = True

Set sapObject1 = sapSession.CreateInstance("WROX.BusObjOne.1")

sapObject1.BAPI1
sapObject1.BAPI2

Set sapObject2 = sapSession.CreateInstance("WROX.BusObjTwo.1")

sapObject2.BAPI1
sapObject2.BAPI2

If OK Then
   sapSession.CommitWork
Else
   sapSession.Rollback
End If
```

The connection to SAP R/3 will be pooled and reused for all BAPI calls within this session. It also lets you better manage transactions. Because BAPIs from older releases and brand-new ones are in the same system, always check the BAPI documentation to find if it supports transactions.

The transactional part of the DCOM CC is being modified rapidly. Moreover, the progress in this area indicates the intention of SAP to transfer more control over to external BAPI programmers, and to enable external programs to emulate transactions in the SAP R/3. The obvious caveat is that you have to be familiar with the workings of the SAP R/3 business objects to correctly implement their transaction-related functionality. However, the technical aspect of programming components generated by the DCOM CC will be the same.

# The DCOM CC and Microsoft Transaction Server

As I mentioned earlier in this chapter, you don't have to use MTS to program components generated by the DCOM CC. It's not imperative, and the functionality of the proxy components will not be in any way diminished. However, if you choose not to use MTS, you obviously will not be able to take advantage of MTS functionality.

MTS is not new as a technology anymore, although for many Visual Basic programmers distributed computing and transaction processing remain something that they don't have to use routinely. You may not have MTS on your workstation at all. If you recall the installation process for the DCOM CC, the message on the installation dialog was very clear – if you have MTS it will install Object Builder and Administrative components as MTS packages, otherwise they will be installed as ordinary DLLs. This gives you implementation flexibility and allows avoiding initial training for your developers.

> *Transaction processing and distributed computing for Visual Basic programmers is a reality, and I strongly recommend you start learning the Microsoft technologies in this area if you don' t know them already. Wrox Press have several titles in this area including, Professional VB6 MTS Progamming and VB6 Business objects.*

There is another subtle subcontext: Windows 2000 will introduce COM+ with the MTS functionality built into it. Therefore, MTS will cease to exist as a separate stand-alone application and will become a system service. Whatever the change, the DCOM CC will accommodate it in future releases. The very architecture of the DCOM CC is open and natively integrated into Windows.

In my opinion the name Transaction Server is a misnomer – it's more of a Component Manager. That's why it is being integrated into COM. It provides plumbing for transaction processing, but the most important functionality of MTS is that it implements a comprehensive framework to deploy COM components, alleviating application programmers from handling pooling, concurrent connection handling, memory management and many other unpleasant and bug prone tasks. It is more of a 'component execution environment' and 'distributed component manager' based on its functionality.

The first obvious reason for DCOM CC developers to go with MTS is because of its DCOM component coordinator's nature. Another very important reason is the MTS by-design support of transaction processing.

Moreover, MTS does a very good job in providing a comprehensive framework and GUI to manage security and user roles for components. Anyone who ever used the DCOM Configuration Utility would notice the difference. MTS has a well-defined security model and you can easily manage users. You can create Roles for packages and then assign users in those Roles. You can then make components inherit those Roles. This model helps to create a robust component deployment framework.

MTS also allows electing for the components to **Support Transactions**, **Require a Transaction**, **Require a New Transaction** or **Not Support Transactions**. This would have fit well into the SAP R/3 implementation of BAPI transactions if DCOM CC business object proxies supported MTS transactions. However, the DCOM CC business object proxies do not support MTS transactions, due to inadequacies of the current implementation of the RFC protocol.

> Do not confuse BAPI transactions and MTS transactions. BAPIs implement
> transactions internally and the DCOM CC generated proxies merely reflect that.
> MTS implements transactions differently, and for these two types of transaction to
> work together, the RFC protocol should support the two-phase commit protocol that
> is required for MTS commits and rollbacks. SAP did a wonderful job fitting SAP
> into COM, but some loose ends still hang out.

The first thing that the DCOM CC installation routine does (provided you have MTS on your
machine) is to install the Administrative and Sample components in MTS. It also creates Roles and
assigns Members to them. At this point, you would have all the components that you need to create a
simple test program based on the sample. Before we do that, let's address some MTS specific issues.

## Roles and Membership for DCOM CC Components

Correct assignment of Roles and Membership for the DCOM CC MTS components is an important
factor that impacts the work of the whole DCOM CC. When you install the components, they have
the following role assignments:

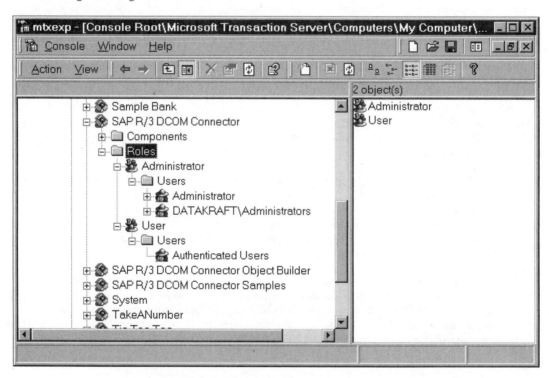

The installation routine will map all users from your workstation's Administrators Group to the
Administrator Role it creates. For the User Role, it will create the Authenticated Users entry. These
settings allow all authenticated users (logged on users) of the workstation to use the component, and
all with administrative credentials to administer (deploy and manage) it.

This is not the most robust implementation schema for security, but it is the least intrusive and will always work without you having to tinker with users and roles from the beginning. It will not create any users or groups for generated proxy components, leaving this noble task to you. I suggest you keep the configuration initially. Once you have mastered MTS and the DCOM CC, you can start implementing your standard access scenario.

> *Refer to the MTS documentation to learn about managing Roles for Packages and Components. For detailed information on DCOM CC MTS related security, please refer to the Expanding the Reach of Your SAP Business Processes article.*
>
> *The settings shown here will be the same for all components that DCOM CC installs into MTS.*

For every component that is part of a package – and no component can be outside of some package – you can inherit Roles from the Package Role for the Component's Role Membership:

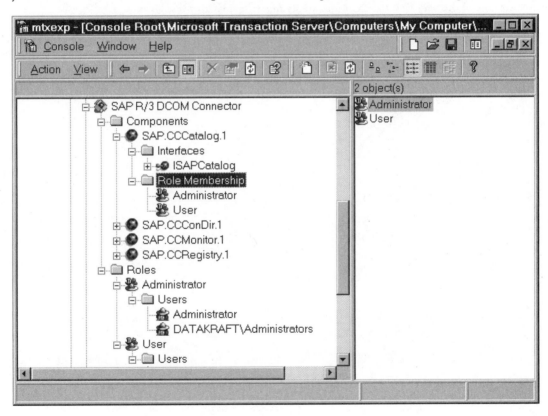

The way MTS implements security – based on the NT security model - allows you to create very elaborate security scenarios. However, a discussion of MTS security and role management is outside the scope of this book. We will keep the installed parameters and replicate them for generated components.

# Summary

In this chapter we started to explore the SAP DCOM Component Connector 4.6. This is an extension to the SAP RFC SDK, and it is the only one developed by SAP to facilitate native integration of business objects into the COM environment. We have learned how to install it on the workstation, and introduced the functionality of the DCOM CC and its configuration.

We learned how to configure DCOM CC to be able to connect to the SAP R/3, browse its Business Object Repository and generate COM proxies for SAP R/3 business objects. It is critical that you comprehend the way DCOM CC implements functionality for those proxies.

This chapter also continued our discussion of BAPIs, providing a view on their transactional nature. We have outlined the role of Microsoft Transaction Server for the DCOM CC implementation, and started to explore the opportunities it opens for Visual Basic developers.

The rest of this book will be devoted to programming with the DCOM CC libraries and the SAP R/3 business object proxies that it generates.

# Programming the Administrative Core of the DCOM Component Connector

As we learned in the previous chapter, the DCOM Component Connector is not an SDK or a set of components that you have to program against. The DCOM CC is a finished application that does not require any programming effort to produce its intended output. However, the DCOM CC is implemented as a set of core DLL components with a web-based front end. This architecture means that we can programmatically access the core component functionality on our own.

When using the DCOM CC, it is assumed that you will stick to the out-of-the-box browser GUI and preferably use MTS. However, there are certain situations where you may need to integrate the DCOM CC's full, or partial, functionality into your own applications. For example, you may wish to integrate the DCOM CC functionality into some other code generators you already have, or use it as a foundation to create some sort of a Visual Basic code generator, or an add-in to generate an entire application based on DCOM CC generated proxies.

The DCOM CC does a very good job of BOR metadata access, in terms of consistency with the internal SAP R/3 implementation, and wins over the SAP Assistant in speed. It lacks all the drill down capabilities of the SAP Assistant but provides the programmable functionality to replicate it easily. This functionality alone is worth integrating into any business analyst oriented SAP R/3 BOR explorer application.

There are many tools currently available, or now being developed, for the purpose of application integration involving SAP R/3. These tools should use DCOM CC as a major building block for the interface with SAP R/3.

*This is providing of course, you want to integrate using the Business Objects Framework.*

# Programming the DCOM CC Core Components

Either way, we need a deeper understanding of the DCOM CCs functionality. As we already know, the DCOM CC installation routine installs several DLLs on your machine. One of them – the `LIBRFC32.DLL` – is the core component from which the other DLLs derive their interfaces. We will not program directly against it, instead we'll use the `CCADMIN.DLL` and the `PROXYGEN.DLL` to replicate the DCOM CC functionality.

> ➢ The `CCADMIN.DLL` is the DCOM CC **Administrative component** that holds the core administrative functionality of the DCOM CC. This library allows us to perform such tasks as setting up Destinations, manage proxy objects, and set environmental settings.

> ➢ On the other hand, `PROXYGEN.DLL` is the **DCOM CC Object Builder** that supplies the proxy object generation functionality, which is at the heart of the DCOM CC.

In this chapter, we are going to concentrate on working with the Administrative component. We shall use a familiar methodology and try to replicate the functionality of the DCOM CC in our own projects.

To do this, create and save a new Visual Basic Standard EXE project, `CCAdmin_Demo`. Add references to the ADO library and to the following DCOM CC library:

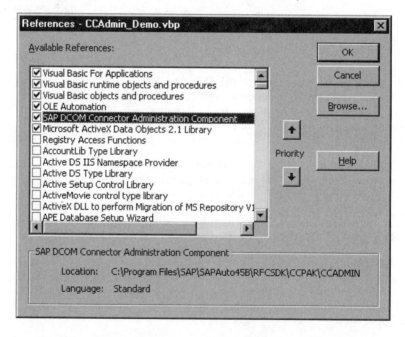

If you can't find the DCOM CC entries in the References dialog, something is wrong with your environment – reinstall the DCOM CC components.

> *Troubleshooting Suggestion: to reinstall DCOM CC components, first delete all the DCOM CC related packages from MTS. Then go to the Task Manager (I assume you are using NT anyway) proceed to Processes and look for any* `mtx.exe` *processes.*

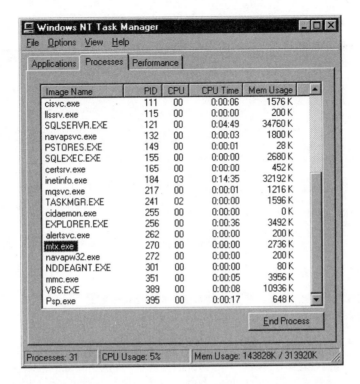

*Select every* `mtx.exe` *process, click on the* <u>E</u>nd Process *button and confirm the termination. Then unregister* `CCADMIN.DLL`, `PROXYGEN.DLL` *and* `CCGEN.DLL`. *Then delete or rename the* `LIBRFC32.DLL`. *To clean up the registry, do a search for the DLLs, and delete whole keys containing entries for those DLLs. Do not forget the* `SALES` *sample DLL and Package – it has to be removed and the DLL unregistered too. After all these operations, you can reinstall DCOM CC components successfully.*

# The DCOM CC Administrative Functionality

Now it is time to use the Object Browser to learn more about this component. Prior to doing so, I recommend you create a couple of destinations using the DCOM CC browser GUI to have something to work with. My approach is simple: to learn the functionality I always try to replicate what the tool does. With this in mind, we have to first learn how to view destinations.

The DCOM CC core component responsible for destinations and installed components is `CCADMIN.DLL`, referred to as the **SAP DCOM CC Administration component**. This component includes the following classes:

>    `CCCatalog`

>    `CCMonitor`

>    `CCRegistry`

>    `SapConDir`

Looking at MTS offers a slightly different picture than the Object Browser:

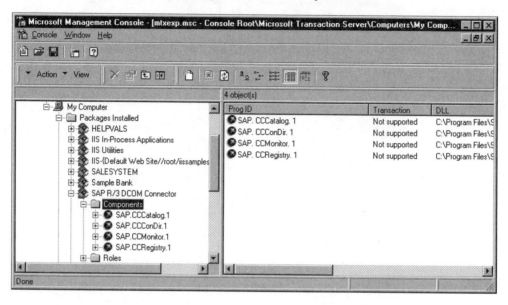

We're going to build a project that shows how to use the described methods for the `CCRegistry`, `CCMonitor` and `SapConDir` classes. This project will basically implement every method in a button click and displays the results in a data grid. However, it will give you enough understanding and sample code to implement the functionality any way you want. The GUI will look something like this:

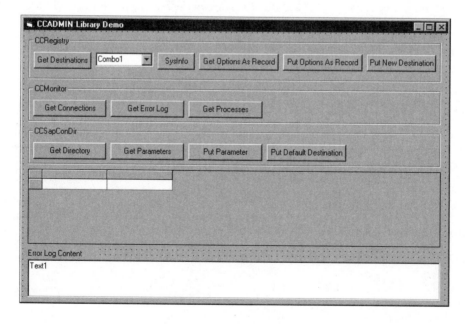

To learn about this component, I have created a destination based on the connection attributes that I have used for all development in this book. It is a connection to the 800 client of the SAP R/3 4.5 IDES, provided courtesy of Microsoft's Enterprise Product Planning group and named MSIDES. Our first task will be to retrieve the list of existing destinations. Destinations are kept locally, and to retrieve them it is not necessary to logon to SAP R/3. The component that we are going to use is the CCRegistry class of the CCADMIN library.

## Programming the CCRegistry Class

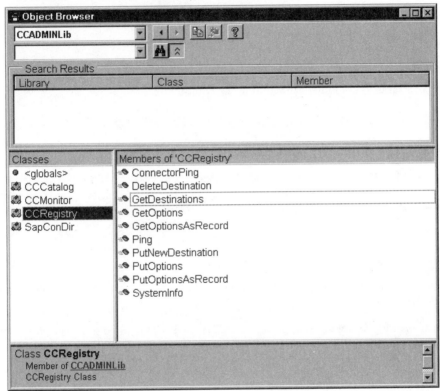

> **The general rule for all the DCOM CC core components is that all data returned is normally in the form of an ADO Recordset.**

Even if it does not say Recordset in the return data type or in the argument, it most likely is an ADO Recordset. This is a very nice standard to adopt. Recordsets are self-describing, and this makes them ideal for studying the data returned by the DCOM CC components.

We will need a member variable for the `CCRegistry` class:

```
Option Explicit
```

```
Dim mdcomRegistry As CCADMINLib.CCRegistry
```

As the `CCADMIN` components may be held in MTS, we'll use the `CreateObject` statement in the form's `Load` event to instantiate instances of this class:

```
Private Sub Form_Load()

   Set mdcomRegistry = CreateObject("SAP.CCRegistry.1")

End Sub
```

Also add a variable to hold the destination in the combo box:

```
Dim mstrDestination As String
```

We need to update this variable every time it changes in the combo box:

```
Private Sub Combo1_Click()

  mstrDestination = Trim(Combo1.List(Combo1.ListIndex))

End Sub
```

## The GetDestinations Method

The `CCRegistry` class contains the aptly named `GetDestinations` method that returns destinations packed into some format.

To experiment with ADO Recordsets, we can define the variable to hold the return value of the `GetDestinations` method as:

```
Dim recDest As ADODB.Recordset
```

Then we can call the method and examine the results.

```
Set recDest = mdcomRegistry.GetDestinations
```

We can now use this recordset to populate a combo box with the values of the destinations. The Destinations recordset comprises two fields:

➢    DESTINATION – Holds the name for the destination

➢    OPTIONS – A 255-character long field that contains options – host server, user name etc.

We can now code the **Get Destinations** command button:

```
Private Sub cmdGetDestinations_Click()

  Dim recDest As ADODB.Recordset

  Combo1.Clear

  Set recDest = mdcomRegistry.GetDestinations()
  Set DataGrid1.DataSource = recDest

  Do Until recDest.EOF
     Combo1.AddItem recDest![DESTINATION]
     recDest.MoveNext
  Loop

  Set recDest = Nothing

End Sub
```

We can then use the OLEDB Data Grid control to display the full set of results:

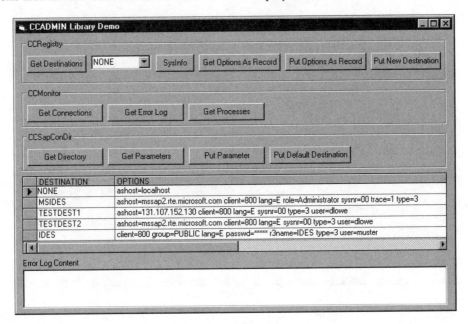

The options are provided as a single line, and to get separate values you would expect to have to parse it. However, this is not necessary, as there is another method provided just for that purpose – GetOptionsAsRecord.

## The GetOptionsAsRecord Method

This method accepts a String argument containing the destination name. It returns an ADO Recordset with 21 fields. The code fragment that produces the Options recordset is shown below:

```
Private Sub cmdGetOptionsAsRecordset_Click()

  Dim recOptions As ADODB.Recordset

  Set recOptions = mdcomRegistry.GetOptionsAsRecord(mstrDestination)

  Set DataGrid1.DataSource = recOptions

  Set recOptions = Nothing

End Sub
```

Executing this code gives the following result:

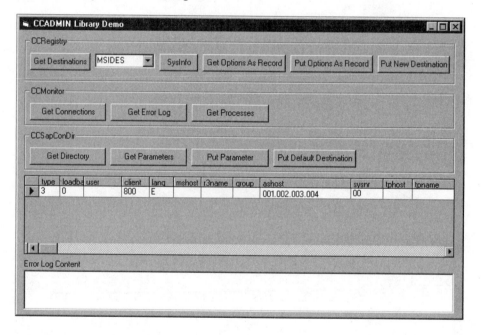

These fields reflect all the possible values that you may need to connect to SAP R/3. The values that we have always used are also present: Server Name (ashost), User Name (user), Language (lang) and System Number (sysnr). Note that the Password is missing from this recordset, because if you save the Password you open up the possibility for unauthorized access. Other fields may contain values indicating whether load balancing or trace functionality is used. As you may notice, the Destination concept is practically identical to what we used for the BAPI control or Logon control Connection object. This is no coincidence – all those controls and the DCOM CC are more or less elaborate extensions to the SAP RFC SDK.

## Creating Deleting and Editing Destinations

Now we have learnt how to view destinations, it's appropriate to learn how to create, delete and edit them. First of all, we have to be able to create a new destination. To do so, we use the `PutNewDestination` method. This method accepts a String value for the new destination name:

```
PutNewDestination(destination As String)
```

If you supply a name that already exists, the new destination will not be created. However, you won't get any warning.

The following method call creates a new destination, `TESTDEST`:

```
Private Sub cmdPutNewDestination_Click()

   mdcomRegistry.PutNewDestination "TESTDEST"

End Sub
```

Once you have created a new destination, it's time to set attributes for it. The most rational way to do it is using the `Options` recordset. The method of the `CCREGISTRY` class that provides this functionality is the `PutOptionsAsRecord` method:

```
PutOptionsAsRecord(destination As String, pIn As Object, passwd As String)
```

As you may notice, this method requires the name of the destination (we just created one), an unspecified object, and a String for the password.

Simple logic suggests that the `Object` parameter is the recordset that has to be populated with valid data prior to the method call. You would expect this class to have some functionality to create an empty recordset with the correct structure – we would simply set values for the fields and call the method. However, this class does not expose such functionality. This should not derail the Visual Basic programmer familiar with ADO.

Remember that we have the recordset returned to us by the `GetOptionsAsRecord` method. It would be perfectly logical to assume that the recordset used to input data would be the same structurally as the one that returns the very same data. If we assume this, we can simply execute the `GetOptionsAsRecord` against an existing destination and get the resultant `Options` recordset:

```
Private Sub cmdPutOptionsAsRecord_Click()

   Dim recNewOptions As ADODB.Recordset
   Dim recClone As ADODB.Recordset

   Set recNewOptions = mdcomRegistry.GetOptionsAsRecord(mstrDestination)
```

Once we have this recordset, we can clone it using the `Clone` method of the ADO Recordset:

```
Set recClone = recNewOptions.Clone
```

`recClone` will be an exact copy of the original recordset. The problem is that we do not need the data in this cloned recordset, so we use the `Delete` method of the ADO Recordset to clean the cloned recordset. Before we do that, we have to close the original recordset so as not to lose it too:

```
recNewOptions.Close
```

We know that it will always have only one record, and we can use the `adAffectCurrent` option of the `Delete` method. After we delete the record, we update the recordset and call the `AddNew` method. Once we have a new record, we can use the regular functionality to set values for required fields:

```
With recClone

    .Delete adAffectCurrent
    .Update

    .AddNew
        ![ashost] = "001.002.003.004"
        ![sysnr] = "00"
        ![user] = "Oleg"
        ![lang] = "E"
        ![client] = "800"
        ![Type] = "3"
        ![loadbal] = "0"
    .Update
End With

Set DataGrid1.DataSource = recClone
```

This routine gives us the `Options` recordset we can use for the `PutOptionsAsRecord` method:

```
mdcomRegistry.PutOptionsAsRecord "TESTDEST", recClone, "yourpwd"

Set recNewOptions = Nothing
Set recClone = Nothing

End Sub
```

This method does not return any value. The only way to check the success of this routine is to call the `GetOptionsAsRecord` with the new name and see if it returns the expected recordset.

Destinations have one caveat related to the password. When you read the options of a destination as records, you do not see the PASSWORD field at all. However, when you create a destination using the DCOM CC GUI or the `PutOptionsAsRecord` method, you can supply a password. If you do so, you will see it in the form of * characters in the DESTINATION field of the `GetDestinations` resultant recordset. When you use the `Options` recordset, you don't have a field to enter the password into and so you need to supply it in the `PutOptionsAsRecord` method call, as shown above. Should you desire, do leave it empty – pass an empty string. If you use the DCOM CC GUI you can create a destination without specifying the password.

## The Ping and SystemInfo Methods

The `Ping` method will ping the connection specified by the destination:

```
Ping(destination)
```

This method will also not return anything. Instead, it will generate a run-time error if the connection is unavailable or the destination not defined. If the destination that you use does not contain a password it will generate a run-time Incomplete Logon Information error.

> Since there is no other argument for the `Ping` method, the only choice you have is to update the destination with the password using the DCOM CC GUI.

This is safe because the DCOM CC GUI does not display the password or implement any "remember password" feature, even if the destination has a password saved. If you do it programmatically, the only thing you can get for the password are * characters in the DESTINATION field of the `GetDestinations` resultant recordset.

Another useful method is the `SystemInfo` method:

```
SystemInfo(destination As String, ppSystemInfo)
```

This method takes a String value for the destination and expects an empty ADO recordset – `ppSystemInfo`:

```
Private Sub cmdSystemInfo_Click()

  Dim recSysInfo As ADODB.Recordset

  mdcomRegistry.SystemInfo mstrDestination, recSysInfo
  Set DataGrid1.DataSource = recSysInfo

  Set recSysInfo = Nothing

End Sub
```

Upon successful execution, this method will return a recordset, in the second argument, containing information on the SAP R/3 system that the destination points to.

The DCOM CC GUI implements this functionality too. Open the DCOM CC home page and follow the `Monitor | Connections` buttons. The DCOM CC will present you with the same values lined up in the table. You can use this feature in administrative types of applications.

## Programming the CCMonitor Class

Another useful
functionality of the
DCOM CC GUI is
the ability to view
and clear the Error
Log file. This
feature is enabled
from the `Monitor`
| `Error Log` link
on the DCOM CC
home page. When
you click on `Error
Log`, the DCOM
CC presents you
with the following
screen:

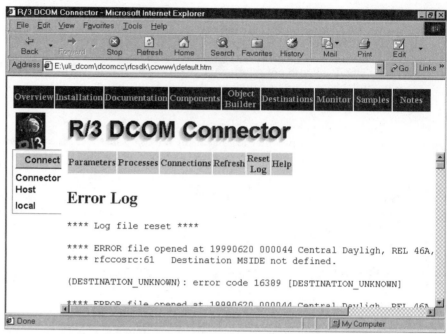

The `Reset Log` option will clear the contents of the Log File. As you may expect, this functionality can also be replicated.

The class that implements this is the
CCMonitor member of the
CCADMINLIB library. The view of this
class from the Object Browser reveals
the following functionality:

Again we will need a member variable for this class:

```
Option Explicit

Dim mstrDestination As String

Dim mdcomRegistry As CCADMINLib.CCRegistry
Dim mdcomMonitor As CCADMINLib.CCMonitor


Private Sub Form_Load()

    Set mdcomRegistry = CreateObject("SAP.CCRegistry.1")
    Set mdcomMonitor = CreateObject("SAP.CCMonitor.1")

End Sub
```

## The GetConnections Method

First on the list is the `GetConnections` method. This method returns an object that we may assume to be an ADO Recordset. The syntax for the method is simple:

```
GetConnections() As Object
```

The code to test this method is shown below, where `mdcomMonitor` is a reference to the `CCMonitor` class:

```
Private Sub cmdGetConnections_Click()

    Dim recConnections As ADODB.Recordset

    Set recConnections = mdcomMonitor.GetConnections
    Set DataGrid1.DataSource = recConnections

    Set recConnections = Nothing

End Sub
```

This method returns **active connections**. Therefore, to meaningfully test it, we have to have an active connection. Don't confuse connection with destination. The destination is a mere connection string, whereas the connection is an established "channel" of communication to SAP R/3. You may have several destinations and no active connections. To ensure that we have active connections, I will `Ping` two legitimate destinations and then call the `GetConnections` method:

```
Private Sub cmdGetConnections_Click()

    Dim recConnections As ADODB.Recordset

    On Error GoTo ErrTrap

    mdcomRegistry.Ping "MSIDES"
    mdcomRegistry.Ping "TESTDEST"
```

```
    Set recConnections = mdcomMonitor.GetConnections
    Set DataGrid1.DataSource = recConnections

    Set reconnections = Nothing

    Exit Sub

ErrTrap:

    MsgBox Err.Description & "From GetConnections"

End Sub
```

The results are shown below:

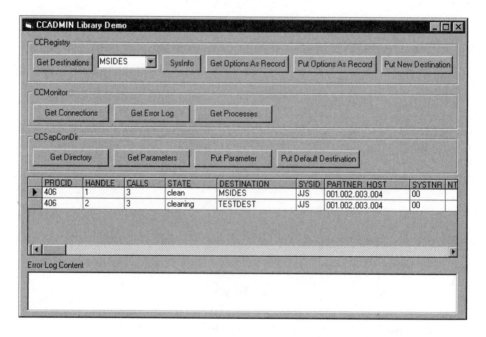

*One side note. I have modified the displayed values of all IP addresses. I have complete trust in the good will of my respected readers, but common courtesy towards the people who provided me with a connection to their server dictates it.*

If you don't have an active connection, you will get an empty recordset. As you will observe, the fields for the resultant recordset of the `GetConnections` method are different from the Destination parameters.

## The GetErrorLog and ResetErrorLog Methods

Next is the `GetErrorLog` method. It returns string data with the contents of the Error Log file and it doesn't take any arguments. The code:

```
Private Sub cmdGetErrorLog_Click()

   Text1 = mdcomMonitor.GetErrorLog

End Sub
```

Will result in the following:

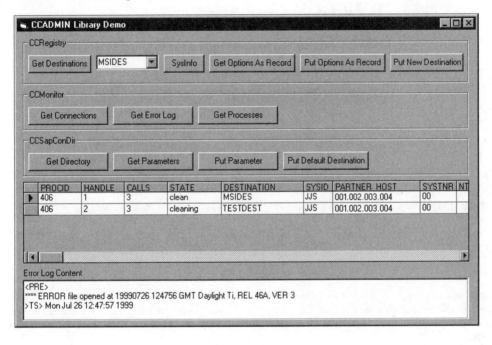

Fairly obviously, the `ResetErrorLog` method will clear the Error Log file.

## *The GetProcesses Method*

The next functionality enabled from the DCOM CC Monitor is the `Processes` link. If you click on it in the DCOM CC GUI you will be presented with the following results:

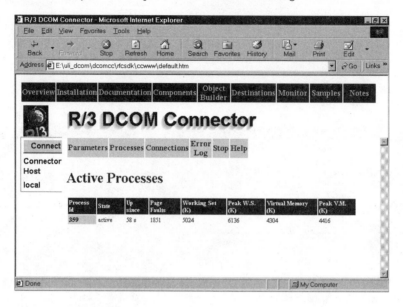

To replicate this functionality, we can use the `GetProcesses` method of the `CCMonitor` class.

The syntax of this method is also very simple:

```
GetProcesses() As Object
```

We can assume, as usual, that it returns an ADO Recordset. This method will return a set of data related to the Windows process that the component uses. This has nothing to do with the connection to SAP R/3 itself. It is the data related to the Windows process that the DCOM CC core component runs in.

> *Note that if your computer does not have the* `psapi.dll` *(normally not present in Windows 95 machines) this feature will not fully function. This is an implementation of the Windows NT Task Manager.*

While this functionality does not explicitly relate to SAP R/3 activities, such as the connection, it is very useful for administering DCOM CC components.

> *If your DCOM CC core components are installed in MTS, then they run in the address space of an instance of* `mtx.exe`*.*

The following code implements the process-related functionality:

```
Private Sub cmdGetProcesses_Click()

   Dim recProcesses As ADODB.Recordset

   Set recProcesses = mdcomMonitor.GetProcesses
   Set DataGrid1.DataSource = recProcesses

   Set recProcesses = Nothing

End Sub
```

After execution of the above code, we will have results similar to those presented via the DCOM CC home page:

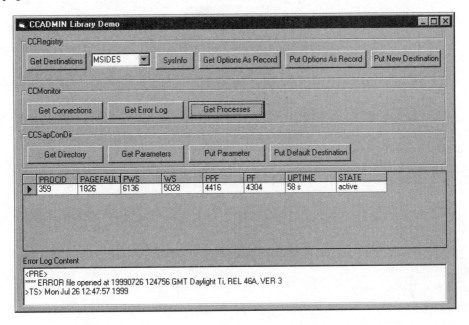

This completes the replication of the reliably implemented functionality of the CCMONITOR class.

# Programming the SapConDir Class

The next class in the CCADMINLIB library that we are going to explore is the SapConDir class. This class encapsulates the functionality that deals with components already installed on your machine. It also deals with options for the DCOM CC configuration, such as trace levels, home directory etc. As with all other classes, this one derives its functionality from LIBRFC32.DLL.

Take a look at the implementation of this class in the Object Browser:

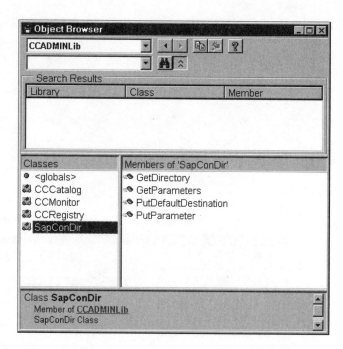

Add another member variable declaration to the form:

```
Option Explicit

Dim mstrDestination As String

Dim mdcomRegistry As CCADMINLib.CCRegistry
Dim mdcomMonitor As CCADMINLib.CCMonitor
Dim mdcomSapConDir As CCADMINLib.SapConDir


Private Sub Form_Load()

   Set mdcomRegistry = CreateObject("SAP.CCRegistry.1")
   Set mdcomMonitor = CreateObject("SAP.CCMonitor.1"
   Set mdcomSapConDir = CreateObject("SAP.CCConDir.1")

End Sub
```

## The GetDirectory Method

The first method is the GetDirectory method. Again, the syntax is simple:

```
GetDirectory() As Object
```

It will also return an ADO Recordset, which contains values of proxy components installed on your machine. To look up the analogous functionality of the DCOM CC, go to the Components selection on the DCOM CC home page and then select Details. You will see all the information on installed components grouped in an HTML table:

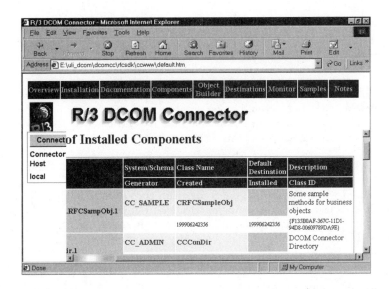

To follow our pattern of learning by replication, I put together the following code:

```
Private Sub cmdGetDirectory_Click()

   Dim recDir As ADODB.Recordset

   Set recDir = mdcomSapConDir.GetDirectory
   Set DataGrid1.DataSource = recDir

   Set recDir = Nothing

End Sub
```

After execution, this returns a recordset populated with all the expected information:

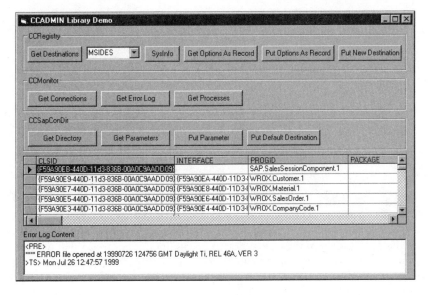

You may notice that the **PACKAGE** field is empty. Moreover, the DCOM CC web GUI doesn't help either. The `Details` option on the `Components` link does not offer the value for the package the component belongs to in MTS.

This is rather inconvenient, because if I need to know what package my component belongs to (in other words, is it installed on MTS or is it a stand alone in-process server) I have to fire up MTS. This is not a big problem in itself, but it would be natural to expect this type of information from the DCOM CC in itself. I am sure that future releases of the DCOM CC will bring us many useful features and fix some minor irritants like this one.

When I started working on this book, I made a promise to myself not to hack and not to extend the functionality beyond that which I am given out-of-the-box – it was a tough one to keep. I made this commitment because I wanted to present the reader with code samples and applications that they could immediately start using without having to set up their environment like mine. However, I don't consider a little function that will populate the **PACKAGE** field of the `GetDirectory` resultant recordset hacking. It's merely a little exercise on registry programming.

### Populating the GetDirectory PACKAGE Field

What happens is that the information on MTS components and DCOM CC components is kept in different places in the registry. What we have as a result of calling the `GetDirectory` method is a list of CLSIDs for the DCOM CC proxies. Should they also be MTS installed components, their CLISD will appear under the `Transaction Server` key in the registry. Every component has a `Package` value in the registry, which is a GUID for the Package component that can be found in the `HKEY_LOCAL_MACHINE\SOFTWARE\Microsoft\Transaction Server\Packages` folder:

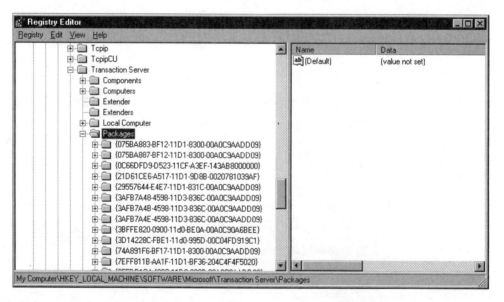

If I therefore query the `Transaction Server\Components` folder using the CLSID value I get from the `CLSID` field of the `GetDirectory` resultant recordset, I will be able to find the GUID for the package that the component belongs to. If it does not belong to any package, the return value will be an empty string.

I can then use the GUID of the package to query the `Transaction Server\Packages` folder to find the name value for the package. This algorithm will either produce the names of the packages that the DCOM CC generated proxy components belong to, or it will return an empty string indicating that they are not installed in MTS. The preceding statement is accurate because you cannot have a component installed in MTS without a package that the component belongs to.

Based on this hypothesis, I wrote a mini-function that performs this registry querying, and uses the results of the registry queries to populate the `PACKAGE` field of the `GetDirectory` method's resultant recordset. I can safely do all this in one swoop, because the recordset is disconnected and nothing but a nicely formatted matrix.

First, I created a subroutine that is going to query the registry. To do this, I use the `Microsoft Visual Studio\Common\Tools\APE\REGTOOL5.DLL` that comes with Visual Studio 6.0.

*If you don't have this handy library, you have to resort to registry API antics. The algorithm will not change, no matter what registry access techniques you use.*

To use this library, you have to add a reference to the appropriate DLL:

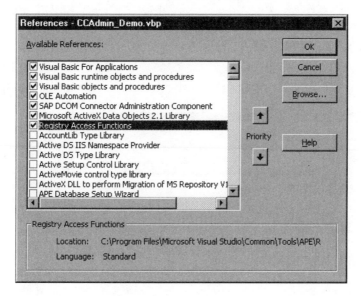

When we have a reference, we can use the single class implemented in the registry functions library:

The key used in this function is HKEY_LOCAL_MACHINE that is defined in the library as a constant:

The two key pathnames are SOFTWARE\Microsoft\Transaction Server\Components and
SOFTWARE\Microsoft\Transaction Server\Packages. The code for the function is
displayed below. It takes the value for the CLSID in one argument, and returns the value for the
package name, or an empty string if the component does not belong to any package (is not installed
on MTS) in the second argument:

```
Dim mxReg As New REGTool5.Registry

Public Sub GetProxyPackage(vCLSID As String, vPackage As String)

  Dim strKeyValue As String

  mxReg.GetKeyValue HKEY_LOCAL_MACHINE, _
                "SOFTWARE\Microsoft\Transaction Server\Components\" & _
                vCLSID, "Package", strKeyValue

  If strKeyValue = "" Then
    vPackage = ""
    Exit Sub
  Else
    mxReg.GetKeyValue HKEY_LOCAL_MACHINE, _
                "SOFTWARE\Microsoft\Transaction Server\Packages\" _
                & strKeyValue, "Name", vPackage
  End If

End Sub
```

To use this routine, I have to modify the procedure that calls the GetDirectory method:

```
Private Sub cmdGetDirectory_Click()

  Dim recDir As ADODB.Recordset
  Dim vPack As String

  Set recDir = mdcomSapConDir.GetDirectory

  recDir.MoveFirst

  Do Until recDir.EOF
     GetProxyPackage recDir![CLSID], vPack
     recDir![package] = vPack
     recDir.Update
     recDir.MoveNext
  Loop

  recDir.MoveFirst

  Set DataGrid1.DataSource = recDir

  Set recDir = Nothing

End Sub
```

I decided against using a second recordset, because it's not necessary in this case. I simply go through the recordset, pass the CLSID of the component to my registry querying routine, GetProxyPackage, and update the PACKAGE field of the current record with the result of the GetProxyPackage. I then display the results in the data grid:

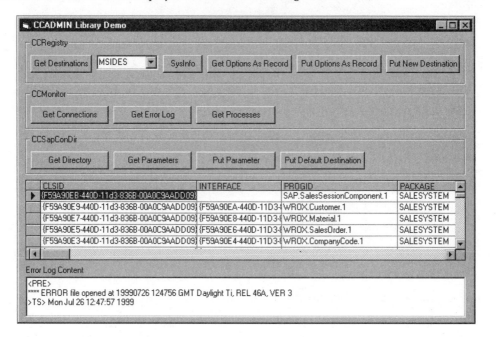

As you can see, the PACKAGE field is now being populated with correct values if the component is installed in MTS.

## The GetParameters Method

The next method we'll look at is `GetParameters`. The functionality implemented by this method can be found on the `Monitor | Parameters` link of the DCOM CC home page:

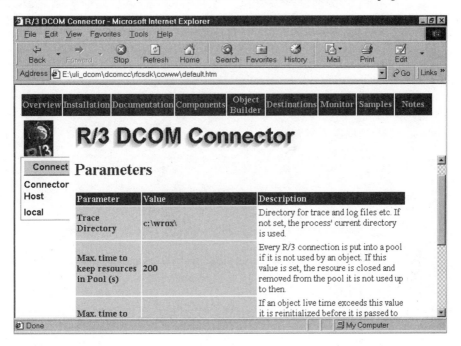

This functionality relates to the DCOM CC parameters, not the proxies. You may modify the DCOM CC parameters regarding trace, timeouts, home directory etc. The syntax of the method is similar to those that we have already seen:

```
GetParameters() As Object
```

And the method also returns an ADO Recordset. If we execute the following code:

```
Private Sub cmdGetParameters_Click()

  Dim recParams As ADODB.Recordset

  Set recParams = mdcomSapConDir.GetParameters
  Set DataGrid1.DataSource = recParams

  Set recParams = Nothing

End Sub
```

The results will be similar to those below (your results may vary depending on your configuration of the DCOM CC):

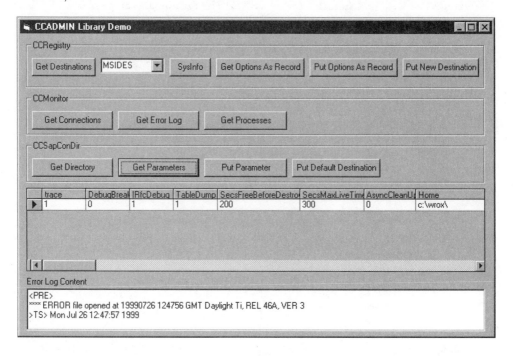

## The PutParameter Method

To change any of the parameter settings you can either use the DCOM CC GUI or do it programmatically. To use the DCOM CC GUI, go to `Monitor | Parameters` and click on the value that you want to change. The web variation of the input box will pop up: enter the new value there and click `OK`:

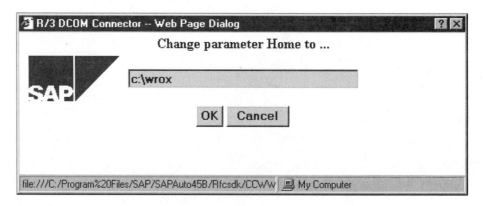

To do it programmatically, you should use the `PutParameter` method of the `SapConDir` class. The syntax of this method is very direct:

```
PutParameter(option As String, value As String)
```

The `option` argument is the name of the field of the recordset that you get from the `GetParameters` method. You can also see it as part of the prompt text in the input box when you attempt to change the parameter using the DCOM CC GUI, right after the words `Change Parameter`. `value` is the new value for the parameter.

The code to change parameter values will look somewhat like the fragment below:

```
Private Sub cmdPutParameter_Click()

   mdcomSapConDir.PutParameter "trace", "1"
   mdcomSapConDir.PutParameter "home", "C:\Wrox\"
   mdcomSapConDir.PutParameter "irfcdebug", "1"
   mdcomSapConDir.PutParameter "tabledump", "1"

End Sub
```

## The PutDefaultDestination Method

The last method of the `SapConDir` class is `PutDefaultDestination`. This method assigns a default destination to a proxy component. It is a convenience feature for the most part, which will force the proxy component to use a particular destination when invoked. If you don't use your components for different SAP R/3 systems, this may prove convenient.

The main premise of the DCOM CC is desktop integration. For the most common scenario – data entry or reporting – you would normally go against the same SAP R/3 instance all the time. If you assign a particular destination to the proxy component, you don't have to explicitly assign a destination or its attributes, provided that your destination is configured fully (including password). The proxy component will use the attributes of the assigned destination every time it needs to contact SAP R/3.

We can assign the destination to the component using the DCOM CC GUI and programmatically. In the DCOM CC GUI, the place to go is the `Components` link:

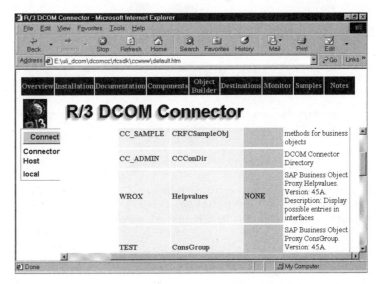

To change the value, hover your mouse cursor over the `Value` field and click there. A dialog window will pop up, to let you select the destination:

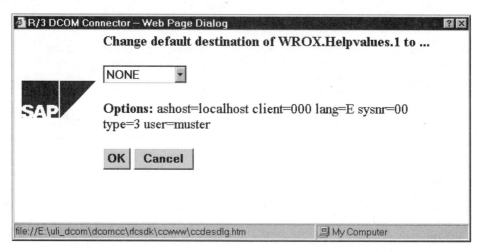

To clear an entry completely, select the last, blank option in the destinations combo box:

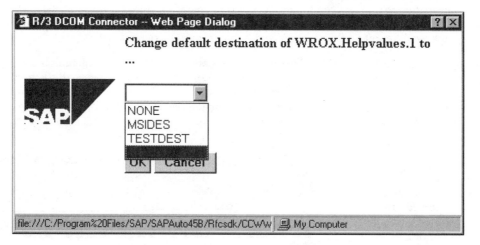

To perform the same activities programmatically we can use the `PutDefaultDestination` method. The syntax for this method is:

```
PutDefaultDestination(clsid As String, destination As String)
```

This method does not return anything. Its `clsid` parameter is expected to be the CLSID of the proxy component. We've already learned how to get those values using the `GetDirectory` method's resultant recordset. The field in that recordset is `CLSID`.

There are some issues to consider with default destinations. First, it would not make much sense to assign different destinations to different components bundled into the same proxy. You can include several SAP R/3 business objects in one DCOM CC generated library component. If you were going to generate a proxy to encapsulate a complex process that spans several business objects, you would normally be going against only one SAP R/3. You would not check for Material in one R/3 and process the Sales Order in another R/3. This makes the assignment of different default destinations to components that belong to the same proxy library useless.

Another issue is that if you were using the Session object, it would make sense to assign a default destination to it and not to bother for the other proxy components. The Session object will handle all connectivity and context functionality, and all other objects will be created using the Session object anyway.

You can assign default destinations any way you like. I will illustrate the use of the default destination in the next chapter.

At this point it's important to learn how to assign the default destination to a proxy programmatically. The code that's going to do that is featured below:

```
Private Sub cmdPutDefaultDestination_Click()

    mdcomSapConDir.PutDefaultDestination _
                "{76D43273-2B8F-11d3-8126-00500462FE37}", "TESTDEST"

End Sub
```

*When calling this method, remember not to modify the class ID value. Do not remove the curly brackets on either end of the class id value – if you do, the call will generate a run-time error, Cannot Open Registry.*

*I would also advise against using mixed case names for destinations. The DCOM CC core components do not appear to be case sensitive for destination names. However, naming consistency always helps – I try to use all upper case for destination names.*

After the `PutDefaultDestination` executes successfully, you can check for the new value using either the DCOM CC GUI or call the `GetDirectory` method, and check the `DESTINATION` field of the resultant recordset.

# Programming the CCCatalog Class

The last class in the `CCADMINLIB` library is `CCCatalog`. This class does what its name implies – it provides the ability to view already generated components and their members – a **catalog**. The functionality of this class does not involve connectivity to SAP R/3. It provides a logical view of metadata from previously generated business object proxies. It can be useful for any administrative type application that has to include object inventory functionality.

To better understand how to use this class, we have to refresh our knowledge of the logic of the DCOM CC object builder functionality. When you prepare to generate a proxy component using the DCOM CC, you have to specify a four-letter namespace parameter. The value of this parameter will be a prefix for all components generated in the proxy library. The `CCCatalog` considers this value to be a **Schemata**.

The choice of word here can be understood better if you consider that the default value for it is the SAP R/3 system name, where the SAP R/3 system is the system you connect to. The recommended value to use as the namespace is the system name or your company abbreviation. This approach correctly reflects the fact that the schemata for business objects will vary from system to system depending on the SAP R/3 release and configuration.

To catalog anything, we have to establish the relational- or hierarchical- order for the objects that we want to catalog. For the CCCatalog class, this hierarchy is as follows:

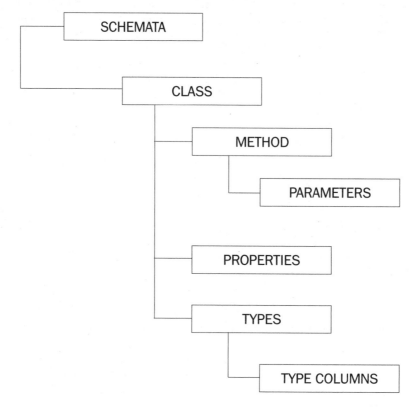

This structure should be familiar because it reflects the SAP R/3 Business Object Repository. The only difference is in the way we refer to the elements:

> A Business Object becomes a **Class**

> A BAPI becomes a **Method**

> Business Object Keys become Properties

This naming structure is much closer to the Visual Basic and COM standards than SAP's so this should make it easier for us to follow. CCCatalog also exposes the metadata of RFC Structures that are referred to as **Types**. The DCOM CC views those structures as User Defined Types. This is a familiar practice to the Visual Basic programmer.

The DCOM CC translates RFC-types into COM-types and it defines COM-structures based on the BOR metadata. `CCCatalog` gives us both Types and **Type Columns** – the structure of Types. This is very useful because it allows us to analyze the structure of the data that the proxy methods expect in a data type and business sense.

To continue with our tradition, we will try to replicate the DCOM CC out-of-the-box functionality, implemented via the DCOM CC web GUI.

## DCOM CC Methodology

To get a sense of what the catalog functionality is all about, open the DCOM CC home page and select the `Components` option:

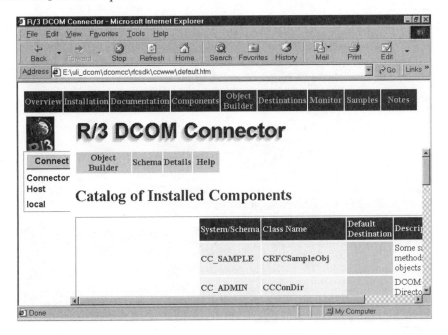

From this page, select the Schema option:

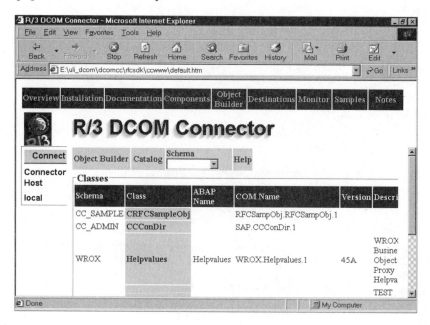

This page is the content of the catalog not sorted by schema. To sort the catalog by the schema, drop the Schema combo-box and select the schema of your choice:

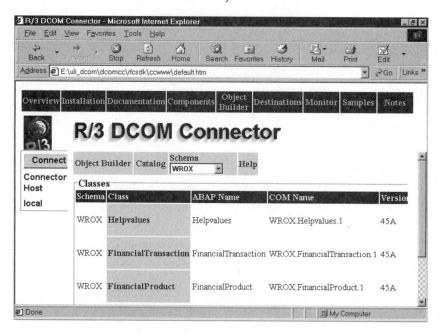

I have selected to look at the component that we generated in Chapter 10 using the namespace WROX.

*The nice feature of the DCOM CC on this page is that if you select Help it will present you with a comprehensive explanation written for somebody outside of the DCOM CC development team.*

At the bottom of this page are option buttons that allow you to select what you want to see should you click on the Class column for the business object:

**No object selected.**
⊙ Methods  ○ Parameters  ○ Types

I will use the Helpvalues object here:

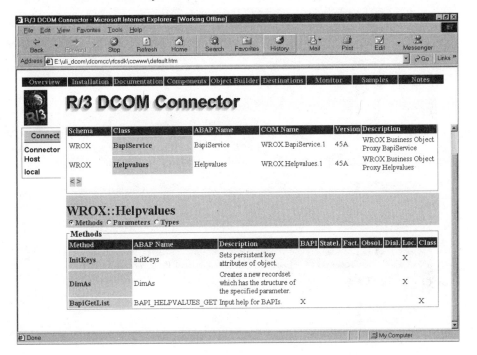

From this point, you can go on and select a particular method and view the results. I selected the `BapiGetList` method:

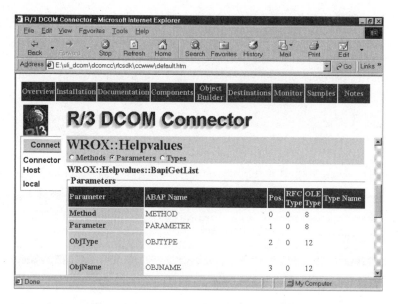

You can elect to view Properties or Types. The `Helpvalues` object does not have keys and therefore no properties, but it has types associated with it and we can select to view them. To do so just click on the `Types` option button and click on any type name. I will use the `BAPIRETURN`:

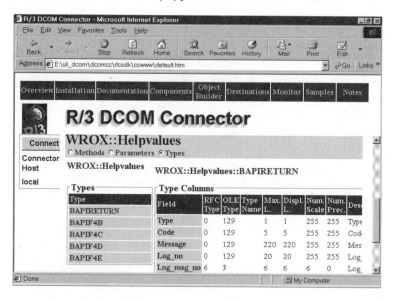

This is as far as the DCOM CC will take you in its catalog functionality.

## Programmatic Methodology

To stay true to form, we will try to programmatically replicate the component catalog functionality of the DCOM CC using the CCADMINLIB library and Visual Basic. I decided against an elaborate GUI implementation here, because it would distract the reader and put too much emphasis on features that are irrelevant to the technology. The main purpose of this part of the book is to familiarize you with the technology and methodology behind the DCOM CC, not to prove Visual Basic's ability to generate an elaborate GUI. Again, the function-per-button approach is good for this exercise.

Start a new Standard EXE project, call it DCOMCC_Cat, and add a reference to the CCADMINLIB library and the ADO library. Add a series of command buttons and an OLEDB Data Grid to the form:

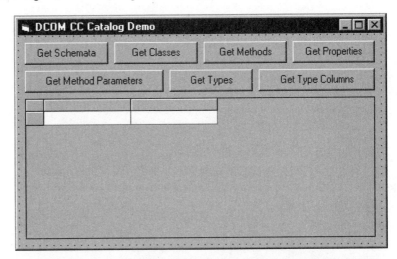

First thing to do is to take a look at the CCCatalog class using the Object Browser:

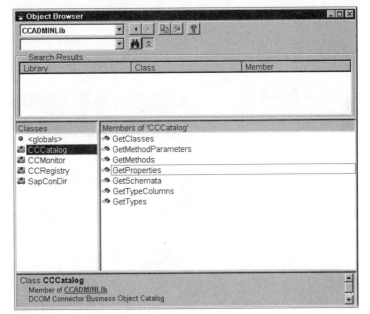

**347**

### The GetSchemata Method

The first method of this class we have to deal with is `GetSchemata`:

```
GetSchemata() As Object
```

As usual, this method will return us an ADO Recordset with schemata names. We first declare a variable to hold the reference to the `CCCatalog` class:

```
Option Explicit
```

```
Dim mdcomCatalog As CCADMINLib.CCCatalog
```

We also need to instantiate it in the `Form_Load` event:

```
Private Sub Form_Load()

   Set mdcomCatalog = CreateObject("SAP.CCCatalog.1")

End Sub
```

After we get this, it is possible to invoke the necessary methods:

```
Private Sub cmdGetSchemata_Click()

   Dim recSchemata As ADODB.Recordset

   Set recSchemata = mdcomCatalog.GetSchemata
   Set DataGrid1.DataSource = recSchemata

   Set recSchemata = Nothing

End Sub
```

The result of this method will be somewhat like the one below:

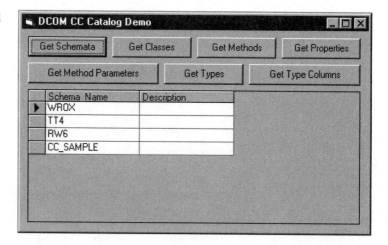

## The GetClasses Method

Once we get names for the Schemata, we can get Classes that belong to a particular Schemata. The method to get all the classes is GetClasses. The syntax is:

```
GetClasses(schemaName As String) As Object
```

This method takes the name of the Schemata and returns an ADO Recordset containing information about classes that belong to the Schemata. The call to this method is also very straightforward:

```
Private Sub cmdGetClasses_Click()

  Dim recClasses As ADODB.Recordset

  Set recClasses = mdcomCatalog.GetClasses("CC_SAMPLE")
  Set DataGrid1.DataSource = recClasses

  Set recClasses = Nothing

End Sub
```

*Please note that I use hard-coded values from the sample business object proxy supplied with the DCOM CC – SAP R/3 DCOM Connector Samples Package – the* Customer *component. This is to ensure that all of us are on the same page.*

The result of this call is shown below:

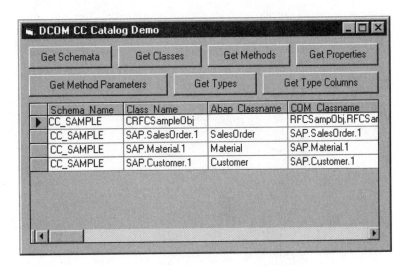

| | Schema Name | Class Name | Abap Classname | COM Classname |
|---|---|---|---|---|
| ▶ | CC_SAMPLE | CRFCSampleObj | | RFCSampObj.RFCSar |
| | CC_SAMPLE | SAP.SalesOrder.1 | SalesOrder | SAP.SalesOrder.1 |
| | CC_SAMPLE | SAP.Material.1 | Material | SAP.Material.1 |
| | CC_SAMPLE | SAP.Customer.1 | Customer | SAP.Customer.1 |

The resultant recordset contains information that is displayed by the DCOM CC via the Component option.

## The GetMethods Method

To drilldown the catalog hierarchy, we have to use the `Class_Name` field provided in the resultant recordset from `GetClasses`. What we need is list of Methods, a.k.a. BAPIs, that are defined in the business object proxies. To do so we have to use the `GetMethods` method of the `CCCatalog` class.

The `GetMethods` has the following syntax:

```
GetMethods(schemaName As String, className As String) As Object
```

This method expects the name of the Schemata and the name of the Class. It will return an ADO Recordset containing data for all Methods defined in the proxy. The call to the method in our example project is shown below:

```
Private Sub cmdGetMethods_Click()

  Dim recMethods As ADODB.Recordset

  Set recMethods = mdcomCatalog.GetMethods("CC_SAMPLE", "Customer")
  Set DataGrid1.DataSource = recMethods

  Set recMethods = Nothing

End Sub
```

After we execute the above code, we will see the following:

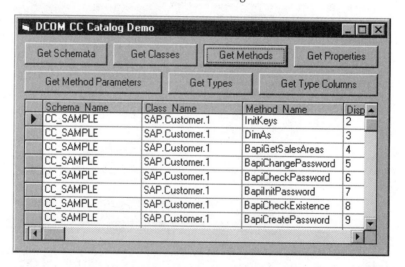

Note that the list of Methods include the DCOM CC specific methods absent from SAP R/3 BOR definitions – `DimAs`, `InitKeys` etc. Remember that the DCOM CC Object Builder utility adds additional methods and properties to business objects to enable some necessary functionality, e.g. connect to SAP R/3 and dimension parameters.

To differentiate between original methods (BAPIs) and DCOM CC specific methods, the resultant recordset returned by `GetMethods` contains the field `IsBapi`. This is populated by an X if the method is an implementation of an original BAPI:

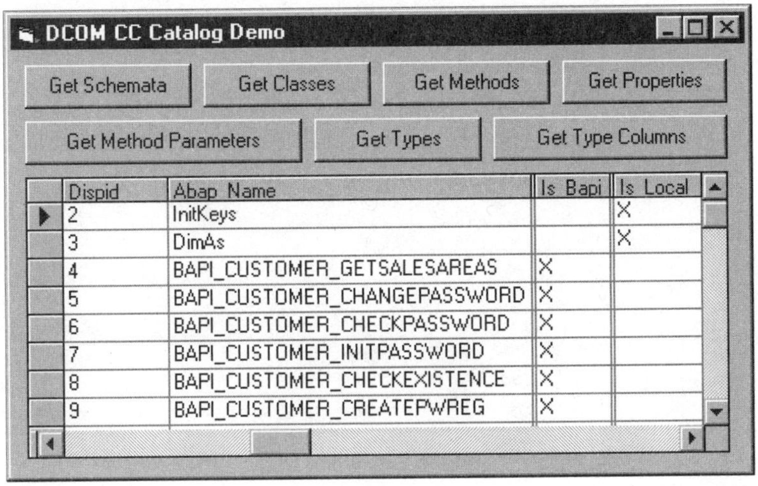

The DCOM CC specific methods will have an X in the `IsLocal` field of the resultant recordset.

## The GetProperties Method

If we need to check whether the object has Properties and retrieve them, the method to use is `GetProperties`. The syntax for this method is shown below:

```
GetProperties(schemaName As String, className As String) As Object
```

This method of `CCCatalog` expects the Schemata name and the Class name to be passed to it, and it will return an ADO Recordset containing data on the Properties of the business object proxy, should it have any. The code for this method call is:

```
Private Sub cmdGetProperties_Click()

  Dim recProps As ADODB.Recordset

  Set recProps = mdcomCatalog.GetProperties("CC_SAMPLE", "Customer")
  Set DataGrid1.DataSource = recProps

  Set recProps = Nothing

End Sub
```

**351**

The results of this code execution are:

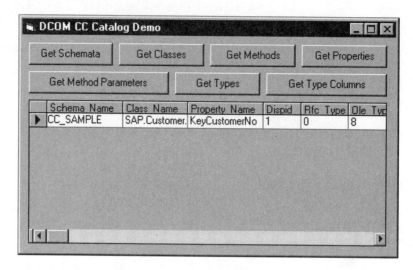

It is easy to see that Properties implement Keys for the business object.

## The GetMethodParameters Method

Once we have the Methods of business objects, it would make perfect sense to go after their Parameters. To get Parameters, we have to employ the `GetMethodParameters` method of the `CCCatalog` class. The syntax for this method is shown below:

```
GetMethodParameters(schemaName As String, className As String, _
                    methodName As String) As Object
```

This method expects the Schema name, the Class name and the Method name. It will return an ADO Recordset containing all the parameters for that particular method. Our sample code for the method call is:

```
Private Sub cmdGetMethodParameters_Click()

  Dim recParams As ADODB.Recordset

  Set recParams = mdcomCatalog.GetMethodParameters _
                        ("CC_SAMPLE", "Customer", "BapiGetDetail")

  Set DataGrid1.DataSource = recParams

  Set recParams = Nothing

End Sub
```

The result of the above code execution is shown below:

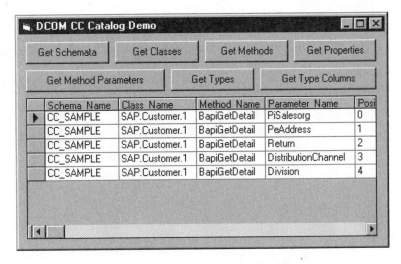

After we get Method Parameters, the only things left are Types and Type Columns.

*Note that Parameters and Types are not related directly in the DCOM CC catalog model.*

The resultant recordset of the `GetMethodParameters` method does have a `Ref_Type_Name` field that contains the Type name corresponding to the Method Parameter. However, not all Parameters have a corresponding Type. This is due to the implementation specifics of BAPIs in SAP R/3. What appears in the BAPI definition as a Parameter, may actually be a member of an RFC structure that is being exposed as a Parameter for the BAPI. That is why you may see several Types for business object but have fewer `Ref_Type_Name` values.

## The GetTypes Method

To get Types for the Class we have to use the `GetTypes` method. The syntax of the method is shown below:

```
GetTypes(schemaName As String, className As String) As Object
```

This method of the `CCCatalog` expects the Schemata name and the Class name. It returns an ADO Recordset containing data for all Types that are defined in the business object proxy. The call to this method can be constructed as shown below:

```
Private Sub cmdGetTypes_Click()

  Dim recTypes As ADODB.Recordset

  Set recTypes= mdcomCatalog.GetTypes("CC_SAMPLE", "Customer")
  Set DataGrid1.DataSource = recTypes

  Set recTypes = Nothing

End Sub
```

The result of the above code execution is shown below:

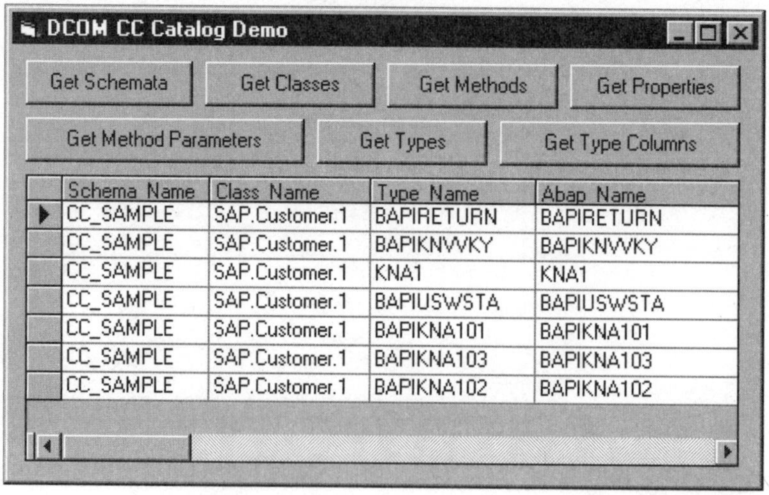

## The GetTypeColumns Method

The last functionality of the DCOM CC Catalog component is to get the structure of the Type. Every Type is an RFC Structure or Table, and we may be interested in its layout. To get this data we have to use the `GetTypeColumns` method of the `CCCatalog` class. The syntax for this method is shown below:

```
GetTypeColumns(schemaName As String, className As String, typeName As String) _
          As Object
```

This method expects the Schemata name, the Class name and the Type name, which we can get from the `GetTypes` resultant recordset in the `Type_Name` field. It returns an ADO Recordset containing metadata on the Type. The code that we use to call the `GetTypeColumns` method is shown below:

```
Private Sub cmdGetTypeColumns_Click()

  Dim recTColumns As ADODB.Recordset

  Set recTColumns= mdcomCatalog.GetTypeColumns _
                            ("CC_SAMPLE", "Customer", "BAPIKNA101")

  Set DataGrid1.DataSource = recTColumns

  Set recTColumns = Nothing

End Sub
```

It retrieves metadata on the BAPIKNA101 Type that corresponds to the PeAddress BAPI parameter. This code produces the following results:

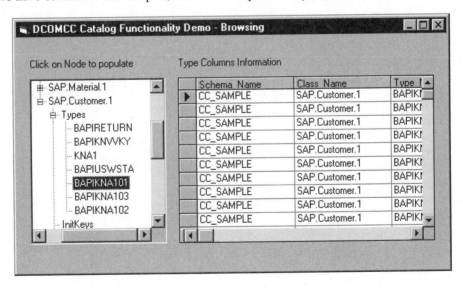

## Dynamic Browsing

In the sample code available for download from the Wrox Press website, I have included an additional project with this chapter – DCOM_Browse. It doesn't use any additional functionality from what we have covered in this chapter, but it does implement dynamic browsing.

This dynamic browsing project has a rudimentary implementation of the Explorer-style UI. You have to click on the node if you want it to be populated. The data grid will display the Type Columns information. In this project, I used the `New GUID` library to generate unique keys for the tree view nodes. This library is the part of the Microsoft Repository SDK that is available as a free download from the MSDN website. It's a very handy library that generates GUID for you. Aside from this, all the functionality used on the dynamic browsing form is identical to what we have discussed and implemented using hard-coded values.

# Summary

This concludes our exploration of the `CCADMINLIB` core component of the DCOM Component Connector. We have learned how to program against this library and what functionality it exposes. We have also implemented all the functionality available via the DCOM CC web GUI. The `CCADMINLIB` component allows us to incorporate the administrative functionality of the DCOM CC into Visual Basic applications, without forcing users to open the DCOM CC web GUI.

Moreover, I don't want to give the impression that the DCOM CC can be used only "as is". What you get with the DCOM CC is a very strong and useful component implementation, and a UI that implements every feature of the DCOM CC. The odd feeling that you get after using this SAP tool is that the DCOM CC is very Microsoft in spirit. It does great things and is needed, but not many people can understand what it is for. What's more, it has somewhat strange naming conventions and UI implementation – however, it lets you use all the functionality you need from your applications.

In the next chapter, we will look at how we can programmatically access the DCOM CC's Object Builder functionality.

# DCOM Component Connector Object Builder Functionality

In the previous chapter, we learned how to use the administrative part of the DCOM Component Connector's core components. We have seen how to browse the catalog of existing proxy components, look up, create and modify destinations and browse the business object proxy metadata. We learned how the DCOM CC persists information in the registry and how we can extend some functionality of the DCOM CC components to better suit our needs. We also went through the feature-by-feature replication of the out-of-the-box DCOM CC functionality.

This information allows us to build custom applications that incorporate the functionality of the DCOM CC administrative component. Although this is very important functionality, if you don't generate any business object proxy components, you have nothing to explore or administer.

The main DCOM CC functionality is online browsing of the SAP R/3 Business Object Repository, and the generation of in-process COM servers that implement the functionality of SAP R/3 business objects. What makes the DCOM CC stand out from the relatively big family of the SAP RFC SDK derived tools is its ability to generate ready-to-use COM components that can be fully utilized as stand-alone or MTS components.

Another very important feature of the DCOM CC is that all the business object proxies that it generates, and its own core components, use the ADO Recordset as the medium of data exchange. This fact provides native integration into Windows data handling. Additionally, with ADO built-in support for XML, the DCOM CC may help to position Windows and COM as a 'common denominator' platform for distributed, heterogeneous OS-based information systems.

*I will not elaborate on the DCOM CC integration with the MS family of desktop and enterprise products for two reasons: physical book space constraints and scope issues. This book is a technology introduction. Should it generate substantial interest, I will follow it up with a more technology implementation focused and business problem oriented development book, with DCOM CC as an enabling tool.*

What we're going to learn in this chapter is how to programmatically use the **Object Builder** functionality of the DCOM CC. We will see how to browse the SAP R/3 BOR and generate SAP R/3 business object proxy components. To do so, I will follow the pattern set in this part of the book – replication of the DCOM CC original web-based functionality. I will basically do nothing more than provide a rudimentary Visual Basic generated GUI for the DCOM CC Object Builder components. This will show us how to use them, and how to incorporate them into other applications you may wish to develop. The sample demo project for this chapter will incorporate the DCOM CC administrative functionality that we have already seen in Chapter 11.

# Programming the PROXYGENERATORLib Library

The library that implements the Object Builder functionality of the DCOM CC is the PROXYGENERATORLib library, physically implemented as a COM compliant DLL – PROXYGEN.DLL. This DLL is installed as a part of the DCOM CC components installation routine that we covered in Chapter 10 (unless you selected not to install it).

If you have correctly installed all the DCOM CC components, you will see the following entry in the Visual Basic **References** dialog – SAP DCOM Object Builder 1.0 Type Library:

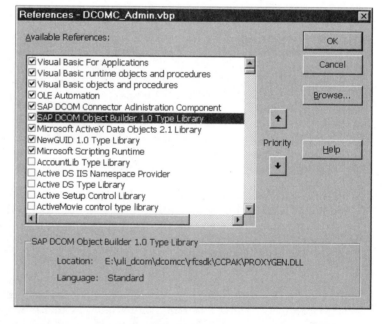

360

If you add a reference to this library and open the Object Browser, you will see the following:

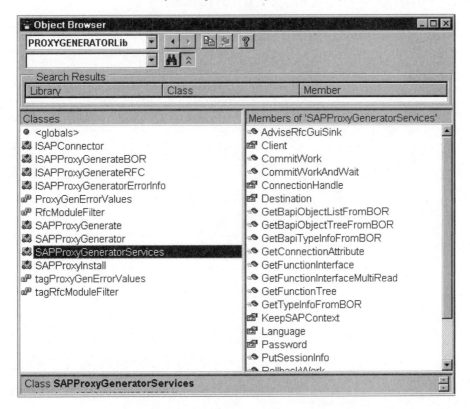

This library implements more functionality than the CCADMINLib and it derives a lot from LIBRFC32.DLL. This is not surprising, because the PROXYGENERATORLib library includes connectivity and BOR browsing functionality.

# DCOMC_Admin – Browsing Functionality

The sample project for this chapter is DCOMC_Admin. It allows you to browse existing components and the SAP R/3 BOR. The GUI for this project is rudimentary, just enough to make calls to methods and view results:

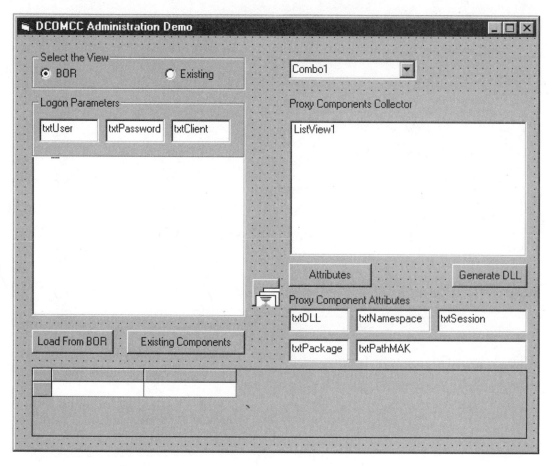

You can choose to browse the created proxy components or the SAP R/3 BOR. The choice is made using the option buttons at the top of the form. The default mode is online BOR browsing. We are implementing this as a first stage in generating proxy components.

If you select the BOR option, you have to specify the destination, which you can select from the combo box. This combo box is populated when the form is loaded, and displays all the defined destinations on your machine. It uses functionality already outlined in the previous chapter. Once you make your choice, you will be prompted to enter the password for the connection:

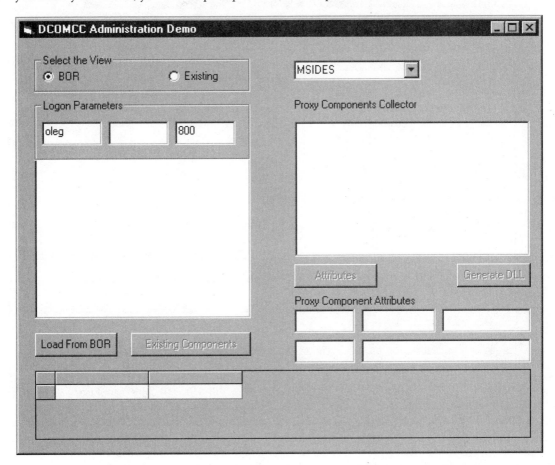

Enter the password and click on the **Load From BOR** button that is now enabled. After some time, depending on your connection, you will see the result below:

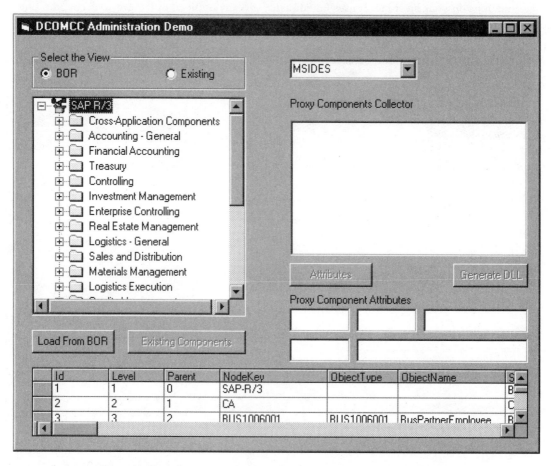

*By the way, the time needed to connect and download BOR metadata using DCOM CC components is an order of magnitude less than using SAP Assistant and its libraries.*

The Data Grid is on the form is used to display different resultant recordsets from method calls for illustrative purposes.

You can browse the metadata as you wish:

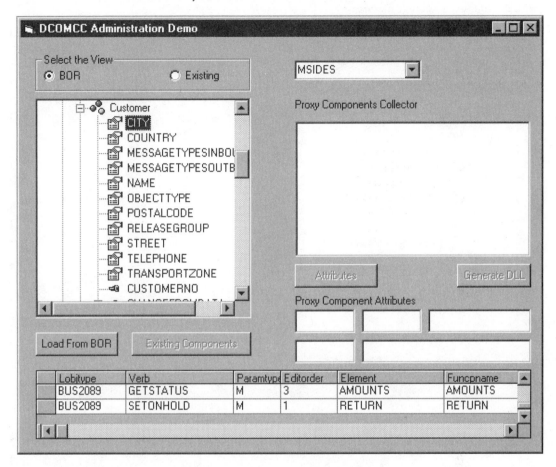

If you select the Existing option and click the Existing Components button, you will be presented with the following familiar picture:

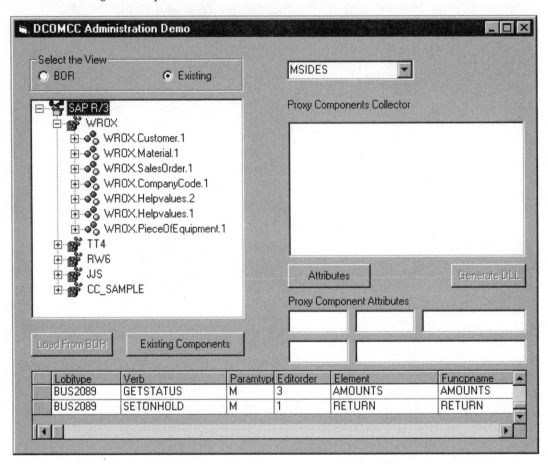

You can toggle the views using the option buttons. You can have a simultaneous view of existing components and the BOR – something the DCOM CC doesn't offer you from a single point of entry.

Let's take look at some of the code behind this functionality.

## Connecting to SAP R/3

We will start from a familiar place – how to establish a connection to SAP R/3 to browse the BOR. The DCOM CC web GUI implements it from the `Object Builder` page – we've already seen it at work in Chapter 10, and you can find the parallel screenshots for the DCOM CC there if you need to refresh your memory on its functionality.

First, we have to find the class in the `PROXYGENERATORLib` library to perform the SAP R/3 BOR browsing. This class is `SAPProxyGeneratorServices` – we can see its implementation in the Object Browser, as shown in our earlier screen shot. We can quickly find the familiar `PutSessionInfo` method that will assign logon attributes, or we can use them directly because they are exposed as properties (`Destination`, `User`, `Password`, `System Number` and `Client`), or employ a fully defined destination that includes the password.

> *You may wonder what the `CommitWork` and `Rollback` methods are doing in what is essentially a BOR browsing class. BOR browsing hardly employs any transaction processing. However, `Rollback` and `CommitWork` are present because it implements the `ISAPConnector` interface, and that one includes all the transaction related methods.*

To use any functionality of this class we have to first get a valid reference to it. Because the `PROXYGENERATOR` library may be installed as an MTS component or stand-alone, we have to consider some issues caused by the differences in the `New` and `CreateObject` functionality as related to MTS.

We could use the `New` keyword and declare the variable for referencing as `Object`. However, if the component is installed in MTS, it is better to use `CreateObject` rather than `New`. Declaring as `Object` is simply mandatory if you don't have the Windows NT 4 Service Pack 4 installed on your machine. If you have Service Pack 4, then you can use the class name without the `New` keyword. If the component is installed as a stand-alone, you may use `New`.

```
Dim mdcomProxySvc As Object
```

I will keep referencing the class as `Object` because it's going to work for both implementations, with or without MTS. For the same reason I will use the `CreateObject` function to create a running instance of the class:

```
Set mdcomProxySvc = CreateObject("SAP.ProxyGeneratorServices.1")
```

Remember that the object that we just instantiated will run in an MTS activity address space.

The next step will be to set up the logon parameters. We can do this using the pre-configured `Destination` property of the `mdcomProxySvc` object, or the `PutSessionInfo` method of the same object. In either case, the Proxy Generator library will use the information from the `Destination` property to logon to SAP R/3. The syntax will look like the fragment below:

```
mdcomProxySvc.PutSessionInfo "destination", "user", "pwd", "lang", "client"
```

Or like:

```
mdcomProxySvc.Destination = "destination"
```

Right after this line of code, we have to allow for multiple connectivity. Just like in my sample project, I may have several destinations that point to different SAP R/3 servers, or I may want to refresh the view of the BOR. To do this, I may invoke the `PutSessionInfo` method or use the `Destination` property more than once.

When I first invoked the `PutSessionInfo` twice I got the run-time error **Object already bound to R/3**. Then I recalled that the `KeepSAPContext` property defaults to `True`, therefore keeping the user context for SAP R/3. Obviously, when I tried to bind it again it refused. I added the following line of code before the previous fragments:

```
mdcomProxySvc.KeepSAPContext = False
```

```
mdcomProxySvc.PutSessionInfo "destination", "user", "pwd", "lang", "client"
```

And the problem went away. Now every time I connect to SAP R/3 I'm given a new context – the old contexts are pooled. This is a good illustration of how context works.

## Browsing the Business Object Repository

Once we have resolved the problems of logging on, we can start exploring the BOR. As you will recall from earlier chapters, the BOR has a hierarchical structure and we can query it externally.

The `SAPProxyGeneratorServices` class has a `GetBapiObjectTreeFromBOR` method. This method retrieves an ADO Recordset – same technology as for the `CCADMINLib` component – that contains the list of all the objects in the SAP R/3 BOR. The syntax for this method is shown below:

```
Sub GetBapiObjectTreeFromBOR(NodeKey As String, pTreeInfo)
```

The `NodeKey` argument refers to the name of the parent node of the BOR object hierarchy. If you pass an empty string it will return the whole hierarchy tree. The call to this method that gets you the whole BOR tree is shown below:

```
Dim recObjTypes As ADODB.Recordset
```

```
mdcomProxySvc.GetBapiObjectTreeFromBOR "", recObjTypes
```

```
Set DataGrid1.DataSource = recObjTypes
```

We can output the results into the Data Grid to see what we get out of the method call and to analyze the data:

| Id | Level | Parent | NodeKey | ObjectType | ObjectName | ShortText | Expandable | IsFolder |
|----|-------|--------|---------|------------|------------|-----------|------------|----------|
| 1 | 1 | 0 | SAP-R/3 | | | Business Application C | | X |
| 2 | 2 | 1 | CA | | | Cross-Application Com | | X |
| 3 | 3 | 2 | BUS1006001 | BUS1006001 | BusPartnerEm | Business partner emplo | | |
| 4 | 3 | 2 | DRAW | DRAW | Document | Document | | |
| 5 | 3 | 2 | BUS1003 | BUS1003 | Class | Class | | |
| 6 | 3 | 2 | BFA_TEST | BFA_TEST | BFA_Test | | | |
| 7 | 3 | 2 | ALEMODEL | ALEMODEL | DistributionMo | ALE distribution model | | |
| 8 | 3 | 2 | HELPVALUES | HELPVALUES | Helpvalues | Display possible entrie | | |
| 9 | 3 | 2 | SAP0001 | SAP0001 | BapiService | General service functio | | |
| 10 | 3 | 2 | BUS1090 | BUS1090 | Currency | Currency | | |
| 11 | 3 | 2 | BUS1093 | BUS1093 | ExchangeRat | Exchange rate | | |
| 12 | 3 | 2 | BUS4001 | BUS4001 | AddressOrg | Addresses of companie | | |
| 13 | 3 | 2 | BUS4002 | BUS4002 | AddressPers | Address of natural oers | | |
| 14 | 3 | 2 | BUS4003 | BUS4003 | AddressContF | Address of "Person in c | | |
| 15 | 2 | 1 | AC | | | Accounting - General | | X |
| 16 | 3 | 15 | BUS6001 | BUS6001 | AcctngService | Accounting Services | | |
| 17 | 3 | 15 | BUS6002 | BUS6002 | AcctngGoods | Accounting Goods Mov | | |
| 18 | 3 | 15 | BUS6003 | BUS6003 | AcctngInvoice | Accounting Invoice Rec | | |
| 19 | 3 | 15 | BUS6004 | BUS6004 | AcctngEmplye | Accounting Employee E | | |

The fields we need to reconstruct the hierarchical view from the table view are the ID, Level and Parent fields. This method outputs a recordset that enables us to perform this reconstruction.

Let's analyze the Level field. During my research for this book, I simply dumped the whole recordset into an Access table and started running various queries against it. This analysis revealed that there is only one record that has a "1" value in the Level field, and the NodeKey for this record is SAP-R/3. That should mean that this is a topmost node – the SAP System node in the BOR. Then I compared the table with the view presented in the DCOM CC Object Builder tree view after logon – the Application Hierarchies with NodeKeys had a "2" in the Level field.

If you recall our BOR diagram, it's easy to understand that the Level field relates to the level in the BOR hierarchy. That means that business objects themselves will have "3" in the Level field. Moreover, every record has a Parent field where entries correspond with the ID values of the Parent objects. And that's all we need to reconstruct the hierarchy tree.

### Application Hierarchies

Armed with the results of my analysis, we can construct a simple routine that populates the tree view control with values for Application Hierarchies:

```
Public Function GetObjTypes()

    Dim ndAppH As Node
    Dim ndDummy As Node

    mdcomProxySvc.KeepSAPContext = False

    'use one of the following, and insert your logon attributes
    mdcomProxySvc.PutSessionInfo Combo1.Text, txtuser, txtpassword, "E", txtclient
    'mdcomProxySvc.Destination = "destination"
```

```
mdcomProxySvc.GetBapiObjectTreeFromBOR "", recObjTypes

Set DataGrid1.DataSource = recObjTypes

Do Until recObjTypes.EOF

  If recObjTypes![Level] = 2 Then

    Set ndAppH = TreeView2.Nodes.Add _
        ("reptop", tvwChild, "APPH" & recObjTypes![ID], _
        recObjTypes![shorttext], 2)

    Set ndDummy = TreeView2.Nodes.Add _
        ("APPH" & recObjTypes![ID], tvwChild, _
        "DUM" & "APPH" & recObjTypes![ID])

  Else
    'Do nothing
  End If

  recObjTypes.MoveNext

Loop

End Function
```

This routine simply checks the Level value of every record and adds a node for each record with the value "2" for the `Level` field. The execution of the above fragment will produce the following results:

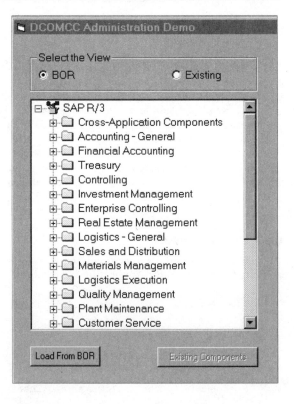

The first part of the problem is resolved. We can get the Parent objects (Application Hierarchies) for the business objects. Now it's time to get the business objects themselves.

## Business Objects

Business objects have their `Parent` field equal the `ID` field of the Application Hierarchy object.

*Note that in the previous code fragment, we incorporated the value of the ID into the key for nodes that reflect the Application Hierarchies.*

Therefore, we can use this value as the criteria to get the records where the `Parent` field matches the ID of the Application Hierarchy. This operation will produce business objects.

The following code is from the `Expand` event of the tree view control:

```
Private Sub TreeView2_Expand(ByVal Node As MSComctlLib.Node)

    Dim ndBusObj As Node


    If Node.Tag = "e" Then

    Else
       Select Case Mid(Node.Key, 1, 4)

          Case "APPH"
             Node.Tag = "e"
             TreeView2.Nodes.Remove "DUM" & Node.Key
             recObjTypes.MoveFirst

             Do Until recObjTypes.EOF

                If CInt(Trim(recObjTypes![Parent])) = _
                      CInt(Trim(Mid(Node.Key, 5))) _
                      And CInt(Trim(Mid(Node.Key, 5))) <> 0 Then

                   Set ndBusObj = TreeView2.Nodes.Add(Node.Key, tvwChild, _
                         "SBOB" & "|" & recObjTypes![ObjectType] & "|" & _
                         recObjTypes![ObjectName], recObjTypes![ObjectName], 5)


                Else
                End If

                recObjTypes.MoveNext

             Loop

          Case Else

       End Select

    End If

End Sub
```

We construct the Key for the business object node using values of the `ObjectType` and `ObjectName` fields separated by the pipe character for future parsing.

Once our business objects are properly displayed, we can go after the BAPIs.

### BAPIs

The `GetBapiObjectTreeFromBOR` method does not provide us with the entire hierarchy. In order to get to the BAPIs, we have to use a different method of the `SAPProxyGeneratorServices` class – `GetBapiTypeInfoFromBOR`.

This method supplies you with several recordsets that include all the information you need to populate the business object properties, BAPIs and BAPI parameters. All data is in the form of ADO Recordsets. The syntax is as follows:

```
Sub GetBapiTypeInfoFromBOR(Language As String, ObjectType As String, _
                       recBaseData, recVerbs, recParameters, recReturn)
```

It expects to be given the `Language` value and the `ObjectType` – we have this from the `GetBapiObjectTreeFromBOR` method's resultant recordset. It will populate the optional arguments: base data, verb data (BAPIs fall into this category), parameters and return. The base data describes the business object itself – we don't need that at this moment. Return contains the status of the RFC call executed by the library to get the metadata – this is irrelevant. The only two arguments we need are verbs and parameters.

First we have to display BAPIs, and the information we need is in the `recVerbs` argument. This recordset brings a lot of data, but the most important for our purpose are the `VerbType` and `IsAPI` fields.

The `VerbType` reflects the type of the verb: **Attribute**, **Key** or **Method** – "A", "K" and "M" respectively. That is what we want to display. Our initial reflex would be that method obviously denotes a BAPI. Not quite. The caveat is that the `GetBapiTypeInfoFromBOR` brings all methods, whether they are implemented as externally accessible BAPIs or not.

Whatever those methods are, we can filter them out using the "X" value in the `IsAPI` field of the `recVerbs` recordset. If the "X" value is present, it's a BAPI. If not, it's not and we don't have to display it.

This logic stands behind the rest of the routine programmed into the `Expand` event of our demo project:

```
Private Sub TreeView2_Expand(ByVal Node As MSComctlLib.Node)

    Dim ndBusObj As Node
    Dim ndBapi As Node
    Dim recReturn As ADODB.Recordset
    Dim recBaseData As ADODB.Recordset


    If Node.Tag = "e" Then
```

```
Else
  Select Case Mid(Node.Key, 1, 4)

    Case "APPH"
      Node.Tag = "e"
      TreeView2.Nodes.Remove "DUM" & Node.Key
      recObjTypes.MoveFirst

      Do Until recObjTypes.EOF

        If CInt(Trim(recObjTypes![Parent])) = _
              CInt(Trim(Mid(Node.Key, 5))) _
              And CInt(Trim(Mid(Node.Key, 5))) <> 0 Then

          Set ndBusObj = TreeView2.Nodes.Add(Node.Key, tvwChild, _
                  "SBOB" & "|" & recObjTypes![ObjectType] & "|" & _
                  recObjTypes![ObjectName], recObjTypes![ObjectName], 5)

          mdcomProxySvc.GetBapiTypeInfoFromBOR "E", _
                  recObjTypes![ObjectType], recBaseData, recVerbs, _
                  recParams, recReturn

          Set DataGrid1.DataSource = recVerbs

                  'enable for practice
                  'Set Form1.DataGrid1.DataSource = recVerbs
                  'Set Form1.DataGrid2.DataSource = recBaseData
                  'Set Form1.DataGrid3.DataSource = recParams
                  'Set Form1.DataGrid4.DataSource = recReturn
                  'Form1.Show

          Do Until recVerbs.EOF
            Select Case UCase(Trim(recVerbs![verbtype]))

              Case "K"
                Set ndBapi = TreeView2.Nodes.Add _
                    ("SBOB" & "|" & recObjTypes![ObjectType] & "|" & _
                    recObjTypes![ObjectName], tvwChild, _
                    "BAPI" & recVerbs![lobjtype] & recVerbs![Verb], _
                    recVerbs![Verb], 9)

              Case "A"
                Set ndBapi = TreeView2.Nodes.Add _
                    ("SBOB" & "|" & recObjTypes![ObjectType] & "|" & _
                    recObjTypes![ObjectName], tvwChild, "BAPI" & _
                    recVerbs![lobjtype] & recVerbs![Verb], _
                    recVerbs![Verb], 10)

              Case "M"
                If recVerbs![isapi] = "X" Then
                  Set ndBapi = TreeView2.Nodes.Add _
                      ("SBOB" & "|" & recObjTypes![ObjectType] & "|" & _
                      recObjTypes![ObjectName], tvwChild, "BAPI" & _
                      recVerbs![lobjtype] & recVerbs![Verb], _
                      mrecVerbs![Verb], 8)

                  GetParams recVerbs![Verb]
                End If

            End Select
```

```
            recVerbs.MoveNext
        Loop

    End If

    recObjTypes.MoveNext

  Loop

 Case Else

 End Select

End If

End Sub
```

After the call to the `GetBapiTypeInfoFromBOR` method, we start to look at the `recVerbs` argument. We build a `Select Case` block using the `VerbType` field's value as a `Case` expression. Again, note that we construct key values as pipe-delimited strings, just in case we have to use them later.

For the case "M" (method) an `If` statement filters out those methods without "X" in the `IsAPI` field. Then, for every qualified BAPI, we invoke the user-defined function `GetParams`. This does what the name implies – it gets the parameters for the BAPI:

```
Public Sub GetParams(strBapi As String)

  Dim ndParam As Node

  recParams.MoveFirst
  Set DataGrid1.DataSource = recParams

  Do Until recParams.EOF

    If recParams![paramtype] = "M" _
        And recParams![Verb] = strBapi Then

      Set ndParam = TreeView2.Nodes.Add _
        ("BAPI" & recVerbs![lobjtype] & recVerbs![Verb], tvwChild, _
        guid.GetGUID, recParams![element], 7)

    End If

    recParams.MoveNext

  Loop

End Sub
```

All this function does is loop through the `recParams` recordset argument of the `GetBapiTypeInfoFromBOR` method, and create nodes based on its values. The function expects the name of the BAPI to compare against the `Verb` field of the `recParams` recordset. It also needs to check whether the `ParamType` field has the value "M" – this indicates that the parameter is normally implemented as a BAPI and we can access it.

If we execute the whole code in the Expand event, the results will be as follows:

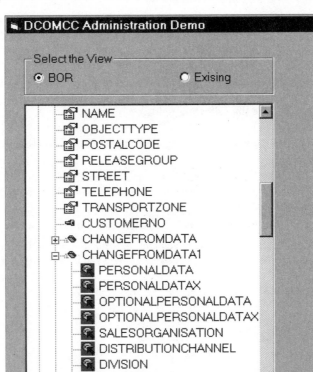

As you can observe, we have attributes (properties), key fields and BAPIs with parameters. The DCOM CC itself stops at BAPIs plus key field. We can now congratulate ourselves for replicating the DCOM CC BOR browsing functionality.

## RFC Browsing

To implement RFC browsing, we have to employ a different set of methods. First you have to call the GetFunctionTree method. The syntax is given below:

```
Sub GetFunctionTree(Language As String, FunctionStatus As RfcModuleFilter, _
                    FunctionName As String, GroupName As String, pTreeInfo)
```

This method populates the pTreeInfo recordset argument with RFC data in the same fashion as the GetBapiObjectTreeFromBOR did.

You can provide the name of a function and/or the name of a Function Group. There is also the enumerated type for the filter. You can select:

> ➤ rfcAccessLevelAll – all function modules

> ➤ rfcAccessLevelCustomer – function modules that are released for customers

> ➤ rfcAccessLevelCustomerWithInternal – function modules that are released for customers and for internal use

Meaningfully combining these search criteria allows you to narrow down the result set.

The pTreeInfo recordset has the following fields:

> ➤ The IsGroup field has values indicating the Function Group – it always contains an "X" if it is a Function Group.

> ➤ Parent and ID fields have the same meaning as those fields did in the GetBapiObjectTreeFromBOR resultant recordset. They help reconstruct hierarchical relations from the flat table structure.

> ➤ The name of the RFC is in the ObjectName field, and a description of it is in ShortText.

> ➤ The Expandable field indicates that you can "expand" the object. It is then pretty obvious that the "X" in it coincides with the "X" in IsGroup. You can find a sample call to this method below:

```
Dim recTreeinfo As ADODB.Recordset

dcomProxySvc.GetFunctionTree "E", rfcAccessLevelAll, "*", "RFC*", recTreeinfo

Set DataGrid1.DataSource = recTreeinfo
```

*Remember to always use "*" unless you know the exact name.*

## The GetFunctionInterface Method

To get to RFC parameters, use the GetFunctionInterface method. It has the following syntax:

```
Sub GetFunctionInterface(Language As String, FunctionName As String, pParameters)
```

You supply the Language and the RFC name. It gets you an ADO Recordset in the pParameters argument, containing all the data for the RFC parameters that we have already discussed earlier in the book. It gives the name (Parameter field), directionality and type (Paramclass field – I = import, E = export, T = table and X = exception). You can analyze the resultant recordset yourself, and you'll find self-explanatory names for fields. You would call this method as follows:

```
Dim recParameters As ADODB.Recordset

mdcomProxySvc.GetFunctionInterface "E", "RFC_CUSTOMER_GET", recParameters

Set DataGrid1.DataSource = recParameters
```

### The GetTypeInfoFromBOR Method

Another very informative method is `GetTypeInfoFromBOR`. This method allows you to read practically any type of metadata you can need for a particular business object type. The syntax for this method is provided below:

```
Sub GetTypeInfoFromBOR(Language As String, ObjectType As String, _
                       WithVerbs As Boolean, WithParameters As Boolean, _
                       WithExceptions As Boolean, WithTexts As Boolean, _
                       WithFormattedDocu As Boolean, [pObjectTypeInfo], _
                       [pKeyFields], [pAttributes], [pMethods], _
                       [pMethodParams], [pMethodExceptions], [pInterfaces], _
                       [pEvents], [pEventParams], [pFormattedDocu])
```

The method expects the language value, the Object Type value and values for the `With*` group of arguments. These arguments regulate the volume of information that you are going to get. If you recall our practice with the BOR using the SAP R/3 front-end, the screens that we have looked at derive values from the same data set as this method does. The best exercise would be to call this method:

```
Dim recObjectTypeInfo As ADODB.Recordset
Dim recKeyFields As ADODB.Recordset
Dim recAttributes As ADODB.Recordset
Dim recMethods As ADODB.Recordset
Dim recMethodParams As ADODB.Recordset
Dim recMethodExceptions As ADODB.Recordset
Dim recInterfaces As ADODB.Recordset
Dim recEvents As ADODB.Recordset
Dim recEventParams As ADODB.Recordset
Dim recFormattedDocu As ADODB.Recordset

mdcomProxySvc.GetTypeInfoFromBOR "E", "KNA1", True, True, True, True, True, _
                      recObjectTypeInfo, recKeyFields, _
                      recAttributes, recMethods, recMethodParams, _
                      recMethodExceptions, recInterfaces, _
                      recEvents, recEventParams, recFormattedDocu
```

And output every recordset argument into a separate data grid or table.

However, the exploration of every field of the multitude of recordsets returned by the `PROXYGENERATORLib` classes is well beyond the scope of this book. I'll demonstrate how to replicate the DCOM CC functionality and try to limit the amount of information to fit the purpose. It's very easy to get carried away with elaboration on every single recordset, plus it is not difficult. However, as far as this book is concerned, there is very little added value in this type of exercise.

The DCOM CC is subject to change as an implementation. It is not going to change as a technology. However, if SAP changes the function signatures in COM components or the structure of ADO Recordsets, an extensive list of fields will be obsolete. What will not change is the technology and the principles of its implementation. And that's what the emphasis of this book is.

# DCOMC_Admin – Proxy Generation

Now we are ready to implement the proxy generation functionality. To do so, we need to implement the following things:

> ➤ We have to set the COM/MTS parameters, as we did with the DCOM CC web GUI in Chapter 10

> ➤ We have to specify the C++ project name, the DLL name, the namespace and (should we employ MTS) the MTS package name

> ➤ We also have to elect to implement the Session object if we want to

> ➤ We have to be able to select business objects from the BOR and kick off the component generation routine

First things first. To implement the COM/MTS attributes setup I have implemented a simple interface, just to enter the necessary values:

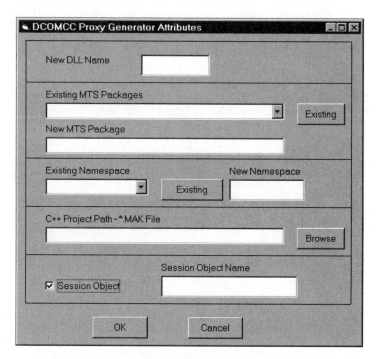

You can toggle the **Existing/New** buttons. This GUI implements all the functionality present in the COM/MTS part of the DCOM CC Object Builder. To get to this window you have to click on the **Attributes** button on the main screen of the DCOMC_Admin project. This button will be enabled after you drag a business object from the tree view on the left of the main screen to the list view control to the right.

*This is done purely for illustrative purposes and does not add any value to the DCOM CC core components. I just wanted to do something more Windows-like for the GUI. All my sample projects have mostly unattractive, functionally challenged UI. This one at least has colorful icons to drag around.*

We can block the ability to drag any image that does not depict a business object. I also block attempts to add the same business object to the list view twice. This is all very simple. The list view generates a run-time error on any attempt to add a list item with the same key. I try to always work with Visual Basic, not against it. This is implemented in the following code fragment:

```
Private Sub ListView1_DragDrop(Source As Control, X As Single, Y As Single)

    Dim lstItem As ListItem

    On Error GoTo ErrGet

    If TypeOf Source Is TreeView Then

        Set lstItem = ListView1.ListItems.Add _
                    (, Source.SelectedItem.Key, _
                    Source.SelectedItem.Text, Source.SelectedItem.Image)

        lstItem.Left = X
        lstItem.Top = Y
        cmdGenerate.Enabled = True
        cmdAttributes.Enabled = True

        Me.MousePointer = vbNormal
    Else
        Me.MousePointer = vbNormal
    End If

ErrGet:

    Select Case Err.Number

        Case 0
        Case 35602
            MsgBox "Component Already Exists!", vbExclamation
            Exit Sub
        Case Else

    End Select

End Sub
```

## Methods and Properties of the SAPProxyGenerator class

What we have to do now is to see how to programmatically generate SAP R/3 business object proxy components. As it turns out, `PROXYGENERATORLib` implements the `SAPProxyGenerator` class. Take a look at this class using the Object Browser:

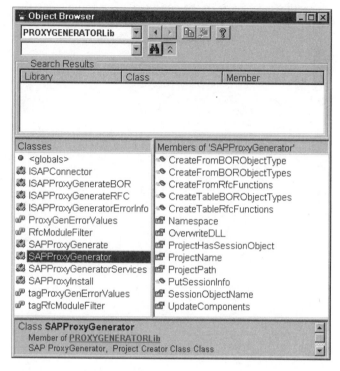

The names of the members of this class are very self-explanatory. However, this is an important class so I will explain each member in some detail.

The `CreateFrom*` group of methods generates the C++ files needed for the DLL.

### The CreateFromBORObjectType Method

Syntax:

```
Sub CreateFromBORObjectType(ObjectName As String, ObjectType As String)
```

This generates all the files necessary to build a DLL for the business object proxy. It requires the `ObjectName` (e.g. Customer) and corresponding `ObjectType` (e.g. KNA1).

### The CreateFromBORObjectTypes Method

Syntax:

```
Sub CreateFromBORObjectTypes(pObjectTypes As Object)
```

This method does the same thing as `CreateFromBORObjectType`. The difference is that when you want to bundle many business objects into one proxy DLL, it lets you do it by providing an ADO Recordset compliant argument `pObjectTypes`. This has two fields – `ObjectName` and `ObjectType`. You may add as many records as you want to it, and pass it to the `CreateFromBORObjectTypes` in one shot. I prefer to use this method even if I have only one business object to work with. It makes the program more generic.

### The CreateFromRfcFunctions Method

Syntax:

```
Sub CreateFromRfcFunctions(ObjectName As String, pFunctionNames As Object)
```

This method generates files based on RFC metadata. The difference here is that for RFC based proxies, you have to supply the class name yourself. The DCOM CC will prompt you to do so on attempting to add the RFC to the list of components.

BAPIs belong to business objects, and the DCOM CC uses the name of the business object for the generated class definition. RFCs don't have any parent business object, therefore the DCOM CC can't pick the class name from any place and it has to ask you for it. You are essentially wrapping the single API into the DLL. You have to supply the name in the `ObjectName` argument – don't give it the same name as the project. The second argument is an ADO Recordset with a single field, `Name`.

### The CreateTableBORObjectTypes Method

Syntax:

```
Sub CreateTableBORObjectTypes(pVal)
```

This method creates an empty table to be populated with values and passed to the `CreateFromBORObjectTypes` method. It's similar to the `DimAs` method. Use it prior to calling `CreateFromBORObjectTypes` to prepare the argument. You can pass an Object or an ADO Recordset type of variable to the `CreateTableBORObjectTypes`.

### The CreateTableRfcFunctions Method

Syntax:

```
Sub CreateTableRfcFunctions(pVal)
```

This method is similar to `CreateTableBORObjectTypes`. It prepares the argument to be populated and passed to the `CreateFromRfcFunctions` method's `pFunctionNames` argument.

### The PutSessionInfo Method

Syntax:

```
Sub PutSessionInfo([Destination], [UserID], [Password], [Language], [Client])
```

This method should be very familiar by now. Call it prior to using the class to actually generate files.

### Properties

The remaining members of the `SAPProxyGenerator` class are properties.

| Property | Description |
|---|---|
| `Namespace` | Requires a four-letter namespace. If it's not set, it will default to the SAP R/3 system name. |
| `OverwriteDLL` | Boolean value. If set to `True` will cause the library to overwrite already existing DLL. Use for modifications of existing proxies. |
| `ProjectHasSessionObject` | If set to `True` will cause the Session object to be generated. Defaults to `False`. |
| `SessionObjectName` | The name for the Session object. |
| `ProjectName` | The name of the MAK file (project file). |
| `ProjectPath` | The path for the MAK file sans the name for the file and the last \. |
| `UpdateComponents` | If set to `True` will cause existing components to be updated. Defaults to `False`. |

## Generating Components using SAPProxyGenerator

A quick look at the above members tells us that we already have all the necessary ingredients to generate the SAP R/3 business object proxy DLL. We also have a functionality to browse the SAP R/3 BOR and extract all the metadata that we need to pass to the `CreateFrom*` methods.

The functionality to generate files and compile DLLs is enabled from the **Generate DLL** button on the main screen:

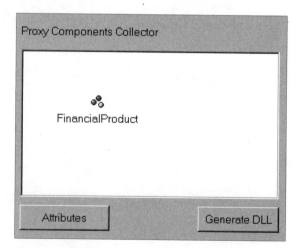

First it checks for business objects added to the list view box:

```
Public Sub BuildObjList()

    Dim recList As New ADODB.Recordset
    Dim lstItem As ListItem
    Dim varObjNames

    mdcomGenerate.CreateTableBORObjectTypes recList

    For Each lstItem In ListView1.ListItems

        varObjNames = Split(lstItem.Key, "|")
        recList.AddNew
        recList![ObjectType] = varObjNames(1)
        recList![ObjectName] = varObjNames(2)
        recList.Update

    Next

    GenerateProxy recList

End Sub
```

All this function does is to go through the ListItems collection of the list view. The keys for its items are pipe-delimited values containing ObjectName and ObjectType. These are parsed using Visual Basic's Split function, and used to populate the ADO Recordset created by the CreateTableBORObjectTypes method. Once we get the required recordset, we can invoke another function:

```
Public Function GenerateProxy(recBoList As ADODB.Recordset)

    On Error GoTo ErrTrap

    With mdcomGenerate

        .ProjectPath = Left(txtPath, InStrRev(txtPath, "\") - 1)

        .ProjectName = txtDll
        .Namespace = txtNameSpace

        If txtSession.Visible Then
            .ProjectHasSessionObject = True
            .SessionObjectName = txtSession

        Else
            .ProjectHasSessionObject = False
        End If

        .PutSessionInfo Combo1.Text, txtUser, txtPassword, "E", txtClient

    End With

    mdcomGenerate.CreateFromBORObjectTypes recBoList

    With makDll
```

```
      .ProjectPath = Left(txtPath, InStrRev(txtPath, "\") - 1)
      .PackageName = Me.txtPackage
      .ProjectName = txtDLL
      .BuildDLL
      .InstallComponents

   End With

ErrTrap:

   Select Case Err.Number

      Case 5008
         mdcomGenerate.UpdateComponents = True
         Resume

      Case 5007
         mdcomGenerate.OverwriteDLL = True
         mdcomGenerate.UpdateComponents = True
         Resume

   End Select

End Function
```

The first half of this function simply assigns values to appropriate properties of the
`SAPProxyGenerator` class. We declare the variable for this class as `Object` and instantiate it in
the form's `Load` event:

```
Dim mdcomGenerate As Object


Private Sub Form_Load()

.......

   Set mdcomProxySvc = CreateObject("SAP.ProxyGeneratorServices.1")
   Set mdcomGenerate = CreateObject("SAP.ProxyGenerator.1")
   Set makDll = CreateObject("SAP.ProxyInstall.1")

.......

End Sub
```

The `GenerateProxy` function also checks if the user elected to generate the Session object and
prepares the Path and Name for the Project. Then we call `PutSessionInfo` and call the
`CreateFromBORObjectTypes` method, passing the prepared recordset to it. The result will be a
directory full of the C++ source, header and other files necessary to build the DLL proxy.

After all files are generated, it's time to compile the DLL. To do so we need another class defined in
the `PROXYGENERATORLib` library – the `SAPProxyInstall` class:

```
Dim makDll As Object
```

```
Private Sub Form_Load()

.......

    Set mdcomProxySvc = CreateObject("SAP.ProxyGeneratorServices.1")
    Set mdcomGenerate = CreateObject("SAP.ProxyGenerator.1")
    Set makDll = CreateObject("SAP.ProxyInstall.1")

.......

End Sub
```

## Properties and Methods of the SAPProxyInstall class

The view of this class from the Object Browser is shown below:

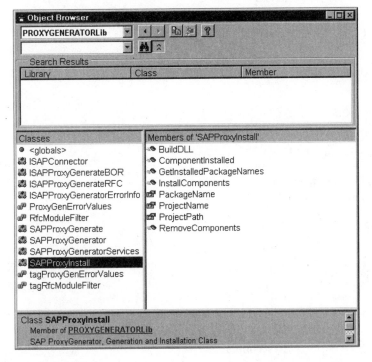

This class has the following members.

### The BuildDLL Method

Syntax:

```
Sub BuildDLL()
```

This method has no arguments. It starts the DLL compilation process.

### The ComponentInstalled Method

Syntax:

```
Sub ComponentInstalled(cmpnt_name As String, remove_if_found As Boolean)
```

This checks if the component that you are about to build is already installed. Pass the name in the first argument. Given `True` for the second argument, the component will be removed. Use it to check for a component's existence or to implement replace functionality.

### The GetInstalledPackageNames Method

Syntax:

```
Sub GetInstalledPackageNames()
```

This method returns an array of the names of packages already installed on your machine. Use it to check for the existence of packages.

### The InstallComponents Method

Syntax:

```
Sub InstallComponents()
```

This installs a generated DLL in MTS.

### The RemoveComponents Method

Syntax:

```
Sub RemoveComponents()
```

This method removes components. Use it to implement the replace functionality for components.

### Properties

The `SAPProxyInstall` class has the following properties:

| Property | Description |
|---|---|
| PackageName | Pass the name of the package you want to generate. |
| ProjectName | Pass the name of the project that you used to build the DLL files – MAK file. |
| ProjectPath | The path to the MAK file sans the name of the file and the last \. This class will have no idea what project you want to use as a source for compilation, and you have to point it to it. |

We have already seen these properties and methods at work in our GenerateProxy function:

```
Public Function GenerateProxy(recBoList As ADODB.Recordset)

......

  With makDll

    .ProjectPath = Left(txtPath, InStrRev(txtPath, "\") - 1)
    .PackageName = Me.txtPackage
    .ProjectName = txtDLL
    .BuildDLL
    .InstallComponents

  End With

......


End Function
```

That's it. We are now fully prepared to generate our first business object proxy using the functionality of the DCOM CC core components programmatically.

## Generating a Proxy

We'll generate a proxy based on the *Employee* business object using our sample project. Upon successful login using our GUI, we can navigate the BOR to the Employee business object located in the Personnel Management area:

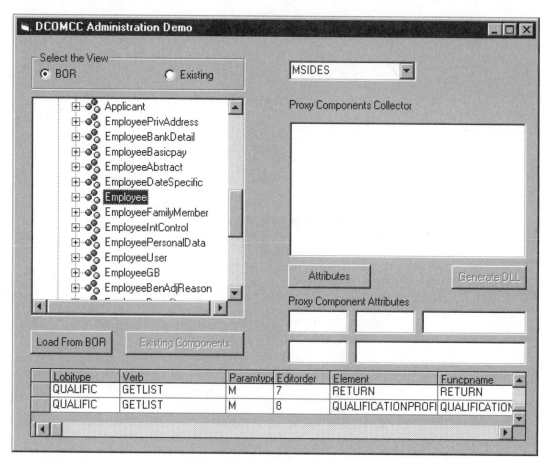

*As a Visual Basic programmer, you're not expected to know all the business objects and their whereabouts by heart. Your ABAP programmers or SAP analysts should tell you that. Nevertheless, your value will increase substantially with the knowledge you gain on SAP R/3 implementation specifics.*

Drag the Employee across the form and drop it into the list view control:

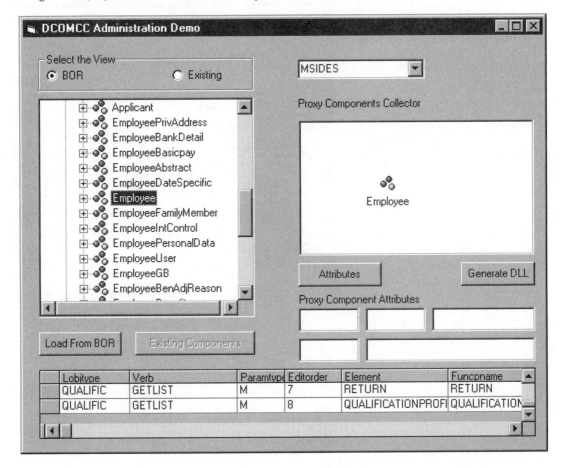

We have the object – now we need
to set up the COM/MTS
environment. To do so, click on
the **Attributes** button and enter all
the necessary values into the
appropriate controls on the
**Attributes** screen:

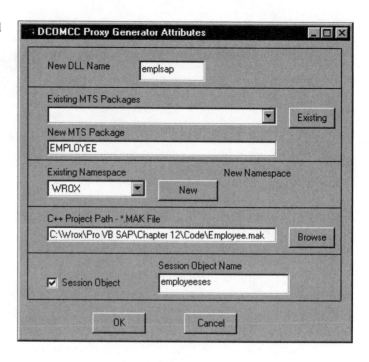

Then click OK to get back to the main form. You can now see all the attributes that you have entered:

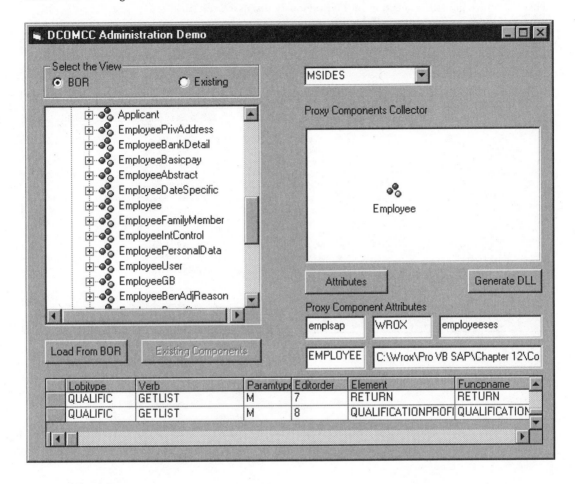

Next click on the **Generate DLL** button and wait for all the files to be created and the DLL generated. This button triggers the execution of the previously discussed routines – `BuildObjList` and `GenerateProxy`. The result will be present in the target directory:

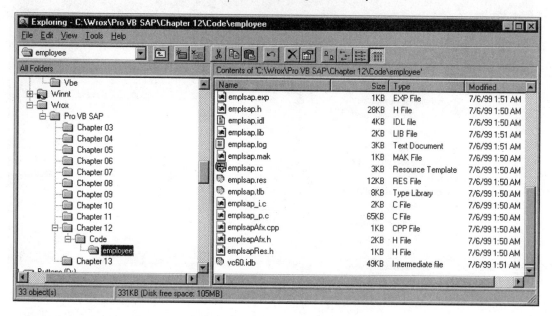

And in the MTS Explorer:

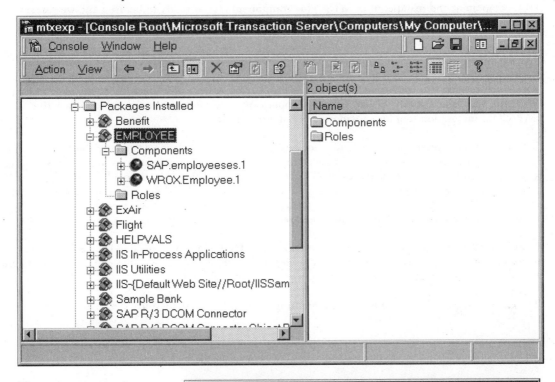

The component is also present in the Visual Basic References dialog:

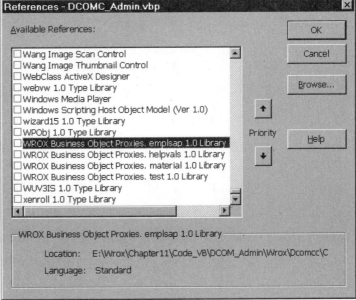

All these signs confirm that we have indeed created a fully legitimate SAP R/3 business object proxy DLL component and installed it in MTS. This component is now ready to be used and we can say that our mission to replicate the functionality of the DCOM CC core components is complete.

# Summary

In this chapter, we have accomplished a significant goal. We were able to replicate the DCOM CC functionality using its own core components as they arrive downloaded from `www.sap.com/bapi`. What this means is that any Visual Basic developer can successfully incorporate the only native SAP/COM integration tool into a wide variety of applications.

It allows the building of custom solutions for business analysts to use for design of integration interfaces. Add a more intuitive and knowledge intensive front-end and business logic, and you have a very powerful solution, virtually for free. COM is free, SAP R/3 is already paid for, the download is free and you already have Visual Basic programmers. The DCOM CC not only reduces the cost and effort involved in SAP R/3–Windows integration, but it also allows for its core components to be reused and incorporated into any Windows based application.

I have tried to give you as much of the mandatory information as possible. The DCOM CC is an exciting tool, and I'm sure you will find more elegant solutions with it. Use these chapters on DCOM CC functionality as a guide to your development, not the cookbook.

The next chapter will be devoted to programming DCOM CC generated proxies using Visual Basic.

# 13

# Programming SAP R/3 Business Object Proxy Components

This chapter concludes the section on the DCOM Component Connector and almost the book itself. In the previous chapters, we have seen what the DCOM CC is and what it can do. We have also been exposed to the core functionality of the DCOM CC and how to incorporate this new tool into our Visual Basic applications. However, the most important benefit of using the DCOM CC is its ability to generate COM proxies for SAP R/3 business objects. This makes the DCOM CC the only tool currently available that enables the native integration of SAP R/3 into Windows.

In this chapter, I'll demonstrate, with some practical examples, how you can use SAP R/3 business object proxy components to create Windows applications for working with SAP R/3. I'll show you examples of both an outbound (data browsing) and inbound (data creation) application.

Before we embark on any coding, I would like to spend a few paragraphs refreshing our knowledge of the subject.

## SAP R/3 Business Objects

SAP R/3 business objects are programmatic structures defined inside the SAP R/3 Application Server, which implement SAP R/3 enterprise functionality. SAP R/3 comprises several Modules (Financial Accounting, Logistics etc.) and every module comprises functions that implement business functionality (create a customer, sell products, etc.). To implement all these business rules, SAP developed a vast layer of robust functions that implemented all the rules.

Every SAP R/3 business object implements a particular functionality. Therefore, if we enable member functions in that business object that are going to perform specific tasks we get what we need. For example the *Customer* business object implements all the functionality related to customers in SAP R/3. You can create customers, view their data and do other things. All this is implemented as member functions of the *Customer* business object, i.e. BAPIs. These are the `CreateFromData`, `CheckExistence`, `GetList` and many other BAPIs that implement particular business functionality. But best of all, is that all we have to do is call the BAPI. It may trigger any number of RFC calls, transactions and any anything else in the SAP R/3, but *all we need to do is call one BAPI*. It's like calling the `OpenDatabase` method of the Workspace object – you do not know, or care, about what is happening.

# DCOM CC Business Object Proxies

> **DCOM CC business object proxies are in-process COM servers, based on SAP R/3 business object metadata.**

Every business object is defined as a class, and every BAPI as a method of that class. COM data types are mapped to RFC data types, and all structured data (BAPI Structure or Table parameters) is presented as ADO Recordsets.

Should you need to manage SAP R/3 customers – no problem. Create a *Customer* proxy component and call the BAPIs defined in the *Customer* object as if they were regular methods of the object. All communication and data conversion issues will be handled by the proxy component. This sounds like one of those 'too good to be true' products but the DCOM CC does it.

We have already seen how to generate proxy components using the DCOM CC. We have also seen how to do it programmatically. In Chapter 10 we discussed the common methods and properties that the DCOM CC implements in every proxy component. We also discussed issues of transaction support for BAPIs.

We are now ready for some sample projects that illustrate business object proxy component programming. All these samples are developed in the 'proof of concept' style, for the following reason. SAP R/3 is not just another RDBMS where you can do pretty much what you want. Every action that you can execute within SAP R/3 – using its own front-end GUI, internal programs that you can write in ABAP, or external RFC or BAPI calls – has a very complex algorithm of execution.

> **This means that you cannot simply click around, or arbitrarily call RFCs or BAPIs, and get meaningful results.**

You have to know *exactly* what you are doing, and what the SAP R/3 predefined way of handling it is.

# Working with SAP R/3

Let's take a simple example that we are going to incorporate into one of our sample projects. There is a very straightforward `CreateFromData1` BAPI for the *Customer* business object. It has one parameter for general data (such as name, address and the like), one parameter for special data, one parameter for the return structure and one for the Reference Customer. Coding against this BAPI, which the DCOM CC will expose as a regular method, is a no-brainer. You populate recordsets for customer data and monitor the returning structure. Code-wise it is elementary. However, if you do just that, the most likely outcome will be an internal SAP R/3 error.

The way SAP R/3 handles the creation of customers is not trivial. There are at least two major 'gotchas' for the Visual Basic programmer not intimately familiar with the specifics of SAP R/3 in this matter.

## The Reference Customer

First of all, you have to select the **Reference Customer**. The new customer will inherit Sales Organization, Distribution Channel and Division information from that Reference Customer. In other words, SAP R/3 will look up the Reference Customer data and create the new customer with the same area-related attributes – and this is the problem. Those Sales Areas, Distribution Channels and Divisions are configurable, and there is no way you would know it for all SAP R/3 systems. Another problem is even more serious.

## Customer Numbering

SAP R/3 implements two mechanisms for assigning unique numbers to customers – **internal** and **external**:

> With the internal mechanism, the user is expected to supply the required data. Upon saving the new customer, SAP R/3 will generate a unique number for it.

> With the external mechanism, the user is expected to provide SAP R/3 with a unique customer number.

So how do you know what mechanism SAP R/3 will engage when you use the BAPI to create a new customer? The answer is in the Reference Customer. SAP R/3 lets you define ranges for customer numbers and assign them to Sales Areas, Distribution Channels and Divisions. For the range you define, you can specify whether SAP R/3 will generate customer numbers internally, or expect them externally. You select the range for the new customer effectively by selecting its Reference Customer – SAP R/3 will attempt to create the new customer within the same range.

If this range requires the external number to be passed and you don't provide it, the call will fail. The very same BAPI call, using the Reference Customer from another range that assigns numbers internally, will succeed.

These types of caveats are everywhere in SAP R/3. Another example: it is not enough to just to have a Material, it has to be "fully configured" and assigned to a proper Sales Area for you to use it in the sales order.

## Using Your Knowledge

This is why I am concentrating on the technology and Visual Basic programming principles for SAP R/3 business object programming, not on the "How to implement my Sales-Order Application on SAP R/3" type of case study. The VB programmer's role in SAP R/3 business object programming is coding, not SAP R/3 functionality research. It should be the SAP R/3 analyst telling the Visual Basic programmer what to do. The VB programmer should know how to do it. The SAP R/3 analyst tells you what BAPIs to call, and in what sequence. You generate proxies using the DCOM CC, or use straight BAPI calls using the SAP Automation BAPI control, and put the code together. In the due course of your BAPI programming, you will gain SAP R/3 knowledge in the area that you work in. Then you will become less dependent on the SAP R/3 specialists.

Another scenario is if you are a strong ABAP programmer, or know some module of SAP R/3 really well. If you learn Visual Basic to the coding extent, after reading this book you will be capable of creating prototype components to use business objects. Your Visual Basic colleagues can then polish and beautify your code. As you gain Visual Basic coding experience, you will become less dependent on help from Visual Basic programmers.

In either case, you need an understanding of the principles of SAP R/3 business object programming using Visual Basic – and this is exactly what this book is all about.

SAP R/3 business objects and BAPI technology simplify coding and integration. They also shield the VB, or any other non-ABAP programmer, from the specifics of SAP R/3's internal implementation. However, you still require some knowledge of how SAP R/3 operates and how it implements particular business processes to create successful applications.

The projects in this chapter will concentrate on the technology behind the DCOM CC generated SAP R/3 business object proxies, and not on any particular SAP R/3 functionality implementation.

> *All values used in this chapter are valid for a particular IDES (SAP R/3). Obviously, values will be different in your particular situation. I strongly recommend consulting with your ABAP programmers and asking them questions outlined in this chapter. Ideally, we all should have had access to the same instance of the SAP R/3. Practically, that is highly unlikely to happen.*

# Creating a Proxy Component

We know that the DCOM CC generated proxies implement the functionality of business objects by exposing BAPIs as methods. However, what they do not do is provide an explicit mechanism to populate the BAPI parameters.

**Fortunately, all these parameters are presented as disconnected ADO Recordsets.**

Therefore it is easy and intuitive for a Visual Basic or any other Windows programmer to write routines to populate and manipulate them. This provides an implicit mechanism for BAPI parameter handling. There is no single recipe on how to handle BAPI parameter manipulation – after all, they are only ADO Recordsets. All the business object cares about is that you call the BAPI using parameters populated with the correct data.

> **Another major advantage of using the DCOM CC over the raw SAP Automation SDK tools is that you don't have to use two different techniques to populate BAPI table parameters and a regular RDBMS table.**

It's therefore possible to either write generic routines to handle BAPI parameters or easily stage data prior to loading or after reading. You could have a small local staging database in Access or SQL Server, and dynamically create tables based on BAPI parameters. You can then populate those tables using any data that you need, and use queries to validate the data.

This may be useful in certain data migration situations when you have to make sure that you are getting the right data. It may also be useful if you need to perform data integration. For example, you may be gathering data from various heterogeneous sources that may not even be relational databases. You may be getting data from any exotic or proprietary data source that doesn't even remotely resemble an ADO Recordset. In this case, it would be useful to be able to have some form of data staging mechanism.

For outbound BAPI processing you will be getting data in ADO Recordsets but in a *non-relational* manner. A BAPI's domain is a single business object, and all the data that the BAPI brings relates to this object only. This means that if you want to see all customers and their sales orders, you cannot have one BAPI call that is going to bring you two related recordsets – one with all the customers and another with all the sales orders. What you will end up doing is first bringing in customers and then getting sales orders for each of them.

If you want to have some reporting functionality built around this data, or you want to integrate SAP R/3 into your existing data mart, you could save all the BAPI generated data into tables and apply your reporting mechanism to those tables. You can then use criteria-related parameters to select data returned by a BAPI, but it will still be per business object. It all stems from the conflict between the 'row and column' relational paradigm and the 'method and property' object paradigm.

# Generating the Component

First of all, we have to use the DCOM CC to generate a COM component based on the SAP R/3 business objects that we need to implement. Logically, we would begin with the specification for the project.

The first project will implement customer browsing and look-up functionality. The user will have the ability to browse customer information in an SAP R/3 database. The information will include the customer and sales order information. The user should be able to see customers' names and view sales orders for a selected customer. This project belongs to the "outbound" or "reporting" category of SAP R/3 related applications. It gets information already present in SAP R/3. The next project will be an "inbound" type. It will actually enter data into SAP R/3.

You also have to decide how you deploy your proxy component. You have the choice between a stand-alone in-process server DLL or an MTS component. My advice is to use MTS to deploy your business object proxies and be consistent with the Service Packs on your server machine.

Another factor is that if you use MTS, you can elect for your components to be activated on the server. This buys you centralized management and your server's resources utilization. Another big plus is that you can enjoy the ability of MTS to export components to client machines, facilitating remote activation for components. That is very important and convenient – otherwise you would have been forced to use the DCOM Component Configuration utility – a tool only a mother could love.

> *No matter how you deploy your components, I strongly recommend getting familiar with MTS. It is there to stay as part of COM+ in Windows 2000 and it is time for all Visual Basic programmers to step out of the desktop sandbox.*

I'll use the MTS deployment option to show you some specific programming considerations and MTS specific functionality.

> *The code presented here will not change should you decide to go with the stand-alone scenario.*

Bring up the DCOM CC and logon to the SAP R/3 of your choice.

> *All illustrations in this chapter are based on SAP R/3 4.5 IDES.*

Upon successful logon you will be presented with the Business Object Repository view in the R/3 **Business Components** tree view.

At this time, we have to select the business objects to include in our proxy component. We will create one proxy component with several business objects to use in several projects in this chapter. We're going to use the following business objects in our proxy component:

> ➤ Customer
> ➤ Sales Order
> ➤ Company Code
> ➤ Material
> ➤ Helpvalues

These objects can be found in:
Customer and Company Code – in Financial
Accounting

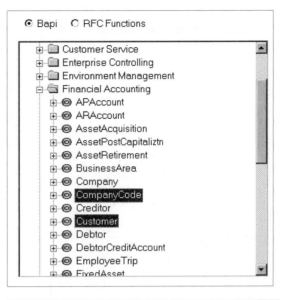

Sales Order – in Sales and Distribution

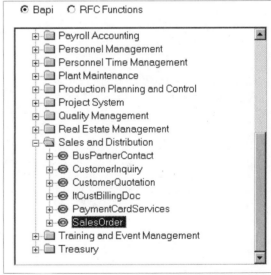

Material – in Logistics – General

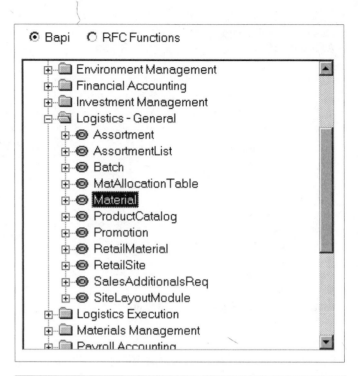

Helpvalues – in Cross-
Applications Components

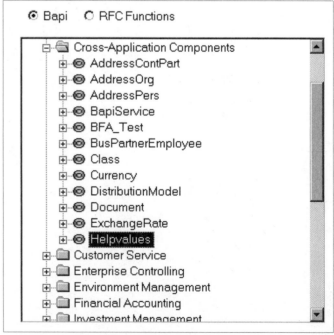

Go to every business object that we listed, click on it, and hit the **ADD>>** button. The resultant view of the **COM Components** tree view should be like the one below:

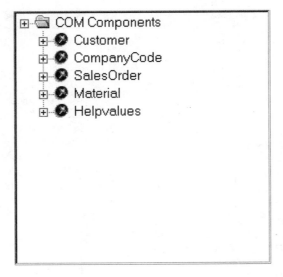

At this point, we have selected all the business objects to be included into the COM proxy component that the DCOM CC will generate.

To proceed with the actual proxy generation we have to specify values for the **COM/MTS** part of the DCOM CC. It requires the full path for the project file, a value for the namespace, a value for the MTS package and a selection for whether to generate the Session component. I have elected to generate the Session component so that I can illustrate its functionality in code.

After I entered all the values, the **COM/MTS** portion looks like the one below:

You can then click on the **Build Component DLL** button, sit back and wait for the confirmation message. Once you've been informed of its success, you can click on the **Install Component DLL in MTS** button. When you get another success message, the full generation and installation of the proxy component is complete.

The next step is to configure the proxy component in MTS. We need to configure roles and users for the package. First, check the package that should have been created, with the MTS Explorer:

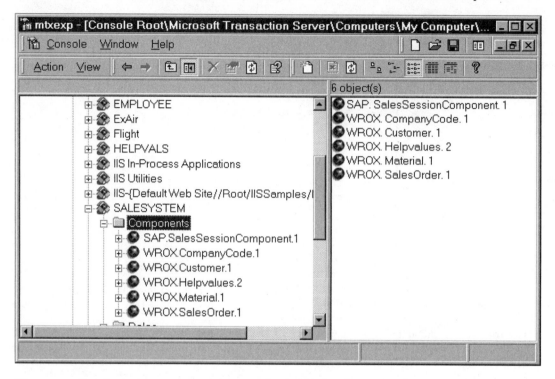

We can see that the proxy component is properly installed in the package and all the classes are present.

> *Note that the* Helpvalues-*based component (WROX.Helpvalues.2) has a 2 instead of 1 at the end of the name. This is because I built one* Helpvalues *component previously and the DCOM CC correctly created another version for it.*

> *During the build, the DCOM CC prompted me with a message that the* Helpvalues *component was already present on my system, and I confirmed my intent to generate another one instead of overwriting the existing component.*

## Configuring the MTS Package

To create roles and assign users to those roles I first created a new user group on my NT machine and called it `DataEntry`. First go to the Start | Programs | Administrative Tools (Common) | User Manager and select the New Local Group menu item.

The user management activities are dependent on the type of NT system that you have – Server or Workstation. I have added a couple of users to this group:

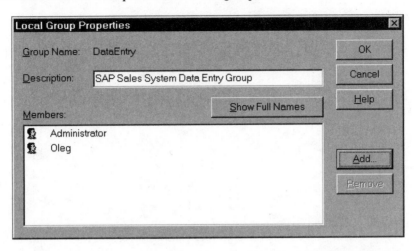

The big advantage of having and employing MTS to deploy DCOM CC proxy components, is that MTS allows you to manage your components in a very intuitive and comprehensive way.

You can easily administer user privileges for using the component, and this is something you have to do in a multi-user distributed environment. You can also configure packages to be run in the creator's process, or to be activated on the server and run in a surrogate process hosted by MTS. The DCOM CC configures its packages to be server activated. The advantage of having this option is that you are getting full support for role-based security, resource sharing, process isolation, and process management.

Check these options or configure them using the **Activation** tab of the **Properties** dialog for the MTS package:

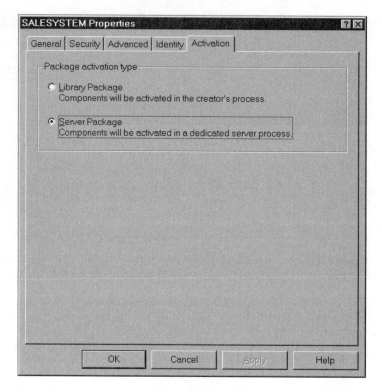

As I have already mentioned, due to the incongruent support of transactions for the RFC protocol and MTS, DCOM CC generated components do not support MTS transactions.

> *For details on configuring MTS components and packages try* Professional VB6 MTS Programming *from Wrox Press.*

Having created a user group for those who will be using the **SALESYSTEM** package, we can now create roles for the package and assign users to those roles. Normally you would have an Administrator role with full rights to the package and some type of Users role. You can have as many roles as you logically need. However, don't get carried away with this task – you may set your components up for access privileges conflicts. I decided to simply have a Users group that will have non-administrative privileges to be defined in the DataEntry role.

To add a new Administrator role to the package, you need to expand the package and right-click on the **Roles** folder of the **SALESYSTEM** package. Then select **Roles | New | Role** and type in `Administrator`:

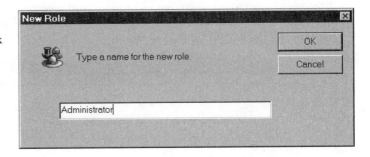

I repeated the same process to create the DataEntry role. What I end up with is the following picture of roles for the **SALESYSTEM** package:

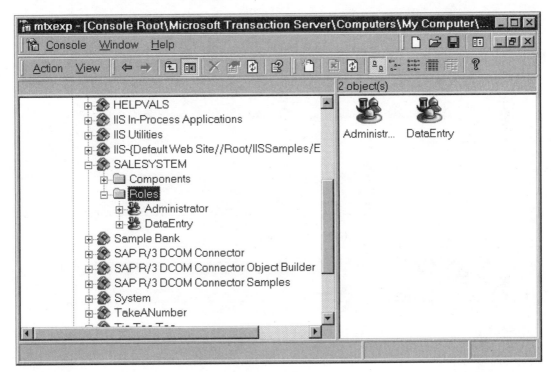

To complete the roles configuration I have to add members to each role. For the Administrator role, I have added the Administrator user, going to Administrator | Users | New | User. You will be prompted with the Add Users and Groups to Role dialog:

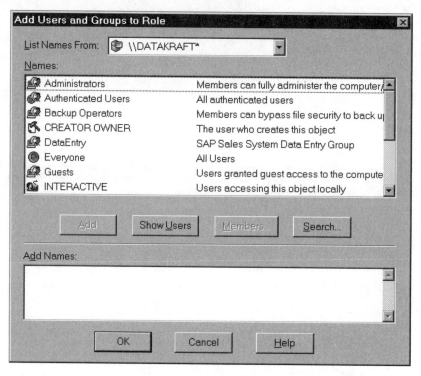

I selected  Administrators and hit the Members button:

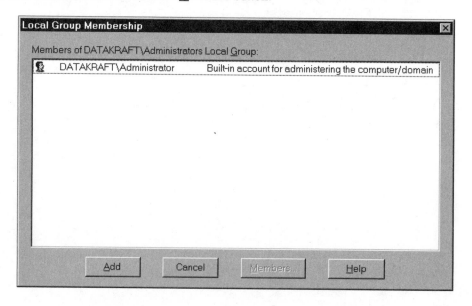

I had little choice to select from, but you may have much bigger selection. I added the only member of Administrators group to the Administrator role of the **SALESYSTEM** package:

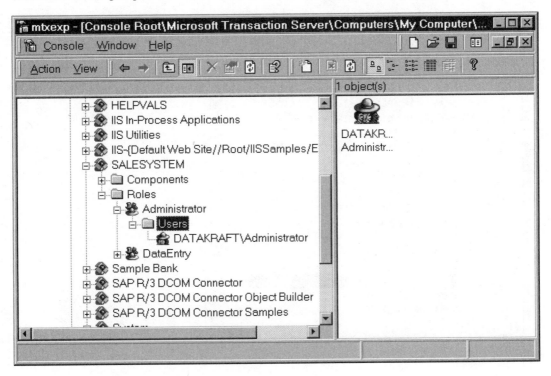

Then I repeated the above steps to add the DataEntry user group, created earlier, as a member of the DataEntry role:

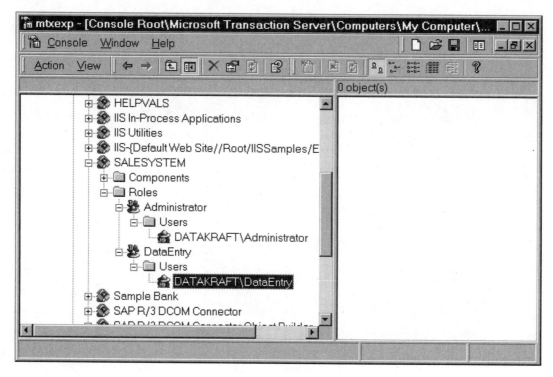

Now I have defined the roles, we can configure the role membership as we see fit for our work environment.

MTS roles configuration is an exciting topic. However, it has minimal impact on Visual Basic coding when it comes to working with DCOM CC generated proxies. At the beginning, I recommend not using any complex security or any other configurations. That is why the DCOM CC configures its own administrative components to have the Administrator account for the Administrator role and All Authenticated Users for the Users role.

Get used to working with the DCOM CC and programming against business object proxies first. Once you have a solid grip on it you can start getting creative with package and component configuration.

# Programming Business Object Proxies

First let's refresh our project specification. It should let us browse customers and look up their details and Sales Orders. Now create a new project group with an **ActiveX DLL** server project to encapsulate the business object proxy functionality and a **Standard EXE** client for the front-end:

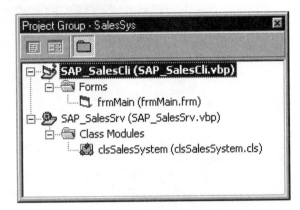

Let's first program the server component. The server component is an ordinary ActiveX DLL that is going to encapsulate all the proxy related functionality. It is not necessary to use a DLL, as you could certainly program the whole project in a form. However, using classes to implement functionality is a much better idea.

Add a reference to the ADO library and our freshly created proxy to the server project. Note that the value that you have entered in the namespace box on the **COM/MTS** portion of the DCOM CC will start the name for the library. In our case, it is **WROX**:

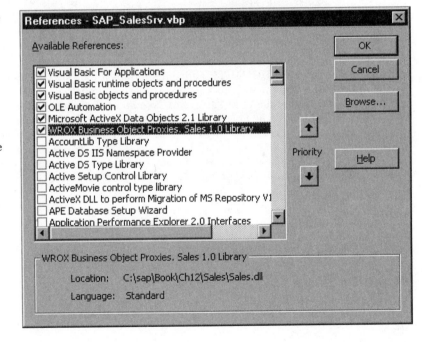

After we have done this, we can take a look at the Object Browser:

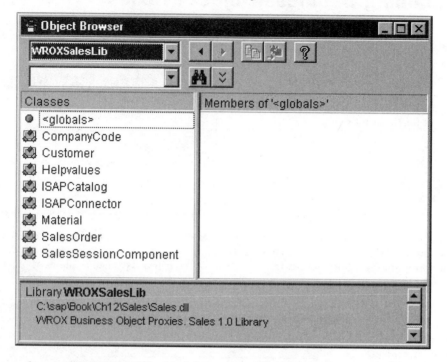

As we can observe, the DCOM CC added definitions for all the business objects that we selected, plus the Session component. It also added two derived interfaces – `ISAPConnector` and `ISAPCatalog` – from the `LIBRFC32.DLL`. We do not use them explicitly so do not declare any variables of their type. The next stage would be to declare the appropriate object variables to hold references to all the classes that implement the business objects that we need.

Our specs say that we have to browse customers, and that means using the *Customer* business object via its definition in the proxy component – the `Customer` class.

> *If you are not using Service Pack 4 or greater, then you need to declare your objects hosted in MTS as a generic `Object` type.*

```
Option Explicit

Private msapCustomer As WROXSalesLib.Customer
```

We now need to instantiate this object: which brings us to the Session object.

# The Session Object

As I explained earlier in Chapter 10, the Session object can be used as a "collector" for operations of all objects that you instantiate within the Session object. The DCOM CC documentation and the "Expanding the Reach of Your SAP Business Processes" article available from the DCOM CC main page compares the Session object to an MTS Activity.

This statement presumes that you are familiar with MTS. If you're not, I would offer a more intuitive analogy. Think of the Session object as something that provides the "container" for other objects and extends certain settings to them. A rough analogy would be the DAO Workspace object. You use it to logon to a database, specify a user, password and system database. You would then instantiate all other DAO objects from within the Workspace object:

```
Set Database = Workspace.OpenDatabase(Name).
```

The database would then "inherit" security information, the version of JET, and the likes, from the Workspace object. You may open multiple databases within one Workspace and they will all "inherit" workspace level attributes. If you close the Workspace you loose all the objects created within it.

The Session object that the DCOM CC will add to your proxy, upon request, will perform similar functionality. It allows you to keep all your business objects within the same RFC context. You also do not have to set any connectivity parameters for the business objects. You can manage context pooling using the KeepContext property of the business objects, but it will not propagate to other business objects. I elected to use the Session object, and it reflects in the code.

## Instantiating with the Session Object

To utilize the Session object I first need to declare a variable and to instantiate it:

```
Option Explicit

Private msapCustomer As WROXSalesLib.Customer
Private msapSession As WROXSalesLib.SalesSessionComponent
```

To instantiate the Session object, use CreateObject in the clsSalesSystem's Initialize event:

```
Private Sub Class_Initialize()

    Set msapSession = CreateObject("SAP.SalesSessionComponent.1")

End Sub
```

You can easily find values for the CreateObject argument using the MTS Explorer. Bring up the MTS Explorer and navigate to the component that you need:

Right-click on the component and select Properties:

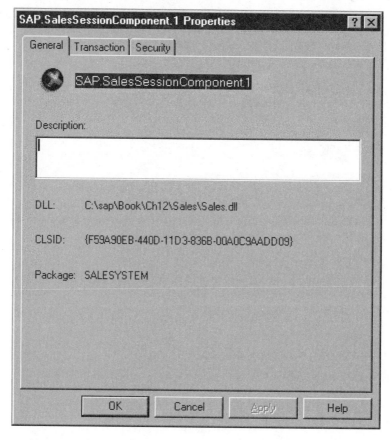

Then highlight the name, copy it to the clipboard and paste it into your Visual Basic code.

*This is a handy technique, because with the proliferation of components having very similar names, it is very easy to make a spelling error.*

Before we can do anything with the Session object, we have to first connect it to SAP R/3.

To do so, if you have a fully configured destination, you would use the Destination property. Alternatively, you can use the PutSessionInfo method if you do not have a fully configured destination or want to override values for some parameters – most commonly the user or the password.

Since I have a fully configured destination and I do not intend to override any of its parameters, I can code the following:

```
Private Sub Class_Initialize()

    Set msapSession = CreateObject("SAP.SalesSessionComponent.1")
    msapSession.Destination = "MSIDES"

End Sub
```

Where `MSIDES` is the name of my fully configured destination.

If you need the `PutSessionInfo` method, your call will look like this:

```
msapSession.PutSessionInfo "MSIDES", "user", "password", "E", "client"
```

We also want to make sure that all the objects we create with this Session object inherit the same context, so we'll set the `KeepSAPContext` property to `True`:

```
Private Sub Class_Initialize()

    Set msapSession = CreateObject("SAP.SalesSessionComponent.1")
    msapSession.Destination = "MSIDES"
    msapSession.KeepSAPContext = True

End Sub
```

Once the Session object is set up, we can begin instantiating the `Customer` object. We can use the `CreateInstance` method of the Session object to get an instance of the `Customer` object. The ProgID for the `Customer` object is `WROX.Customer.1`. Therefore, the call for this method will be as follows:

```
Private Sub Class_Initialize()

    Set msapSession = CreateObject("SAP.SalesSessionComponent.1")
    msapSession.Destination = "MSIDES"
    msapSession.KeepSAPContext = True

    Set msapCustomer = msapSession.CreateInstance("WROX.Customer.1")

End Sub
```

Because of the Session object, the newly created `msapCustomer` object will use all the connectivity parameters the same as the Session object when necessary, and you do not have to explicitly initialize them.

*This works in a very similar manner to the `CreateInstance` method of the MTS Context object.*

We can create instance for all the business objects we will need in the same manner:

```
Option Explicit

Dim msapSession As WROXSalesLib.SalesSessionComponent
Dim msapCustomer As WROXSalesLib.Customer
Dim msapSaleOrg As WROXSalesLib.CompanyCode
Dim msapSalesOrder As WROXSalesLib.SalesOrder

Dim mstrError As String

Private Sub Class_Initialize()

  On Error GoTo SAP_Error

  Set msapSession = CreateObject("SAP.SalesSessionComponent.1")
  msapSession.Destination = "MSIDES"
  msapSession.KeepSAPContext = True

  Set msapCustomer = msapSession.CreateInstance("WROX.Customer.1")
  Set msapSaleOrg = msapSession.CreateInstance("WROX.CompanyCode.1")
  Set msapSalesOrder = msapSession.CreateInstance("WROX.SalesOrder.1")

  Exit Sub

SAP_Error:

  mstrError = Err.Description
  MsgBox mstrError

End Sub
```

*Note that there is also a member variable to hold error information.*

Having done that we can move on to prepare the parameters for the BAPI call.

*To determine which BAPI to call, consult your SAP R/3 analyst or ABAP programmer, read documentation or experiment. I recommend against experimentation because it may be very time consuming, irrational and may never bring you results if you do not know what you are doing. It is like trying to guess the value of the constant for the window style without looking up the appropriate header file or Windows SDK documentation.*

## Getting a List of Customers

The BAPI that is going to bring us customers is GetList, and it is presented as the BapiGetList method of the Customer class in the proxy library. The DCOM CC prefixes all BAPI names with Bapi when creating names for the methods. A look at BapiGetList reveals the following syntax:

```
Sub BapiGetList(IdRange, [MaxRows], [Return], [AddressData], [SpecialData])
```

It does not return anything itself. The data that we are after will be returned in the AddressData argument. Although, it doesn't say so, all arguments are exposed as ADO Recordsets. The only required argument is IdRange.

You can use the Helpvalues project from Chapter 8 to get the values for the OPTION and SIGN fields of IdRange. For the HIGH and LOW fields consult an ABAP programmer or look up the ranges in SAP R/3. I have already discussed the difference between coding and SAP R/3 implementation. To save time, we will be using the following values for these fields:

- ➢  OPTION = EQ
- ➢  SIGN = E
- ➢  HIGH = " "
- ➢  LOW = *

First, I created a method for the clsSalesSystem class to implement the BapiGetList functionality – GetCustomers:

```
Public Function GetCustomers(recCust As ADODB.Recordset) As Integer
```

This method will expect a single argument for the resultant recordset with the list of customers. Next we have to create arguments for the BAPI call. Because all the arguments are disconnected ADO Recordsets I can safely code the following:

```
Dim pIdRange As ADODB.Recordset
Dim ret As ADODB.Recordset
```

I prefixed the name of the BapiGetList with p to make reading the code easier. The ret is for the return parameter. To initialize these recordsets I use the familiar DimAs method. The DCOM CC adds this method to all the classes it generates in the proxy library.

> The big difference with DimAs in the proxy classes is that it expects you to pass the proxy class's member name, not the actual name of the BAPI. In our case, it should be BapiGetList not GetList. Note that DimAs is also case sensitive.

I recommend simply copying names for methods and arguments from the Object Browser. The code for DimAs will be as follows:

```
msapCustomer.DimAs "BapiGetList", "IdRange", pIdRange
msapCustomer.DimAs "BapiGetList", "Return", ret
```

The first argument is the proxy defined method name; the second is the proxy-defined argument name; and the third is the variable for the BAPI-based method's argument. If these lines of code fail, it is either because the *Customer* object is not initialized properly, or you misspelled or used the wrong letter case for the method or parameter.

After a successful execution of the above code, you can check what you have by simply putting a breakpoint after the first line and typing something like this into the Immediate window:

```
? pIdRange.Fields.Item(0).Name
```

You should see "Sign" after you hit *Return*.

> *I strongly recommend performing this type of incremental validation to prevent some errors from sneaking into the code.*

Once we have valid ADO Recordsets for the BAPI method parameters, we can populate them. Remember that while they are recordsets, therefore presumably multiple records, not all BAPI parameters are tables. Many of them are structures and so it does not make sense to add more than one record or try to read more than one record from them. In our case, IdRange is a table. We know this because you may want to look for customers that fall within two or more ranges. Moreover, you may want to exercise different options. For example the BT (Between) value for the OPTION field of IdRange will get you customers between the LOW and HIGH customer numbers. The following code:

```
pIdRange.AddNew
  pIdRange![SIGN] = "I"
  pIdRange![Option] = "BT"
  pIdRange![LOW] = "0000020000"
  pIdRange![HIGH] = "0000030000"
pIdRange.Update

pIdRange.AddNew
  pIdRange![SIGN] = "I"
  pIdRange![Option] = "BT"
  pIdRange![LOW] = "0000070000"
  pIdRange![HIGH] = "0000090000"
pIdRange.Update
```

will cause `BapiGetList` to bring those customers who fall into both intervals. How do you know what intervals you have? Well, ask your ABAP programmer. To get you started on this – and only on this one – do the following. Fire up your SAP R/3 front-end and follow the Tools | Business Engineer | Customizing menu choices:

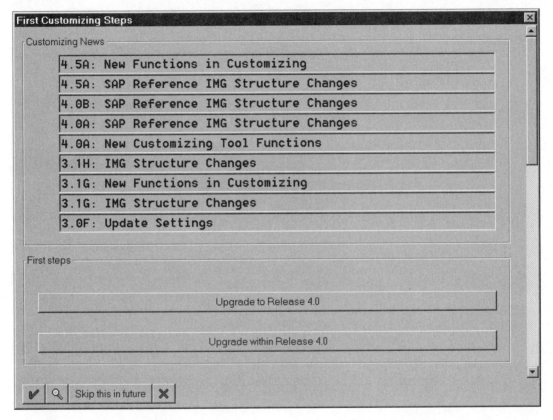

Click on the green check button to dismiss the dialog. Then go to the Implement Projects | SAP Reference IMG menu item.

Expand Logistics General | Logistics Basic Data: Business Partners | Customers | Control and you should get the following:

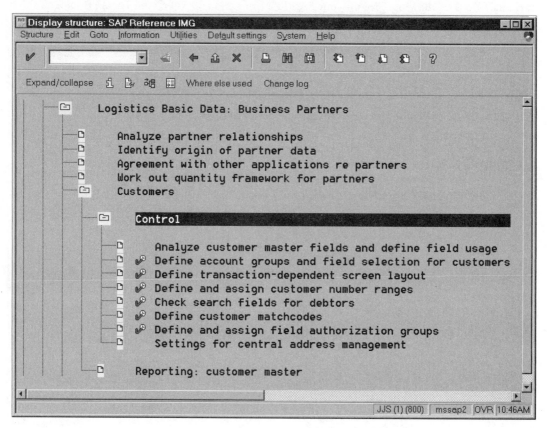

Select the Define and assign customer number ranges cherry-check and you should see the following:

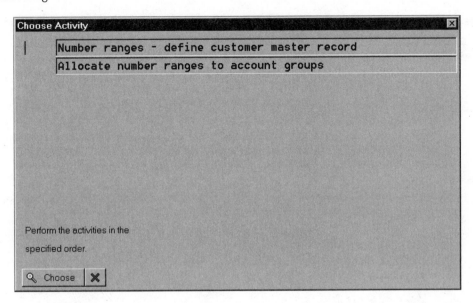

Double-click on `Number ranges - define customer master record` and hit the **Intervals** button and you should see the something like this:

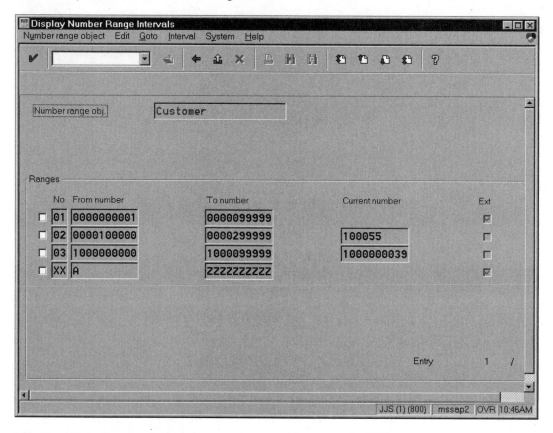

These are the ranges for the customer numbers complete with the **Ext** check box on the far-right. This tells you whether you have to assign customer numbers externally when creating customers, or if SAP R/3 will do it internally for you.

> *I performed this little SAP R/3 exploration just to illustrate how complex and non-trivial R/3 is. This is why I strongly recommend consulting somebody who really knows SAP R/3 before experimenting with BAPI-related code. I'll show you how to program against DCOM CC generated proxies, or how to use the SAP Automation Desktop SDK, but I am not attempting to teach SAP R/3 in this book.*

After our exploration of `IdRange` values we are ready to populate the `IdRange` Table:

```
pIdRange.AddNew
  pIdRange![SIGN] = "E"
  pIdRange![Option] = "EQ"
  pIdRange![LOW] = "*"
  pIdRange![HIGH] = ""
pIdRange.Update
```

The above values for the `IdRange` fields will return all customers available. We have to also prepare the resultant recordset: `AddressData`. We do it the same way as for all the rest:

```
msapCustomer.DimAs "BapiGetList", "AddressData", recCust
```

The BAPI call will not fail if we simply pass the ADO Recordset to the method without using the `DimAs` method. However, it is strongly recommended to use `DimAs`. Not only does it format the argument correctly, it also allows us to know the metadata of the resultant or inbound parameter. This allows us to correctly prepare the data.

After all the pre-processing we can finally call the `BapiGetList` method that implements the original `GetList` BAPI.

> *It is recommended to adapt calling the BAPI based methods of proxy components using named arguments. We have already discussed why, when we discussed BAPI programming using the SAP Automation toolkit. The major benefit of using named arguments is that as long as SAP does not change the function interface your code will work. The only caveat with named arguments is that they do not allow you to use empty placeholders for optional parameters. Named argument names are not case sensitive.*

The code for the `BapiGetList` method will look like this:

```
msapCustomer.BapiGetList IDRANGE:=pIdRange, RETURN:=ret, ADDRESSDATA:=recCust
```

The result of this call will be an ADO Recordset containing all customers with their address data. We'll see how we can display this data when we get to the client.

This is the first part of the project. We were able to selectively extract the customer data from SAP R/3 using the DCOM CC generated proxy component. We can now select customers to look up their data.

# Getting Customer Details

Instead of simply displaying the data that we already have in the `AddressData` recordset, I decided to put together a routine to retrieve the whole set of a customer's **Personal Data**. The Address Data is simply a subset of the Personal Data. The `PersonalData` recordset is an argument of the `BapiGetDetail1` method of the `Customer` class. If you are using an SAP R/3 release older than 4.5 you will not find the `GetList` BAPI and should use `GetDetail`. Both `GetList` and `GetDetail1` appear in SAP R/3 4.5 or greater.

A look at the `BapiGetDetail1` method reveals that we need a value for the Sales Organization, and we're better off providing values for the Distribution Channel and Division. These three values would identify a customer for a particular Sales Organization. The specifics of SAP R/3 mean that while you may have a customer, it may not be defined in a certain Sales Area, Distribution Channel and Division.

Therefore, the task of getting Personal Data is dependent on our ability to retrieve the Sales Organization data for a particular customer. The BAPI to use for this task is GetSalesAreas, which is implemented as the BapiGetSalesAreas method of the Customer class. The syntax for this method is as follows:

```
Sub BapiGetSalesAreas([Return], [SalesAreas])
```

The SalesAreas argument, that is also implemented as an ADO Recordset, will bring us the necessary information. The Return argument – also an ADO Recordset – will as usual bring the status of the BAPI's execution. The returned SalesArea recordset will have the following fields:

> ➢ Customer
> ➢ Salesorg
> ➢ Distrchn
> ➢ Division

> *A favorite technique that I use to discover a recordset's fields is to use a simple piece of code to loop through the recordset and dump the field names and length into the Immediate window, and then copy those values into a text file for future reference.*

As you can see, the SalesArea recordset has all we need to correctly identify a customer for the BapiGetDetail1 method:

> ➢ The Salesorg field will bring the Sales Organization
> ➢ The Distrchn field will bring the Distribution Channel
> ➢ The Division field will provide a Division

The only problem now is how do we make this method bring us data for a specific customer. The syntax for the method does not provide any argument for the customer number. If you recall the SAP BAPI control library, the GetSAPObject method had arguments for up to 10 optional keys that you could supply to get a reference not to an abstract customer, but to a particular customer.

The same functionality is implemented a little differently in DCOM CC generated proxies. Every class definition generated by the DCOM CC has a common method, InitKeys(keyval). This method will initialize the key for the business object and when you use the reference to the business object, it will not be an abstract reference anymore. You can always check if the InitKeys method was successful by checking the value of the KeyCustomerNo read-only property defined for the Customer class.

To get a reference to a particular customer, we have to pass the customer number to the routine that is going to execute InitKeys prior to calling BapiGetSalesAreas. We can then use those values of the SalesAreas records to get details for the customer.

*Note that this is not the whole story. Due to the nature of SAP R/3, one customer can be defined in several Sales Organizations, Divisions or Distribution Channels. This would create more than one record in the* SalesAreas *recordset. In this case, I will assume that every customer will only have a single record in the* SalesAreas *recordset.*

The routine that is going to provide us with customer Sales Area information is coded as the GetCustSalesAreas method for our server component:

```
Public Sub GetCustSalesAreas(strCust As String, recSalesA As ADODB.Recordset, _
                             strErr As String)

    Dim ret As ADODB.Recordset

    On Error GoTo SAP_Error

    msapCustomer.InitKeys strCust

    msapCustomer.BapiGetSalesAreas SALESAREAS:=recSalesA, RETURN:=ret

    If ret(0) = "E" Then
        strErr = ret(2)
    End If


    Set ret = Nothing

    Exit Sub

SAP_Error:

    mstrError = Err.Description
    MsgBox mstrError

End Sub
```

This method expects the customer number to be passed to it and it will return a recordset with Sales Areas information. It also has an argument for the BAPI error message.

This routine is called before the routine that has to provide us with customer details. I created the GetCustDetails routine as another method of our server component to call the BapiGetDetail1 method:

```
Public Sub GetCustDetails(strCust As String, strSOrg As String, _
                          strDistCh As String, strDv As String, _
                          recDet As ADODB.Recordset, strErr As String)

    Dim ret As ADODB.Recordset

    On Error GoTo SAP_Error

    msapCustomer.InitKeys strCust
```

```
      msapCustomer.BapiGetDetail1 SALESORGANIATION:=strSOrg, _
                                  DISTRIBUTIONCHANNEL:=strDistCh, _
                                  DIVISION:=strDv, PERSONALDATA:=recDet, _
                                  RETURN:=ret

   If ret(0) = "E" Then
      strErr = ret(2)
   End If

   Set ret = Nothing

   Exit Sub

SAP_Error:

   mstrError = Err.Description
   MsgBox mstrError

End Sub
```

As you see this method expects the Customer Number, Sales Organization, Distribution Channel and Division. To get these values, I simply call the `GetCustSalesAreas` method from the GUI prior to calling the `GetCustDetails` method.

You may get the feeling that BAPIs are like APIs. You should use them in specific sequence and process the output of one in the input for another. The order and relation of BAPI calls is where a knowledge of SAP R/3 comes in.

> Please do not confuse the user-defined methods in the server component with the methods of the proxy component based on the BAPIs. All DCOM CC generated BAPI based methods have a `BAPI` prefix. My user-defined methods never begin with BAPI, but more closely resemble the underlying BAPI call.

This completes the second phase of our outbound project, retrieving details on individual customers. The final step is to also retrieve Sales Orders.

# Getting Sales Orders

So far, it has been sufficient to use the `Customer` class defined in our proxy component. We now want to display sales orders for customers, and so we have to use another class defined in the proxy component – `SalesOrder`. Take a look at this class in the Object Browser:

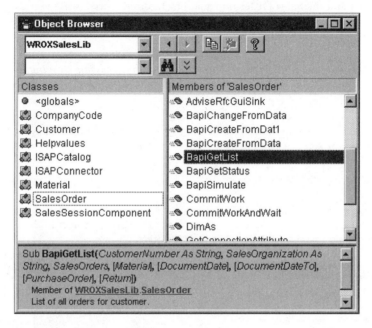

The `BapiGetList` method, that obviously implements the `GetList` BAPI, is what we are looking for. The syntax for this method is as follows:

```
Sub BapiGetList(CustomerNumber As String, SalesOrganization As String, _
            SalesOrders, [Material], [DocumentDate], [DocumentDateTo], _
            [PurchaseOrder], [Return])
```

It requires the Customer Number and the Sales Organization, and gives you the list of Sales Orders in the `SalesOrders` argument. Needless to say, the `SalesOrders` argument is implemented as an ADO Recordset.

I created the `GetSalesOrder` method for our server component to implement the `BapiGetList` method of the `SalesOrder` class:

```
Public Function GetSalesOrder(strCust As String, strSalesOrg As String, _
                        recSalesOrder As ADODB.Recordset)

    Dim ret As ADODB.Recordset

    msapSalesOrder.BapiGetList CUSTOMERNUMBER:=strCust, _
                        SALESORGANIZATION:=strSalesOrg, _
                        SALESORDERS:=recSalesOrder, RETURN:=ret
```

```
    Set ret = Nothing

  End Function
```

The specifics of the `BapiGetList` method are that it returns a recordset that contains the line items for the Sales Order and the Sales Order information. In other words, what you get are repetitive entries for the Sales Order and different data for the Material that was in a line item. It's basically the merged Orders and Line Items tables.

> *This is, by the way, the perfect candidate for some sort of staging – saving the result into a relational database and performing data normalization. For our purposes, I just got rid of duplicate Order Number entries.*

This completes the server component for our first exercise. At this point, it makes sense to start creating a client for our server component.

# The Client

The client is a single form **Standard EXE** project (`SAPSales_Cli`) that I added to the project group. Because they belong to the same group, I can reference the server project in the client project, thereby making development and debugging very intuitive:

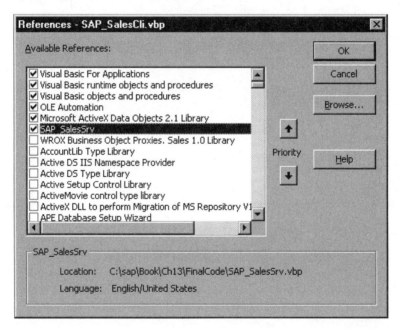

I added a few controls to the client form to facilitate the display of customer data: a tree view control (with an associated image list control), a list box control, and an OLEDB Data Grid:

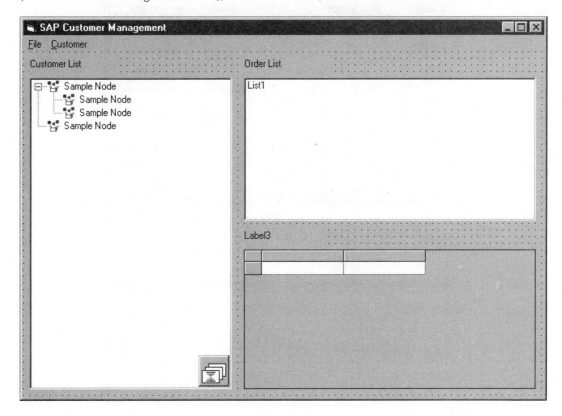

The menu contains the following items:

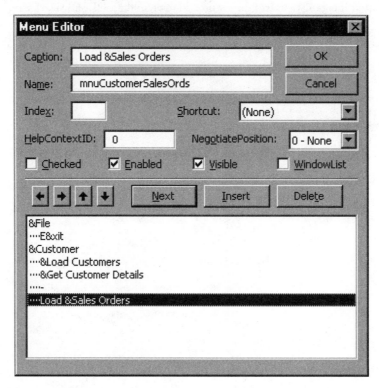

The first thing to do is to get the list of customers to populate the tree view. We'll start by declaring a variable to hold a reference to our server component in the form's General Declarations section:

```
Option Explicit

Dim mobjSrv As New clsSalesSystem
```

## Listing Customers

Next we need to get a list of customers. In our server component, we created the GetCustomers method that will return a list of customers in a recordset. We therefore need to first call this method, passing in an ADO Recordset variable, and then use the returned AddressData recordset to load the tree view control:

```
Private Sub mnuCustomerLoad_Click()

   Dim recCust As ADODB.Recordset

   mobjSrv.GetCustomers recCust

   DisplayCust recCust
```

```
    Set recCust = Nothing

End Sub
```

To display the content of this recordset properly, I coded a simple routine to populate a tree view control with customer names:

```
Private Sub DisplayCust(recCust As ADODB.Recordset)

    Dim ndCust As Node

    On Error GoTo ErrTrap

    recCust.Sort = "Name ASC"

    Do Until recCust.EOF
        Set ndCust = TreeView1.Nodes.Add("topnod", tvwChild, "CUST" & _
                                    recCust![Customer], recCust![Name], 2)
        recCust.MoveNext
    Loop

    Exit Sub

ErrTrap:

    MsgBox Err.Description

End Sub
```

This routine simply adds nodes to the tree view using the Name field of the passed AddressData recordset for the text of the node, and the unique customer number from the Customer field of the same recordset.

*I used the Sort method of the recordset to arrange the customer names alphabetically and make customer browsing easier.*

The result of all these operations will be as follows. Remember not to expect the same customer names in your SAP R/3:

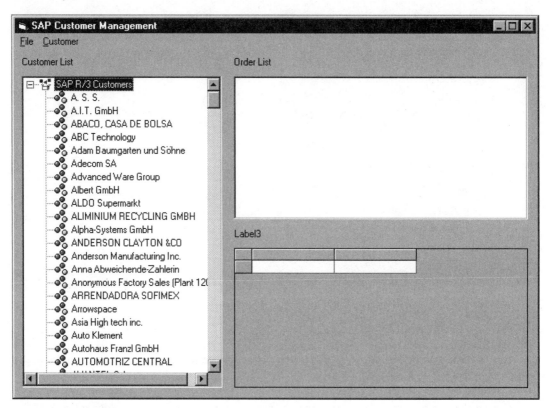

## Customer Details

The next step is to display the details for a particular customer. To implement this, we created the `GetCustDetails` method in our server component. However, as you should recall, before we can use this method we need some additional parameters that we can get by calling our `GetCustSalesAreas` method.

Before we can call either of these methods, we need to store a reference to the particular customer that the user has highlighted in the tree view. I've coded this in the tree view's `NodeClick` event:

```
Private Sub TreeView1_NodeClick(ByVal Node As MSComctlLib.Node)

   mstrOrdKey = Mid(Node.Key, 5)

End Sub
```

The `mstrOrdKey` variable holds the value of the selected node's key sans the prefix `CUST`.

*I constructed the keys for the nodes to display customers, by appending the customer number to the letters "CUST". Now I have to shed the "CUST".*

Then we can call the methods of the server component to load the details for a customer. I've implemented this in a menu item, but if you want a more dynamic interface you could code it in the `NodeClick` event:

```
Private Sub mnuCustomerDetails_Click()

    Dim recDet As ADODB.Recordset
    Dim strErr As String

    mobjSrv.GetCustSalesAreas mstrOrdKey, mrecSA, strErr

    If Trim(strErr) = "" Then

        mobjSrv.GetCustDetails mstrOrdKey, mrecSA![Salesorg], mrecSA![Distrchn], _
                           mrecSA![Division], recDet, strErr

        If Trim(strErr) = "" Then
            Label3 = "Customer Details"
            ShowProps recDet
        Else
            MsgBox strErr
        End If

    Else

        MsgBox strErr

    End If


    Set recDet = Nothing

End Sub
```

Since we'll need a SalesAreas recordset when we retrieve Sales Orders I stored this recordset as a member variable:

```
Option Explicit

Dim mobjSrv As New clsSalesSystem
Dim mrecSA As ADODB.Recordset
```

The routine that displays the results from the `GetCustDetails` method of our server component is very simple. The idea is to display the recordset in Name-Value pairs because it contains one record anyway and viewing one record is more convenient vertically. To do so I make an ADO recordset with two fields – `Name` and `Value` – and populate it with the field names for the `Name` and `Value` fields of the resultant recordset:

```
Private Sub ShowProps(recProps As ADODB.Recordset)

    Dim recRs As New ADODB.Recordset
    Dim intCount As Integer

    MakeAdoRs recRs
    recRs.Open
```

```
      For intCount = 0 To recProps.Fields.Count - 1
         recRs.AddNew
         recRs![Name] = recProps.Fields.Item(intCount).Name
         recRs![Value] = recProps.Fields.Item(intCount).Value
         recRs.Update
      Next
      recRs.MoveFirst

      Set DataGrid1.DataSource = recRs

      Set recRs = Nothing

   End Sub
```

The call to make the recordset is simple:

```
   Public Sub MakeAdoRs(ret As ADODB.Recordset)

      ret.Fields.Append "Name", adChar, 50
      ret.Fields.Append "Value", adChar, 120
      ret.CursorLocation = adUseClient

   End Sub
```

The result of all these manipulations will be as follows:

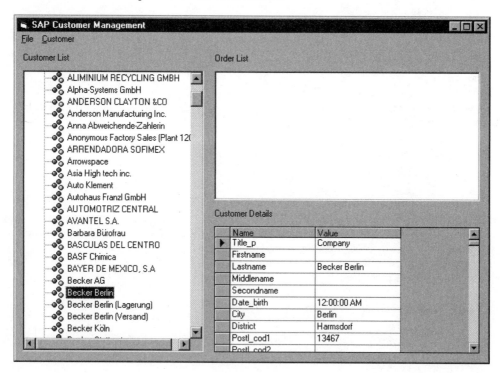

## Sales Orders

The final step is to display Sales Orders for a particular customer. To do this we created the `GetSalesOrder` method in our server component:

```
Private Sub mnuCustomerSalesOrds_Click()

    Dim recSO As ADODB.Recordset
    Dim recM As ADODB.Recordset
    Dim intCount As Integer
    Dim strCurrentCust As String
    Dim strPreviousCust As String

    On Error GoTo ErrTrap

    mobjSrv.GetSalesOrder mstrOrdKey, mrecSA![Salesorg], recSO

    Label3 = "Orders' Details"

    If recSO Is Nothing Then
        MsgBox "The Customer " & mstrOrdKey & " has no Sales Orders"
    Else
        List1.Clear

        Do Until recSO.EOF
            strCurrentCust = recSO![sd_doc]
            If strPreviousCust <> strCurrentCust Then
                List1.AddItem recSO![sd_doc] & vbTab & recSO![doc_date]
            End If
            strPreviousCust = recSO![sd_doc]
            recSO.MoveNext
        Loop

        Set DataGrid1.DataSource = recSO

    End If

    Set recSO = Nothing
    Set recM = Nothing

    Exit Sub

ErrTrap:

    MsgBox Err.Description

End Sub
```

We basically loop trough the resultant recordset with repetitive Sales Orders data and filter out repetitive Sales Order numbers. The result is presented below:

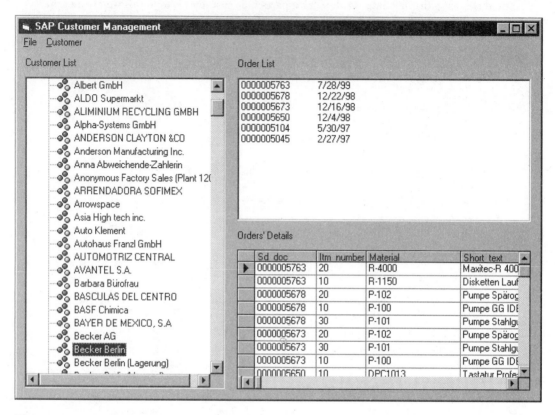

The raw recordset is displayed in the data grid with repetitive information, while the list box above the data grid presents the filtered out Order Numbers and Order Dates.

That completes the first, outbound, project. Now we are going to look at how to use our business object proxy component to add data to SAP R/3.

# Creating Customers

The task of creating anything in SAP R/3 is much more complex and error prone than the outbound tasks that pull data out of SAP R/3. To create something we have to find the appropriate business object and select one of its BAPIs. The most time consuming yet most important task is to learn what predefined values the `Create*` BAPI expects, and what the format and type for the rest of the data are. SAP R/3 is notorious for its maze of internally defined or configured values that are not normally exposed or intuitive.

I decided to implement the creation of customers for two reasons:

> I believe it is important functionality that many people will implement first. It is critical for any sales oriented SAP R/3 integration and I think these types of applications will be early targets for integration.

> The DCOM CC comes with very a solid Create Sales Order example located in the `\rfcsk\ccsamp` folder. You are encouraged to study those examples. I figured that if I give you an example on how to create customers, you can combine the two types of projects and you've got yourself a Sales System.

I have already showed how to browse the customer and sales orders data. Thus, instead of giving you a variation of the existing sample project, I decided to create something complimentary to the DCOM CC RFC SDK. Creating customers would also allow us to utilize the SAP R/3 knowledge that we have accumulated so far.

I decided to implement a no-frills GUI and not even get creative with ActiveX components for a change. This is a small demo that concentrates on the core programming issues. I created user-defined functions for every operation, so all you have to do to wrap it into a class is copy and paste the code.

# Programming Considerations

Before we can begin programming this project, there are a few issues we need to discuss before hand.

## Session Object

In this project, I will not implement the Session object. My reasoning is simple. With this type of data entry application, the operator may spend significant time entering data or maybe even go and have a coffee in the middle of the process. If I were to use a Session object, it would be to take advantage of maintaining context with SAP R/3. I need exactly the opposite. I want to establish the connection only at the moment I submit the data. I do not want to maintain context during idle-time.

Another consideration is that I will be creating several business objects simultaneously, so I cannot use the ability of the Session object to instantiate other business objects in its own process.

## Customer Numbering Revisited

To successfully create customers I have to resolve one important question that I have already described – do I generate customer numbers or do I delegate the process to SAP R/3?

I tend to upload as much functionality as possible to SAP R/3, so I decided to go with internal customer number assignment. I have already shown you where to go to determine what range is configured to generate numbers internally. Once you find that out, it's trivial to look up a well-defined customer in that range to serve as a Reference Customer. If you have problems doing it yourself, ask your ABAP colleagues. You have to phrase the question somewhat like this – "Please find me the customer that belongs to the range configured to assign customer numbers automatically".

Alternatively, you can follow these SAP R/3 front-end screenshots to do it yourself. Find the range and then go to the Accounting | Accounts Receivable | Master Records | Display and find yourself a legitimate customer:

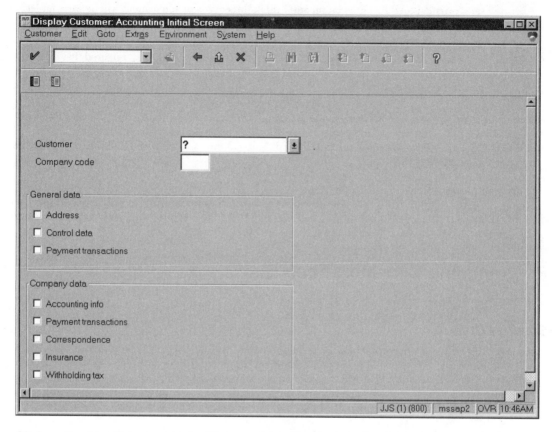

Click on the drop-down next to the Customer box. Then, on the Customers per account group screen, hit the Multiple Search Criteria button ->...:

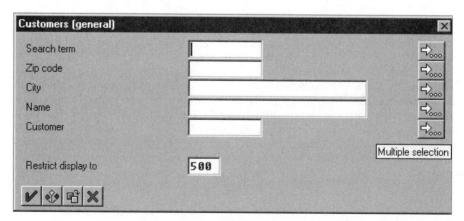

Then select the **Ranges** tab:

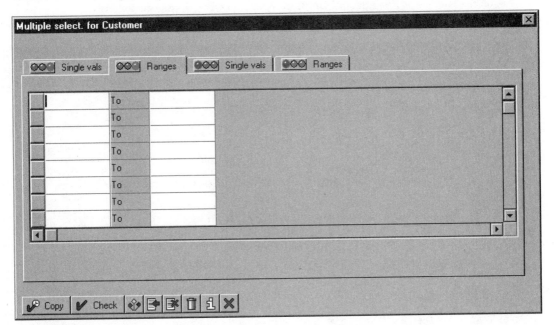

Enter values for the range of Customer numbers, hit Check and then Copy. Proceed to the green check on the Customer Per Account Group screen. You will get your customers:

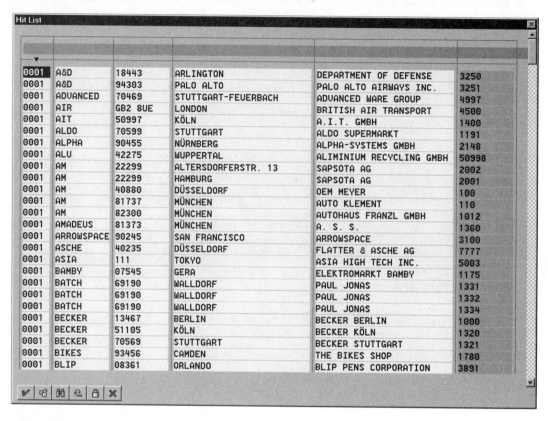

| Hit List | | | | | |
|---|---|---|---|---|---|
| 0001 | A&D | 18443 | ARLINGTON | DEPARTMENT OF DEFENSE | 3250 |
| 0001 | A&D | 94303 | PALO ALTO | PALO ALTO AIRWAYS INC. | 3251 |
| 0001 | ADVANCED | 70469 | STUTTGART-FEUERBACH | ADVANCED WARE GROUP | 4997 |
| 0001 | AIR | GB2 8UE | LONDON | BRITISH AIR TRANSPORT | 4500 |
| 0001 | AIT | 50997 | KÖLN | A.I.T. GMBH | 1400 |
| 0001 | ALDO | 70599 | STUTTGART | ALDO SUPERMARKT | 1191 |
| 0001 | ALPHA | 90455 | NÜRNBERG | ALPHA-SYSTEMS GMBH | 2148 |
| 0001 | ALU | 42275 | WUPPERTAL | ALIMINIUM RECYCLING GMBH | 50998 |
| 0001 | AM | 22299 | ALTERSDORFERSTR. 13 | SAPSOTA AG | 2002 |
| 0001 | AM | 22299 | HAMBURG | SAPSOTA AG | 2001 |
| 0001 | AM | 40880 | DÜSSELDORF | OEM MEYER | 100 |
| 0001 | AM | 81737 | MÜNCHEN | AUTO KLEMENT | 110 |
| 0001 | AM | 82300 | MÜNCHEN | AUTOHAUS FRANZL GMBH | 1012 |
| 0001 | AMADEUS | 81373 | MÜNCHEN | A. S. S. | 1360 |
| 0001 | ARROWSPACE | 90245 | SAN FRANCISCO | ARROWSPACE | 3100 |
| 0001 | ASCHE | 40235 | DÜSSELDORF | FLATTER & ASCHE AG | 7777 |
| 0001 | ASIA | 111 | TOKYO | ASIA HIGH TECH INC. | 5003 |
| 0001 | BAMBY | 07545 | GERA | ELEKTROMARKT BAMBY | 1175 |
| 0001 | BATCH | 69190 | WALLDORF | PAUL JONAS | 1331 |
| 0001 | BATCH | 69190 | WALLDORF | PAUL JONAS | 1332 |
| 0001 | BATCH | 69190 | WALLDORF | PAUL JONAS | 1334 |
| 0001 | BECKER | 13467 | BERLIN | BECKER BERLIN | 1000 |
| 0001 | BECKER | 51105 | KÖLN | BECKER KÖLN | 1320 |
| 0001 | BECKER | 70569 | STUTTGART | BECKER STUTTGART | 1321 |
| 0001 | BIKES | 93456 | CAMDEN | THE BIKES SHOP | 1780 |
| 0001 | BLIP | 08361 | ORLANDO | BLIP PENS CORPORATION | 3891 |

### Fixed Values

SAP R/3 maintains a huge number of fixed values for various fields and parameters. Some of them are configurable, some are not. In either case, any attempt to assign a value to a field in a BAPI parameter that is different from the predefined value will cause the BAPI to fail. A good example would be the Currency and Language parameters. SAP R/3 expects a value of USD for US Dollar and E for English. SAP R/3 maintains internal check tables and obviously employs function modules to validate the data being entered, whether it be via a GUI, RFC or BAPI. SAP implements the *Helpvalues* business object that can retrieve most fixed values via its GetList BAPI.

## Coding the Project

I created a single form Standard EXE project (Cust_Create) to implement creating customers. We already have the *Customer* and *Helpvalues* business objects defined in the proxy component that we created and used in the previous project. I added a reference to it and started coding.

First – variable definitions:

```
Option Explicit

Dim msapHelp As WROXSalesLib.Helpvalues
Dim msapCustomer As WROXSalesLib.Customer
```

Then I have to look up the BAPI-based method I will use to create customers. The method is `BapiCreateFromData1` for releases 4.5 and after. For releases prior to 4.5, you will have `BapiCreateFromData`. A look at the method shows the following syntax:

```
Sub BapiCreateFromData1(PersonalData, CopyReference, [OptionalPersonalData], _
                        [Return])
```

The required arguments are `PersonalData` and `CopyReference`, both implemented as ADO Recordsets. Remember that they are based on structures not tables, so don't attempt to add more than one record and slip it to the BAPI. The structure of `CopyReference` is as follows:

- ➤ `SALESORG` field – The Sales Organization
- ➤ `DISTR_CHAN` field – The Distribution Channel
- ➤ `DIVISION` field – The Division
- ➤ `REF_CUSTMR` field – The Reference Customer number

We already know how to get these values and what they are for.

The `PersonalData` argument is much bigger and I have assembled the minimal list of fields required to create customers:

- ➤ `FIRSTNAME`
- ➤ `LANGU_P` – Predefined abbreviation
- ➤ `STREET` – Street Name
- ➤ `CITY`
- ➤ `COUNTRY` – Fixed
- ➤ `POSTL_COD1` – Postal Code
- ➤ `LASTNAME` –
- ➤ `CURRENCY` – Predefined abbreviation
- ➤ `REGION` – Predefined abbreviation
- ➤ `E_MAIL`
- ➤ `HOUSE_NO` – House Number

As you can see `LANGUAGE`, `CURRENCY`, `COUNTRY` and `REGION` have fixed values that we have to use. Moreover, `COUNTRY` and `REGION` are interconnected.

What I decided to do is to perform on-line value lookup. To do this, we will use the *Helpvalues* business object to load fixed values into combo boxes, thus minimizing human error. This is better than having to go online for field level validation, plus it reduces network traffic.

## The GUI Implementation

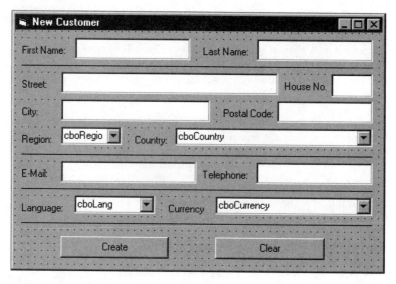

### Loading Fixed Values – Countries

The GUI contains combo boxes to display the fixed values. This is done using several routines, identical in functionality:

```
Public Sub GetCountries()

  Dim recCountrs As ADODB.Recordset
  Dim ret As ADODB.Recordset


  msapHelp.DimAs "BapiGetList", "Helpvalues", recCountrs

  msapHelp.BapiGetList METHOD:="CreateFromData1", _
                  PARAMETER:="PERSONALDATA", OBJNAME:="Customer", _
                  FIELD:="COUNTRY", RETURN:=ret, _
                  HELPVALUES:=recCountrs

  Do Until recCountrs.EOF

    cboCountry.AddItem Mid(recCountrs![Helpvalues], 4, 3) & _
                  " " & Mid(recCountrs![Helpvalues], 8, 15)

    recCountrs.MoveNext

  Loop

  cboCountry.ListIndex = 1
```

```
      Set recCountrs = Nothing
      Set ret = Nothing

End Sub
```

Note than unlike the `DimAs` method of the proxy objects, `GetList` of the *Helpvalues* object requires real BAPI names. For details on the *Helpvalues* `GetList` BAPI implementation see Chapter 8. The `Mid` statement that I use to populate the combo box gets its values from the `Description4HV` parameter of the `GetList` BAPI.

Here we use the proxy component of the *Helpvalues* business object and it implements the BAPI based method `BapiGetList` that has identical parameters with BAPI `GetList` for the same business object. To look up all the values I actually used the sample project from Chapter 8 – it is indeed handy.

The results of the execution of `GetCountries` is shown below:

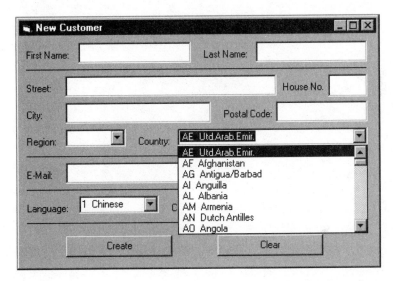

We're going to be a bit clever here and limit the entries in the Region combo box to only those belonging to the selected country. Therefore, code the Country combo box's `Click` event to call `GetRegions`:

```
Private Sub cboCountry_Click()

    cboRegion.Clear
    GetRegions Trim(Left(cboCountry, 3))

End Sub
```

### Loading Fixed Values –Regions

The next routine to consider is `GetRegions`:

```
Public Sub GetRegions(vCountry As String)

    Dim recRegions As ADODB.Recordset
    Dim ret As ADODB.Recordset
    Dim recSelect As ADODB.Recordset

    msapHelp.DimAs "BapiGetList", "Values4Field", recRegions
    msapHelp.DimAs "BapiGetList", "Selection4Helpvalues", recSelect

    recSelect.AddNew
        recSelect![Select_fld] = "LAND1"
        recSelect![Sign] = "I"
        recSelect![Option] = "EQ"
        recSelect![LOW] = vCountry
        recSelect![HIGH] = ""
    recSelect.Update

    msapHelp.BapiGetList METHOD:="CreateFromData1", _
                    PARAMETER:="PERSONALDATA", OBJNAME:="Customer", _
                    FIELD:="REGION", RETURN:=ret, _
                    SELECTION4HELPVALUES:=recSelect, _
                    VALUES4FIELD:=recRegions

    If recRegions Is Nothing Then
        MsgBox "No Regions"
    Else

        Do Until recRegions.EOF
            cboRegion.AddItem recRegions![Values]
            recRegions.MoveNext
        Loop

        cboRegion.ListIndex = 1

    End If

    Set recRegions = Nothing
    Set ret = Nothing
    Set recSelect = Nothing

End Sub
```

This routine has a little twist in it. We use the `SELECTION4HELPVALUES` argument to select only those regions that belong to the country that the user should select first. This argument acts like a criteria table.

*Refer to Chapter 8 for details on the `SELECTION4HELPVALUES` argument.*

The name of the criteria is filed in LAND1, which I got from the DESCRIPTION4HV data. DESCRIPTION4HV also provided me with Offsets and Lengths for fields that I use in the Mid statements to populate combo boxes. I pass the name of the country and set the LOW field to it. Because there is no from X to Y type of selection, the HIGH field is empty, the OPTION is EQ (equals), and the SIGN is I (inclusive). For an extensive elaboration on these values, please again refer back to Chapter 8.

We then call the BapiGetList method using the SELECTION4HELPVALUES argument. The results after first selecting US as the country are shown below:

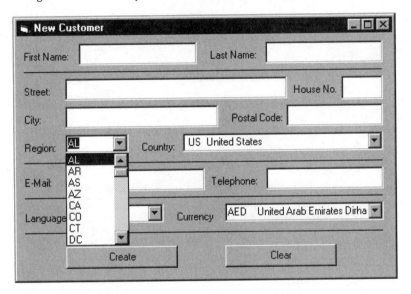

## Loading Fixed Values – Languages

For the Language value, I created another routine – GetLang:

```
Public Sub GetLang()

  Dim recLang As ADODB.Recordset
  Dim ret As ADODB.Recordset

  msapHelp.DimAs "BapiGetList", "Helpvalues", recLang

  msapHelp.BapiGetList METHOD:="CreateFromData1", _
              PARAMETER:="PERSONALDATA", OBJNAME:="Customer", _
              FIELD:="langu_p", RETURN:=ret, _
              HELPVALUES:=recLang

Do Until recLang.EOF

  cboLang.AddItem Mid(recLang![Helpvalues], 1, 1) & _
              " " & Mid(recLang![Helpvalues], 2, 16)

  recLang.MoveNext

Loop
```

```
    cboLang.ListIndex = 1

    Set recLang = Nothing
    Set ret = Nothing

End Sub
```

Nothing new here either. I call `BapiGetList` passing the name of the field in question – `langu_p`. The rest of the method call stays the same because the BAPI, Parameter and business object are the same. The results of this routine are displayed below:

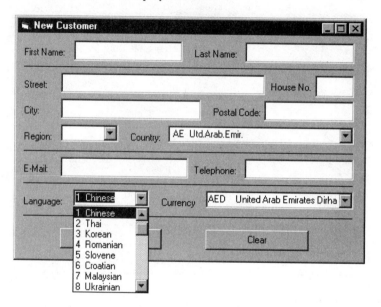

### Loading Fixed Values – Currency

The last lookup function is `GetCurr`:

```
Public Sub GetCurr()

   Dim recCurr As ADODB.Recordset
   Dim ret As ADODB.Recordset

   msapHelp.DimAs "BapiGetList", "Helpvalues", recCurr

   msapHelp.BapiGetList METHOD:="CreateFromData1", PARAMETER:="PERSONALDATA", _
                   OBJNAME:="Customer", FIELD:="currency", RETURN:=ret, _
                   HELPVALUES:=recCurr

   Do Until recCurr.EOF

      cboCurrency.AddItem Mid(recCurr![Helpvalues], 1, 5) & _
                   " " & Mid(recCurr![Helpvalues], 6, 40)
      recCurr.MoveNext

   Loop
```

```
    cboCurrency.ListIndex = 1

    Set recCurr = Nothing
    Set ret = Nothing

End Sub
```

This one gets us the list of predefined currencies. The results are shown below:

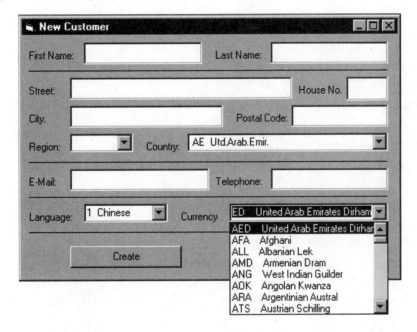

I have not given elaborate explanations because these functions are so redundant you may feel the compulsion to write a wrapper for them.

We set a `Destination` for the `msapHelp` object in the `Connect` subroutine:

```
Public Sub Connect()

  msapHelp.Destination = "MSIDES"

End Sub
```

Because we load fixed values on start up, we call the `Connect` routine from the form's `Load` event:

```
Private Sub Form_Load()

  Set msapHelp = CreateObject("WROX.Helpvalues.2")

  Connect
  GetCountries
  GetCurr
```

```
      GetLang

End Sub
```

## Creating Customers

The last function to discuss is `CreateCust`, that actually implements the call to the `BapiCreateFromData1` method of the *Customer* business object:

```
Public Sub CreateCust(strCustNum As String, strError As String)

   Dim recAddr As ADODB.Recordset
   Dim recCopRef As ADODB.Recordset

   Dim ret As Object

   On Error GoTo SAP_Error

   msapCustomer.DimAs "BapiCreateFromData1", "CopyReference", recCopRef
   msapCustomer.DimAs "BapiCreateFromData1", "PersonalData", recAddr

   recAddr.AddNew
       recAddr![FIRSTNAME] = txtFName
       recAddr![langu_p] = UCase(Trim(Left(Trim(cboLang.Text), 1)))
       recAddr![STREET] = txtStreet
       recAddr("CITY") = txtCity
       recAddr("COUNTRY") = UCase(Trim(Left(Trim(cboCountry.Text), 2)))
       recAddr("POSTL_COD1") = txtPostCode
       recAddr("LASTNAME") = txtLName
       recAddr("CURRENCY") = UCase(Trim(Left(Trim(cboCurrency.Text), 5)))
       recAddr("REGION") = UCase(Trim(Left(Trim(cboRegion.Text), 2)))
       recAddr("FAX_EXTENS") = Trim(txtTel)
       recAddr("E_MAIL") = UCase(Trim(txtEmail))
       recAddr("HOUSE_NO") = txtHouseN
   recAddr.Update

   recCopRef.AddNew
       recCopRef("SALESORG") = "R300"
       recCopRef("DISTR_CHAN") = "R1"
       recCopRef("DIVISION") = "R1"
       recCopRef("REF_CUSTMR") = "0000100041"
   recCopRef.Update

    msapCustomer.BapiCreateFromData1 COPYREFERENCE:=recCopRef, _
                            PERSONALDATA:=recAddr, RETURN:=ret

   Select Case ret(0)

      Case "E"
          msapCustomer.RollbackWork

      Case Else
          msapCustomer.CommitWork

   End Select

   Set recAddr = Nothing
   Set recCopRef = Nothing
```

```
SAP_Error:

    If Err.Number <> 0 Then
        strError = Err.Description
        MsgBox strError
        Exit Sub
    Else
        strCustNum = msapCustomer.KeyCustomerNo
        strError = ret("MESSAGE")
    End If

End Sub
```

*Note that some fields have rather elaborate validation code due to SAP R/3 sensitivity to their values.*

This function is long but simple. We first prepare arguments for the method call using the `DimAs` method – do not forget that it is case sensitive and you have to pass the names as defined in the proxy. Then we assign values for the fields of the single record of the `PersonalData` argument, using processed values from the GUI. We use `Trim`, `Mid` and `UCase` to make sure that the correct data is passed with no trailing or leading spaces.

The same process applies to the `CopyReference` parameter, except that here I use fixed values that I fished out of the IDES SAP R/3 client. This Reference Customer belongs to the range that is configured to assign customer numbers internally. After all these preparations, we finally call the BAPI-based method `BapiCreateFromData1`, passing all the prepared parameters.

At the end, we monitor the return structure. If it brings an error, we call a `RollbackWork` method of the *Customer* object. If everything is correct, we call the `CommitWork` method of the *Customer* object. These methods belong to the group of common methods added by the DCOM CC to every proxy component. Please refer to Chapter 10 and the DCOM CC documentation for more details.

At the very end, we check the value of the `KeyCustomerNo` property of the *Customer* object that has the value of the new customer's number. This value is passed back to the calling procedure (command button's `Click` event) and displayed in a message box.

The client's GUI calling routine is shown below:

```
Private Sub cmdCreate_Click()

    Dim newCustomer As String
    Dim strErr As String

    Set msapCustomer = CreateObject("WROX.Customer.1")

    msapCustomer.Destination = "MSIDES"

    CreateCust newCustomer, strErr

    If Trim(strErr) <> "" Then
        MsgBox strErr
    Else
```

```
      MsgBox "New Customer Number: " & newCustomer
   End If

End Sub
```

Note that we instantiate a *Customer* object and assign the `Destination` to it every time we call the create routine.

Sample entries are shown below:

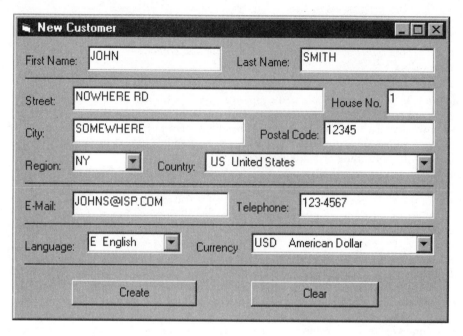

After entry, click on the **Create** button and wait for the results. Soon you get a message box with the new customer's number:

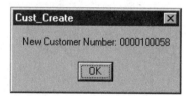

Now we can bring up our earlier project and confirm the results:

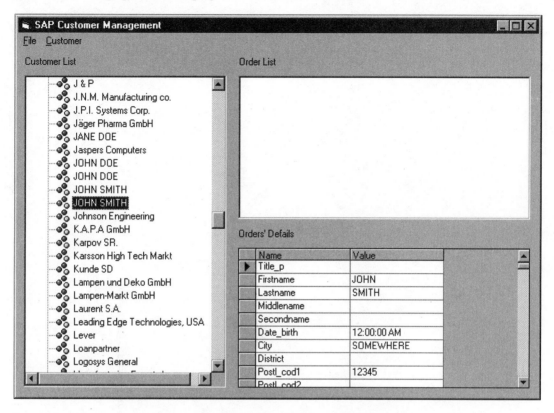

As you can see, we successfully entered a new customer into SAP R/3.

# Summary

In this chapter, we have learned how to program DCOM CC generated business object proxies. I also tried to demonstrate how to employ various aspects of MTS component deployment. You can experiment with exporting DCOM CC generated MTS packages to different computers that do not have to have MTS as long as DCOM is configured correctly. You can then enjoy remote invocation of business object proxies functionality across the network.

We also came across some of the hidden problems with working with SAP R/3. I hope you can begin to see why SAP R/3 programming can be such a complex process even for relatively simple tasks.

This chapter and the whole DCOM CC part of this book should serve as a primer on this exciting new technology. You should use it to learn how to apply the technology, and then implement it in your integration projects.

# 14

# Where to go from here

To write the conclusion for books on new technologies is both exciting and difficult. Exciting because new technologies offer new solutions in previously unexplored territory. Difficult because it is unclear along which exact route the new technology will take us. To avoid speculation, I will try to outline a few ideas that are the most natural progression for utilizing the technology described in this book.

First of all, I am positive that the Open Business Framework, as a technology, is a success with a bright future. As SAP continues to add more-and-more business objects and BAPIs to its Repository, then more-and-more developers will turn to business objects and BAPIs to deliver SAP R/3 solutions.

Initially developers will use this technology to integrate desktop applications with SAP R/3. However, as the technology matures, more emphasis will be placed on true application and data integration. With the evolution of Windows and COM+, there will be fewer valid arguments against using COM components to deliver scalable enterprise solutions involving SAP R/3.

As you could have gathered from the book, the new SAP R/3 business object related technology, and tools such as the DCOM Component Connector, can nicely fit into the Windows DNA paradigm. These components and tools can easily be integrated into Internet and intranet applications allowing remote-client access to SAP R/3.

The first candidates for development will be traditional problem areas for SAP R/3 – reporting and data exchange with external applications. We can easily create powerful reporting applications using BAPIs and RFC components encapsulated into COM proxy components. The argument against these technologies will be that BAPIs do not yet cover every possible scenario for reporting. However, this will be resolved by SAP, who have committed themselves to releasing more BAPIs and business objects with every release.

There exists enormous potential in integrating existing Information Systems with SAP R/3 using the SAP Automation Toolkit and the DCOM CC. These allow for more than just putting an attractive GUI in front of the user. The key will be in the real-time data exchange between existing applications and SAP R/3.

To solve all these problems we do not have to look any further than Microsoft Visual Studio, Microsoft Office and Microsoft BackOffice. We have messaging functionality in MSMQ, transaction support in MTS, and robust RDBMS with OLAP capabilities in SQL Server 7.0. We have Internet Information Server to deploy Internet solutions. Microsoft Office provides productivity tools that can be easily integrated into SAP R/3 using the DCOM CC. Moreover, if you use the DCOM CC to generate business object proxies you get XML support by-design. Because the DCOM CC uses ADO Recordsets to represent data, we can convert result data into XML natively using ADO 2.1.

Another effect of these new SAP technologies and tools is that they allow traditional programmers to leverage their existing skills and program against BAPIs without needing any specific SAP R/3 knowledge. It is now possible to create a 100% Windows Information System using SAP R/3.

I am certain that we are at the beginning of a very interesting and promising branch of SAP R/3 related development, and I hope that this book will somehow contribute to your future success.

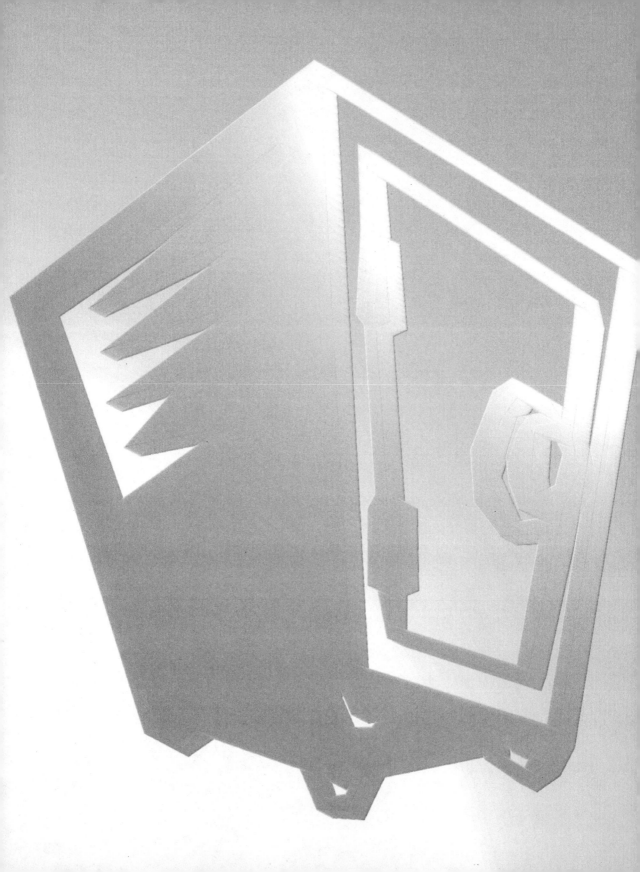

# SAP R/3 Business Object Diagram

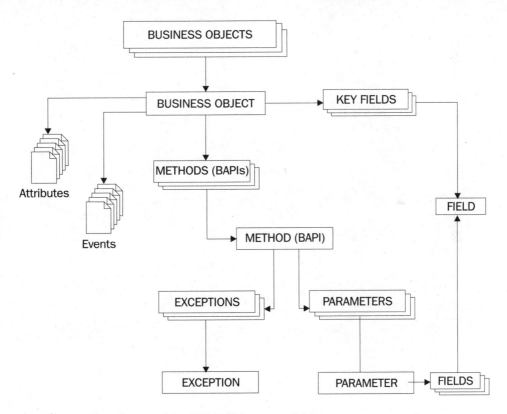

*Events are not yet implemented for SAP R/3 business objects

# SAP Automation Toolkit Components

The available SAP OCX controls and DLL components that form the SAP Automation Toolkit are listed below:

- ➤ The **Logon control** provides a Connection object that enables logon to R/3.
- ➤ The **BAPI control** provides functionality to create instances of SAP R/3 business objects, prepare BAPI parameters and execute BAPIs.
- ➤ The **Function control** provides functionality to execute RFCs and view the results of the execution.
- ➤ The **Transaction control** provides screen and field object management, and remote calling of R/3 transactions. The Transaction control only allows transaction calls in batch-input mode – an external program can send input field values to an R/3 screen, but output field values are not returned.
- ➤ The **Table View control** provides functionality to view an RFC table as a spreadsheet.
- ➤ The **Table Factory control** encapsulates Table/Structure objects for easier access by the client application.
- ➤ The **Table Tree control** makes visible those tables that contain hierarchically structured data (trees of parent nodes and their children). Table Trees allow the programmer and user to manage tables containing directory trees.
- ➤ The **SAP Browser control** provides functionality for browsing SAP R/3 BOR and RFC metadata information. It has Online and Offline modes.
- ➤ The **SAP Online Repository Services library** provides Online and Offline SAP R/3 BOR and RFC metadata browsing functionality. The SAP Browser Control uses it. It also encapsulates the functionality to save metadata into the local MDB database, and to generate C++ or Java code to implement business object's and RFC proxies.

# Setting Up The Tools

## SAP Automation Toolkit

You may get this toolkit either as part of the SAP front-end installation or as a free download from the following web sites:

➢  www.sap.com/bapi -> COM Section
➢  www.saplabs.com/usa/download.htm

Before downloading the installation files, check the date to get the latest version. I also recommend monitoring the SAPLABS web site for updates.

You can choose to install the toolkit using the Web Install option. I recommend downloading the installation file to your local drive. You may have to reuse it. I also recommend uninstalling any previous version of the SAP Automation Toolkit prior to installing a new one.

The installation will result in creating the entry in your Start menu – SAP Automation 4.xY, where x is the minor release number and the Y is the letter for the version of SAP, e.g. SAP Automation 4.5A.

The sure way to test the installation is to fire up the SAP Assistant and try to logon. If it is successful, try to import SAP R/3 metadata and execute an RFC from the SAP Assistant. If all these things are successful it is most likely a valid installation. Another test would be to start Visual Basic, open a Standard EXE and look up the Components list. This list should contain all the SAP controls. Next open the References dialog and you should see the SAP Online Repository Services library.

The ultimate test would be to run any of the projects that accompany the SAP Automation part of the book.

# DCOM Component Connector

You can get the DCOM Component Connector via the same resources and web sites. The DCOMCC is currently available as 4.5, 4.6A and beta 4.6B. This book reflects the 4.6A version.

Should you have 4.5, beware that it will generate a run-time error if you use the Internet Explorer 5.0. I recommend upgrading to version 4.6A.

After you download the installation file, you should carefully read the documentation prior to installing the DCOM CC. One caveat is that the DCOM CC installation routine will attempt to install `LIBRFC32.DLL` into your system directory. If this library is already there the installation will fail. Rename the old version of the `LIBRFC32.DLL` prior to installing the DCOM CC.

The test for a correct installation would be to bring up the Object Builder. If this is works correctly, then try to create a Destination. If you are using MTS with the DCOM CC you can use the MTS Explorer to look up the DCOM CC components. The ultimate test would be to create a business object proxy and develop a Visual Basic project to test the proxy's functionality.

# D

# Integrating the DCOM Component Connector with Visual Component Manager

Version 4.6B of the DCOM Component Connector includes integration with **Visual Component Manager (VCM)**. This is the first step in the integration of the DCOM CC with Visual Studio. It means that SAP has developed the first native integration with the Microsoft development environment.

> *Note that all material in this appendix was written based on a beta version of the product. This beta is available for download from* www.sap.com/bapi.

To integrate the DCOM CC with VCM, SAP had to first provide the **Open Information Models (OIM)** to be imported into the **Microsoft Repository**. This was necessary because the MS Repository did not contain the model for DCOM CC generated SAP R/3 business object proxy components.

You need to have the following requirement to enable VCM integration:

- ➢ SQL Server 7.0
- ➢ Microsoft Data Access Components 2.1
- ➢ Microsoft Repository 2.1 – comes with the MS Repository SDK

# The Integration Process

The process of making the MS Repository DCOM CC aware is straightforward. If you have a 4.6B release of the DCOM CC, it will prompt you to enable the VCM integration during the installation process:

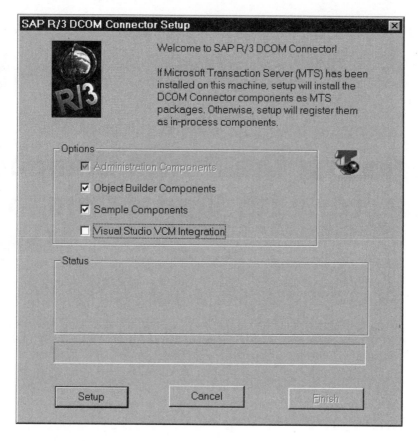

Once you check Visual Studio VCM Integration, the following dialog will come up:

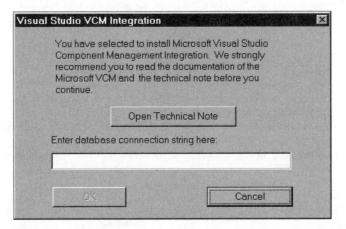

This dialog will not let you enter any values or click OK until you use the Open Technical Note button. Then you have to enter:

```
SERVER=ServerName;DATABASE=DatabaseName
```

These values represent the name of your SQL Server and the name of the Database that you'd like the DCOM CC to import the OIM files into.

Then you are all set to go. After you click OK, the installation routine will accept the parameters, and import OIM files supplied from the RFC SDK that comes with the DCOM CC download. All this is performed transparently.

After you complete the installation with the VCM integration, you will have a Visual Studio VCM Integration check box on the DCOM CC Object Builder web GUI:

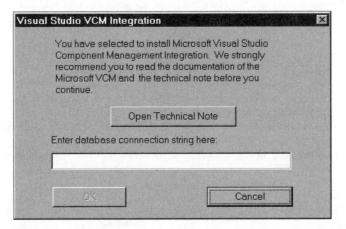

The rest of the DCOM CC functionality remains the same. You configure destinations, logon, and select business objects and generate proxies the same way you did before. The only difference will be that you will have values for newly created components entered into the Repository database you created.

You can import OIM files into your MS Repository database that comes with the SQL Server. However, I would suggest having a separate database for your DCOM CC generated SAP R/3 business object proxy components.

# Importing Proxies into the Repository

If you already have an earlier version of the DCOM CC but still want to use the VCM, follow the advice provided in the documentation and import the OIM files manually using the provided Visual Basic code. You can then import proxies that you have already built into the Repository database.

To do it manually first create a new database in SQL Server 7.0. Then if you look in the documentation you will find the source code that you can use to build a project called REPOSTST. It includes a single form:

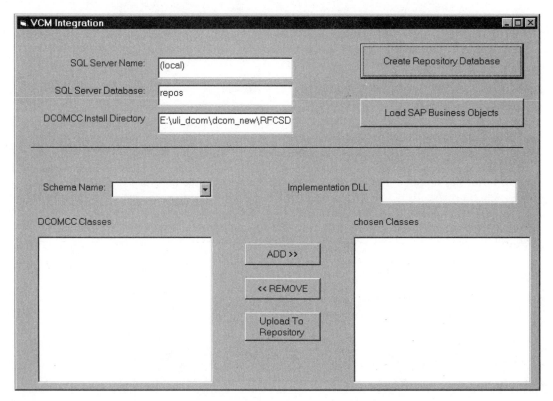

You are expected to enter the name of your SQL Server and the name of a newly created empty database. Then click on the **Create Repository Database** button and the application will import all the OIM files – these files have an RDM extension and are supplied with the DCOM CC installation:

> *Be careful with the connection string attributes. They should be the same as for a regular DSN you create with the ODBC32 utility. Also correct the path values for these files depending on your directory structure.*

After you have successfully imported all the RDM files, click on the **Load SAP Business Objects** button. It will populate a **Schema Name** combo box with your Namespace values. Select the one you need and the list box under the combo box will be populated with proxy names according to the Namespace:

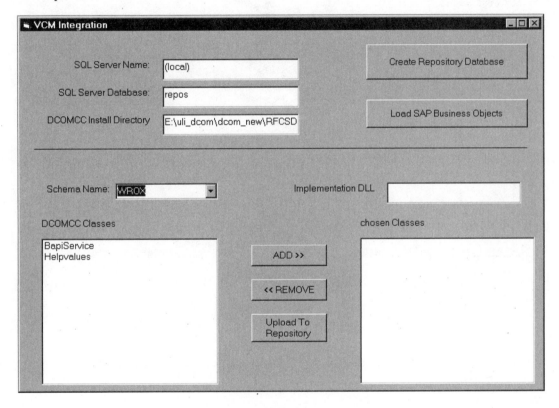

Select the classes you want to import in the left list box, and click on the **Add >>** button to move the class to the **Chosen Classes** list box on the right. You have to also enter the full path for the DLL that the class is implemented in, into the **Implementation DLL** text box above the list box:

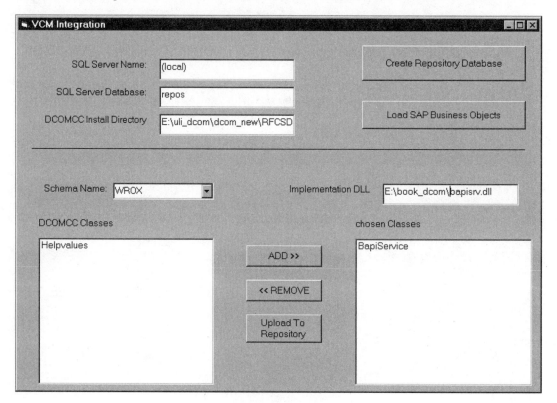

Click on the **Upload To Repository** button and this application will upload the component into the Repository database. You can then bring up the VCM add-in from Visual Basic and look up the newly imported component:

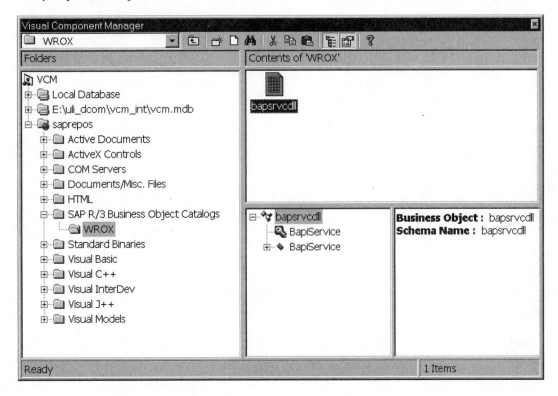

# Index

## wrox
PROGRAMMER TO PROGRAMMER™

Wrox writes books for you. Any suggestions, or ideas about how you want information given in your ideal book will be studied by our team.
Your comments are always valued at Wrox.

Free phone in USA 800-USE-WROX
Fax (312) 893 8001

UK Tel. (0121) 687 4100        Fax (0121) 687 4101

---

### Professional Visual Basic SAP R/3 Programming - Registration Card

Name _____

Address _____

_____

_____

City_____ State/Region _____

Country_____ Postcode/Zip _____

E-mail _____

Occupation _____

How did you hear about this book? _____

☐ Book review (name) _____

☐ Advertisement (name) _____

☐ Recommendation _____

☐ Catalog _____

☐ Other _____

Where did you buy this book? _____

☐ Bookstore (name)_____ City _____

☐ Computer Store (name)_____

☐ Mail Order _____

☐ Other _____

What influenced you in the purchase of this book?

☐ Cover Design

☐ Contents

☐ Other (please specify) _____

How did you rate the overall contents of this book?

☐ Excellent        ☐ Good

☐ Average          ☐ Poor

What did you find most useful about this book? _____

What did you find least useful about this book? _____

Please add any additional comments. _____

What other subjects will you buy a computer book on soon? _____

What is the best computer book you have used this year?

_____

*Note: This information will only be used to keep you updated about new Wrox Press titles and will not be used for any other purpose or passed to any other third party.*

**wrox**
PROGRAMMER TO PROGRAMMER™

**NB.** If you post the bounce back card below in the UK, please send it to:

Wrox Press Ltd., Arden House, 1102 Warwick Road,
Acocks Green, Birmingham B27 6BH. UK.

*Computer Book Publishers*

# BUSINESS REPLY MAIL
FIRST CLASS MAIL      PERMIT#64      CHICAGO, IL

POSTAGE WILL BE PAID BY ADDRESSEE

**WROX PRESS INC.,**
**29 S. LA SALLE ST.,**
**SUITE 520**
**CHICAGO IL 60603-USA**